VISUALIZING
BANKRUPTCY

VISUALIZING
BANKRUPTCY

Laura B. Bartell
Professor of Law
Wayne State University Law School

ISBN: 978-1-4224-8229-2

Library of Congress Cataloging-in-Publication Data
Bartell, Laura B. Visualizing bankruptcy / Laura B. Bartell. p. cm. Includes index. ISBN 978-1-4224-8229-2 (soft cover) 1. Bankruptcy--United States. I. Title. KF1524.85.B37 2011 346.7307'8--dc23   2011032493

NOTE TO USERS

To ensure that you are using the latest materials available in this area, please be sure to periodically check the LexisNexis Law School web site for downloadable updates and supplements at www.lexisnexis.com/lawschool.

Editorial Offices
121 Chanlon Rd., New Providence, NJ 07974 (908) 464-6800
201 Mission St., San Francisco, CA 94105-1831 (415) 908-3200
www.lexisnexis.com

MATTHEW◆BENDER

(2011–Pub.3316)

PREFACE

Bankruptcy law is inherently political. This is hardly surprising; the law creates winners and losers, and the subject over which they are battling is money. But the political process does not always produce the most elegantly drafted legislation. Our current federal bankruptcy law, 11 U.S.C. §§ 101-1532, is a telling example of that fact.

Although permanent federal bankruptcy legislation in the United States dates back to 1898 (the Bankruptcy Act of 1898, ch. 541, 30 Stat. 544 (1989) (repealed 1978)), our modern bankruptcy law, created by the Bankruptcy Reform Act of 1978, Pub. L. No. 95-598, 92 Stat. 2549 (1978) (familiarly known as the "Bankruptcy Code"), was the product of many years of political debate. Since its enactment it, has been amended in significant respects several times, most recently by the enactment of the Bankruptcy Abuse Prevention and Consumer Protection Act of 2005 (BAPCPA), Pub. L. No. 109-8, 119 Stat. 23 (2005), which was motivated in large part by the efforts of the consumer credit industry to make bankruptcy less hospitable to consumer debtors. The process by which our current bankruptcy laws have been enacted has resulted in statutory provisions that are often lengthy, convoluted, difficult to parse and sometimes incoherent.

Under the best of circumstances, statutory analysis is difficult for anyone unused to it, and for a student taking a course in bankruptcy law, reading provisions of the Bankruptcy Code and the Federal Rules of Bankruptcy Procedure can be a daunting task. During my many years of teaching bankruptcy, I have found that a summary of statutory provisions in visual form makes those provisions much easier to grasp for my students. Law students tend to be visual learners, craving visual aids to make sense out of language and intellectual concepts. The more difficult the language or concepts, the more useful a visual aid may be.

I am the first to admit that visualizing the Bankruptcy Code and Rules requires a loss of nuance, a simplification of concepts that were intended to be more complex. No one would try to practice bankruptcy law from the charts included in this book. But for a law student, who is generally given a broad survey of how bankruptcy works, without getting into a great deal of depth, visualizing legislative language can be very helpful.

This book contains the many charts and other visual aids I have used in my classes. They are organized not by chapter of the Bankruptcy Code (for the most part) but chronologically by the normal course of a bankruptcy case. I have included some specialized bankruptcy topics (chapters 9, 12 and 15) at the end of the book; they are not ordinarily included in a law school bankruptcy course, but are of sufficient general interest to visualize.

TABLE OF CONTENTS

TABLE OF CONTENTS

TABLE OF CONTENTS

TABLE OF CONTENTS

Chapter 1

THE BEGINNING OF A BANKRUPTCY CASE

Financial distress does not always lead to the filing of a bankruptcy case. State law provides remedies both for creditors whose debtors fail to fulfill their obligations, and for debtors who find themselves unable to satisfy all creditors.

Creditors who have the benefit of security interests in, or liens on, specific property of the debtor, may be afforded the ability under state law to exercise self-help remedies, that is, taking possession of their collateral without breach of the peace and/or the selling the collateral in a commercially reasonable manner. See Article 9 of the Uniform Commercial Code. Similar private remedies — the ability under state law to foreclose without judicial intervention — may be given to creditors with a mortgage on real property of the debtor.

Those creditors without interests in property of the debtor must seek judicial help to collect unpaid debts. First, they must sue the debtor and get a judgment. Then, after whatever period is specified by state law for appealing from the judgment (often 21–30 days), they may seek to collect that judgment through judicial means from assets of the debtor. To reach physical assets of the debtor, the judgment creditor typically obtains a writ of execution from the clerk of court, which directs the sheriff to execute on (seize or levy on) the debtor's assets to satisfy the judgment. Exempt assets, specified by state statute, are exempt from judicial process. Seizure of the property by the sheriff creates a lien on the seized property in favor of the judgment creditor, called an execution lien, which gives the judgment creditor priority over other creditors who do not have a lien with respect to the seized property. After appropriate notice, the seized assets are sold by the sheriff and the proceeds of the sale (after the sheriff is reimbursed for the costs of seizure and sale) are used to satisfy the judgment. Special protection may be given to real property under state execution law, such as providing for a right of redemption. Many states also provide for recordation of judgment liens against title to real property, which gives the judgment creditor a right to be paid out of the proceeds of any sale or financing of the property before the debtor receives anything.

To capture assets consisting of money owing to the debtor held by third parties (such as bank accounts and wages), the judgment creditor can obtain a writ of garnishment which is served on the third party holding the debtor's assets and directing that they be paid over to the creditor or to the court for the creditor's benefit. Wage garnishments may be limited by federal law (Consumer Credit Protection Act, 15 U.S.C. § 1673).

The major problem of state law remedies from the creditor's standpoint is that they are individual in nature. Each creditor may pursue remedies on its own, and keeps what it receives without any obligation to share with other creditors who may be slower to take action, or who may not yet have a legal right to do so. Not only does individual action by many creditors lead to perceived unfairness in result, it is also economically inefficient because the total costs of individual actions are likely to exceed the costs of collective action.

State law remedies for insolvent debtors may include the right to make an assignment for the benefit of creditors (often referred to as an "ABC"). Typically, the debtor conveys all non-exempt property to an assignee who acts as trustee for benefit of creditors. The assignee sells the assets and notifies the creditors of their right to file proofs of claim with the assignee. Those who do so share the proceeds ratably in accordance with their respective priorities. While property is in the hands of the assignee, it is protected from individual creditor action. A similar state law proceeding with respect to anticipated wages is the receivership for voluntary assignment of wages under which a debtor/wage-earner assigns future wages to the court for ratable distribution to creditors, who are precluded from garnishing those wages.

Although these state law mechanisms do provide a means for a debtor to deal with its creditors collectively, the major deficiency of state law remedies from the debtor's standpoint is that they do not provide a discharge of the debtor's obligations. As a result, absent contractual undertakings to forgive any deficiency by the creditors receiving payments, the debtor remains at risk to the extent the creditors are not paid in full.

Federal bankruptcy law is designed to minimize the flaws inherent in state law proceedings. The Bankruptcy Code provides a mandatory collective procedure to realize upon the value of the debtor's assets or business, and treats similarly situated creditors the same. For the individual debtor, the Code provides a discharge from most pre-bankruptcy debts, even over the objection of some creditors. Therefore, bankruptcy may be seen as more desirable than state remedies both by the debtor and by creditors.

A. THE BANKRUPTCY SYSTEM AND JURISDICTION

The Bankruptcy Code is a federal law, codified at 11 U.S.C. §§ 101 *et seq.*., and is administered by the federal courts. Under the Bankruptcy Act of 1898, the bankruptcy courts had jurisdiction over the bankruptcy case itself, but only limited jurisdiction over disputes relating to bankruptcy. The bankruptcy courts exercised summary jurisdiction only when the court had actual or constructive possession of the property involved in the dispute, or the parties had expressly or constructively consented to the exercise of jurisdiction, as by filing a claim. Matters outside the summary jurisdiction of the court were called "plenary" and had to be tried in the same locale as would be required if there were no bankruptcy case (a federal district court or state court).

In enacting the Bankruptcy Code of 1978, Congress attempted to get rid of this summary/plenary distinction, which spawned considerable litigation, by conferring on bankruptcy courts broad jurisdiction over bankruptcy cases and related disputes. However, the Supreme Court concluded in *Northern Pipeline Construction Co. v. Marathon Pipe Line Co.*, 458 U.S. 50 (1982), that conferring jurisdiction on a non-Article III court over state common law causes of action (such as the right to recover contract damages) was unconstitutional. As a result, Congress reworked the jurisdictional scheme of the Code by amendments which were enacted in the Bankruptcy Amendments and Federal Judgeship Act of 1984, and have so far withstood constitutional challenge.

To avoid conferring jurisdiction on non-Article III courts, jurisdiction over all bankruptcy cases was vested in Article III United States district courts. 28 U.S.C. § 1334. Those courts exercise exclusive jurisdiction over the bankruptcy case itself (the actual civil proceeding created by a bankruptcy filing), 28 U.S.C. § 1334(a), and over property of the debtor and property of the estate and over claims or causes of action involving § 327 of the Code (employment of professional persons), 28 U.S.C. § 1334(e). The district courts are given nonexclusive jurisdiction over civil proceedings arising under the Code or arising in or related to cases under the Code. 28 U.S.C. § 1332(b).

The terms "arising under," "arising in" and "related to" are terms of art that have well-developed meanings. "Arising under" jurisdiction involves causes of action created or determined by the Code itself. "Arising in" jurisdiction involves administrative matters that arise only in bankruptcy proceedings and would have no existence outside of bankruptcy. "Related to" jurisdiction has been defined in a test developed by Third Circuit in *Pacor, Inc. v. Higgins*, 743 F.2d 984 (3d Cir. 1984) (and adopted by most other circuits) — "whether the outcome of that proceeding could conceivably have any effect on the estate being administered in bankruptcy."

Bankruptcy judges are designed as "units" of the district court, 28 U.S.C. § 151, and are appointed by the courts of appeals for terms of 14 years, 28 U.S.C. § 152. All bankruptcy matters within district court jurisdiction are referred to bankruptcy judges under local rule. 28 U.S.C. § 157(a). But the bankruptcy judges have different roles with respect to those matters depending on whether those matters can be definitively resolved by a non-Article III court. With respect to the bankruptcy case itself, and any proceeding arising under the Code or arising in a bankruptcy case that constitutes a "core" proceeding (defined in 28 U.S.C. § 157(b)(2)) as to which a non-Article III judge may constitutionally render a final judgment, the bankruptcy judge may "hear and determine" the matter. 28 U.S.C. § 157(b)(1). If the proceeding is noncore, unless the parties consent to have the bankruptcy judge hear and determine the proceeding, the bankruptcy judge can "hear" the matter but can only submit proposed findings of fact and conclusions of law to the district court for determination. The Article III district court then reviews the matter de novo as to any issue to which a party objects. 28 U.S.C. § 157(c)(1).

A visualization of the jurisdictional allocation with respect to bankruptcy between the district court and the bankruptcy judges follows.

JURISDICTION
28 U.S.C. § 1334

	CASES UNDER TITLE 11	CIVIL PROCEEDINGS ARISING UNDER TITLE 11	CIVIL PROCEEDINGS ARISING IN CASES UNDER TITLE 11	CIVIL PROCEEDINGS RELATED TO CASES UNDER TITLE 11
DISTRICT COURT	ORIGINAL AND EXCLUSIVE JURISDICTION	ORIGINAL BUT NOT EXCLUSIVE JURISDICTION	ORIGINAL BUT NOT EXCLUSIVE JURISDICTION	ORIGINAL BUT NOT EXCLUSIVE JURISDICTION
BANKRUPTCY JUDGES	CORE: HEAR AND DETERMINE § 157(b)(1)	CORE: HEAR AND DETERMINE § 157(b)(1)	CORE: HEAR AND DETERMINE § 157(b)(1)	NONCORE: HEAR OR, WITH CONSENT, HEAR AND DETERMINE § 157(c)

Core proceedings are those that are seen by Congress to be at the core of the bankruptcy power of the district courts, central to a bankruptcy case. Although other proceedings may be labeled as core, 28 U.S.C. § 157(b) lists sixteen proceedings as nonexclusive core proceedings. Even with respect to proceedings labeled as "core," the bankruptcy judge may not "hear and determine" proceedings — such as state common law claims — that must be resolved by an Article III judge. *Stern v. Marshall*, 131 S. Ct. 2594 (2011). Section 157(b) is visualized below.

CORE PROCEEDINGS
28 U.S.C. § 157(b)(2)

1) MATTERS CONCERNING THE ADMINISTRATION OF THE ESTATE;

2) ALLOWANCE OR DISALLOWANCE OF CLAIMS AGAINST THE ESTATE OR EXEMPTIONS, AND ESTIMATION OF CLAIMS OR INTERESTS, BUT NOT LIQUIDATION OR ESTIMATION OF CONTINGENT OR UNLIQUIDATED PERSONAL INJURY TORT OR WRONGFUL DEATH CLAIMS AGAINST THE ESTATE

3) COUNTERCLAIMS BY THE ESTATE AGAINST PERSONS FILING CLAIMS

4) ORDERS IN RESPECT TO OBTAINING CREDIT

5) ORDERS TO TURN OVER PROPERTY OF THE ESTATE

6) PREFERENCE PROCEEDINGS

7) MOTIONS REGARDING AUTOMATIC STAY

8) FRAUDULENT TRANSFER PROCEEDINGS

9) DETERMINATIONS AS TO DISCHARGEABILITY OF DEBTS

10) OBJECTIONS TO DISCHARGES

11) DETERMINATIONS OF VALIDITY, EXTENT OR PRIORITY OF LIENS

12) CONFIRMATION OF PLANS

13) ORDERS APPROVING USE OR LEASE OF PROPERTY

14) ORDERS APPROVING SALE OF PROPERTY

15) OTHER PROCEEDINGS AFFECTING LIQUIDATION OF ASSETS OF THE ESTATE OR ADJUSTMENT OF DEBTOR-CREDITOR OR EQUITY SECURITY HOLDER RELATIONSHIPS, EXCEPT PERSONAL INJURY TORT OR WRONGFUL DEATH CLAIMS

16) RECOGNITION OF FOREIGN PROCEEDINGS AND OTHER MATTERS UNDER CHAPTER 15

Even if a bankruptcy matter falls within the jurisdiction of the United States district courts, Congress determined that under some circumstances, those courts (and their adjuncts, the bankruptcy courts) either may or must decline to exercise jurisdiction and allow the matter to be resolved by the applicable state courts. The action of declining to exercise jurisdiction under these circumstances is called "abstention."

Under 28 U.S.C. § 1334(c)(1), the district court may abstain from hearing any proceeding arising under title 11 or arising in or related to a case under title 11 "in the interest of justice, or in the interest of comity with State courts or respect for State law." In deciding whether to abstain as a permissive matter, courts may consider such matters as whether the federal forum or state forum is more convenient to the parties, whether piecemeal litigation can be avoided by abstaining or declining to abstain, which court assumed jurisdiction over the matter first, whether one court has jurisdiction over property involved in the litigation, whether the applicable law is state or federal, the relationship of the matter to the rest of the bankruptcy case, whether there is a right to a jury trial, whether one of the parties appears to be engaged in forum-shopping, whether there is a basis for federal jurisdiction in the absence of bankruptcy, and whether there are non-debtor parties involved who would not have other involvement in the bankruptcy case. These considerations are listed in the visualization below:

PERMISSIVE ABSTENTION 28 U.S.C. § 1334(c)(1)	
STANDARD	FACTORS
IN THE INTEREST OF JUSTICE, OR IN THE INTEREST OF COMITY WITH STATE COURTS OR RESPECT FOR STATE LAW	1) CONVENIENCE OF FEDERAL FORUM 2) AVOIDANCE OF PIECEMEAL LITIGATION 3) ORDER IN WHICH COURTS ASSUMED JURISDICTION 4) JURISDICTION OVER PROPERTY 5) SOURCE OF APPLICABLE LAW 6) RELATIONSHIP TO BANKRUPTCY CASE 7) RIGHT TO JURY TRIAL 8) AVOIDANCE OF FORUM-SHOPPING 9) NON-BANKRUPTCY BASIS FOR FEDERAL JURISDICTION 10) PRESENCE OF NON-DEBTOR PARTIES

Under some circumstances, the district court (and bankruptcy judge adjunct) is required to abstain from exercising its bankruptcy jurisdiction. Under 28 U.S.C. § 1334(c)(2), the district court, upon motion, must abstain from hearing a state cause of action otherwise solely within its related-to jurisdiction when an action "is commenced, and can be timely adjudicated, in a State forum of appropriate jurisdiction." If the bankruptcy proceeding meets the five requirements set out in the following visualization, mandatory abstention is required.

One type of proceeding is excluded from the requirement for mandatory abstention even if it meets all these requirements. Noncore proceedings under 28 U.S.C. § 157(b)(2)(B) (proceedings for the liquidation or estimation of contingent or unliquidated personal injury tort or wrongful death claims against the estate) are not subject to mandatory abstention pursuant to 28 U.S.C. § 157(b)(4). These claims must be tried in the district court under 28 U.S.C. § 157(b)(5).

MANDATORY ABSTENTION 28 U.S.C. § 1334(c)(2)	
REQUIREMENTS FOR ABSTENTION	EXCEPTION
1) PROCEEDING IS BASED ON STATE LAW CLAIM 2) NO FEDERAL JURISDICTIONAL BASIS OVER PROCEEDING OTHER THAN BANKRUPTCY 3) PROCEEDING IS COMMENCED IN STATE FORUM 4) STATE FORUM CAPABLE OF TIMELY ADJUDICATION OF PROCEEDING 5) PROCEEDING IS NONCORE	PROCEEDING TO LIQUIDATE OR ESTIMATE CONTINGENT OR UNLIQUIDATED PERSONAL INJURY TORT OR WRONGFUL DEATH CLAIMS AGAINST ESTATE 28 U.S.C. § 1334(b)(4)

If the district court decides to abstain (either mandatory or permissive) or not to abstain (permissive), the decision is not reviewable by the court of appeals pursuant to 28 U.S.C. § 1334(d).

Although all district courts have provided for the referral of bankruptcy cases and proceedings to the bankruptcy judges by local rule, the district courts may, if they wish to do so, take the case or a proceeding back. The return of a bankruptcy case or proceeding to the district court is called "withdrawal of the reference." The district court may, under 28 U.S.C. § 157(d), withdraw, in whole or in part, any case or proceeding referred to the bankruptcy court "for cause shown." Some of the factors considered by the district court in deciding whether cause is shown are listed in the following visualization.

Withdrawal of the reference is required if "resolution of the proceeding requires consideration of both title 11 and other laws of the United States," 28 U.S.C. § 157(d). The language has been interpreted to mean that withdrawal of the reference is mandatory if substantial and material consideration of nonbankruptcy federal law is required. The burden is on the party seeking withdrawal to establish its necessity.

WITHDRAWAL OF THE REFERENCE 28 U.S.C. § 157(d)			
DISCRETIONARY		MANDATORY	
STANDARD	FACTORS	STANDARD	MEANING
FOR CAUSE SHOWN	1) EFFICIENCY 2) DELAY 3) COST 4) JURY TRIAL 5) FORUM-SHOPPING 6) UNIFORM ADMINISTRATION	RESOLUTION OF PROCEEDING REQUIRES CONSIDERATION OF BOTH TITLE 11 AND OTHER LAWS OF THE UNITED STATES	SUBSTANTIAL AND MATERIAL CONSIDERATION OF NONBANKRUPTCY FEDERAL LAW IS REQUIRED

When a bankruptcy judge enters a final order or judgment, there are three possible routes for an appeal of that order or judgment. The first, which is always available to the litigants, is an appeal to the district court, 28 U.S.C. § 158(a), and from there to the Court of Appeals, 28 U.S.C. § 158(d). With respect to core proceedings, the district court reviews the bankruptcy court determination with significant deference and will affirm unless the decision was "clearly erroneous." For non-core (related) proceedings, the bankruptcy judge can only submit proposed findings of fact and conclusions of law to the district court, and the final order or judgment must be entered by the district court after de novo review of all matters as to which any party has objected. 28 U.S.C. § 157(c)(1).

Congress provided for an alternative means of appeal from bankruptcy court orders or judgments by a specialized appellate panel. Under 28 U.S.C. § 158(b)(1), the judicial council of each circuit was required to create a Bankruptcy Appellate Panel to hear and determine bankruptcy appeals unless the circuit found there are insufficient judicial resources available in the circuit, or establishment would increase delay or cost to the parties in bankruptcy cases. Bankruptcy Appellate Panels (BAPs) are currently operating in the First, Sixth, Eighth, Ninth and Tenth Circuits. These BAPs are composed of bankruptcy judges in the circuit appointed by the judicial council of the circuit and who sit as three-judge panels to hear appeals under 28 U.S.C. § 158(b)(5).

The BAPs hear appeals only from those districts within their circuit in which a majority of the district court judges have authorized such appeals. 28 U.S.C. § 158(b)(6). Even if such authorization is provided by the district court judges, each appellant and appellee has the right to elect to have the appeal heard by the district court instead. 28 U.S.C. § 158(d)(1). Appeals from a decision of the BAP goes to the court of appeals, just as would an appeal from a decision of the district court. 28 U.S.C. § 158(d)(1).

In the 2005 BAPCPA amendments, Congress created limited circumstances under which appeals may go directly to the court of appeals from the bankruptcy judge. 28 U.S.C. § 158(d)(2). First, either the bankruptcy court, district court or BAP, or all appellants and appellees acting jointly, must certify that one of three situations exists: (a) the judgment, order or decree involves a question of law as to which there is no controlling decision or involves a matter of public importance; (b) the judgment, order or decree requires resolution of conflicting decisions on a question of law; or (c) immediate appeal may materially advance the progress of the case or proceeding. Second, the court of appeals must authorize the direct appeal. 28 U.S.C. § 158(d)(2)(A). The bankruptcy court, district court or BAP may make the required certification on its own motion or on the request by a party, and must make the certification if requested to do so by a majority of the appellants and a majority of the appellees. 28 U.S.C. § 158(d)(2)(B).

The bankruptcy appeal process is visualized below.

APPEALS 28 U.S.C. § 158				
APPEAL FROM BANKRUPTCY JUDGE				APPEAL FROM DISTRICT COURT OR BAP
DISTRICT COURT HAS JURISDICTION OVER APPEALS	BANKRUPTCY APPELLATE PANEL (BAP) HAS JURISDICTION OVER APPEALS WITH CONSENT OF ALL PARTIES IF MAJORITY OF DISTRICT JUDGES IN DISTRICT HAVE AGREED	COURT OF APPEALS HAS JURISDICTION OVER APPEALS IF IT AUTHORIZES DIRECT APPEAL AND REQUIRED CERTIFICATION MADE		COURT OF APPEALS HAS JURISDICTION OVER APPEALS FROM DISTRICT COURT OR BAP JUDGMENTS, ORDERS OR DECREES
		CERTIFICATION BY WHOM	CRITERIA FOR CERTIFICATION	
		BANKRUPTCY COURT, DISTRICT COURT, OR BAP, OR ALL APPELLANTS AND APPELLEES ACTING JOINTLY	QUESTION OF LAW AS TO WHICH THERE IS NO CONTROLLING DECISION OR INVOLVES MATTER OF PUBLIC IMPORTANCE, OR QUESTION OF LAW REQUIRING RESOLUTION OF CONFLICTING DECISIONS, OR IMMEDIATE APPEAL MAY MATERIALLY ADVANCE PROGRESS OF CASE OR PROCEEDING	

B. THE LAWYER-CLIENT RELATIONSHIP

Generally the regulation of the lawyer-client relationship is a matter left to the states. However, in the 2005 BAPCPA amendments to the Bankruptcy Code, Congress imposed significant new obligations on lawyers who represent consumer debtors.

First, Congress created a new definition in the Code, "debt relief agency," which is defined in § 101(12A) as any person who provides bankruptcy assistance (defined in § 101(4A)) to an assisted person (defined in § 101(3) as any person whose debts consist primarily of consumer debts and the value of whose nonexempt property is less than $175,750*) in return for the payment of money or other valuable consideration, or who is a bankruptcy petition preparer. Explicitly excluded are officers, directors, employees or agents of such persons, nonprofit organizations, creditors of assisted persons, depository institutions or credit unions or their affiliates or subsidiaries, or authors, publisher, distributors or sellers of copyrighted works. The Supreme Court has recently rejected an argument that lawyers should not be deemed to be included in the definition. *See Milavetz, Gallop & Milavetz, P.A. v. United States,* 130 S. Ct. 1324, 1332-33 (2010).

Congress then made debt relief agencies subject to restrictions on their advertising, the contracts into which they enter with their clients, disclosures they must make to their clients, advice they may give their clients and services they must perform. Failure to comply with these new restrictions can subject the debt relief agency to civil penalties. Challenges to several of these requirements on First Amendment and due process grounds have been rejected. *See Connecticut Bar Association v. United States,* 620 F.3d 81 (2d Cir. 2010).

Advertising includes all forms of communication directed either to the general public (such as general media or seminars) or directed to prospective clients (such as direct mailing, or telephone or electronic messages). § 528(a)(3). Advertising includes descriptions of chapter 13 relief even if chapter 13 is not mentioned, and statements that could lead a reasonable consumer to believe that the services offered involved debt counseling when in fact bankruptcy assistance was contemplated. § 528(b)(1). When a debt relief agency offers assistance in connection with credit defaults, mortgage foreclosures, eviction proceedings, excessive debt, debt collection pressure, or inability to pay any consumer debt, it is required to make the same disclosures as if the advertisement explicitly offered bankruptcy assistance. § 528(b)(2). The advertising restrictions are summarized in the following visualization.

---

* This dollar figure, like many of the dollar figures in the Code, is subject to adjustment every three years under § 104(b) of the Code to reflect change in the Consumer Price Index for the most recent three years, and was most recently adjusted effective April 1, 2010 and will be adjusted again in 2013.

ADVERTISING RESTRICTIONS ON DEBT RELIEF AGENCIES		
WHAT CONSTITUTES ADVERTISING § 528(a), (b)(1) & (2)	CONTENT OF ADVERTISING § 528(a)(3) & (b)(2)(A)	LEGEND ON ADVERTISING § 528(a)(4) & (b)(2)(B)
ADVERTISING INCLUDES: GENERAL MEDIA, SEMINARS, SPECIFIC MAILINGS, TELEPHONIC OR ELECTRONIC MESSAGES, AND DESCRIPTIONS OF BANKRUPTCY ASSISTANCE IN CONNECTION WITH CHAPTER 13 PLAN, AND STATEMENTS THAT COULD LEAD REASONABLE CONSUMER TO BELIEF THAT DEBT COUNSELING IS BEING OFFERED IF SERVICES ARE DIRECTED AT BANKRUPTCY ASSISTANCE, AND OFFER TO PROVIDE ASSISTANCE WITH RESPECT TO CREDIT DEFAULTS, MORTGAGE FORECLOSURES, EVICTION PROCEEDINGS, EXCESSIVE DEBT, DEBT COLLECTION PRESSURE, OR INABILITY TO PAY CONSUMER DEBT	MUST DISCLOSE THAT SERVICES OR BENEFITS OFFERED ARE WITH RESPECT TO OR MAY INVOLVE BANKRUPTCY RELIEF UNDER BANKRUPTCY CODE	ADVERTISING MUST INCLUDE STATEMENT: "WE ARE A DEBT RELIEF AGENCY. WE HELP PEOPLE FILE FOR BANKRUPTCY RELIEF UNDER THE BANKRUPTCY CODE" OR SUBSTANTIALLY SIMILAR STATEMENT

A debt relief agency is required to execute a written contract with an assisted person for whom it proposes to provide bankruptcy assistance services not later than five business days after the first date on which it provides any such services, and prior to the assisted person filing a bankruptcy petition. § 528(a)(1). Any such contract must explain "clearly and conspicuously" the services the debt relief agency will provide to the assisted person, and the fees for such services and terms of payment. § 528(a)(1)(A) & (B). The debt relief agency must provide a copy of the fully-executed contract to the assisted person. § 528(a)(2). These requirements are visualized below.

RESTRICTIONS ON CONTRACTS BETWEEN DEBT RELIEF AGENCIES AND ASSISTED PERSONS § 528(a)		
TIMING	CONTENT	DELIVERY
WRITTEN CONTRACT MUST BE EXECUTED NOT LATER THAN FIVE BUSINESS DAYS AFTER PROVIDING ANY BANKRUPTCY ASSISTANCE SERVICES, AND BEFORE FILING BANKRUPTCY PETITION	WRITTEN CONTRACT MUST EXPLAIN CLEARLY AND CONSPICUOUSLY 1) SERVICES TO BE PROVIDED, AND 2) FEES OR CHARGES AND TERMS OF PAYMENT	FULLY-EXECUTED COPY MUST BE DELIVERED TO ASSISTED PERSON

Congress has imposed four different disclosure obligations on debt relief agencies. The first, under § 527(a)(1), is to provide the assisted persons to whom they provide bankruptcy assistance the written notice required to be delivered by the clerk to an individual consumer debtor before the commencement of a bankruptcy case under § 342(b)(1). This notice contains a brief description of chapters 7, 11, 12, and 13 of the Code and the general purpose, benefits and costs of proceeding under each chapter and the types of services available from credit counseling agencies. The debt relief agency must retain a copy of this notice for two years after it is given to the assisted person. § 527(d).

Second, to the extent that the first notice does not cover these matters, the debt relief agency must, not later than three days after first offering to provide bankruptcy assistance, provide the assisted person a "clear and conspicuous" written notice advising them of the requirement that information they provide during the case must be complete, accurate and truthful, that all assets and liabilities must be completely and accurately disclosed and replacement value of each asset must be stated after reasonable inquiry, that current monthly income and all figures used in the means test (*see* section 1(D) *infra*) and disposable income must be stated after reasonable inquiry, and that all information provided by the assisted person may be audited and sanctions imposed (including dismissal and criminal sanctions) for failure to provide such information. § 527(a)(2). The debt relief agency must retain a copy of this notice for two years after it is given to the assisted person. § 527(d).

Third, Congress provided a statutory form of statement that must be provided to each assisted person at the same time as the first notice, describing that person's rights with respect to the bankruptcy case and the duties of the debt relief agency towards the assisted person. § 527(b).

Finally, the debt relief agency is required to provide to the assisted person at the time the first notice is given reasonably sufficient information in a clear and conspicuous writing on how to provide all the information the assisted period is required to provide under § 521 (such as the list of creditors, schedule of assets and liabilities, schedule of current income and current expenditures, and statement of financial affairs), including how to value assets at replacement value, how to determine current monthly income and all figures used in the means test and disposable income, how to complete the list of creditors and determine what is owed to them and their addresses, and how to determine what property is exempt and how to value exempt property at replacement value. § 527(c).

A visualization of these disclosure requirements follows:

DISCLOSURE REQUIREMENTS FOR DEBT RELIEF AGENCIES § 527			
WRITTEN NOTICE REQUIRED UNDER § 342(b)(1)	NOT LATER THAN THREE BUSINESS DAYS AFTER FIRST OFFERING TO PROVIDE BANKRUPTCY ASSISTANCE SERVICES, CLEAR AND CONSPICUOUS WRITTEN NOTICE ADVISING THAT: 1) ALL INFORMATION PROVIDED MUST BE COMPLETE, ACCURATE AND TRUTHFUL, AND 2) ALL ASSETS AND LIABILITIES MUST BE COMPLETELY AND ACCURATELY DISCLOSED AND REPLACEMENT VALUE OF ASSETS STATED AFTER REASONABLE INQUIRY, AND 3) CURRENT MONTHLY INCOME AND MEANS TESTING AMOUNTS AND DISPOSABLE INCOME MUST BE STATED AFTER REASONABLE INQUIRY, AND 4) ALL INFORMATION PROVIDED MAY BE AUDITED AND PENALTIES ASSESSED	STATUTORY STATEMENT IN FORM OF § 527(b)	REASONABLY SUFFICIENT INFORMATION IN CLEAR AND CONSPICUOUS WRITING ON HOW TO PROVIDE ALL INFORMATION REQUIRED UNDER § 521, INCLUDING: 1) HOW TO VALUE ASSETS AT REPLACEMENT VALUE, DETERMINE CURRENT MONTHLY INCOME AND MEANS TESTING AMOUNTS, AND HOW TO DETERMINE DISPOSABLE INCOME, AND 2) HOW TO COMPLETE LIST OF CREDITORS, INCLUDING AMOUNTS OWED AND ADDRESSES, AND 3) HOW TO DETERMINE WHAT PROPERTY IS EXEMPT AND HOW TO VALUE EXEMPT PROPERTY

The limitation on advice a debt relief agency may give to an assisted person is contained in § 526. The debt relief agency is barred from making any statement, or counseling or advising any assisted person or prospective assisted person to make any statement, in a filed document that is untrue or misleading or, upon the exercise of reasonable care, should have been known to be so. § 526(a)(2). Nor may a debt relief agency advise an assisted person or prospective assisted person to incur more debt in contemplation of bankruptcy or to pay for services performed in preparing for or representing a debtor in a bankruptcy case. § 526(a)(4). The Supreme Court has recently upheld this provision from constitutional attack under the First Amendment, interpreting the language narrowly to bar only advice to incur debt because the debtor is filing for bankruptcy (presumably in order to obtain a discharge of the debt, or more favorable treatment under the means test) rather than for a legitimate purpose. *See Milavetz, Gallop & Milavetz, P.A. v. United States*, 130 S. Ct. 1324, 1336 (2010).

The debt relief agency is statutorily precluded from misrepresenting to an assisted person, whether directly or by material omission, the services that will be provided by the debt relief agency, or the benefits and risks resulting from bankruptcy. § 526(a)(3). On the other hand, the debt relief agency is affirmative required to perform all services that the debt relief agency informed the assisted person or prospective assisted person it would provide in connection with a bankruptcy case or proceeding. § 526(a)(1). No waiver of these protections given to the assisted person is enforceable. § 526(b).

The restrictions on debt relief agencies are visualized below.

RESTRICTIONS ON DEBT RELIEF AGENCIES § 526				
PROHIBITIONS § 526(a)				WAIVERS § 526(b)
DRA MAY NOT FAIL TO PERFORM ANY SERVICE THAT IT UNDERTOOK TO PROVIDE	DRA MAY NOT MAKE ANY STATEMENT, OR ADVISE ASSISTED PERSON TO MAKE ANY STATEMENT, IN FILED DOCUMENT THAT IS UNTRUE AND MISLEADING OR SHOULD HAVE BEN KNOWN TO BE SO UPON EXERCISE OF REASONABLE CARE	DRA MAY NOT MISREPRESENT TO ANY ASSISTED PERSON DIRECTLY OR INDIRECTLY WITH RESPECT TO SERVICES TO BE PROVIDED, OR BENEFITS AND RISKS OF BANKRUPTCY	DRA MAY NOT ADVISE ASSISTED PERSON TO INCUR MORE DEBT IN CONTEMPLATION OF BANKRUPTCY OR PAY FEES FOR SERVICES PERFORMED AS PART OF PREPARING FOR OR REPRESENTING DEBTOR IN BANKRUPTCY	NO WAIVER BY AN ASSISTED PERSON OF PROTECTION OR RIGHT UNDER § 526 IS ENFORCEABLE AGAINST DEBTOR

The remedies available if a debt relief agency breaches any of its new obligations range from contract nullification to injunctive relief to damages and civil penalties. A visualization of the various sanctions that may be provided follows.

REMEDIES FOR VIOLATIONS OF DEBT RELIEF AGENCY (DRA) PROVISIONS § 526(c) & (d)				
CONTRACT THAT VIOLATES MATERIAL REQUIREMENTS OF §§ 526, 527 OR 528 IS VOID	DRA IS LIABLE FOR FEES RECEIVED, ACTUAL DAMAGES AND REASONABLE ATTORNEYS' FEES AND COSTS IF: 1) DRA INTENTIONALLY OR NEGLIGENTLY FAILED TO COMPLY WITH §§ 526, 527 OR 528, OR 2) CASE IS DISMISSED OR CONVERTED BECAUSE OF DRA'S INTENTIONAL OR NEGLIGENT FAILURE TO FILE REQUIRED DOCUMENT, OR 3) DRA INTENTIONALLY OR NEGLIGENTLY DISREGARDED MATERIAL REQUIREMENTS OF CODE OR BANKRUPTCY RULES	STATE OFFICER MAY SEEK TO ENJOIN VIOLATION OF § 526 AND SEEK ACTUAL DAMAGES, FEES AND COSTS ON BEHALF OF RESIDENTS	IF COURT FINDS PERSON INTENTIONALLY VIOLATED § 526 OR ENGAGED IN A CLEAR AND CONSISTENT PATTERN OR PRACTICE OF VIOLATING § 526, COURT MAY ENJOIN VIOLATION OR IMPOSE AN APPROPRIATE CIVIL PENALTY	STATE AUTHORITIES AND FEDERAL COURT RETAIN POWER TO DETERMINE AND ENFORCE QUALIFICATIONS FOR PRACTICE OF LAW

C. ELIGIBILITY

A debtor is eligible to file for bankruptcy under a chapter of the Bankruptcy Code only if the debtor meets the eligibility requirements for that chapter under § 109. In addition, if the debtor is an individual or family farmer (§ 101(18)), he or she must satisfy other requirements to be eligible to file for bankruptcy protection. For all debtors, there must be a satisfactory connection to the United States in order to take advantage of the provisions of the Code.

The protection of the United States Bankruptcy Code is available only to those prospective debtors who have a sufficient jurisdictional connection to the United States. That connection may be created by a domicile (the permanent residence of an individual or the jurisdiction in which a legal entity is created, such as the state of incorporation), residence (where an individual lives or where the chief executive offices of a legal entity are located), a place of business, or property in the United States. In addition, "municipalities" (§ 101(40)) are eligible to file. § 109(a). A visualization of this eligibility requirement follows.

ELIGIBILITY FOR BANKRUPTCY BASED ON CONNECTION TO UNITED STATES § 109(a)				
RESIDENCE	DOMICILE	PLACE OF BUSINESS	PROPERTY	MUNICIPALITY

Chapter 7 is available to all persons (§ 101(41)) who are prospective debtors other than those falling within three categories. § 109(b). First, a railroad may not file under chapter 7 because chapter 11 includes a subchapter specifically dealing with railroad reorganizations, §§ 1161 *et seq.* These provisions contain specific protections to ensure the integrity of the national railroad system in the event a particular carrier has financial difficulties. Second, certain domestic insurance companies and banking institutions are excluded, because their dissolutions are covered by other laws. These other laws also cover foreign insurance companies and banks that are doing business in the United States, and they are therefore also excluded from eligibility for chapter 7. If a foreign insurance company or bank is not doing business in the United States but has property in the country, it would be eligible to file under chapter 7. A visualization of eligibility for chapter 7 follows.

ELIGIBILITY FOR CHAPTER 7 § 109(b)	
WHO IS ELIGIBLE	WHO IS NOT ELIGIBLE
A PERSON (§ 101(41)), INCLUDING INDIVIDUALS, PARTNERSHIPS, AND CORPORATIONS, BUT NOT GOVERNMENTAL UNITS (§ 101(27))	RAILROAD DOMESTIC INSURANCE COMPANY, BANK, SAVINGS BANK, COOPERATIVE BANK, SAVINGS AND LOAN ASSOCIATION, AND SIMILAR BANKING ORGANIZATIONS FOREIGN INSURANCE COMPANIES ENGAGED IN BUSINESS IN U.S. OR FOREIGN BANK, SAVINGS, BANK, COOPERATIVE BANK, SAVINGS AND LOAN ASSOCIATION AND SIMILAR BANKING ORGANIZATIONS THAT HAVE A BRANCH IN THE U.S.

Chapter 9 is available only to municipalities. § 109(c)(1). A "municipality" is defined in § 101(40) as a "political subdivision or public agency or instrumentality of a state." Political subdivisions include political units of a state, such as counties (or parishes), cities, towns, villages, boroughs, and townships, all of which exercise sovereign powers, like the power to tax and the police power. Public agencies are authorities, commissions, or agencies organized for the purpose of constructing, maintaining and operating revenue producing enterprises, generally in connection with the issuance of bonds. Instrumentalities include local improvement districts (school districts, port districts, library districts). The definition would not include non-profit corporations created to issue bonds used to finance the acquisition of land and construction of public buildings which are then leased to the governmental entity.

A municipality may be a debtor under chapter 9 only if it meets four additional requirements. First, the municipality must be "specifically authorized, in its capacity as a municipality or by name," to be a debtor under chapter 9 by state law or by someone empowered by state law to make such an authorization. § 109(c)(2). Prior to 1994, the Code only required a municipality to be "generally authorized" to be a debtor under chapter 9 in order to be eligible. This language had been interpreted in some cases to permit municipalities to file under chapter 9 without specific authorization from the state merely because state law gave them general powers over their finances, and the right to sue and be sued, to enter into contracts, to incur debts, and to exercise all powers necessary to further their purposes. Congress amended § 109(c)(2) to require specific authorization in order to give states more control over their local municipalities. Since the amendment, some states have enacted specific authorization to allow chapter 9 filings by local municipalities without approval at the state level (including Alabama, Arizona, Arkansas, California, Colorado, Florida, Idaho, Missouri, Montana, Nebraska, Oklahoma, South Carolina, Texas and Washington). Some other states require approval by a designated state agency, commission or officer before a chapter 9 filing may be made. Most other states either affirmatively preclude chapter 9 filings by state law, or have no legislation at all (which has the same result of barring chapter 9 filings by their municipalities).

The second additional requirement for a municipality to file under chapter 9 is that the municipality be "insolvent." § 109(c)(3). With respect to a municipality, insolvent means one of two things is true. Either the municipality is "generally not paying its debts as they become due" (unless subject to a bona fide dispute), or the municipality is "unable to pay its debts as they become due." § 101(32)(C). The test of insolvency for municipalities is different from that applied to non-municipalities (other than partnerships), where insolvency is based on a balance sheet test comparing an entity's debts to its property at a fair valuation. § 101(32)(A). The reason for the different approach is that in a chapter 9 case, the municipality is not expected to liquidate its property to satisfy its debts.

To be eligible for chapter 9, a municipality must also "desire[] to effect a plan to adjust [its] debts." § 109(c)(4). Such desire can be shown by testimony by municipal officers or directors. It can also be demonstrated by production of a draft plan of reorganization.

The final requirement for a municipality to be eligible for chapter 9 is that the prospective debtor meets one of four alternative tests in connection with its dealings with its creditors. § 109(c)(5). First (and least likely), it must obtain the agreement of creditors holding a majority in amount of the claims of each class that will be impaired by the municipality under a reorganization plan. In the absence of such an agreement, the municipality must show that it has negotiated in good faith with creditors and failed to get such agreement. If it cannot show such negotiation, the municipality must demonstrate that it is unable to negotiate with creditors because such negotiation is impracticable (such as because there is such a large number of creditors or there are severe time constraints or negotiations are pointless, *see In re Valley Health System*, 383 B.R. 156 (Bankr. C.D. Cal. 2008)). Finally, eligibility is established without regard to such an agreement or negotiations if the municipality demonstrates that it reasonably believes that a creditor may attempt to obtain a preferential transfer.

The eligibility requirements for chapter 9 are visualized as follows.

ELIGIBILITY FOR CHAPTER 9 § 109(c)				
MUNICIPALITY (§ 101(40))	SPECIFICALLY AUTHORIZED TO BE DEBTOR UNDER CHAPTER 9 BY STATE LAW OR BY AUTHORIZED GOVERNMENTAL OFFICER OR ORGANIZATION	INSOLVENT (§ 101(32)(C))	DESIRES TO EFFECT A PLAN TO ADJUST DEBTS	RELATIONS WITH CREDITORS: 1) HAS OBTAINED AGREEMENT OF MAJORITY OF CLAIMS OF EACH CLASS TO BE IMPAIRED, OR 2) HAS NEGOTIATED IN GOOD FAITH BUT FAILED TO OBTAIN SUCH AGREEMENT, OR 3) IS UNABLE TO NEGOTIATE BECAUSE IMPRACTICABLE, OR 4) REASONABLY BELIEVES THAT CREDITOR MAY ATTEMPT TO OBTAIN PREFERENTIAL TRANSFER

The eligibility requirements for chapter 11 are coextensive with the eligibility requirements for chapter 7 with only three exceptions. First, a railroad (not eligible for chapter 7) is eligible for chapter 11. As was previously mentioned, chapter 11 has a specific subchapter, §§ 1161–1174, that deals with railroad reorganizations. Second, a stockbroker or a commodity broker (eligible for chapter 7) is not eligible for chapter 11. Chapter 7 has a specific subchapter (§§ 741–753) dealing with stockbroker liquidations, and another (§§ 761–767) dealing with commodity broker liquidations. Congress did not want the protective provisions included in chapter 7 for customers of those types of debtors to be circumvented by a chapter 11 filing. Third, an uninsured state member bank or multilateral clearing organization is permitted to file under chapter 11 although it may not file under chapter 7 unless it does so by a petition filed at the direction of the Board of Governors of the Federal Reserve System. § 109(d). The eligibility requirements for chapter 11 are visualized as follows.

ELIGIBILITY FOR CHAPTER 11 § 109(d)	
WHO IS ELIGIBLE	WHO IS NOT ELIGIBLE
PERSON (§ 101(41)) WHO IS ELIGIBLE UNDER CHAPTER 7 RAILROAD UNINSURED STATE MEMBER BANK OR MULTILATERAL CLEARING ORGANIZATION	STOCKBROKER COMMODITY BROKER

Under § 109(e), chapter 13 is available only to an "individual with regular income" or such an individual and such individual's spouse. This term is defined in § 101(30) to mean an individual (meaning a natural person rather than a legal entity) with income "sufficiently stable and regular to enable such individual to make plan payments" under a chapter 13 plan. Stockbrokers and commodity brokers are explicitly excluded, for the same reason that they are excluded from eligibility for chapter 11.

In addition to limiting chapter 13 to individuals with regular income (or such individuals and their spouses), Congress imposed debt limitations on chapter 13 debtors. In order to qualify for chapter 13, a debtor or joint debtors must have noncontingent, liquidated, unsecured debts of less than $360,475[*] and noncontingent, liquidated, secured debts of less than $1,081,400.[*] "Noncontingent" means that debtor's liability is unconditional; debtor will have to pay (whether the amount is ascertained or not, as when there has been an admission of liability or a determination of liability, but damages are yet to be assessed). "Liquidated" means the amount of the liability is ascertained (whether or not it is certain the debtor will have to pay it, such as a guaranty of a certain amount which will not be payable unless the primary obligor defaults). If an individual with regular income exceeds the debt limitations, he or she must file either under chapter 7 or under chapter 11.

A visualization of the chapter 13 eligibility requirements follows.

---

[*] These dollar figures, like many of the dollar figures in the Code, are subject to adjustment every three years under § 104(b) of the Code to reflect change in the Consumer Price Index for the most recent three years, and were most recently adjusted effective April 1, 2010 and will be adjusted again in 2013.

ELIGIBILITY FOR CHAPTER 13 § 109(e)		
TYPE OF DEBTOR	DEBT LIMITATIONS	
INDIVIDUAL WITH REGULAR INCOME (§ 101(30)), OR SUCH INDIVIDUAL AND SPOUSE, BUT NOT STOCKBROKER OR COMMODITY BROKER	NONCONTINGENT, LIQUIDATED, UNSECURED DEBTS LESS THAN $360,475*	NONCONTINGENT, LIQUIDATED, SECURED DEBTS LESS THAN $1,081,400*

Only a family farmer with regular income (§ 101(19)) or family fisherman with regular income (§ 101(19B)) is eligible to file for protection under chapter 12. § 109(f). In each case, the definition requires that the prospective debtor have "annual income sufficiently stable and regular" to enable the debtor to make payments under a chapter 12 plan. A visualization of the eligibility requirements for chapter 12 follows.

ELIGIBILITY FOR CHAPTER 12 § 109(f)	
FAMILY FARMER WITH REGULAR INCOME (§ 101(19))	FAMILY FISHERMAN WITH REGULAR INCOME (§ 101(19B))

"Family farmer" is defined in § 101(18). A family farmer may be either an individual (or an individual and his or her spouse) or a corporation or partnership. For an individual (or individual and spouse), the first requirement to constitute a "family farmer" is that he, she or they be "engaged in a farming operation." "Farming operation" is defined in § 101(21) as including "farming, tillage of the soil, dairy farming, ranching, production or raising of crops, poultry, or livestock, and production of poultry or livestock products in an unmanufactured state."

The second requirement for an individual or individual and spouse to be a family farmer is that his, her or their aggregate debts do not exceed $3,792,650.* Note that, unlike the debt limitations for chapter 13 in § 109(e), this figure includes all debts, not merely noncontingent, liquidated debts, and there is no separate limit for secured and unsecured debts.

---

* These dollar figures, like many of the dollar figures in the Code, are subject to adjustment every three years under § 104(b) of the Code to reflect change in the Consumer Price Index for the most recent three years, and were most recently adjusted effective April 1, 2010 and will be adjusted again in 2013.

The third requirement for an individual or individual and spouse to be a family farmer is that not less than 50% of his, her or their aggregate noncontingent, liquidated debts (excluding debt on the debtor's or debtors' principal residence unless the debt arises out of a farming operation) at the time of filing arises out of a farming operation "owned or operated" by the individual or the individual and spouse. The 50% figure was reduced from 80% in the 2005 BAPCPA amendments to make chapter 12 available to more potential debtors.

The final requirement for an individual or individual and spouse to qualify as a "family farmer" is that at least 50% of gross income be received from the farming operation. The 50% figure may be satisfied in either of two periods: (i) the taxable year preceding the tax year of filing, or (ii) each of the second and third taxable years preceding the tax year of filing.

A corporation or partnership may qualify as a "family farmer" if it meets five requirements (plus a sixth for a corporation that issues stock). First, more than 50% of the outstanding stock or equity must be held by a single family or by a single family and relatives of the members of the family. Second, the family or relatives holding the stock or equity must "conduct the farming operation." Note that this bars family corporations from filing for chapter 12 if they rent their farm to a tenant farmer. Third, more than 80% of the value of the assets of the corporation or partnership must consist of assets relating to the farming operation. There is no requirement that a specified percentage of income be farm-related, as there is for individual family farmers. Fourth, aggregate debts may not exceed $3,792,650.* And finally, not less than 50% of the aggregate noncontingent, liquidated debts (excluding a debt for one dwelling owned by the corporation or partnership in which a shareholder or partner maintained a principal residence, unless the debt arose out of a farming operation) as of the filing date must arise out of the farming operation owned or operated by the corporation or partnership. If the proposed debtor is a corporation that issues stock, the stock may not be publicly traded.

The following is a visualization of the definition of "family farmer."

---

* These dollar figures, like many of the dollar figures in the Code, are subject to adjustment every three years under § 104(b) of the Code to reflect change in the Consumer Price Index for the most recent three years, and were most recently adjusted effective April 1, 2010 and will be adjusted again in 2013.

DEFINITION OF "FAMILY FARMER" § 101(18)

INDIVIDUAL OR INDIVIDUAL AND SPOUSE			
ENGAGED IN FARMING OPERATION (§ 101(21))	AGGREGATE DEBTS DO NOT EXCEED $3,792,650*	NOT LESS THAN 50% AGGREGATE NONCONTINGENT, LIQUIDATED DEBTS ARISE OUT OF FARMING OPERATION	MORE THAN 50% GROSS INCOME FROM FARMING OPERATION

CORPORATION OR PARTNERSHIP					
MORE THAN 50% OUTSTANDING STOCK OR EQUITY HELD BY ONE FAMILY OR ONE FAMILY AND RELATIVES	FAMILY OR RELATIVES CONDUCT FARMING OPERATION	MORE THAN 80% OF ASSETS ARE RELATED TO FARMING OPERATION	AGGREGATE DEBTS DO NOT EXCEED $3,792,650*	NOT LESS THAN 50% AGGREGATE NONCONTINGENT, LIQUIDATED DEBTS ARISE OUT OF FARMING OPERATION	IF CORPORATION ISSUES STOCK, STOCK IS NOT PUBLICLY TRADED

* These dollar figures, like many of the dollar figures in the Code, are subject to adjustment every three years under § 104(b) of the Code to reflect change in the Consumer Price Index for the most recent three years, and were most recently adjusted effective April 1, 2010 and will be adjusted again in 2013.

One of the major changes in the 2005 BAPCPA amendments was to expand the availability of chapter 12 to a "family fisherman with regular income" in § 109(f). "Family fisherman" is defined in § 101(19A) to parallel the definition of "family farmer" in § 101(18) in providing separate requirements depending on whether the family fisherman is an individual or individual and spouse, or a corporation or partnership.

For an individual or individual and spouse, there are four requirements to qualification as a "family fisherman." First, he, she or they must be "engaged in a commercial fishing operation." "Commercial fishing operation" is defined in § 101(7A) as meaning (not "including") one of two activities: (i) the "catching or harvesting of fish, shrimp, lobsters, urchins, seaweed, shellfish, or other aquatic species or products of such species"; or (ii) aquaculture activities consisting of raising for market any species or product described in the definition. Second, the individual or individual and spouse cannot have aggregate debts exceeding $1,757,475.* As was true for family farmers, this figure includes all debts, not merely noncontingent, liquidated debts like the debt limits in § 109(e) for chapter 13, and there is no separate limit for secured and unsecured debts.

Third, not less than 80% of the proposed debtor's aggregate noncontingent, liquidated debts (excluding debt on the debtor's principal residence unless the debt arose out of a commercial fishing operation) at the time of filing must arise out of a commercial fishing operation "owned or operated" by the individual or the individual and spouse. Fourth, the individual or the individual and spouse must receive from the commercial fishing operation more than 50% of gross income for the taxable year preceding the taxable year of filing.

If the prospective family fisherman is a corporation or partnership, there are five requirements (with a sixth in the case of a corporation that issues stock). First, more than 50% of the outstanding stock or equity must be held by a single family or by a single family and relatives of the members of the family. Second, such family or relatives must conduct the commercial fishing operation. Third, more than 80% of the value of the assets of the corporation or partnership must consist of assets relating to the commercial fishing operation. Fourth, aggregate debts can not exceed $1,757,475.* Fifth, not less than 80% of the aggregate noncontingent, liquidated debts (excluding a debt for one dwelling owned by the corporation or partnership in which a shareholder or partner maintained a principal residence, unless the debt arose out of a commercial fishing operation) as of the filing date must arise out of the commercial fishing operation owned or operated by the corporation or partnership. Finally, if the proposed debtor is a corporation, the stock may not be publicly traded.

A visualization of the definition of "family fisherman" follows:

---

* These dollar figures, like many of the dollar figures in the Code, are subject to adjustment every three years under § 104(b) of the Code to reflect change in the Consumer Price Index for the most recent three years, and were most recently adjusted effective April 1, 2010 and will be adjusted again in 2013.

DEFINITION OF "FAMILY FISHERMAN" § 101(19A)

	INDIVIDUAL OR INDIVIDUAL AND SPOUSE			CORPORATION OR PARTNERSHIP					
ENGAGED IN COMMERCIAL FISHING OPERATION (CFO) (§ 101(7A))	AGGREGATE DEBTS DO NOT EXCEED $1,757,475*	NOT LESS THAN 80% AGGREGATE NONCONTINGENT, LIQUIDATED DEBTS ARISE OUT OF CFO	MORE THAN 50% GROSS INCOME FROM CFO	MORE THAN 50% OUTSTANDING STOCK OR EQUITY HELD BY ONE FAMILY OR ONE FAMILY AND RELATIVES	FAMILY OR RELATIVES CONDUCT CFO	MORE THAN 80% OF ASSETS ARE RELATED TO CFO	AGGREGATE DEBTS DO NOT EXCEED $1,757,475*	NOT LESS THAN 80% AGGREGATE NONCONTINGENT, LIQUIDATED DEBTS ARISE OUT OF CFO	IF CORPORATION ISSUES STOCK, STOCK IS NOT PUBLICLY TRADED

* These dollar figures, like many of the dollar figures in the Code, are subject to adjustment every three years under § 104(b) of the Code to reflect change in the Consumer Price Index for the most recent three years, and were most recently adjusted effective April 1, 2010 and will be adjusted again in 2013.

Section 109(g) is intended to preclude individuals or family farmers from becoming so-called "serial filers" under circumstances where Congress deemed repeated filings an abuse of the bankruptcy system. If an individual or family farmer was a debtor in a bankruptcy case pending at any time during the 180 days preceding a new filing, the individual or family farmer is ineligible if the prior case was dismissed either by the court for willful failure of the debtor to abide by court orders or to appear before the court and properly prosecute the case, or on a voluntary basis by the debtor after the filing of a request for relief from the stay under § 362. This provision is visualized below.

INELIGIBILITY BASED ON DISMISSAL OF PRIOR CASE § 109(g)		
TYPE OF DEBTOR	WHEN PRIOR CASE WAS PENDING	CIRCUMSTANCES OF DISMISSAL
INDIVIDUAL OR FAMILY FARMER	DURING 180-DAY PERIOD PRIOR TO CURRENT FILING	1) DISMISSAL BY COURT FOR WILLFUL FAILURE TO ABIDE BY COURT ORDERS OR TO APPEAR 2) VOLUNTARY DISMISSAL BY DEBTOR AFTER FILING OF MOTION FOR RELIEF FROM STAY

The final eligibility provision, § 109(h), added by the 2005 BAPCPA amendments, is applicable only to individual prospective debtors, and requires under most circumstances that such debtors receive a briefing from an approved nonprofit budget and credit counseling agency in the 180 days before filing for bankruptcy with respect to available credit counseling. This briefing is distinct from the instructional course concerning personal financial management required as a condition to discharge under § 727(a)(11) and § 1328(g). See Chapter 10[A], *infra*. Such a briefing may be either individual or in a group, and may be given in person, by telephone, or by the internet. § 109(h)(1). The clerk is required to maintain a publicly available list of approved nonprofit budget and credit counseling agencies that provide the services described in § 109(h). § 111(a). The standards for approving such agencies are set out in § 111.

The prospective debtor is excused from complying with this requirement for prebankruptcy credit counseling only if the debtor resides in a district for which the U.S. trustee or bankruptcy administrator has determined that the approved nonprofit budget and credit counseling agencies for such district are not reasonably able to provide adequate services, § 109(h)(2), or if the prospective debtor is exempt. A prospective debtor is exempt if the court determines, after notice and a hearing, that the debtor is unable to complete the credit counseling briefing for any of three reasons: (1) incapacity (meaning mental illness or mental deficiency rendering the debtor incapable of realizing and making rational decisions with respect to financial responsibilities), (2) disability (meaning debtor is so physically impaired as to be unable, after reasonable effort, to participate in the briefing), or (3) active military duty in a military combat zone. § 109(h)(4).

A debtor may receive a temporary waiver of the requirement if the debtor submits to the court a certification, satisfactory to the court, setting forth exigent circumstances that merit a waiver and stating that the debtor requested credit counseling services from an approved nonprofit budget and credit counseling agency, but was unable to obtain the services for five days after the request was made. § 109(h)(3)(A). If a waiver is granted, the debtor is required to obtain the required briefing no later than 30 days after filing a bankruptcy petition (a period that may be extended by the court for cause for an additional 15 days). § 109(h)(3)(B).

Exhibit D to Official Bankruptcy Form 1 implements the requirements of § 109(h) and must be filed with every bankruptcy petition. The following is a visualization of the new prebankruptcy credit counseling requirements.

PREBANKRUPTCY CREDIT COUNSELING ELIGIBILITY REQUIREMENT § 109(h)				
TYPE OF DEBTOR	REQUIREMENT		EXCEPTIONS	WAIVER	
INDIVIDUAL	TIMING	TYPE OF BRIEFING	DEBTOR RESIDES IN DISTRICT FOR WHICH U.S. TRUSTEE DETERMINES THAT APPROVED NONPROFIT BUDGET AND CREDIT COUNSELING AGENCIES ARE NOT REASONABLY ABLE TO PROVIDE ADEQUATE SERVICES, OR COURT DETERMINES THAT DEBTOR IS UNABLE TO COMPLETE REQUIREMENTS BECAUSE OF • INCAPACITY, • DISABILITY, OR • ACTIVE MILITARY DUTY IN COMBAT ZONE	WHEN GRANTED	DURATION
	DURING 180-DAY PERIOD PRECEDING DATE OF FILING	INDIVIDUAL OR GROUP BRIEFING OUTLINING OPPORTUNITIES FOR AVAILABLE CREDIT COUNSELING AND ASSISTANCE IN PERFORMING BUDGET ANALYSIS FROM APPROVED NONPROFIT BUDGET AND CREDIT COUNSELING AGENCY (§ 111)		DEBTOR CERTIFIES THAT: 1) EXIGENT CIRCUM-STANCES EXIST THAT MERIT WAIVER, AND 2) DEBTOR REQUESTED BRIEFING BUT WAS UNABLE TO OBTAIN IT FOR NEXT FIVE DAYS, AND COURT IS SATISFIED WITH CERTIFICATION	UP TO 30 DAYS AFTER FILING OF PETITION UNLESS COURT, FOR CAUSE, GRANTS 15 DAYS MORE

D. MEANS TESTING

Since the enactment of the Bankruptcy Code in 1978, Congress has amended it twice in order to force more consumer debtors to use chapter 13 (where it was assumed that creditors would receive more of their debt than in chapter 7). The first amendment, in 1984, added § 707(b) which at the time permitted the court, *sua sponte* or on motion of the U.S. trustee, to dismiss the chapter 7 case if a case is filed by an individual debtor whose debts were primarily consumer debts and the court concluded that granting a chapter 7 discharge would be "a substantial abuse of the provisions of this chapter [7]"; the presumption was in favor of allowing the debtor to file under chapter 7.

Despite the existence of § 707(b), the vast majority of consumer debtors nationwide continued to file under chapter 7 rather than chapter 13. Many creditors began to think that too many debtors who had an ability to pay back their debts out of future earnings were filing under chapter 7 and getting an immediate discharge of those debts. After years of unsuccessful attempts to obtain amendments to the Code, the creditor lobby was ultimately successful in pushing through the 2005 BAPCPA amendments to § 707(b) which make it much more difficult for a consumer debtor to take advantage of chapter 7.

Under the amended § 707(b)(1), any party in interest (not just the U.S. trustee or the court *sua sponte*) may seek dismissal of a chapter 7 case for abuse unless the "current monthly income" (§ 101(10A)) of the debtor times 12 is equal or less than the median family income in the applicable state for a same size household. For these below-median debtors, only the court, the U.S. trustee or the bankruptcy trustee may bring such a motion, § 707(b)(6).

The revised § 707(b)(1) also changes the standard for dismissal. Formerly the case was dismissed only if chapter 7 relief would be "a substantial abuse"; the new language changed to a standard to direct dismissal if granting relief would be "an abuse" of chapter 7.

Rather than retaining the explicit presumption that the debtor who files for chapter 7 protection should be able to continue in chapter 7, Congress created a new presumption against the availability of chapter 7 if the consumer debtor has the means to repay a certain portion of his or her debts. This presumption is familiarly called "means testing," and appears in the new § 707(b)(2)(A)(i). The court must presume abuse exists warranting dismissal under § 707(b)(1) if debtor's income available to satisfy unsecured claims over a five-year period is not less than the lesser of (a) 25% of the debtor's nonpriority unsecured claims or $7,025,[*] whichever is greater, or (b) $11,725.[*]

No one may bring a motion seeking dismissal based on the presumption of abuse if the current monthly income (§ 101(10A)) of the debtor and the debtor's spouse combined times 12 is not greater than the highest median family income (§ 101(39A)) for the applicable state for a household of the same size. § 707(b)(7). The vast majority of debtors fall below the median (more poor people file for bankruptcy than rich people) and therefore will not be subject to a motion to dismiss based on the means test. The current median family income used in the means test is available online, posted on the Department of Justice U.S. Trustees website.

The means test is applied by mathematical computation. It begins with the debtor's (or in a joint case, the debtor's and the debtor's spouse's) current monthly income. "Current monthly income" is defined in § 101(10A) by looking backward to the six

---

[*] These dollar figures, like many of the dollar figures in the Code, are subject to adjustment every three years under § 104(b) of the Code to reflect change in the Consumer Price Index for the most recent three years, and were most recently adjusted effective April 1, 2010 and will be adjusted again in 2013.

calendar months ending before the month in which the bankruptcy filing occurred, and averaging actual monthly income from all sources during those months. The debtor must include as income amounts paid by others on a regular basis for household expenses of debtor or debtor's dependants. Social security benefits are explicitly excluded, as are compensatory payments to victims of war crimes or crimes against humanity and payments to victims of international terrorism. A visualization of the definition of "current month income" follows:

CURRENT MONTHLY INCOME § 101(10A)	
AVERAGE MONTHLY INCOME THAT DEBTOR OR JOINT DEBTORS RECEIVED DURING 6 MONTHS ENDING ON LAST DAY OF CALENDAR MONTH IMMEDIATELY PRECEDING COMMENCEMENT OF CASE	
INCLUDING	EXCLUDING
AMOUNTS PAID BY OTHERS ON REGULAR BASIS FOR HOUSEHOLD EXPENSES OF DEBTOR OR DEBTOR'S DEPENDENTS	SOCIAL SECURITY BENEFITS, PAYMENTS TO VICTIMS OF WAR CRIMES OR CRIMES AGAINST HUMANITY OR DOMESTIC TERRORISM

Current monthly income is then multiplied by 12 to obtain an annual figure, and that annual figure is compared to the applicable median family income for the state in which the debtor lives and household size of the debtor's household. If the debtor's annualized current monthly income is equal to or below the applicable median, no motion may be made based on the means test and the presumption of abuse does not arise.

If the debtor is an above-median debtor (meaning the debtor's annualized current monthly income exceeds the applicable median family income), application of the means test continues by reducing current monthly income by certain expenses; the expenses that are subtracted from debtor's current monthly income are of three types.

First are the debtor's applicable monthly expense amounts allowed by the Internal Revenue Service (IRS) in its National and Local Standards and Other Necessary Expenses for the relevant area in which the debtor lives for the same size family. § 707(b)(2)(A)(ii). These are also available on the U.S. trustee website, and include standard allowances for food, clothing, and other items; health care; housing and utilities; mortgage expense; and transportation.

The Supreme Court decided in *Ransom v. FIA Credit Card Services, N.A.*, 131 S. Ct. 716 (2011), that a chapter 13 debtor who is not making any debt or lease payments on his car may not deduct transportation ownership expenses itemized in the National and Local Standards with respect to that car in computing projected disposable income. *See* Chapter 8[D], *infra*. It is currently unclear whether *Ransom* applies in chapter 7 cases, *see In re Ross-Tousey*, 549 F.3d 1148 (7th Cir. 2008) (allowing debtors to deduct transportation ownership expenses for cars they owned outright), and whether it is applicable to other expenses used in the means test computations.

The IRS also allows the debtor to deduct actual additional amounts paid for taxes, required deductions for employment (like mandatory retirement contributions, union dues and uniform costs), life insurance costs, court-ordered payments (such as spousal or child support), education expenses required for employment or for a mentally or physically challenged child, childcare costs, unreimbursed health care costs, and telecommunication services other than basic telephone and cell phone service necessary to debtor's health and welfare.

In addition to these expenses allowed by the IRS, Congress provided in § 707(b)(2)(A)(ii) for seven additional categories of expenses that may be deducted in the means test computations. These include reasonably necessary health insurance, disability insurance and health savings account expenses; the debtor's reasonably necessary expenses incurred to maintain the safety of the debtor and his or her family from family violence; if debtor demonstrates that such additional expenses are reasonable and necessary, an additional allowance for food and clothing of up to 5% of the food and clothing allowance under the IRS National Standards; continuation of actual expenses that are reasonable and necessary paid by the debtor for the care and support of elderly, chronically ill, or disabled household members who are unable to pay for themselves; if the debtor is eligible for chapter 13, actual administrative expenses of a chapter 13 plan in the applicable district up to 10% of the projected plan payments; actual expenses for each dependent minor child to attend a private or public elementary or secondary school up to $1,775* per year to the extent the expenses are reasonable and necessary; and actual expenses for home energy costs in excess of the IRS Local Standards amounts for housing and utilities in the relevant area if such expenses are documented and are reasonable and necessary. Congress has also specified that the court may not consider debtor's charitable contributions in deciding whether the chapter 7 filing is abusive, § 707(b)(1), so charitable contributions may be deducted as well.

The next category of deductions is for actual average amounts payable monthly during the five years following the filing date on account of secured debt, § 707(b)(2)(A)(iii), including auto payments and mortgage expenses, plus any additional amounts that would be payable to the secured creditor under a chapter 13 plan in order to maintain possession of collateral necessary for the support of the debtor and the debtor's dependents.

The final category of expenses deducted from current monthly income is for amounts payable monthly on priority claims (including alimony and child support claims) over the next five years. § 707(b)(2)(A)(iv).

---

* These dollar figures, like many of the dollar figures in the Code, are subject to adjustment every three years under § 104(b) of the Code to reflect change in the Consumer Price Index for the most recent three years, and were most recently adjusted effective April 1, 2010 and will be adjusted again in 2013.

A visualization of expenses deducted from current monthly income in applying the means test follows:

EXPENSES DEDUCTED FROM CURRENT MONTHLY INCOME IN APPLYING MEANS TEST § 707(b)(2)(A)(ii) – (iv)

EXPENSE AMOUNTS UNDER IRS NATIONAL STANDARDS	EXPENSE AMOUNTS UNDER IRS LOCAL STANDARDS	EXPENSE AMOUNTS UNDER IRS OTHER NECESSARY EXPENSES	ADDITIONAL EXPENSES	PAYMENTS ON SECURED DEBT	PAYMENTS ON PRIORITY CLAIMS
FOOD, CLOTHING AND OTHER ITEMS	HOUSING AND UTILITIES: NON-MORTGAGE EXPENSES, MORTGAGE EXPENSE, ADJUSTMENT	TAXES	HEALTH INSURANCE, DISABILITY INSURANCE AND HEALTH SAVINGS ACCOUNT EXPENSES	AVERAGE MONTHLY AMOUNT DUE TO SECURED CREDITORS OVER 60 MONTHS FOLLOWING FILING DATE, AND	AVERAGE MONTHLY EXPENSES OVER NEXT FIVE YEARS FOR PAYMENT OF ALL PRIORITY CLAIMS
HEALTH CARE		INVOLUNTARY DEDUCTIONS FOR EMPLOYMENT	CARE AND SUPPORT OF ELDERLY, CHRONICALLY ILL OR DISABLED FAMILY MEMBER		
		LIFE INSURANCE	PROTECTION AGAINST FAMILY VIOLENCE	ANY ADDITIONAL PAYMENTS TO MAINTAIN POSSESSION OF COLLATERAL NECESSARY FOR SUPPORT IN CHAPTER 13	
	TRANSPORTATION: VEHICLE OPERATION, PUBLIC TRANSPORTATION, ADDITIONAL EXPENSES, OWNERSHIP/LEASE EXPENSE	COURT-ORDERED PAYMENTS	HOME ENERGY		
		EDUCATION FOR EMPLOYMENT OR FOR PHYSICALLY OR MENTALLY CHALLENGED CHILD	EDUCATION EXPENSES FOR MINORS UP TO $1,775* A YEAR		
		CHILDCARE	ADDITIONAL FOOD AND CLOTHING UP TO 5% OF ALLOWED AMOUNT		
		HEALTH CARE	CHAPTER 13 ADMINISTRATIVE EXPENSES		
		TELECOMMUNICATION SERVICES	CHARITABLE CONTRIBUTIONS		

* This dollar figure, like many of the dollar figures in the Code, are subject to adjustment every three years under § 104(b) of the Code to reflect change in the Consumer Price Index for the most recent three years, and were most recently adjusted effective April 1, 2010 and will be adjusted again in 2013.

After current monthly income is reduced by the permitted expenses, we are left with monthly disposable income (the excess amount that is available every month to pay unsecured creditors). That amount gets multiplied by 60 to obtain the amount of available income to pay unsecured debt over the next five years. If that figure is less than $7,025,[*] the presumption of abuse does not apply and debtor's chapter 7 case will not be dismissed on that basis. If that figure is greater than $11,725,[*] the presumption of abuse arises, and the chapter 7 case will be dismissed unless the debtor can rebut the presumption as discussed below. If the figure is neither less than $7,025[*] nor greater than $11,725,[*] then the debtor must compute the amount that equals 25% of the debtor's nonpriority unsecured claims. If the figure is at least as much as that 25% figure, the presumption of abuse arises. A visualization of the application of the presumption of abuse to the monthly disposable income figures follows:

PRESUMPTION OF ABUSE BASED ON FIVE YEARS OF MONTHLY DISPOSABLE INCOME § 707(b)(2)(A)(i)			
MONTHLY DISPOSABLE INCOME TIMES 60 IS LESS THAN $7,025[*]	MONTHLY DISPOSABLE INCOME TIMES 60 IS MORE THAN $11,725*	MONTHLY DISPOSABLE INCOME TIMES 60 IS NOT LESS THAN $7,025* NOR MORE THAN $11,725*	
PRESUMPTION OF ABUSE DOES NOT ARISE	PRESUMPTION OF ABUSE ARISES	MONTHLY DISPOSABLE INCOME TIMES 60 IS LESS THAN 25% OF DEBTOR'S NONPRIORITY UNSECURED CLAIMS	MONTHLY DISPOSABLE INCOME TIMES 60 IS NOT LESS THAN 25% OF DEBTOR'S NONPRIORITY UNSECURED CLAIMS
		PRESUMPTION OF ABUSE DOES NOT ARISE	PRESUMPTION OF ABUSE ARISES

---

[*] These dollar figures, like many of the dollar figures in the Code, are subject to adjustment every three years under § 104(b) of the Code to reflect change in the Consumer Price Index for the most recent three years, and were most recently adjusted effective April 1, 2010 and will be adjusted again in 2013.

The presumption of abuse may be rebutted only upon a showing of "special circumstances that justify additional expenses or adjustments of current monthly income for which there is no reasonable alternative." § 707(b)(2)(B)(i). These special circumstances (such as "a serious medical condition or a call or order to active duty in the Armed Forces") must be documented and explained and the debtor must attest to the accuracy of the information under oath. The presumption of abuse may be rebutted by these special circumstances only if the additional expenses or adjustments of current monthly income would cause the monthly disposable income times 60 to be less than the lesser of (i) 25% of the debtor's nonpriority unsecured claims, or $7,025,[*]

---

[*] These dollar figures, like many of the dollar figures in the Code, are subject to adjustment every three years under § 104(b) of the Code to reflect change in the Consumer Price Index for the most recent three years, and were most recently adjusted effective April 1, 2010 and will be adjusted again in 2013.

whichever is greater, or (ii) $11,725,* so that the presumption of abuse would not arise. § 707(b)(2)(B). A visualization of the special circumstances doctrine follows:

REBUTTAL OF PRESUMPTION OF ABUSE § 707(b)(2)(B)			
STANDARD FOR REBUTTAL OF PRESUMPTION OF ABUSE	EXAMPLES OF SPECIAL CIRCUMSTANCES	DEBTOR'S DUTIES TO REBUT PRESUMPTION	MINIMUM REQUIREMENTS FOR REBUTTAL
SPECIAL CIRCUMSTANCES THAT JUSTIFY ADDITIONAL EXPENSES OR ADJUSTMENT OF CURRENT MONTHLY INCOME FOR WHICH THERE IS NO REASONABLE ALTERATIVE	SERIOUS MEDICAL CONDITION CALL OR ORDER TO ACTIVE DUTY IN THE ARMED FORCES	DOCUMENTATION FOR EXPENSE OR ADJUSTMENT TO INCOME DETAILED EXPLANATION OF SPECIAL CIRCUMSTANCES MAKING EXPENSE OR ADJUSTMENT REASONABLE AND NECESSARY ATTESTATION UNDER OATH TO ACCURACY OF INFORMATION PROVIDED	PRESUMPTION WOULD NOT ARISE AFTER GIVING EFFECT TO ADDITIONAL EXPENSE OR ADJUSTMENT TO INCOME

In every chapter 7 case filed by an individual debtor, the U.S. trustee is required by § 704(b)(1) to review all materials filed by the debtor, including Official Form 22, and not later than 10 days after the first meeting of creditors file with the court a statement as to whether the debtor's chapter 7 case should give rise to a presumption of abuse under § 707(b)(2). The U.S. trustee is then required within 30 days after filing such statement either to file a motion to dismiss or convert the case, or to file a statement explaining why the trustee does not consider such a motion to be appropriate. § 704(b)(2).

If a trustee files a motion for dismissal or conversion and the court grants the motion, and the court finds that the action of the attorney for the debtor in filing a chapter 7 case violated Fed. R. Bankr. P. 9011, the court may order the attorney for the debtor to reimburse the trustee for all reasonable costs incurred in prosecuting the motion, including reasonable attorneys' fees. § 707(b)(4)(A). In addition, if the court concludes that the attorney violated Rule 9011, the court may assess an appropriate

---

* This dollar figure, like many of the dollar figures in the Code, is subject to adjustment every three years under § 104(b) of the Code to reflect change in the Consumer Price Index for the most recent three years, and were most recently adjusted effective April 1, 2010 and will be adjusted again in 2013.

civil penalty against the attorney and may order payment of such penalty to the trustee or the U.S. trustee. § 707(b)(4)(B). By signing a bankruptcy petition, the attorney for the debtor is deemed to certify that the attorney has performed a reasonable investigation into the circumstances that gave rise to the petition and determined that the petition is well grounded in fact and warranted by existing law or a good faith argument for the extension, modification, or reversal of existing law and does not constitute an abuse of chapter 7. § 707(b)(4)(C). The attorney's signature on a chapter 7 petition is also a certification that the attorney has no knowledge after an inquiry that the information in the schedules filed with the petition is incorrect. § 707(b)(4)(D).

If any party in interest (other than the trustee or U.S. trustee) makes a motion to dismiss the chapter 7 case under § 707(b) and the court denies the motion, the court may award the debtor all reasonable costs, including reasonable attorneys' fees, incurred in contesting the motion if the position of the movant violated Rule 9011 or the attorney who filed the motion did not perform a reasonable investigation into the circumstances that gave rise to the motion and did not determine that the motion was well grounded in fact and warranted by existing law or a good faith argument for the extension, modification, or reversal of existing law and did not constitute an abuse of chapter 7, and the motion was made solely for the purpose of coercing a debtor into waiving a right guaranteed to the debtor under chapter 7. § 707(b)(5)(A).

The presumption of abuse is considered at the onset of a chapter 7 case, but a motion to dismiss or convert a case under § 707(b)(1) may be made at any time during the case. A further discussion of dismissal or conversion is included in Chapter 11, *infra*.

E. VENUE

The concept of "venue" is designed to direct cases over which a federal court has jurisdiction into the federal court located in a district in which there is an appropriate connection to the party seeking redress. The appropriate venue for a bankruptcy case is set forth in 28 U.S.C. § 1408(1); this identifies the proper federal district or districts in which a person or persons may file a petition commencing a bankruptcy case.

The indicia of an appropriate connection to the district are any of the following: (1) debtor's domicile (for an individual, that individual's permanent home, and for a legal person, the state of organization or incorporation); (2) debtor's residence (for an individual, where that individual is actually living, and for a legal person, where the chief executive offices are located); (3) debtor's principal place of business in the United States; or (4) the location of debtor's principal assets in the United States.

But in order to avoid forum-shopping (selecting a favorable district for the bankruptcy filing by moving to that district immediately before filing), 28 U.S.C. § 1408(1) makes venue appropriate in a particular district only if one of the four factors listed above has been located in that district for 180 days prior to the filing of the bankruptcy petition. If one of those factors was not located in a district during the full 180 days, the filer may choose a district in which a factor was located for the longer part of the 180-day period prior to filing.

Prospective debtors are given an additional option for the location of their bankruptcy filings in 28 U.S.C. § 1408(2). Instead of filing based on the location of their own domicile, residence, principal place of business or principal assets, they may file in any district in which there is pending a bankruptcy case concerning their affiliate or general partner or partnership. Under § 101(2) of Code, an "affiliate" means an entity that controls or is controlled by the debtor, as determined by ownership or control of voting stock (with a 20% threshold), operation of business or operation of substantially all property. A visualization of the definition of "affiliate" follows.

DEFINITION OF AFFILIATE § 101(2)			
PERSONS CONTROLLED BY DEBTOR		PERSONS CONTROLLING DEBTOR	
CORPORATION 20% OR MORE OF WHOSE OUTSTANDING VOTING SECURITIES ARE OWNED, CONTROLLED OR HELD WITH POWER TO VOTE BY DEBTOR OR BY ENTITY THAT OWNS, CONTROLS OR HOLDS WITH POWER TO VOTE 20% OR MORE OF OUTSTANDING VOTING SECURITIES OF DEBTOR (OTHER THAN ENTITY HOLDING SECURITIES AS FIDUCIARY OR AS SECURED PARTY)	PERSON WHOSE BUSINESS IS OPERATED UNDER A LEASE OR OPERATING AGREEMENT BY DEBTOR, OR PERSON SUBSTANTIALLY ALL OF WHOSE PROPERTY IS OPERATED UNDER AN OPERATING AGREEMENT WITH DEBTOR	ENTITY THAT OWNS, CONTROLS, OR HOLDS WITH POWER TO VOTE 20% OR MORE OF OUTSTANDING VOTING SECURITIES OF DEBTOR (OTHER THAN ENTITY HOLDING SECURITIES AS FIDUCIARY OR AS SECURED PARTY)	ENTITY THAT OPERATES THE BUSINESS OR SUBSTANTIALLY ALL OF THE PROPERTY OF THE DEBTOR UNDER A LEASE OR OPERATING AGREEMENT

Although this provision is intended to promote judicial economy, by allowing consolidation of related cases in one district, it has the practical effect of allowing forum-shopping by entities with numerous affiliates by allowing an initial filing of a bankruptcy petition by the affiliate in a district where venue is appropriate for the affiliate but not for the often-much-larger entity, followed by filing of the entity in the same district. A classic example of this tactic was the bankruptcy case of Enron Corp., an Oregon corporation based in Houston, Texas, which had no connection to New York except for its subsidiary Enron Metals & Commodity Corp. (EMC), a Delaware corporation, which had its principal place of business in New York and whose assets constituted less than .5% of the consolidated assets of Enron and its affiliates. EMC filed a bankruptcy petition in the Southern District of New York (long a favored venue for bankruptcy cases) based on EMC's principal place of business under § 1408(1), and then filed petitions for Enron Corp. and the other Enron subsidiaries in the same district under § 1408(2). The following visualizes the venue provisions for bankruptcy cases:

VENUE OF BANKRUPTCY CASE 28 U.S.C. § 1408	
FACTORS RELATING DEBTOR TO DISTRICT OF FILING § 1408(1)	AFFILIATE (§ 101(2)) EXCEPTION § 1408(2)
DISTRICT IN WHICH ANY OF THE FOLLOWING HAS BEEN LOCATED FOR 180 DAYS IMMEDIATELY PRECEDING FILING (OR LONGER PORTION OF SUCH 180-DAY PERIOD THAN ANY OTHER DISTRICT): 1) DEBTOR'S DOMICILE 2) DEBTOR'S RESIDENCE 3) DEBTOR'S PRINCIPAL PLACE OF BUSINESS IN U.S. 4) DEBTOR'S PRINCIPAL ASSETS IN U.S.	DEBTOR MAY FILE IN DISTRICT IN WHICH THERE IS PENDING A BANKRUPTCY CASE CONCERNING DEBTOR'S AFFILIATE, GENERAL PARTNER, OR PARTNERSHIP

Even if a bankruptcy petition is filed in a district where venue is proper, the court has the power, either on its own motion or a motion by a party in interest, to transfer the bankruptcy case to another district "in the interest of justice or for the convenience of the parties" under 28 U.S.C. § 1412 and Fed. R. Bankr. P. 1014(a)(1). When the motion for transfer is made by a party in interest, that party has the burden of showing that the transfer meets the statutory standard. If the standard is not met, the original court retains the filed bankruptcy case.

If a bankruptcy filing is made in a district in which venue is improper, 28 U.S.C. § 1412 is not entirely clear on what should happen. Prior to 1984, the Judicial Code explicitly authorized a bankruptcy court to retain a case filed in a jurisdiction in which venue was improper "in the interests of justice and for the convenience of the parties"; that provision was repealed in 1984. Fed. R. Bankr. P. 1014(a)(2), intended to implement 28 U.S.C. § 1412, states that if a petition is filed in an improper district, the court may dismiss it, or transfer it to another district if the transfer is in the interest of justice or for the convenience of the parties; Rule 1014(a)(2) does not explicitly authorize the court to retain jurisdiction. Under the general venue provision of the Judicial Code (28 U.S.C. § 1406(a)), when a case is filed in an improper venue, the district court must dismiss the case or transfer it upon objection by a party in interest. The prevailing view is that a bankruptcy judge has the same powers with respect to a case filed in a district where venue does not lie and may not retain the case. The following visualization shows the change of venue provision:

CHANGE OF VENUE
28 U.S.C. § 1412

DISTRICT COURT MAY TRANSFER BANKRUPTCY CASE OR PROCEEDING TO ANOTHER
DISTRICT IN THE INTEREST OF JUSTICE OR FOR THE CONVENIENCE OF THE PARTIES

Section 1408 of the Judicial Code deals with venue of the bankruptcy case itself. The Judicial Code includes two separate venue provisions relating to bankruptcy cases, one for bankruptcy proceedings arising under the Code or arising in or related to bankruptcy cases, and one for bankruptcy cases ancillary to foreign proceedings.

Generally, a proceeding arising under title 11 or arising in or related to a bankruptcy case is appropriately brought in the district in which the bankruptcy case is pending. 28 U.S.C. § 1409(a). However, there are two exceptions to that rule, and two other cases in which an alternative venue is also appropriate.

The first exception is for small claims. Under § 1409(b), a trustee may commence a proceeding arising in or related to a bankruptcy case to recover a money judgment or property worth less than $1,175,* or a consumer debt of less than $17,575,* or a non-consumer debt against a noninsider (*see* definition of "insider" in § 101(31)) of less than $11,725,* only in the district court for the district in which the defendant resides. The justification for this exception is that it is unfair to compel the defendant to incur the cost of defending an action to recover a relatively small amount of money or property in what may be a distant jurisdiction where the bankruptcy case is pending. If the trustee wishes to pursue these actions, the trustee should go to the defendant's district rather than forcing the defendant to come to the trustee's district.

The second exception relates to claims from the operation of the business of the debtor brought by the trustee arising after the commencement of the bankruptcy case. These postpetition claims may be asserted by the trustee only in the district court for the district where a state or federal court is located in which an action on such claim could have been brought under applicable nonbankruptcy venue provisions. § 1409(d).

The two alternative provisions permit, but do not require, a proceeding to be commenced in a district other than the district in which the bankruptcy case is pending. The first, § 1409(c), allows the trustee to bring claims (other than small claims covered by § 1409(b)) as statutory successor to the debtor or creditors under § 541 or § 544(b) of the Code in the district court for the district where a state or federal court is located in which an action on such claim could have been brought by the debtor or creditors, as the case may be, under applicable nonbankruptcy venue provisions. The second, § 1409(e), allows a person with a claim from the operation of the business of the debtor arising after the commencement of the bankruptcy case to commence a

---

* These dollar figures, like many of the dollar figures in the Code, are subject to adjustment every three years under § 104(b) of the Code to reflect change in the Consumer Price Index for the most recent three years, and were most recently adjusted effective April 1, 2010 and will be adjusted again in 2013.

proceeding in the district court for the district where a state or federal court is located in which an action on such claim could have been brought under applicable nonbankruptcy venue provisions, as well as in the district in which the bankruptcy case is pending.

As was true for bankruptcy cases, a district court may transfer a bankruptcy proceeding to a district court for another district "in the interest of justice or for the convenience of the parties" under 28 U.S.C. § 1412.

A visualization of the venue provisions relating to proceedings in bankruptcy follows:

VENUE OF BANKRUPTCY PROCEEDINGS 28 U.S.C. § 1409		
GENERAL VENUE PROVISION § 1409(a)	EXCEPTIONS § 1409(b) & (d)	ALTERNATIVES § 1409(c) & (e)
PROCEEDING ARISING UNDER TITLE 11 OR ARISING IN OR RELATED TO BANKRUPTCY CASE MAY BE COMMENCED IN DISTRICT COURT IN WHICH CASE IS PENDING	PROCEEDING BY TRUSTEE TO RECOVER MONEY JUDGEMENT OR PROPERTY WORTH LESS THAN $1,175* OR CONSUMER DEBT LESS THAN $17,575* OR NONCONSUMER DEBT AGAINST NONINSIDER LESS THAN $11,725* MAY BE BROUGHT ONLY IN DISTRICT IN WHICH DEFENDANT RESIDES PROCEEDING BY TRUSTEE ON POSTPETITION CLAIM ARISING FROM OPERATION OF DEBTOR'S BUSINESS MAY BE BROUGHT ONLY IN DISTRICT WHERE IT COULD HAVE BEEN BROUGHT UNDER NONBANKRUPTCY VENUE PROVISIONS	PROCEEDING BY TRUSTEE AS STATUTORY SUCCESSOR TO DEBTOR OR CREDITORS UNDER § 541 OR § 544(b) (OTHER THAN SMALL CLAIM UNDER § 1409(b)) MAY BE BROUGHT IN DISTRICT WHERE IT COULD HAVE BEEN BROUGHT UNDER NONBANKRUPTCY VENUE PROVISIONS PROCEEDING BROUGHT AGAINST REPRESENTATIVE OF ESTATE ON POSTPETITION CLAIM ARISING FROM OPERATION OF DEBTOR'S BUSINESS MAY BE BROUGHT IN DISTRICT WHERE IT COULD HAVE BEEN BROUGHT UNDER NONBANKRUPTCY VENUE PROVISIONS OR IN DISTRICT WHERE BANKRUPTCY CASE IS PENDING

---

* These dollar figures, like many of the dollar figures in the Code, are subject to adjustment every three years under § 104(b) of the Code to reflect change in the Consumer Price Index for the most recent three years, and were most recently adjusted effective April 1, 2010 and will be adjusted again in 2013.

The venue provision for cases ancillary to foreign proceedings under chapter 15 of the Bankruptcy Code, 28 U.S.C. § 1410, provides three alternative districts for venue, the second to be applicable only if the first is not, and the third to be applicable only if the two prior alternatives are not. The first choice for venue of a chapter 15 case is the district in which the debtor has its principal place of business or principal assets in the United States. If the debtor does not have a U.S. place of business or assets, venue is appropriate in a district in which there is pending against the debtor an action or proceeding in federal or state court. If neither of those alternatives is applicable, venue is appropriate in any district in which venue will be "consistent with the interests of justice and the convenience of the parties, having regard to the relief sought by the foreign representative." A visualization of these provisions follows:

VENUE OF CASES ANCILLARY TO FOREIGN PROCEEDINGS 28 U.S.C. § 1410		
DISTRICT IN WHICH DEBTOR HAS PRINCIPAL PLACE OF BUSINESS OR PRINCIPAL ASSETS IN U.S.	IF DEBTOR HAS NO U.S. PLACE OF BUSINESS OR ASSETS, DISTRICT IN WHICH THERE IS PENDING AGAINST THE DEBTOR AN ACTION OR PROCEEDING IN STATE OR FEDERAL COURT	IN ALL OTHER CASES, ANY DISTRICT IN WHICH VENUE WILL BE CONSISTENT WITH THE INTERESTS OF JUSTICE AND THE CONVENIENCE OF THE PARTIES, HAVING REGARD TO THE RELIEF SOUGHT BY THE FOREIGN REPRESENTATIVE

F. FILING REQUIREMENTS AND DEBTOR DISCLOSURE DUTIES

1. The Petition (Voluntary and Involuntary)

A voluntary bankruptcy case is commenced by the filing with the clerk of the bankruptcy court of a petition under a chapter of the Code by an entity eligible to be a debtor under that chapter. § 301, Fed. R. Bankr. P. 1002. If an individual who is an eligible debtor and that individual's spouse wish to file for bankruptcy jointly, they may do so by filing a single petition that so indicates. § 302. The overwhelming majority of bankruptcy cases are voluntary cases, commenced voluntarily by the debtor or debtors. Official Form 1 is the form of petition for a voluntary filing.

The Code does, however, provide for debtors to be forced into bankruptcy, a so-called "involuntary case." § 303. Official Form 5 is the form of petition for an involuntary filing. Involuntary cases may be commenced only under chapter 7 or chapter 11 of the Code. Farmers (§ 101(20)), family farmers (§ 101(18)) and corporations that are not moneyed, business, or commercial corporations cannot be the subject of an involuntary bankruptcy, nor can a person who is ineligible to be a debtor under the chapter for which the petition is filed.

If the person against whom the involuntary petition is being filed has at least 12 holders of claims against the prospective debtor that are not contingent as to liability or the subject of a bona fide dispute as to liability or amount, and which aggregate at least $14,425* more than the value of any lien on debtor's property securing such claims (meaning the claims are unsecured to that extent), then an involuntary petition can be filed only by three or more such holders (or indenture trustees representing such holders).

If the person against whom the involuntary petition is being filed has fewer than 12 such holders (excluding holders who are employees or insiders of the prospective debtor, and any transferee of a claim who received the claim in a transfer that is voidable under the Code), any one or more of such holders holding in the aggregate at least $14,425* of noncontingent, undisputed, unsecured claims may file an involuntary petition.

The filing of a petition in a voluntary bankruptcy case constitutes an "order for relief," meaning that the bankruptcy case is legally commenced at that time. § 301(b). However, the filing of a petition in an involuntary bankruptcy is only the first step in the determination of whether a bankruptcy case is appropriate. The debtor against whom the petition has been filed has the right to file an answer to the petition, § 303(d), and the court may, for cause, order the creditors who filed the involuntary petition to post a bond to indemnify the debtor for any damages caused by an unjustified petition. § 303(e). Meanwhile, until an order for relief is granted by the court, the debtor may continue to operate its business and use, acquire or dispose of property to the same extent as before the petition was filed, unless the court orders otherwise. § 303(f). Any party in interest may move for the appointment of an interim trustee to take possession of the estate property and to run debtor's business, but such a motion will be granted only "if necessary to preserve the property of the estate or to prevent loss to the estate." § 303(g).

If the debtor chooses not to contest the involuntary petition within the time period provided by Fed. R. Bankr. P. 1011, the court must order relief against the debtor under the chapter pursuant to which the petition was filed. But if the debtor opposes the petition, the court will hold a trial to determine whether to order relief. There are only two grounds for ordering relief. The first is if the court finds that the debtor is "generally not paying such debtor's debts as such debts become due unless such debts are the subject of a bona fide dispute as to liability or amount." The second is if the court concludes that during the 120 days prior to the filing of the petition, a custodian was appointed or took possession of the property of the debtor. § 303(h).

If the court orders relief, the bankruptcy case continues and the debtor is required to file all required information under § 521 and Fed. R. Bankr. P. 1007. If the court dismisses the petition (other than with the consent of all petitioners and the debtor), the bankruptcy case ends and the court may impose sanctions against the petitioners unless the debtor waives them. All petitioners may be liable for debtor's costs or a reasonable attorney's fee. Any petitioner that filed the petition in bad faith may be liable for damages caused by the filing or punitive damages. § 303(i). In unusual cases, the petitioners may also be charged with bankruptcy crimes under 18 U.S.C. § 152(2)

---

* This dollar figure', like many of the dollar figures in the Code, are subject to adjustment every three years under § 104(b) of the Code to reflect change in the Consumer Price Index for the most recent three years, and were most recently adjusted effective April 1, 2010 and will be adjusted again in 2013.

(for making a false oath), 18 U.S.C. § 152(3) (for making a false statement under penalty of perjury) or 18 U.S.C. § 152(4) (for presenting a false claim).

If a petition filed against an individual is dismissed, other remedies may also be available. If the petition is false or contains any statement that is materially false, fictitious or libelous, the court must also, upon motion by the debtor, seal all records of the court relating to the petition. § 303(k)(1). The court may also enter an order prohibiting all consumer reporting agencies from making any consumer report containing information relating to the petition or the bankruptcy case commenced by the filing of the petition. § 303(k)(2).

A visualization of the provisions relating to involuntary bankruptcies follows:

INVOLUNTARY PETITIONS

BY WHOM § 303(b)	AGAINST WHOM § 303(a)	GROUNDS § 303(h)	SANCTIONS § 303(i) & (k)		
			ALL PETITIONS	PETITIONS FILED IN BAD FAITH	PETITIONS AGAINST INDIVIDUAL DEBTOR
IF DEBTOR HAS 12 OR MORE CREDITORS, THREE OR MORE CREDITORS HOLDING NON-CONTINGENT, NON-DISPUTED UNSECURED CLAIMS AGGREGATING AT LEAST $14,425*	PERSON NOT A FARMER, FAMILY FARMER OR NON-MONEYED, NON-BUSINESS OR NON-COMMERCIAL CORPORATION	GENERALLY NOT PAYING DEBTS AS THEY BECOME DUE UNLESS SUBJECT TO BONA FIDE DISPUTE, OR	COSTS, OR	DAMAGES, OR	SEAL RECORDS THAT ARE FALSE
OTHERWISE, ANY ONE CREDITOR HOLDING A NON-CONTINGENT, NON-DISPUTED CLAIM OF AT LEAST $14,425*		CUSTODIAN APPOINTED OR TOOK POSSESSION OF DEBTOR'S PROPERTY IN LAST 120 DAYS	REASONABLE ATTORNEYS' FEES	PUNITIVE DAMAGES	BAR USE IN CREDIT REPORTS

* These dollar figures, like many of the dollar figures in the Code, are subject to adjustment every three years under § 104(b) of the Code to reflect change in the Consumer Price Index for the most recent three years, and were most recently adjusted effective April 1, 2010 and will be adjusted again in 2013.

2. Debtor Disclosure Duties

At the beginning of a bankruptcy case, all debtors (including those filing under chapter 9, § 925) are required to file a list of creditors. § 521(a)(1)(A). In a voluntary case, the list (including each creditor's name and address) must be filed with the petition; in an involuntary case, the list must be filed within 14 days after entry of the order for relief. Fed. R. Bankr. P. 1007(a). If the debtor is a corporation, it must file a corporate ownership statement (*see* Fed. R. Bankr. P. 7007.1) with the petition, and if the filing is under chapter 11, must file within 14 days after the order for relief a list of equity security holders of each class showing the number and kind of equity interests each owns and the owner's address or place of business. Fed. R. Bankr. P. 1007(a)(1) and (3). A chapter 9 or chapter 11 debtor must also file a list of its 20 largest creditors (excluding insiders) by name, address and claim on Official Form 4. Fed. R. Bankr. P. 1007(d). A chapter 15 foreign representative must file a corporate ownership statement and a list of persons authorized to administer foreign proceedings of the debtor, parties to litigation pending by or against the debtor in the U.S. and all entitles against whom provisional relief is being sought under § 1519. Fed. R. Bankr. P. 1007(a)(4).

Each debtor (other than a chapter 9 debtor) is also required to file various schedules, statements and other documents shortly after the order for relief. § 521(a)(1)(B) and Fed. R. Bankr. P. 1007(b)(1). These include schedules of assets and liabilities (Official Form 6), a schedule of current income and current expenditures (Official Form 6), a schedule of executory contracts and unexpired leases (Official Form 6), and a statement of debtor's financial affairs (Official Form 7). Debtor must also file copies of all payment advices or other evidence of payments received in the last 60 days before filing from any employer, a statement of the amount of monthly net income (showing its computation), and a statement disclosing any reasonably anticipated increase in income or expenditures over the 12-month period following the filing date. If the debtor is an individual whose debts are primarily consumer debts, the debtor must also file a certificate of debtor's attorney or bankruptcy petition preparer indicating that debtor received the notice required by § 342(b).

If an individual debtor filing a voluntary petition under chapter 7 or chapter 13 fails to file all of the information required by § 521(a)(1) within 45 days after filing (or within an additional 45 days if the court finds justification for extending the period of filing, § 521(i)(3)), the case is automatically dismissed effective as of the next day. § 521(i)(1). Any party in interest may request an order dismissing the case effective as of such 46th day, and the court must act on such a motion within five days after it is made. However, on motion of the trustee filed before the expiration of the time for filing, the court may decline to dismiss the case if the debtor attempted in good faith to provide all payment advices and the best interests of creditors would be served by administering the case. § 521(i)(4).

An individual debtor has additional disclosure obligations. An individual debtor must submit a verified statement setting forth debtor's social security number or stating that the debtor does not have one. Fed. R. Bankr. P. 1007(f). Such a debtor must also file a statement of compliance with the prebankruptcy credit counseling requirement of § 109(h) on Exhibit D to Official Form 1, together with a certificate from the approved nonprofit budget and credit counseling agency that provided the required prebankruptcy briefing on credit counseling services under § 109(h), and a copy of any debt repayment plan developed through such counseling services. § 521(b) and Fed. R. Bankr. P. 1007(b)(3).

If the individual chapter 7 debtor's schedule of assets and liabilities includes debts secured by property of the estate, before the earlier of 30 days after filing or the date of the meeting of creditors (or such later date as the court for cause determines), the debtor must file a statement of intention (Official Form 8) with respect to the retention or surrender of such property and whether the debtor intends to redeem any such property that is exempt or reaffirm debts secured by such property. § 521(a)(2)(A) and Fed. R. Bankr. P. 1007(b)(2). The debtor must perform his or her intention with respect to such property within 30 days after the first date set for the meeting of creditors under § 341(a) (or within such additional time as the court, for cause, fixes). § 521(a)(2)(B).

If the individual debtor files under chapter 7, the debtor must complete a statement of current monthly income and means-test calculation on Official Form 22 to permit the implementation of § 707(b)(2) discussed in Chapter 1[D], *supra*. An individual chapter 11 filer must complete a statement of current monthly income on Official Form 22B, and the chapter 13 filer must complete a statement of current monthly income and calculation of commitment period and disposable income on Official Form 22C. Fed. R. Bankr. P. 1007(b)(4)–(6).

The debtor must also provide to the trustee (and to any creditor that timely requests a copy), not later than seven days before the date first set for the meeting of creditors under § 341, a copy of debtor's federal income tax return for the most recently ended tax year before filing for which such a return was filed. § 521(e)(2)(A). Failure to do so warrants dismissal of the case unless the debtor demonstrates that the failure to comply is due to circumstances beyond the debtor's control. § 521(e)(2)(B) & (C).

A visualization of the debtor's disclosure duties upon filing follows:

DEBTOR DISCLOSURE DUTIES § 521 & RULE 1007					
ALL NON-CHAPTER 9 DEBTORS	INDIVIDUAL DEBTORS	CORPORATE DEBTORS	CHAPTER 9 DEBTORS	CHAPTER 11 DEBTOR	CHAPTER 15 FOREIGN REPRESENTATIVE
LIST OF CREDITORS SCHEDULES STATEMENT OF FINANCIAL AFFAIRS PAYMENT ADVICES STATEMENT OF MONTHLY NET INCOME STATEMENT OF ANTICIPATED CHANGES IN INCOME OR EXPENDITURES DURING NEXT 12 MONTHS STATEMENT OF INTEREST IN EDUCATION IRA OR STATE TUITION PROGRAM FEDERAL INCOME TAX RETURN FOR MOST RECENT TAX YEAR	§ 342(b) STATEMENT CERTIFICATE ON PRE-BANKRUPTCY CREDIT COUNSELING STATEMENT OF INTENTION WITH RESPECT TO PROPERTY SECURING DEBT IN CHAPTER 7 CURRENT MONTHLY INCOME CALCULATION ON FORM 22 (CHAPTER 7), 22B (CHAPTER 11) OR 22C (CHAPTER 13) STATEMENT OF SOCIAL SECURITY NUMBER	CORPORATE OWNERSHIP STATEMENT	LIST OF CREDITORS LIST OF 20 LARGEST CREDITORS	LIST OF EQUITY INTEREST HOLDERS LIST OF 20 LARGEST CREDITORS	CORPORATE OWNERSHIP STATEMENT LIST OF THOSE AUTHORIZED TO ADMINISTER FOREIGN PROCEEDINGS OF DEBTOR LIST OF PARTIES TO LITIGATION PENDING IN U.S. IN WHICH DEBTOR IS A PARTY LIST OF ALL ENTITIES AGAINST WHOM PROVISIONAL RELIEF IS BEING SOUGHT

G. EARLY CASE MANAGEMENT ISSUES

1. Trustees and Examiners and Debtor in Possession

As soon as the debtor has filed for bankruptcy, control over the debtor's property and affairs changes. The extent to which it changes depends on the chapter under which the filing was made.

If the debtor files under chapter 7, the U.S. trustee must appoint a disinterested person (§ 101(14)) from the panel of private trustees in the district to serve as interim trustee in the case. § 701(a). In most cases, the interim trustee continues to serve as the permanent trustee in the case. But on rare occasions, the interim trustee is replaced by a trustee elected by creditors at the meeting of creditors held under § 341 if eligible creditors holding at least 20% in amount of eligible claims so request. § 702. Eligible creditors are those holding allowable, undisputed, fixed, liquidated, unsecured, nonpriority claims other than insiders. § 101(31).

An individual is eligible to serve as a trustee if he or she is competent to perform the duties and, in the case of a chapter 7, 12 or 13 case, if the individual resides or has an office either in the judicial district in which the case is pending or an adjacent judicial district. § 321(a). A person who has served as an examiner in a case is not eligible to serve as trustee in that case. § 321(b). Anyone other than the U.S. trustee selected to serve as trustee qualifies if, before seven days after being selected, that person files with the court a bond in favor of the United States conditioned on faithful performance of the trustee's official duties. § 322(a). The U.S. trustee determines the amount of the bond and the sufficiency of the surety on the bond. § 322(b)(2).

A trustee is the representative of the estate in any bankruptcy case, § 323(a), and may sue and be sued in the case. § 323(b). The court, for cause, may remove a trustee (other than the U.S. trustee serving in that role), and if the court does so, the trustee is automatically removed from all other cases in which the trustee is serving unless the court orders otherwise. § 324.

The trustee is entitled to reasonable compensation for services rendered. In a chapter 7 or 11 case, the amount of the trustee's (or trustees') aggregate compensation awarded under § 330 is based on a sliding scale of percentages of moneys disbursed to parties in interest, ranging from 25% of the first $5,000 or less down to 3% of amounts in excess of $1,000,000. § 326(a). The trustee in a chapter 7 case is also entitled to $45 from the filing fee. § 330(b)(1). In a chapter 12 or 13 case, a trustee or trustees other than the U.S. trustee or a standing chapter 13 trustee may receive reasonable compensation under § 330 not to exceed 5% of plan payments in the aggregate, § 326(b), but in no event less than $5 a month from any distribution under the plan. § 330(c). The court may deny the trustee compensation for services and reimbursement of expenses if the trustee knowingly hires a professional person who is not a disinterested person or who represents or holds an interest adverse to the interest of the estate, or if the trustee fails to make diligent inquiry into those facts. § 326(d). For a discussion of retention of professional persons, see Chapter 1[G][3], *infra*.

The chapter 7 trustee administers the debtor's property and business during the chapter 7 case. Duties under § 704 include collecting property of the estate and reducing it to money for distribution, investigating the financial affairs of the debtor, examining and objecting to proofs of claim, providing appropriate reports and information to the court and creditors, and closing the estate as expeditiously as possible. Section 704 imposes additional duties on the trustee in cases involving individual debtors or health care businesses. A visualization of the duties of the chapter 7 trustee follows:

DUTIES OF CHAPTER 7 TRUSTEE § 704		
DUTIES IN ALL CASES	ADDITIONAL DUTIES IN INDIVIDUAL DEBTOR CASES	DUTIES FOR CASES INVOLVING HEALTH CARE BUSINESS
COLLECT AND REDUCE TO MONEY ALL PROPERTY OF THE ESTATE CLOSE THE ESTATE EXPEDITIOUSLY BE ACCOUNTABLE FOR ALL PROPERTY RECEIVED INVESTIGATE FINANCIAL AFFAIRS OF DEBTOR EXAMINE PROOFS OF CLAIM AND MAKE APPROPRIATE OBJECTIONS FURNISH INFORMATION REQUESTED BY PARTY IN INTEREST IF BUSINESS IS AUTHORIZED TO BE OPERATED, FILE PERIODIC REPORTS AND SUMMARIES OF OPERATIONS MAKE FINAL REPORT AND FILE FINAL ACCOUNT CONTINUE TO PERFORM ANY OBLIGATIONS AS ADMINISTRATOR OF EMPLOYEE BENEFIT PLAN	ENSURE DEBTOR PERFORMS INTENTION SPECIFIED IN STATEMENT OF INTENTION UNDER § 521(a)(2)(B) IF APPROPRIATE, OPPOSE DISCHARGE IF THERE IS CLAIM FOR DOMESTIC SUPPORT OBLIGATION, PROVIDE NOTICE DESCRIBED IN § 704(c) TO HOLDER OF CLAIM	USE BEST EFFORTS TO TRANSFER PATIENTS TO ALTERNATIVE FACILITY

Most districts have standing trustees appointed by the U.S. trustee to serve as trustees in chapter 13 cases. 28 U.S.C. § 586(b). In those districts without standing trustees, the U.S. trustee must appoint a disinterested person (§ 101(14)) to serve as trustee in a chapter 13 case, or the U.S. trustee must serve in that capacity. § 1302(a). Unlike in chapter 7, creditors may not replace the appointed trustee with a trustee of their own choosing.

The duties of a chapter 13 trustee under § 1302(b) and (c) are similar to those of a chapter 7 trustee, but the chapter 13 trustee does not collect and reduce to money property of the estate. A visualization of the duties of a chapter 13 trustee follows:

DUTIES OF CHAPTER 13 TRUSTEE § 1302(b) & (c)	
DUTIES IN ALL CASES	ADDITIONAL DUTIES IF DEBTOR IS ENGAGED IN BUSINESS
BE ACCOUNTABLE FOR ALL PROPERTY RECEIVED ENSURE DEBTOR PERFORMS INTENTION SPECIFIED IN STATEMENT OF INTENTION UNDER § 521(a)(2)(B) INVESTIGATE FINANCIAL AFFAIRS OF DEBTOR EXAMINE PROOFS OF CLAIM AND MAKE APPROPRIATE OBJECTIONS IF ADVISABLE, OBJECT TO DEBTOR'S DISCHARGE FURNISH INFORMATION REQUESTED BY PARTY IN INTEREST MAKE FINAL REPORT AND FILE FINAL ACCOUNT APPEAR AND BE HEARD AT HEARINGS ON: 1) VALUE OF PROPERTY SUBJECT TO LIEN 2) CONFIRMATION OF PLAN, OR 3) POST-CONFIRMATION MODIFICATION OF PLAN ADVISE AND ASSIST DEBTOR IN PERFORMANCE OF PLAN ENSURE DEBTOR BEGINS MAKING TIMELY PAYMENTS IF THERE IS CLAIM FOR DOMESTIC SUPPORT OBLIGATION, PROVIDE NOTICE DESCRIBED IN § 1302(d) TO HOLDER OF CLAIM	INVESTIGATE ACTS, CONDUCT, ASSETS, LIABILITIES, AND FINANCIAL CONDITION OF DEBTOR, OPERATION OF DEBTOR'S BUSINESS AND DESIRABILITY OF CONTINUING IT, AND OTHER MATTERS RELEVANT TO THE CASE OR TO FORMULATION OF A PLAN FILE STATEMENT OF ANY INVESTIGATION AND TRANSMIT COPY OR SUMMARY TO ANY ENTITY COURT DESIGNATES

A trustee may also be appointed in a chapter 11 case at any time after the commencement of the case and before confirmation of a plan. § 1104(a). Procedurally, the appointment of a trustee in a chapter 11 case requires a motion by a party in interest or the U.S. trustee and notice and a hearing, Fed. R. Bankr. P. 2007.1 and 9014. If the court determines that a trustee should be appointed, either the U.S. trustee will appoint one, or (on request of a party in interest) the U.S. trustee will convene a meeting of creditors to elect a trustee in the same manner as a trustee is elected in a chapter 7 case. § 1104(b).

There are two bases for appointment of a trustee. The first is for cause, including "fraud, dishonesty, incompetence, or gross mismanagement of the affairs of the debtor by current management, either before or after" filing. § 1104(a)(1). The type of mismanagement that warrants appointment is generally something more than that which led to the failure of the business, something that includes indications of self-dealing and gross negligence. The U.S. trustee is required to move for appointment of a trustee if there are reasonable grounds to suspect management or those selecting management participated in actual fraud, dishonesty or criminal conduct in debtor's management or public financial reporting. § 1104(e).

The second basis for appointment of a trustee is when appointment would be in the interests of creditors, equity holders and other interests. § 1104(a)(2). Although this is drafted as an alternative standard to the first, in practice it is rarely invoked because the same conduct would satisfy both bases for appointment.

A visualization of the grounds for appointment of a trustee follows:

GROUNDS FOR APPOINTMENT OF A TRUSTEE § 1104(a)	
§ 1104(a)(1)	§ 1104(a)(2)
FOR CAUSE, INCLUDING FRAUD, DISHONESTY, INCOMPETENCE, GROSS MISMANAGEMENT	IN THE INTERESTS OF CREDITORS, EQUITY SECURITY HOLDERS AND OTHER INTERESTS OF ESTATE

If the events giving rise to the appointment of a trustee disappear, the court may order that the debtor in possession be restored to possession and management of the estate and operation of the business. § 1105.

The duties of a chapter 11 trustee combine some of the duties of a chapter 7 trustee with some additional duties. § 1106(a). The trustee is authorized to operate the debtor's business unless the court orders otherwise. § 1108. A visualization of those duties follows:

DUTIES OF CHAPTER 11 TRUSTEE § 1106		
DUTIES IN ALL CASES	INDIVIDUAL DEBTOR CASES	HEALTH CARE BUSINESS CASES
BE ACCOUNTABLE FOR ALL PROPERTY RECEIVED EXAMINE PROOFS OF CLAIM AND MAKE APPROPRIATE OBJECTIONS FURNISH INFORMATION REQUESTED BY PARTY IN INTEREST IF BUSINESS IS AUTHORIZED TO BE OPERATED, FILE PERIODIC REPORTS AND SUMMARIES OF OPERATIONS MAKE FINAL REPORT AND FILE FINAL ACCOUNT CONTINUE TO PERFORM ANY OBLIGATIONS AS ADMINISTRATOR OF EMPLOYEE BENEFIT PLAN FILE § 521(a)(1) LISTS, SCHEDULES AND STATEMENT IF DEBTOR HAS NOT DONE SO INVESTIGATE ACTS, CONDUCT, ASSETS, LIABILITIES, AND FINANCIAL CONDITION OF DEBTOR, OPERATION OF DEBTOR'S BUSINESS AND DESIRABILITY OF CONTINUING IT, AND OTHER MATTERS RELEVANT TO THE CASE OR TO FORMULATION OF A PLAN FILE STATEMENT OF ANY INVESTIGATION AND TRANSMIT COPY OR SUMMARY TO ANY ENTITY COURT DESIGNATES FILE PLAN OF REORGANIZATION AS SOON AS PRACTICABLE OR STATEMENT WHY NOT OR RECOMMEND CONVERSION OR DISMISSAL FURNISH INFORMATION TO GOVERNMENTAL UNITS FOR YEARS IN WHICH TAX RETURN NOT FILED AFTER CONFIRMATION FILE NECESSARY REPORTS	IF THERE IS CLAIM FOR DOMESTIC SUPPORT OBLIGATION, PROVIDE NOTICE DESCRIBED IN § 1106(c) TO HOLDER OF CLAIM	USE BEST EFFORTS TO TRANSFER PATIENTS TO ALTERNATIVE FACILITY

In most chapter 11 cases, a trustee is not appointed or elected. Instead, the pre-bankruptcy debtor becomes something called the debtor in possession or DIP (§ 1101(1)) and has all the rights and powers (other than the right to compensation), and performs all the duties, of a trustee in the case (other than the duties set forth in § 1106(a)(2), (3) and (4)) until or unless another trustee is appointed. § 1107(a).

The debtor in possession operates under the direction of the management of the debtor. Retaining key management personnel is one of the principal objectives of a debtor in possession early in the ease, and the DIP may seek court approval of a program that provides financial incentives to those managers who continue their employment with the DIP during the bankruptcy case. Prior to the 2005 BAPCPA amendments to the Code, these programs (called key employee retention programs, or

"KERPs") were approved so long as they reflected a reasonable business judgment on the part of the DIP. But in the 2005 amendments, Congress imposed very strict limitations on KERPs in § 503(c). Payments to induce an insider to stay with the debtor during the bankruptcy (sometimes called "pay to stay") cannot be made under § 503(c)(1) unless the court determines that three conditions are met. First, the insider must have a bona fide job offer from another business at the same or greater rate of compensation. Second, the person's services must be essential to the survival of the business. Third, the amount paid that person must not be greater than 10 times the mean amount given to non-management employees or, if none are being given them, not greater than 25% of the amount of any payment to the insider in the prior calendar year. Severance payments are precluded under § 503(c)(2) unless two conditions are met: (i) the program is applicable to all full-time employees, and (ii) the amount is not greater than 10 times the amount of the mean severance pay given to non-management employees. A visualization of the limitations on KERPs follows:

LIMITATIONS ON KERPs
§ 503(c)

RETENTION TRANSFERS & OBLIGATIONS	SEVERANCE PAYMENTS	OTHER TRANSFERS & OBLIGATIONS
NONE UNLESS 1) BONA FIDE COMPETING JOB OFFER FOR AT LEAST SAME COMPENSATION, 2) SERVICES ESSENTIAL TO SURVIVAL OF BUSINESS, AND 3) EITHER: • AMOUNT ≤ 10 TIMES AMOUNT TO NONMANAGEMENT EMPLOYEES DURING SAME CALENDAR YEAR, OR • IF NONE MADE, AMOUNT ≤ 25% AMOUNT FOR THAT INSIDER DURING PRIOR CALENDAR YEAR	NONE UNLESS 1) PART OF PROGRAM FOR ALL FULL-TIME EMPLOYEES, AND 2) AMOUNT ≤ 10 TIMES MEAN SEVERANCE FOR NONMANAGEMENT EMPLOYEES DURING SAME CALENDAR YEAR	NONE OUTSIDE ORDINARY COURSE OF BUSINESS AND NOT JUSTIFIED BY FACTS AND CIRCUMSTANCES OF CASE, INCLUDING POSTPETITION OFFICERS, MANAGERS, CONSULTANTS

If there are no grounds for appointment of a trustee, but there are specific transactions involving management that require an independent investigation, the court may order the appointment of an examiner under § 1104(c). The procedural steps for appointment are the same as for a trustee — a motion by a party in interest or the U.S. trustee, notice and a hearing. Fed. R. Bankr. P. 2007.1 and 9014.

There are two grounds for appointment of an examiner. The first is when appointment is in the interests of creditors, equity holders and other interests of estate. § 1104(c)(1). In practice, this requires a determination of whether there is some evidence of fraud, misconduct, dishonesty, incompetence, or other management problems that would give rise to claims against management. The second ground is if the debtor's fixed, liquidated, unsecured debts (other than debts for goods, services, taxes or to an insider) exceed $5 million. § 1104(c)(2). Although the language suggests that there should be mandatory appointment of an examiner in all large cases, in practice courts will not make such an appointment unless they determine that the investigation is "appropriate," given the facts of each case and the cost of an examiner. The grounds for appointment of an examiner are visualized below:

GROUNDS FOR APPOINTMENT OF AN EXAMINER § 1104(c)	
§ 1104(c)(1)	§ 1104(c)(2)
IN THE INTERESTS OF CREDITORS, EQUITY SECURITY HOLDERS AND OTHER INTERESTS OF ESTATE	DEBTOR'S FIXED, LIQUIDATED UNSECURED DEBTS OTHER THAN FOR GOODS, SERVICES, TAXES, OR TO INSIDER > $5 MILLION

Like the trustee, an examiner may be removed by the court for cause. When the court so removes an examiner, the examiner is automatically removed in all other cases in which the examiner is serving unless the court orders otherwise. § 324.

2. Committees

The organization of creditors and other interested parties into committees is most often seen in cases filed under chapter 11. However, chapter 7 creditors may elect a committee of not fewer than three and not more than eleven creditors holding allowable unsecured nonpriority claims to serve as a creditors' committee. § 705(a). Such a committee may consult with the trustee or the U.S. trustee in connection with the administration of the debtor's estate, make recommendations with respect to the trustee's duties, and submit to the court or to the U.S. trustee any question about the administration of the estate. § 705(b).

But in chapter 11 cases, the U.S. trustee must appoint a committee of creditors holding unsecured claims as soon as practicable after the order for relief. § 1102(a)(1). This committee ordinarily consists of the persons holding the seven largest claims against the debtor of the kind represented by the committee who are willing to serve.

§ 1102(b)(1). The court may order that a committee of creditors not be appointed upon request by a party in interest if the debtor is a small business debtor (§ 101(51D)). § 1102(a)(3).

The U.S. trustee may (but need not) appoint additional committees of creditors and/or committees of equity security holders as the U.S. trustee deems appropriate. § 1102(a)(1). A committee of equity security holders ordinary consists of the persons holding the seven largest amounts of equity securities of the debtor of the kind represented on such committee. § 1102(b)(2).

If the U.S. trustee does not appoint additional committees, upon the request of a party in interest, the court may order such appointment by the U.S. trustee if "necessary to assure adequate representation of creditors or of equity security holders." § 1102(a)(2). The court may also order the U.S. trustee to change the membership of a committee based on the same considerations. § 1102(a)(4).

The following visualizes the provisions relating to appointment of committees in chapter 11:

APPOINTMENT OF CHAPTER 11 COMMITTEES § 1102				
OFFICIAL UNSECURED CREDITORS' COMMITTEE § 1102(a)(1)		OTHER COMMITTEES § 1102(a)(2)		
APPOINTMENT	COMPOSITION	APPOINTMENT	COMPOSITION	
MUST BE APPOINTED AS SOON AS PRACTICABLE AFTER ORDER FOR RELIEF BY U.S. TRUSTEE COURT MAY ORDER NO APPOINTMENT FOR SMALL BUSINESS DEBTOR CASE	ORDINARILY PERSONS HOLDING SEVEN LARGEST UNSECURED CLAIMS AGAINST DEBTOR COURT MAY ORDER CHANGE IN MEMBERSHIP TO ENSURE ADEQUATE REPRESEN-TATION	ADDITIONAL COMMITTEES OF CREDITORS OR EQUITY SECURITY HOLDERS AS U.S. TRUSTEE DEEMS APPROPRIATE OR AS DIRECTED BY COURT IF NECESSARY TO ENSURE ADEQUATE REPRESEN-TATION	FOR CREDITORS' COMMITTEES, ORDINARILY PERSONS HOLDING SEVEN LARGEST UNSECURED CLAIMS AGAINST DEBTOR OF THAT TYPE COURT MAY ORDER CHANGE IN MEMBERSHIP TO ENSURE ADEQUATE REPRESEN-TATION	FOR EQUITY COMMITTEES, ORDINARILY PERSONS HOLDING SEVEN LARGEST AMOUNTS OF EQUITY SECURITIES OF THAT KIND COURT MAY ORDER CHANGE IN MEMBERSHIP TO ENSURE ADEQUATE REPRESEN-TATION

A committee appointed under § 1102 has both rights and obligations. It must provide access to information to creditors it represents who are not appointed to the committee, and it must solicit and receive comments from those creditors. It is also subject to any court order compelling additional disclosure to those creditors. § 1102(b)(3). On the other hand, the committee has the right to hire attorneys, accountants, or other agents, to represent or perform services for the committee. § 1103(a). It may also perform various other services in the interest of those it represents. A visualization of the rights and duties of a committee follows:

RIGHTS AND DUTIES OF CHAPTER 11 COMMITTEES § 1102(b)(3) & § 1103	
DUTIES OF COMMITTEES TO REPRESENTED CREDITORS	RIGHTS OF COMMITTEES
PROVIDE ACCESS TO INFORMATION SOLICIT AND RECEIVE COMMENTS BE SUBJECT TO COURT ORDER COMPELLING ADDITIONAL REPORT OR INFORMATION BE MADE	EMPLOY ATTORNEYS, ACCOUNTANTS, OR OTHER AGENTS TO REPRESENT OR PERFORM SERVICES CONSULT WITH TRUSTEE OR DIP CONCERNING ADMINISTRATION OF ESTATE INVESTIGATE ACTS, CONDUCT, ASSETS, LIABILITIES, AND FINANCIAL CONDITION OF DEBTOR, OPERATION OF DEBTOR'S BUSINESS AND DESIRABILITY OF CONTINUING IT, AND OTHER MATTERS RELEVANT TO THE CASE OR TO FORMULATION OF A PLAN PARTICIPATE IN FORMULATION OF PLAN, ADVISE THOSE REPRESENTED ABOUT PLAN, AND COLLECT AND FILE ACCEPTANCES OR REJECTIONS OF PLAN REQUEST APPOINTMENT OF TRUSTEE OR EXAMINER PERFORM SUCH OTHER SERVICES AS ARE IN THE INTEREST OF REPRESENTED PARTIES

The trustee is obligated to meet with each committee as soon as practicable after its appointment to "transact such business as may be necessary or proper." § 1103(d).

3. Retention of Professionals

The Bankruptcy Code provides explicit authorization to the trustee to employ "one or more attorneys, accountants, appraisers, auctioneers, or other professional persons, that do not hold or represent an interest adverse to the estate, and that are disinterested persons." § 327(a). Because a debtor in possession has all the rights and powers of a trustee (with limited exceptions), § 1107(a), the debtor in possession also has the right to employ professional persons. A committee appointed under § 1102 may also employ attorneys, accountants or other agents. § 1103(a). The court may authorize the trustee to act as attorney or accountant for the estate if that is in the best interest of the estate, § 327(d), and may allow the trustee compensation for such services to the extent they are not within the general scope of a trustee's duties. § 328(b).

There are three requirements that must be met in order to be employed pursuant to § 327(a). First, the professional person must be offering the right type of service — the section authorizes retention of "attorneys, accountants, appraisers, auctioneers, or other professional persons." The Code does not define "professional persons," but courts tend to look to whether the person is performing services unique to the bankruptcy process, rather than general services that would be performed for the debtor in the absence of a bankruptcy filing.

Second, a professional person cannot be retained if that person holds or represents an interest adverse to the estate. This principle is similar to the limitations on lawyers with respect to conflicts of interest in representation under the Model Rules of Professional Conduct. For example, a retained professional would represent an interest adverse to the estate if such professional had an economic interest that would tend to lessen the value of the bankrupt estate or that would create either an actual or potential dispute in which the estate would be a rival claimant, or if the professional had any sort of bias against the estate. Some examples of situations in which an adverse interest has been found include representation of both a debtor corporation and its major shareholder or officers or directors where there are potential claims by the debtor against those other persons or entities, and representation of both a corporation debtor and its subsidiary debtors if there are significant inter-company claims and/or a likelihood of substantive consolidation. A professional person is not necessarily disqualified from retention by the trustee in a case under chapter 7, 11 or 12 because of such person's employment by or representation of a creditor. However, if another creditor or the U.S. trustee objects to such retention, the court must disapprove the retention if there is an actual conflict of interest. § 327(c).

Third, a professional person retained under § 327(a) must be a "disinterested person" under § 101(14). The definition defines a disinterested person by identifying three categories of persons who do not qualify: (1) anyone who is a creditor, equity holder, or insider (§ 101(31)); (2) anyone who is or has been a director, officer, or employee of debtor in the last two years before the bankruptcy filing; and (3) anyone with an interest materially adverse to the estate or any class of creditors or equity security holders. A visualization of the definition of "disinterested person" follows:

DISINTERESTED PERSON § 101(14)	
1)	NOT CREDITOR, EQUITY HOLDER, INSIDER (§ 101(31)),
2)	SINCE 2 YEARS PRIOR TO FILING HAS NOT BEEN DIRECTOR, OFFICER OR EMPLOYEE OF DEBTOR, AND
3)	NO MATERIALLY ADVERSE INTEREST TO ESTATE, OR ANY CLASS OF CREDITORS OR EQUITY HOLDERS

A summary visualization of the requirements for retention of professional persons under § 327(a) follows:

QUALIFICATIONS FOR RETENTION § 327(a)	
1)	PROFESSIONAL PERSON
2)	DOES NOT HOLD OR REPRESENT AN INTEREST ADVERSE TO ESTATE
3)	DISINTERESTED PERSON (§ 101(14))

In a case filed under chapter 11, a person is not disqualified from retention under § 327(a) by the debtor in possession solely because that person was employed by or represented the debtor prior to the bankruptcy filing. § 1107(b). This exception is probably not intended to permit retention of a professional with a claim against the estate based on prepetition services. Under § 327(e), the trustee is specifically authorized to employ, with the court's approval, for a specified purpose more limited than general representation of the trustee in the case, an attorney who has represented the debtor if such representation is in the best interest of the estate and if such attorney does not represent or hold any interest adverse to the debtor or to the estate with respect to the specified purpose.

The court must approve employment of any professional by the trustee, debtor in possession or committee. To obtain such approval, the trustee, debtor in possession or committee files an application seeking retention of the professional person. This application must include the detailed information specified in Fed. R. Bankr. P. 2014, including why the appointment is necessary, who is to be employed, why that person was selected, what services are to be provided, any proposed arrangement for compensation, and (to the best knowledge of the party seeking approval of the retention) all of the person's connections with the debtor, creditors, any other party in interest, their respective attorneys and accountants, the U.S. trustee or any person employed by U.S. trustee's office. Additional requirements for retention may be established by local rule of the bankruptcy court in which retention is sought. The application must be accompanied by a verified statement of the person to be retained setting forth the person's connections to the debtor, creditors, any other party in interest, their respective attorneys and accountants, the U.S. trustee or any person employed by U.S. trustee's office.

The requirements of Rule 2014 are visualized below:

APPLICATION FOR RETENTION
Fed. R. Bankr. P. 2014(a)

1)	NECESSITY FOR APPOINTMENT
2)	NAME OF PERSON TO BE EMPLOYED
3)	REASONS FOR SELECTION
4)	PROFESSIONAL SERVICES TO BE RENDERED
5)	ANY PROPOSED ARRANGEMENT FOR COMPENSATION
6)	TO THE BEST OF APPLICANT'S KNOWLEDGE, ALL CONNECTIONS WITH DEBTOR, CREDITORS, ANY OTHER PARTY IN INTEREST, THEIR ATTORNEYS AND ACCOUNTANTS, U.S. TRUSTEE, OR ANY PERSON EMPLOYED BY U.S. TRUSTEE
7)	ACCOMPANIED BY VERIFIED STATEMENT OF PERSON TO BE EMPLOYED SETTING OUT ALL CONNECTIONS WITH DEBTOR, CREDITORS, ANY OTHER PARTY IN INTEREST, THEIR ATTORNEYS AND ACCOUNTANTS, U.S. TRUSTEE, OR ANY PERSON EMPLOYED BY U.S. TRUSTEE

If the court approves the retention of a professional person and the professional person willfully fails to make the required disclosures under Rule 2014 that would have made the professional person ineligible for retention, the court may revoke the retention and deny or reduce the fees awarded or even require disgorgement of fees already paid. Any individual signing an application under Rule 2014 who intentionally fails to disclose material information may be charged with perjury.

The trustee or an official committee appointed under § 1102 may, with the court's approval, employ a professional person under § 327 or § 1103 "on any reasonable terms and conditions of employment, including on a retainer, on an hourly basis, on a fixed or percentage fee basis, or on a contingent fee basis." § 328(a). Even if the court approves those terms and conditions, if they turn out to be "improvident in light of developments not capable of being anticipated at the time of the fixing of such terms and conditions," the court may award compensation other than that provided under the agreed terms and conditions. *Id.* The court may deny compensation and reimbursement of expenses of a professional person if at any time during that person's employment that person is not a disinterested person or represents or holds an interest adverse to the interest of the estate. § 328(c).

Any attorney representing a debtor in or in connection with a bankruptcy case, whether or not such attorney seeks compensation pursuant to the Code, must file a statement of compensation paid or agreed to be paid for services in connection with the case and the source of such compensation if the payment or agreement was made within one year before the date of the filing of the petition. § 329(a). If the agreed or paid compensation exceeds the reasonable value of the services rendered, the court may cancel any such agreement, and may order the return of excessive funds paid. § 329(b).

The trustee or a professional person retained under § 327 or § 1103 may seek reasonable compensation for actual, necessary services rendered and reimbursement of actual, necessary expenses under § 330(a)(1). In determining the amount of compensation that is reasonable, the court must consider "the nature, the extent, and the value of such services," and must take into account not only the time spent and the rates charged for the services, but also such additional factors as the customary compensation charged by comparably skilled practitioners in other cases, and whether a professional person is board certified. § 330(a)(3). The court may award less than the amount sought, § 330(a)(2), and is specifically directed to disallow compensation for unnecessary duplication of services and services that were not reasonably likely to benefit the estate or not necessary to the administration of the case. § 330(a)(4)(A).

A person entitled to compensation under § 330 may apply for compensation for services rendered or expenses incurred to date not more than once every 120 days after the order for relief (more often if the court permits). § 331. The court may allow and disburse this interim compensation, but the final compensation awarded under § 330 is reduced by the amount of any interim compensation previously awarded. § 330(a)(5). If the amount of interim compensation exceeds the reasonable compensation awarded under § 330, the recipient must return the excess to the estate. *Id.*

A visualization of the provisions relating to compensation of professional persons follows.

COMPENSATION OF OFFICERS AND PROFESSIONAL PERSONS § 328 & § 330				
LIMITS ON COMPENSATION OF PROFESSIONAL PERSONS		COMPENSATION OF OFFICERS		
APPROVAL OF TERMS AND CONDITIONS § 328(a)	EXCEPTIONS § 328(a) & (c)	STANDARD § 330(a)(1)	FACTORS TO BE CONSIDERED § 330(a)(3)	EXCEPTIONS § 330(a)(4)(A)
TRUSTEE OR COMMITTEE MAY EMPLOY PROFESSIONAL PERSON ON ANY REASONABLE TERMS AND CONDITIONS OF EMPLOYMENT WITH COURT'S APPROVAL	IF TERMS AND CONDITIONS ARE IMPROVIDENT IN LIGHT OF DEVELOPMENTS NOT CAPABLE OF BEING ANTICIPATED AT TIME, COURT MAY AWARD DIFFERENT COMPENSATION COURT MAY DENY COMPENSATION FOR TIME PROFESSIONAL PERSON WAS NOT DISINTERESTED PERSON OR HELD ADVERSE INTEREST TO ESTATE	COURT MAY AWARD TRUSTEE OR PROFESSIONAL PERSON EMPLOYED UNDER § 327 OR § 1103 REASONABLE COMPENSATION FOR ACTUAL, NECESSARY SERVICES RENDERED AND REIMBURSE-MENT FOR ACTUAL, NECESSARY EXPENSES	COURT MUST CONSIDER NATURE, EXTENT AND VALUE OF SERVICES, INCLUDING: 1) TIME SPENT, 2) RATES CHARGED, 3) WHETHER SERVICES WERE NECESSARY OR BENEFICIAL, 4) WHETHER SERVICES WERE PERFORMED WITHIN REASONABLE AMOUNT OF TIME, 5) WHETHER PERSON IS BOARD CERTIFIED, AND 6) COMPENSATION OF OTHER COMPARABLY SKILLED PRACTITIONERS IN OTHER CASES	COURT MAY NOT AWARD COMPENSATION FOR UNNECESSARY DUPLICATION OF SERVICES, OR SERVICES THAT WERE NOT REASONABLY LIKELY TO BENEFIT ESTATE OR NOT NECESSARY TO ADMINISTRATION OF CASE

4. Meeting of Creditors

Unless the debtor has filed a plan and solicited acceptances prior to the commencement of the case and the court for cause orders that such a meeting need not be held, *see* § 341(e), the U.S. trustee must convene a meeting of creditors "within a reasonable time" after the order for relief in a bankruptcy case. § 341(a). The time for scheduling such a "§ 341 meeting" depends on the chapter under which the filing is made. Fed. R. Bankr. P. 2003(a). The meeting is held at the bankruptcy court or at another place designated by the U.S. trustee within the district convenient for the parties in interest. The U.S. trustee or the designee of the U.S. trustee presides over the meeting, and the bankruptcy judge may not attend any such meeting. § 341(c). The debtor is required to attend the meeting and submit to examination under oath by creditors, any indenture trustee, any trustee or examiner, or the U.S. trustee. § 343. Pursuant to local rule, the debtor may be required to bring certain documentation (such as tax returns, proof of earnings, appraisals, copies of leases, and cancelled checks for various payments) to support the information contained on the debtor's schedules.

The principal purpose of the meeting is to permit examination of the debtor under oath with respect to any facts bearing on the debtor's financial position. In a chapter 7 case, the creditors may also elect a trustee in bankruptcy, if they wish to replace the interim trustee, § 702(b), and may also elect a creditors' committee. § 705(a). The U.S. trustee must orally examine a chapter 7 debtor, asking whether the debtor is aware of the consequences of a bankruptcy discharge, the debtor's ability to file under another chapter of the Code, the effect of a bankruptcy discharge, and the effect of a reaffirmation (including the provisions of § 524(d)). § 341(d).

The § 341 meeting may be adjourned or continued when necessary to permit the debtor to obtain further documentation in response to the creditors' questions or to enable the creditors to make objections. Various other time periods for taking action in the bankruptcy case are determined by the time the § 341 meeting is held. *See, e.g.,* Fed. R. Bankr. P. 3002(c) (time for filing proofs of claim); Fed. R. Bankr. P. 4003(b) (time for filing objections to exemptions); Fed. R. Bankr. P. 4004(a) (time for filing objection to discharge); Fed. R. Bankr. P. 4007(c) (time for filing complaint to determine dischargeability of debt under § 523(c)).

A visualization of the § 341 meeting of creditors follows:

MEETING OF CREDITORS
§ 341 AND RULE 2003

WHEN			WHERE	WHO	ROLE OF CREDITORS	ROLE OF U.S. TRUSTEE	EXCEPTION
CH. 7 & 11	CH. 12	CH. 13					
NO FEWER THAN 21 OR MORE THAN 40 DAYS AFTER ORDER FOR RELIEF	NO FEWER THAN 21 OR MORE THAN 35 DAYS AFTER ORDER FOR RELIEF	NO FEWER THAN 21 OR MORE THAN 50 DAYS AFTER ORDER FOR RELIEF	REGULAR PLACE FOR HOLDING COURT OR ANY OTHER PLACE SET BY U.S. TRUSTEE IN DISTRICT CONVENIENT FOR PARTIES IN INTEREST	U.S. TRUSTEE OR DESIGNEE PRESIDES DEBTOR MUST BE PRESENT CREDITORS MAY ATTEND TRUSTEE MAY ATTEND COURT MAY NOT ATTEND	MAY ELECT TRUSTEE § 702(b) MAY ELECT CREDITORS' COMMITTEE § 705(a) MAY EXAMINE DEBTOR UNDER OATH	ADMINISTER OATHS MAY EXAMINE DEBTOR UNDER OATH RECORD EXAMINATION OF DEBTOR FILE REPORT OF ELECTION OF TRUSTEE OR CREDITORS' COMMITTEE OR REPORT OF DISPUTED ELECTION ORALLY EXAMINE CHAPTER 7 DEBTOR ON EFFECTS OF BANKRUPTCY	IF COURT FOR CAUSE ORDERS NO § 341 MEETING BECAUSE DEBTOR HAS FILED PLAN AND SOLICITED ACCEPTANCES PREPETITION

Chapter 2

THE ESTATE AND THE AUTOMATIC STAY

The filing of a bankruptcy petition has two immediate statutory consequences — it creates an estate (the property that becomes subject to the court's supervision), and operates as a stay (referred to as the "automatic stay") of certain acts, actions and proceedings. We will now look at the provisions relating to the bankruptcy estate and the automatic stay.

A. THE BANKRUPTCY ESTATE

1. Included and Excluded Property

Section 541(a) of the Code states that "[t]he commencement of a case . . . creates an estate." This estate is comprised of certain property in which the debtor had a legal or equitable interest prior to the bankruptcy filing or acquires an interest after the case commences. Seven different categories of property are described as part of the estate in § 541(a).

The first and most inclusive category of property included in the estate by the statute is legal or equitable interests of the debtor in property as of the commencement of the case. § 541(a)(1). Notice that there are three aspects of this broad inclusionary language: we must have something called "property," there must be some connection between that property and the debtor in the form of a legal or equitable interest, and this connection must exist at the applicable moment in time, i.e., as of the commencement of the case. Whether something qualifies as "property" is a question of federal law, and the term has been interpreted very broadly, sometimes more broadly than applicable state law. Whether the debtor has a legal or equitable interest in the property is an issue solely of state law. If the debtor has a legal interest (such as legal title) but no equitable interest in property, the property is included in the estate only to the extent of the debtor's legal interest. § 541(d).

Under § 541(a)(2), the estate may include some interests in property that belong to someone other than the debtor. If the debtor and the debtor's spouse hold community property that is either under the sole, equal, or joint management and control of the debtor or is liable for an allowable claim against the debtor or for allowable claims against both the debtor and the debtor's spouse (to the extent it is so liable), the interests of both the debtor and the debtor's spouse in that community property are included in the estate.

Generally, the debtor must have had an interest in the property as of the commencement of the case for the interest to be included in the estate, § 541(a)(1), but the remaining sections of § 541(a) sweep into the estate property in which the debtor or the trustee acquires an interest after the case is begun. Sections 541(a)(3) and (4) bring into the estate interests in property that are recovered by the trustee or preserved for the benefit of the estate during the case. Section 541(a)(5) includes interests in property acquired by the debtor (or to which the debtor becomes entitled) within 180 days after the filing of the petition in any of three ways: (1) by bequest, devise, or inheritance; (2) under a property settlement agreement with the debtor's spouse or a divorce decree; or (3) as a beneficiary of a life insurance policy or death benefit plan. If current property of the estate generates any proceeds, product, offspring, rents, or profits, those are also included in the estate under § 541(a)(6) (unless they are earnings from services performed by an individual debtor after the commencement of the case). And if the estate acquires an interest in property after commencement of the case, that interest also becomes part of the estate under § 541(a)(7).

Interests in property described in § 541(a) become part of the estate even if the debtor would be precluded from transferring the debtor's interest in the property outside of bankruptcy under an applicable agreement, transfer instrument, or nonbankruptcy law. The Code also renders ineffective any provision of such an agreement, instrument or nonbankuptcy law that would cause the debtor's interest in the property to terminate, or would give someone else the option to terminate debtor's interest, based on debtor's insolvency or financial condition, or filing for bankruptcy, or the appointment of a trustee or custodian. § 541(c)(1).

A visualization of the property included in the estate under § 541(a) follows:

PROPERTY INCLUDED IN THE ESTATE § 541(a)	
PROPERTY HELD AS OF COMMENCEMENT OF CASE	PROPERTY ACQUIRED AFTER COMMENCEMENT OF CASE
ALL LEGAL OR EQUITABLE INTERESTS OF THE DEBTOR IN PROPERTY § 541(a)(1) ALL INTERESTS OF THE DEBTOR AND DEBTOR'S SPOUSE IN COMMUNITY PROPERTY: • UNDER SOLE, EQUAL OR JOINT MANAGEMENT AND CONTROL OF DEBTOR, OR • LIABLE FOR AN ALLOWABLE CLAIM AGAINST DEBTOR OR ALLOWABLE CLAIMS AGAINST DEBTOR AND DEBTOR'S SPOUSE TO THE EXTENT SO LIABLE § 541(a)(2) INTERESTS IN PROPERTY THAT ARE NONASSIGNABLE UNDER AGREEMENT, TRANSFER INSTRUMENT OR APPLICABLE NONBANKRUPTCY LAW § 541(c)(1)	PROPERTY RECOVERED BY TRUSTEE OR PRESERVED FOR BENEFIT OF ESTATE § 541(a)(3) & (4) PROPERTY ACQUIRED BY DEBTOR WITHIN 180 DAYS AFTER FILING: • BY BEQUEST, DEVISE OR INHERITANCE, • BY DIVORCE DECREE OR PROPERTY SETTLEMENT AGREEMENT, OR • BY LIFE INSURANCE OR DEATH BENEFIT § 541(a)(5) PROCEEDS OF ESTATE PROPERTY (OTHER THAN POSTPETITION EARNINGS) § 541(a)(6) PROPERTY ACQUIRED BY ESTATE AFTER CASE COMMENCES § 541(a)(7)

In a chapter 13 case (or an individual chapter 11 case), in addition to the property described in § 541, two additional types of property are included in the estate. The first is all property of the kind described in § 541 that the debtor acquires after the case begins and before the case is closed, dismissed or converted. § 1306(a)(1) and § 1115(a)(1). The second is earnings from services performed by the debtor after commencement of the case and before the case is closed, dismissed, or converted. § 1306(a)(2) and § 1115(a)(2). Inclusion of this postpetition property in the estate is consistent with the approach of chapter 13 and an individual chapter 11, which allows the individual debtor to retain prepetition property in exchange for dedication of postpetition earnings to a plan. The chapter 13 debtor and the chapter 11 debtor (unlike the chapter 7 debtor) remain in possession of all property of the estate. § 1306(b) and § 1115(b). A visualization of the chapter 13 and individual chapter 11 estate follows:

PROPERTY INCLUDED IN THE CHAPTER 13 AND INDIVIDUAL CHAPTER 11 ESTATE § 1306 AND § 1115
ALL PROPERTY SPECIFIED IN § 541 ALL PROPERTY OF THE KIND SPECIFIED IN § 541 THAT DEBTOR ACQUIRES AFTER COMMENCEMENT OF CASE AND BEFORE CASE IS CLOSED, DISMISSED OR CONVERTED ALL EARNINGS FROM SERVICES PERFORMED BY DEBTOR AFTER COMMENCEMENT OF CASE AND BEFORE CASE IS CLOSED, DISMISSED OR CONVERTED

Certain property that would fall within the broad provisions of § 541(a) is explicitly excluded from the estate. As mentioned above, § 541(a)(6) includes within the estate any property derived from property of the estate (such as proceeds), but explicitly excludes "earnings from services performed by an individual debtor after the commencement of the case." Congress determined that postpetition earnings are particularly necessary to an individual debtor to get a fresh start coming out of bankruptcy and should not be swept into the estate.

Other exclusions from the estate are specifically enumerated in § 541(b). There are nine different interests in property which are excluded from the estate under § 541(b). All exclusions other than the first have been added since the enactment of the Code in 1978. Four were added by the 2005 BAPCPA amendments. A visualization of these § 541(b) exclusions follows:

EXCLUSIONS FROM PROPERTY OF THE ESTATE § 541(b)

POWER EXERCISABLE BY DEBTOR ONLY FOR BENEFIT OF ANOTHER	INTEREST AS LESSEE UNDER NON-RESIDENTIAL PROPERTY LEASE TERMINATED AT END OF TERM PRIOR TO OR DURING CASE	ELIGIBILITY UNDER HIGHER EDUCATION ACT PROGRAM OR ACCREDI-TATION AS EDUCATIONAL INSTITUTION	CERTAIN INTERESTS IN LIQUID OR GASEOUS HYDRO-CARBONS	FUNDS IN EDUCATIONAL IRA ACCOUNT DEPOSITED NOT LATER THAN 365 DAYS BEFORE FILING IF: • FOR BENEFIT OF CHILD OR GRANDCHILD, AND • NOT PLEDGED AS SECURITY, AND • IF DEPOSITED BETWEEN 365 AND 720 DAYS BEFORE FILING, FUNDS DO NOT EXCEED $5,850*	FUNDS IN TUITION CREDIT OR 529(b) ACCOUNT OR STATE TUITION PROGRAM DEPOSITED NOT LATER THAN 365 DAYS BEFORE FILING IF: • FOR BENEFIT OF CHILD OR GRANDCHILD, AND • IF DEPOSITED BETWEEN 365 AND 720 DAYS BEFORE FILING, FUNDS DO NOT EXCEED $5,850*	WAGES WITHHELD FOR OR CONTRIBU-TIONS TO EMPLOYEE BENEFIT PLANS OR DEFERRED COMPENSA-TION PLANS OR TAX-DEFERRED ANNUITIES OR HEALTH INSURANCE PLANS	INTEREST IN TANGIBLE PERSONAL PROPERTY PLEDGED OR SOLD AS COLLATERAL FOR LOAN FROM LICENSED LENDER IF: • PROPERTY HELD BY LENDER, • DEBTOR HAS NO OBLIGATION TO REPAY LOAN OR REDEEM PROPERTY, AND • NO RIGHT TO REDEEM EXERCISED	PROCEEDS OF MONEY ORDER SOLD WITHIN 14 DAYS PRIOR TO FILING UNDER AGREEMENT PROVIDING FOR NO COMINGLING OF PROCEEDS
§ 541(b)(1)	§ 541(b)(2)	§ 541(b)(3)	§ 541(b)(4)	§ 541(b)(5)	§ 541(b)(6)	§ 541(b)(7)	§ 541(b)(8)	§ 541(b)(9)

* This dollar figure, like many of the dollar figures in the Code, is subject to adjustment every three years under § 104(b) of the Code to reflect change in the Consumer Price Index for the most recent three years, and was most recently adjusted effective April 1, 2010 and will be adjusted again in 2013.

Section 541(c)(2) provides another exclusion from property of the estate — debtor's beneficial interest in a trust that restricts its transfer if, as a matter of applicable nonbankruptcy law, those restrictions are enforceable. This is the only situation in which a contractual provision limiting transfer, which is generally unenforceable in bankruptcy under § 541(c)(1), is given effect to exclude a property interest from the estate. The Supreme Court held in *Patterson v. Shumate*, 504 U.S. 753 (1992), that the "nonbankruptcy law" referred to in § 541(c)(2) may be federal law, such as the Employee Retirement Income Security Act of 1974 ("ERISA"), which requires any qualified pension plan to include a provision prohibiting benefits from assignment. As a result, a debtor's interest in an ERISA-qualified pension plan is excluded from the estate. Nonbankruptcy law also includes state spendthrift laws, which generally prevent a beneficiary of a trust satisfying certain requirements from alienating the beneficial interest (designed to protect these beneficiaries from impoverishing themselves by selling or pledging their trust interests for immediate capital).

One final exclusion is described in § 541(d) which excludes from the estate the equitable interest in property in which the debtor has only legal title and not an equitable interest. The debtor's legal interest in the property is included.

PROPERTY EXCLUDED FROM BANKRUPTCY ESTATE
EARNINGS FROM SERVICES PERFORMED BY INDIVIDUAL DEBTOR AFTER COMMENCEMENT OF CASE § 541(a)(6)
ITEMIZED EXCLUSIONS IN § 541(b)
NONASSIGNABLE BENEFICIAL INTEREST IN TRUST § 541(c)(2)
BENEFICIAL INTEREST IN PROPERTY OF WHICH DEBTOR HAS LEGAL INTEREST ONLY § 541(d)

2. Turnover of Property

Any entity having possession, custody or control of property of the estate at any time during the case, including the debtor, must turn that property or its value over to the trustee (or debtor in possession functioning as trustee) unless the property is of "inconsequential value or benefit to the estate." § 542(a). The goal of the turnover provision is to permit the trustee to use, sell or lease the property under § 363, or to permit the debtor to claim it as exempt under § 522.

If the property is in the form of a debt owing to the debtor that is either matured or is payable on demand or payable to order, the obligor on such debt must pay the debt to or to the order of the trustee (subject to any right of setoff against a claim owed to the obligor by the debtor recognized by § 553). § 542(b). Although not constituting property of the estate, the court may order an attorney, accountant, or anyone else who is holding records related to the debtor's property or financial affairs to turn over or disclose such records to the trustee, subject to any applicable privilege. § 542(e).

There are three exceptions to the general turnover obligations imposed by § 542. The first is for a custodian of property of the estate, who is subject to the requirements of § 543, discussed below. The second is for an entity that has no actual notice or knowledge of the bankruptcy case. Such an entity is permitted to transfer property of the estate or pay a debt owing to the debtor in good faith to someone other than the trustee just as if the case had not been commenced. § 542(c). The third exception is for a life insurance company which has a prepetition contract with the debtor that is property of the estate under which automatic transfers are made to pay a premium or to carry out a nonforfeiture insurance option. The life insurance company may continue to make such transfers of property of the estate or property of the debtor to such company in good faith as if the bankruptcy case had not been commenced. § 542(d).

A visualization of the turnover requirements of § 542 follows:

TURNOVER REQUIREMENTS OF § 542					
PROPERTY SUBJECT TO TURNOVER			EXCEPTIONS		
PROPERTY (OR ITS VALUE) THAT THE TRUSTEE MAY USE, SELL OR LEASE UNDER § 363 OR DEBTOR MAY EXEMPT UNDER § 522	DEBT THAT IS PROPERTY OF ESTATE THAT IS MATURED, PAYABLE ON DEMAND OR PAYABLE TO ORDER (EXCEPT TO EXTENT SUBJECT TO § 553 SETOFF)	ON COURT ORDER, RECORDS RELATING TO DEBTOR'S PROPERTY OR FINANCIAL AFFAIRS, SUBJECT TO ANY APPLICABLE PRIVILEGE	CUSTODIAN	ENTITY THAT HAS NO ACTUAL NOTICE OR KNOWLEDGE OF BANKRUPTCY CASE FOR GOOD FAITH TRANSFERS OF PROPERTY OF ESTATE OR PAYMENTS OF DEBT OWING TO DEBTOR	LIFE INSURANCE COMPANY FOR GOOD FAITH AUTOMATIC TRANSFERS OF PROPERTY OF ESTATE OR OF DEBTOR TO PAY PREMIUM OR NONFORFEITURE OPTION UNDER PREPETITION CONTRACT CONSTITUTING PROPERTY OF ESTATE

A custodian having possession, custody or control of property of the debtor or property of the estate and who has knowledge of the commencement of the case is barred from taking any further action with respect to that property, including making any further distributions or administering that property except as necessary to preserve it. § 543(a). Instead, as soon as the custodian obtains knowledge of the bankruptcy case, the custodian is required to deliver any such property to the trustee and file an accounting of such property. § 543(b)(1) and (2). A custodian (other than an assignee for the benefit of creditors appointed more than 120 days prior to the commencement of the bankruptcy case) who has made any improper or excessive disbursement, other than a disbursement made in accordance with applicable law or approved by an appropriate court prior to the bankruptcy case, may be surcharged for that disbursement. § 543(c)(3).

There are two exceptions to the turnover obligation of custodians. First, the court may allow the custodian to remain in possession, custody or control of property if the interests of creditors and (if the debtor is solvent) equity security holders would be better served by that action. Second, the court must allow the custodian to remain in possession, custody or control of property if the custodian is an assignee for the benefit of creditors who was appointed more than 120 days before the filing of the bankruptcy petition, unless turnover is "necessary to prevent fraud or injustice." § 543(d).

The interests of the custodian are protected by the requirement that the court provide for payment of reasonable compensation for services rendered and costs and expenses of the custodian. § 543(c)(2). The court must also protect all entities to whom the custodian has become liable with respect to the property or its proceeds. § 543(c)(1).

A visualization of the custodian's turnover obligations under § 543 follows:

TURNOVER OBLIGATIONS OF CUSTODIANS § 543

OBLIGATIONS OF CUSTODIAN § 543(a) AND (b)(1) & (2)			EXCEPTIONS § 543(d)		PROTECTIONS FOR CUSTODIANS AND OTHERS § 543(c)(1) AND (2)		SURCHARGE OF CUSTODIAN § 543(c)(3)	
							OBLIGATION TO SURCHARGE	**EXCEPTIONS**
NOT MAKE ANY DISBURSEMENT OR TAKE ANY ACTION IN ADMINISTRATION EXCEPT ACTION NECESSARY TO PRESERVE PROPERTY	DELIVER TO TRUSTEE ANY PROPERTY OF DEBTOR OR PROCEEDS	FILE AN ACCOUNTING	COURT MAY EXCUSE COMPLIANCE IF RETENTION OF PROPERTY BY CUSTODIAN WOULD BETTER SERVE INTERESTS OF CREDITORS AND EQUITY SECURITY HOLDERS	COURT MUST EXCUSE COMPLIANCE (OTHER THAN ACCOUNTING) BY ASSIGNEE FOR BENEFIT OF CREDITORS APPOINTED > 120 DAYS PRIOR TO FILING DATE	COURT MUST PROTECT ALL ENTITIES TO WHICH CUSTODIAN HAS BECOME OBLIGATED WITH RESPECT TO PROPERTY OR PROCEEDS	COURT MUST PROVIDE FOR PAYMENT OF CUSTODIAN'S REASONABLE COMPENSATION AND COSTS AND EXPENSES	COURT MUST SURCHARGE CUSTODIAN FOR ANY IMPROPER OR EXCESSIVE DISBURSEMENT	NOT APPLICABLE TO ASSIGNEE FOR BENEFIT OF CREDITORS APPOINTED > 120 DAYS PRIOR TO FILING DATE NOT APPLICABLE TO DISBURSEMENTS MADE IN ACCORDANCE WITH APPLICABLE LAW OR APPROVED BY COURT OF COMPETENT JURISDICTION

3. Removal of Property From Estate

Property initially included in the estate may be removed from the estate by various means. For example, as discussed in Section 2[B][5], *infra*, a party in interest may obtain relief from the stay with respect to acts against property of the estate in which it has an interest under § 362, and may then seize and sell such property to the same extent as it could had the bankruptcy not occurred. Alternatively, the stay may terminate with respect to an individual debtor's personal property securing a claim or subject to an unexpired lease under § 362(h), as a result of which the personal property is no longer property of the estate.

Another way in which property is removed from the estate is through the use, sale or lease of the property by the trustee under § 363. *See* Chapter 6[B], *infra*. If the property constitutes the debtor's interest in an executory contract or unexpired lease, the trustee may reject the contract or lease under § 365, resulting in the interest being removed from the estate and the other party to the contract or lease obtaining a prepetition claim for breach. *See* Chapter 6[D], *infra*. In the case of an individual debtor's bankruptcy, the debtor may claim certain property of the estate as exempt, resulting in its being removed from property of the estate available to creditors under § 522(b). *See* Chapter 3[C], *infra*.

If the trustee concludes that property of the estate "is burdensome" or is "of inconsequential value and benefit," the trustee may, after notice and a hearing (*see* Fed. R. Bankr. P. 6007(a)), abandon any property of the estate. § 554(a). The trustee must abandon property of the estate meeting the same standard if the court orders the trustee to do so upon request of a party in interest pursuant to Fed. R. Bankr. P. 6007(b). § 554(b). When property of the estate is abandoned, it reverts to anyone with an interest in that property, such as a secured creditor or the debtor. At the conclusion of a bankruptcy case, unless the court orders otherwise, any property which was listed on the debtor's schedules under § 521(a)(1) and which was not otherwise administered by the trustee during the case is abandoned to the debtor. § 554(c).

A visualization of ways in which property is removed from the estate follows.

REMOVAL OF PROPERTY FROM THE ESTATE

RELIEF FROM STAY § 362	USE, SALE OR LEASE BY TRUSTEE § 363	REJECTION OF EXECUTORY CONTRACT OR UNEXPIRED LEASE § 365	CLAIM OF EXEMPTION § 522(b)	ABANDONMENT § 554		
				WHY	HOW	END OF CASE
ON REQUEST OF PARTY IN INTEREST § 362(d) — AUTOMATIC WITH RESPECT TO PERSONAL PROPERTY OF INDIVIDUAL DEBTOR SECURING CLAIM OR SUBJECT TO UNEXPIRED LEASE § 362(h)				PROPERTY IS BURDENSOME OR OF INCONSEQUENTIAL VALUE TO ESTATE	VOLUNTARY BY TRUSTEE OR BY COURT ORDER ON REQUEST OF PARTY IN INTEREST — RULE 6007	ALL SCHEDULED PROPERTY NOT OTHERWISE ADMINISTERED IS ABANDONED TO DEBTOR WHEN CASE IS CLOSED UNLESS COURT ORDERS OTHERWISE

B. THE AUTOMATIC STAY

The filing of a petition for protection under the Code not only creates an estate comprised of all of the debtor's prepetition interests in property, but also protects that property, the debtor's property, and the debtor from further actions by prepetition creditors and others by imposing an automatic stay (like a statutory injunction) under § 362 of the Code.

The stay obviously protects the debtor. It stops all efforts to collect on debts, including calls, harassment, foreclosure actions, lawsuits, and garnishment, without regard to the stage to which any such action has progressed. It also frees the debtor from most obligations to pay current debts, because the creditor has no remedy for that default. (Indeed, postpetition transfers of property of the estate are avoidable by the trustee under § 549.)

But the stay also protects creditors to some extent. All priorities among creditors, whether based on state law priority or on legal action to enforce obligations, are frozen as of the filing; grabby competitors are precluded from taking further action to improve their position over others, furthering the Code's policy of treating similarly-situated creditors the same. The stay provides an opportunity for orderly identification of property, turnover, and liquidation of the assets (if they are to be liquidated), which is likely to generate more proceeds and benefit everyone.

Of course, the stay can also hurt creditors. The value of the debtor's property may decline, rather than increase, during the course of the case, and the stay delays distribution of that value both to those with interests in specific property and to unsecured creditors. For a creditor who is secured, the delay in realizing on its collateral costs it the money it would have made had it been able to take the proceeds of a sale of the collateral and reinvest those proceeds in other income-producing ways.

In looking at the stay, we will examine what actions are barred, what actions are excluded from the scope of the stay, when the stay does not come into effect or terminates automatically, how a party in interest may obtain relief from the stay from the court, and the penalties for violation of the stay.

1. What Actions Are Stayed

Eight acts are prevented by the stay under § 362(a). These acts are barred without regard to who performs them (that is, the stay is applicable to "all entities," not merely creditors). Some protect the debtor individually, some protect property of the estate, and some protect property of the debtor. Three relate to various types of proceedings and judgments. Two relate to the creation, perfection or enforcement of liens. Acts barred by the automatic stay often fall into more than one category.

The first category, § 362(a)(1), bars "the commencement or continuation . . . of [an] action or proceeding against the debtor" that was or could have been brought prepetition or is to collect a prepetition debt. This clause obviously covers all civil litigation, the normal lawsuit against the debtor, whether in state or federal court, and whatever stage it has reached. But this clause also covers non-litigation adjudication, including legislative, administrative, or regulatory or adjudication by arbitration or mediation. Note that the litigation or other adjudicative proceeding need not be to collect a debt; it just has to be "against the debtor" (and thus would cover such things as an eviction proceeding). However, the stay protects only the debtor; if the action or proceeding is against the debtor and nondebtors, it may continue against the nondebtors. In only one situation are nondebtors protected by the automatic stay. In a chapter 13 case, until the case is closed, dismissed or converted to chapter 7 or chapter 11, a creditor is barred from seeking to collect a consumer debt of the debtor from any individual who is liable on the consumer debt with the debtor, or who provided security for such consumer debt unless that individual became liable on or secured the debt in the ordinary course of the individual's business. § 1301(a).

The second clause of § 362(a) prevents the "enforcement, against the debtor or against property of the estate, of a [prepetition] judgment." Even if all adjudication has been completed and the litigant has obtained a judicial or administrative determination of the debtor's liability, the litigant cannot turn that determination into money by execution, garnishment, or any other collection mechanism without violating the automatic stay.

Section 362(a)(3) is the broad protection given to property of the estate; it precludes "any act to obtain possession of property of the estate or . . . from the estate or to exercise control over" it. The concept of "exercising control" is a broad one. It precludes actions taken with respect to intangible assets as to which possession is impossible, such as trademarks and copyrights and accounts receivable. With respect to tangible assets, it prevents the retention of property of the estate even if possession was obtained lawfully prior to the bankruptcy filing. Failure to turn the property of the estate over to the trustee under § 542 of the Code also constitutes a violation of the automatic stay.

The fourth clause, § 362(a)(4), prevents any "act to create, perfect, or enforce any lien against property of the estate." This prohibition is applicable to all liens, consensual security interests on personal property or real property mortgages, as well as nonconsensual judicial or statutory liens. It prevents all actions that might be taken by a secured creditor or in order to become a secured creditor — attachment, filing, recording — as well as any exercise of remedies available to such a creditor.

Section 362(a)(5) is similar to § 362(a)(4), but protects property of the debtor to the extent that the act to create, perfect or enforce a lien is taken with respect to a prepetition claim. The theory behind this clause is that prepetition claims are to be satisfied out of property of the estate; the property of the debtor which is excluded from property of the estate is intended to be available to the debtor for the debtor's "fresh start" coming out of bankruptcy and should not be used to satisfy prepetition claims. The clause protects not only property which is never included in the estate (such as property which comes into existence after filing) but also property which is originally part of the estate but is then returned to the debtor (such as exempt or abandoned property).

The sixth clause of § 362(a) prohibits acts to "collect, assess, or recover a [prepetition] claim against the debtor." Many of these acts would be prohibited either by § 362(a)(1) (if those acts are taken through an action or proceeding) or by § 362(a)(2) (if those acts are an attempt to enforce a prepetition judgment). But

§ 362(a)(6) prohibits even informal collection efforts, and includes acts directed at third parties if they are acts intended to coerce or induce or encourage debtor into paying a prepetition claim.

Section 362(a)(7) forbids the exercise of any right of setoff of a prepetition debt owing to the debtor (and thus an asset of the estate) against a debt owed by the debtor. The most common right of set-off is that claimed by a bank against its depositor/borrower. Rights of setoff are generally recognized in bankruptcy to the same extent as they exist under state law (§ 553), but subject to the limitations imposed by § 362 (meaning that the right of setoff cannot be exercised without getting relief from the automatic stay). The Supreme Court held in *Citizens Bank of Maryland v. Strumpf*, 516 U.S. 16 (U.S. 1995), that, although a bank cannot exercise its right of setoff with respect to the debtor's bank account without violating the automatic stay, it could place an administrative freeze on the account to maintain the status quo in preparation for seeking relief from the stay under § 362(d).

Finally § 362(a)(8) prevents the commencement or continuation of a proceeding before the U.S. Tax Court concerning the debtor's tax liability for a prepetition taxable period (in the case of an individual) or for a taxable period determined by the bankruptcy court (in the case of a debtor that is a corporation).

A visualization of the acts barred by the automatic stay of § 362(a) follows.

ACTS BARRED BY AUTOMATIC STAY § 362(a)
1)   COMMENCEMENT OR CONTINUATION OF PREPETITION ACTION OR PROCEEDING AGAINST DEBTOR OR TO RECOVER PREPETITION CLAIM AGAINST DEBTOR
2)   ENFORCEMENT AGAINST DEBTOR OR PROPERTY OF ESTATE OF PREPETITION JUDGMENT
3)   ACT TO OBTAIN POSSESSION OF OR EXERCISE CONTROL OVER PROPERTY OF ESTATE
4)   CREATION, PERFECTION OR ENFORCEMENT OF LIEN AGAINST PROPERTY OF ESTATE
5)   CREATION, PERFECTION OR ENFORCEMENT OF LIEN SECURING PREPETITION CLAIM AGAINST PROPERTY OF DEBTOR
6)   ACT TO COLLECT PREPETITION CLAIM
7)   SETOFF OF PREPETITION DEBT OWING TO DEBTOR AGAINST CLAIM AGAINST DEBTOR
8)   COMMENCEMENT OR CONTINUATION OF U.S. TAX COURT PROCEEDING CONCERNING PREPETITION TAX LIABILITY

2. What Actions Are Excluded from Stay

Certain actions that might otherwise be precluded by § 362(a) are explicitly permitted, notwithstanding the filing of the bankruptcy petition, under § 362(b). There are currently 28 separate exceptions listed (although one numbered exception has been repealed). When the Code was first enacted in 1978, there were only nine; ten new exceptions were added in the BAPCPA amendments. Ensuring that a particular activity is excluded from the scope of the automatic stay is the next best thing to immunizing that activity from the bankruptcy case entirely. This explains the intense lobbying to expand the exclusions in § 362(b).

The first exclusion is for "commencement or continuation of a criminal action or proceeding against the debtor." § 362(b)(1). Congress wished to ensure that bankruptcy did not become a refuge for all those charged with a crime seeking to delay their trials. The exception reflects a more general legislative philosophy that essential governmental functions cannot be stayed merely to promote the orderly administration of a bankruptcy case.

The second exclusion concerns certain domestic relations matters. It permits the "commencement or continuation of a civil action or proceeding" with respect to paternity, domestic support obligations (§ 101(14A)), child custody or visitation, dissolution of a marriage (other than orders for division of estate property), or domestic violence. § 362(b)(2)(A). It also allows someone to collect a domestic support obligation from non-estate property, § 362(b)(2)(B), withholding of income for payment of a domestic support obligation under an order or statute, § 362(b)(2)(C), as well as certain other remedies against a debtor who has not paid a domestic support obligation or medical obligation, § 362(b)(2)(C)-(E). These provisions reflect the view of Congress that domestic relations matters should be left to state law.

Section 362(b)(3) permits a secured party to take any act to perfect its security interest in property, or maintain or continue that perfection, after the filing of a bankruptcy petition "to the extent that the trustee's rights and powers are subject to such perfection under section 546(b) of this title or to the extent that such act is accomplished within the period provided under section 547(e)(2)(A) of this title." Section 546(b) makes the trustee's avoiding powers subject to any applicable non-bankruptcy law that would allow a creditor to obtain perfection (and maintain and continue that perfection) effective against an entity that acquires rights in the property prior to the date of perfection. For example, under Article 9 of the Uniform Commercial Code, a purchase money security interest in non-inventory, non-livestock can get priority over a lien creditor (the trustee in bankruptcy qualifies as a lien creditor) who obtains rights in the collateral prior to the date of perfection if the secured creditor perfects within 20 days after attachment. Because of the first part of § 362(b)(3), the purchase money secured creditor is allowed to perfect within that 20-day period despite the existence of the automatic stay.

Under the second part of § 362(b)(3), any secured creditor — even one who could not prevail against an entity acquiring rights in the collateral prior to the date of perfection — is permitted to perfect its security interest within the period provided under § 547(e)(2)(A). That section provides that if a secured creditor perfects its security interest within 30 days after the security interest takes effect between the debtor and the secured party (familiarly known as the time of "attachment" under Article 9 of the Uniform Commercial Code), the "transfer" of that security interest is deemed to have occurred at the time of attachment. Presumably, the reference to the period provided under § 547(e)(2)(A) allows a secured creditor to perfect its security interest within 30 days after attachment, even if the bankruptcy filing has intervened, without violating the automatic stay. However, if it is not perfected at the time of filing, its security interest will be subject to avoidance under § 544(a) unless § 546(b) is applicable.

Section 362(b)(4) excludes from the stay "the commencement or continuation of an action or proceeding by a governmental unit" to enforce "police and regulatory power." The exception is aimed at situations when the government is seeking to prevent or stop the violation of fraud, environmental protection, consumer protection, safety or similar laws enacted to protect the public or to fix damages for violations. If the government prevails in the action, § 362(b)(4) allows enforcement of the judgment by injunction, but precludes enforcement of a money judgment. (This provision used to be included in a separate clause, § 362(b)(5), which was deleted when its substance was incorporated into § 362(b)(4)). In its capacity as a judgment creditor for money, the government must wait with all other creditors.

The next clause, § 362(b)(6), permits the exercise by commodity brokers, forward contract merchants, stockbrokers, financial institutions, financial participants and securities clearing agencies of a contractual right conferred by a security agreement or other credit enhancement to offset or net out any termination value, payment amount or other transfer obligation arising under or in connection with any commodity contract, forward contract or securities contract. Similar rights were given to repo participants or financial participants with respect to repurchase agreements under § 362(b)(7), to swap participants or financial participants with respect to swap agreements under § 362(b)(17), and under § 362(b)(27), to master netting agreement participants with respect to master netting agreements to the extent the participant is eligible under § 362(b)(6), (7) or (17) to exercise such rights under the individual contracts covered by the master netting agreements. A court or administrative agency may not issue a stay of the actions permitted by § 362(b)(6), (7), (17) or (27). § 362(o).

Section 362(b)(8) allows the Secretary of Housing and Urban Development to commence an action to foreclose a mortgage or deed of trust insured under the National Housing Act covering property of five or more living units. The commencement of such an action was deemed necessary for tax purposes, but the action may not be pursued once it is commenced.

Section 362(b)(9) permits government units to take certain actions with respect to the debtor's taxes. They may audit, issue a notice of tax deficiency, make a demand for tax returns, and make an assessment of tax due and provide notice and demand for payment. A tax lien does not attach as a result of such assessment unless the tax is not dischargeable and the property against which the lien would arise revests in the debtor. However, the governmental unit may create or perfect a statutory lien for an ad valorem property tax or a special tax or special assessment on real property if such tax or assessment comes due postpetition. § 362(b)(18).

The lessor under a lease of nonresidential real property that has terminated at the conclusion of its stated term either prepetition or during the case is allowed under § 362(b)(10) to take any act against the debtor to obtain possession of the property.

Section 362(b)(11) allows the holder of a negotiable instrument to make presentment of such instrument and give notice of and protest dishonor of such instrument without violating the automatic stay.

The next two clauses, § 362(b)(12) and (13), are applicable only in chapter 11 cases. They permit the Secretary of Transportation or Secretary of Commerce to commence and continue to conclusion an action to foreclose a preferred ship or fleet mortgage in a vessel, or a security interest in or relating to a vessel held by the Secretary of Transportation or in a fishing facility held by the Secretary of Commerce.

If the debtor is an educational institution, § 362(b)(14) and (15) allow any action by an accrediting agency regarding debtor's accreditation status or by a state licensing body regarding debtor's licensure without violating the automatic stay. A guaranty agency or the Secretary of Education is also allowed to take action regarding the eligibility of the debtor to participate in programs authorized by the Higher Education Act of 1965. § 362(b)(16).

Section 362(b)(19) allows for automatic withholding from a debtor's wages pursuant to the debtor's agreement for the benefit of a pension, profit-sharing, stock bonus or similar employer-sponsored plan solely to make payments on a loan from such plan.

The next two clauses allow enforcement of a lien on real property against certain serial filers (debtors who have recently been in a prior bankruptcy case and seem to be abusing the bankruptcy process). Under § 362(b)(20), if in the debtor's prior bankruptcy case the court entered an order providing relief from the stay to the holder of an interest in debtor's real property under § 362(d)(4) (because the filing of the petition in that case was part of a scheme to delay, hinder, and defraud creditors by transferring an interest in real property without consent of the secured party or court approval or there have been serial bankruptcy filings affecting such real property), the holder of the interest in debtor's real property is not precluded by the automatic stay from taking action against such real property anytime within two years after the date of entry of such order for relief. The debtor may seek to prevent any such action by motion showing changed circumstances or other good cause.

Section 362(b)(21) applies to individual debtors who are ineligible to be a debtor under § 109(g) (because a prior case pending during the 180 days prior to filing was dismissed for willful failure to abide by court orders or to prosecute the case or because a party in interest filed a motion for relief from the stay and the debtor thereupon dismissed the prior case) and to any debtors who filed for bankruptcy protection in violation of a prior bankruptcy court order prohibiting such a filing. In such situations, any act to enforce any lien against or security interest in real property is permitted despite the automatic stay.

The next two clauses permit certain eviction proceedings. Section 362(b)(22) allows continuation of an eviction proceeding by a lessor against a tenant in residential property if the lessor obtained a prepetition judgment for possession. This provision is effective upon filing of the bankruptcy petition unless the debtor files with the petition and serves on the lessor a certification that, under applicable non-bankruptcy law, the debtor would still be permitted to cure the monetary default that gave rise to the judgment for possession and the debtor has deposited with the clerk of court any rent that would become due within the 30-day period after filing. § 362(l)(1). Official Form 1 includes the required certification. If the debtor files such a certification, § 362(b)(22) becomes effective 30 days after the bankruptcy petition is filed unless the debtor cures such default within the 30-day period and so certifies. If the debtor does so, § 362(b)(22) does not become applicable to permit eviction unless the court upholds any objection by the lessor to a certification filed by the debtor. § 362(l)(3).

Section 362(b)(23) permits pursuit of an eviction action seeking possession of residential property by lessor based on the debtor/tenant's endangerment of property or drug use within 30 days prior to filing. This provision becomes applicable only if the lessor files with the court, and serves on the debtor, a certification that such an eviction action has been filed, or that the debtor, during the immediately preceding 30-day period, has endangered property or illegally used or allowed to be used a controlled substance on the property. If the lessor files and serves such a certification, § 362(b)(23) becomes applicable 15 days thereafter unless the debtor files and serves an objection to such certification. § 362(m)(1) and (2)(A). If the debtor objects, the court must hold a hearing within 10 days after the filing of the objection. § 362(m)(2)(B). If the debtor demonstrates that the situation giving rise to the lessor's certification did not exist or has been remedied, § 362(b)(23) does not become applicable. § 362(m)(2)(C). If the debtor fails to make such a showing, § 362(b)(23) becomes immediately applicable. § 362(m)(2)(D).

A visualization of these new provisions dealing with evictions of a debtor/tenant from residential property follows:

EXCLUSION FOR EVICTION OF TENANTS FROM RESIDENTIAL PROPERTY
§ 362(b)(22) AND (23)

SECTIONS	GROUNDS	DUTIES OF LESSOR TO TRIGGER EXCLUSION	DUTIES OF DEBTOR TO AVOID EXCLUSION	WHEN EXCLUSION IS EFFECTIVE
§ 362(b)(22) AND § 362(l)	LESSOR OBTAINED PREPETITION JUDGMENT FOR POSSESSION	NONE	1) FILE AND SERVE CERTIFICATION THAT DEFAULT CAN BE CURED UNDER NONBANKRUPTCY LAW AND RENT FOR 30 DAYS AFTER FILING IS DEPOSITED WITH CLERK, 2) CURE DEFAULT WITHIN 30 DAYS AFTER FILING, AND 3) FILE AND SERVE CERTIFICATION STATING THAT DEFAULT WAS CURED	30 DAYS AFTER DATE ON WHICH BANKRUPTCY PETITION IS FILED OR DATE ON WHICH LESSOR'S OBJECTION TO ONE OF DEBTOR'S CERTIFICATIONS IS UPHELD
§ 362(b)(23) AND § 362(m)	ENDANGER-MENT OF PROPERTY OR ILLEGAL USE OF CONTROLLED SUBSTANCES ON PROPERTY	FILE AND SERVE CERTIFICATION THAT EVICTION ACTION HAS BEEN FILED OR DEBTOR ENDANGERED PROPERTY OR ILLEGAL USE OF CONTROLLED SUBSTANCES ON PROPERTY WITHIN PRIOR 30 DAYS	FILE AND SERVE OBJECTION TO LESSOR'S CERTIFICATION WITHIN 15 DAYS AFTER IT IS FILED	IF NO OBJECTION TO LESSOR'S CERTIFICATION IS FILED, 15 DAYS AFTER IT IS FILED IF OBJECTION TO LESSOR'S CERTIFICATION IS FILED, COURT MUST HOLD HEARING WITHIN 10 DAYS AND § 362(b)(23) BECOMES EFFECTIVE ONLY IF OBJECTION IS REJECTED

Section 362(b)(24) allows any transfer that is not avoidable under § 544 or § 549 (*see* Chapter 5, *infra*).

A securities self-regulatory organization is permitted to pursue an investigation or action to enforce its regulatory power, enforce any order or decision (other than for monetary sanctions) in any such action, and take any act to delist, delete or refuse to permit quotation of a stock by the debtor if the debtor does not meet applicable regulatory requirements. § 362(b)(25).

Under § 362(b)(26), a governmental unit is allowed to set off an income tax refund with respect to a prepetition taxable period against a prepetition tax liability to the same extent as it could do so under applicable nonbankruptcy law. However, if applicable nonbankruptcy law would not permit the setoff because of a pending action to determine the amount or legality of debtor's tax liability, the governmental unit is permitted to hold the refund pending resolution of the action unless it is granted adequate protection of its interest in the refund.

The final clause, § 362(b)(28), allows the Secretary of Health and Human Services to exclude the debtor from participation in the medicare program or any other federal health care program.

A visualization of the exclusions from the automatic stay follows:

EXCLUSIONS FROM AUTOMATIC STAY § 362(b)
(1)   CRIMINAL ACTION OR PROCEEDING
(2)   DOMESTIC RELATIONS MATTERS
(3)   PERFECTION EFFECTIVE AGAINST PRIOR HOLDER OF INTEREST IN PROPERTY UNDER 546(b) OR WITHIN 30 DAYS OF ATTACHMENT UNDER 547(e)(2)(A)
(4)   GOVERNMENTAL POLICE OR REGULATORY POWERS AND NON-MONETARY ENFORCEMENT OF GOVERNMENTAL POLICE OR REGULATORY JUDGMENTS
(5)   REPEALED
(6)   COMMODITY/SECURITIES/ FORWARD CONTRACT SETOFFS
(7)   REPURCHASE AGREEMENT SETOFFS
(8)   HUD FORECLOSURES ON FIVE OR MORE LIVING UNITS
(9)   TAXING AUTHORITY AUDIT, ISSUANCE OR NOTICE OF DEFICIENCY AND MAKING ASSESSMENT
(10)   EVICTION FROM EXPIRED NONRESIDENTIAL REAL PROPERTY LEASE
(11)   PRESENTMENT OF NEGOTIABLE INSTRUMENTS AND PROTEST OF DISHONOR
(12)-(13) FORECLOSURE OF SHIP MORTGAGE OR VESSEL OR FISHING FACILITY SECURITY INTEREST BY SECRETARY OF TRANSPORTATION OR SECRETARY OF COMMERCE
(14)-(16) ACCREDITATION, LICENSURE OR PARTICIPATION IN GUARANTY PROGRAMS BY EDUCATIONAL INSTITUTIONS
(17)   SWAP SETOFFS
(18)   LIENS FOR POSTPETITION AD VALOREM PROPERTY TAXES OR SPECIAL TAXES OR ASSESSMENTS ON REAL PROPERTY
(19)   PENSION, PROFIT-SHARING, STOCK BONUS WITHHOLDINGS TO REPAY LOAN FROM PLAN
(20)   ENFORCEMENT OF LIEN AGAINST REAL PROPERTY FOR TWO YEARS FOLLOWING LIFT STAY ORDER IN PRIOR CASE UNLESS DEBTOR SHOWS CHANGED CIRCUMSTANCES OR GOOD CAUSE
(21)   ENFORCEMENT OF LIEN AGAINST REAL PROPERTY IF DEBTOR INELIGIBLE OR PROHIBITED FROM FILING BECAUSE OF PRIOR CASE
(22)   EVICTION ACTION AGAINST RESIDENTIAL TENANT IF PREPETITION JUDGMENT FOR POSSESSION, SUBJECT TO LIMITATIONS OF § 362(l)
(23)   EVICTION ACTION AGAINST RESIDENTIAL TENANT BASED ON ILLEGAL USE OF DRUGS OR ENDANGERMENT OF PROPERTY IF LESSOR SUBMITS CERTIFICATION, SUBJECT TO LIMITATIONS OF § 362(m)
(24)   NON-AVOIDABLE TRANSFER UNDER § 544 OR § 549
(25)   SECURITIES SELF-REGULATORY ORGANIZATION INVESTIGATION OR ACTION OR ENFORCEMENT OF ORDER OR DECISION, OR DELISTING
(26)   SETOFF BY GOVERNMENTAL UNIT OF PREPETITION INCOME TAX REFUND AGAINST PREPETITION TAXES OWING
(27)   MASTER NETTING AGREEMENT SETOFFS
(28)   EXCLUSION FROM MEDICARE PROGRAM OR OTHER HEALTH CARE PROGRAM BY SECRETARY OF HEALTH AND HUMAN SERVICES

3. When Stay Does Not Come Into Effect

In the 2005 BAPCPA amendments to the Code, Congress imposed certain sanctions on serial bankruptcy filers (those who file for bankruptcy multiple times within a relatively short period). Among those sanctions was denial of the protection of the automatic stay to an individual debtor who is the subject of a single or joint case and who had two or more single or joint cases pending within the previous year which were dismissed (except pursuant to § 707(b)). § 362(c)(4)(A)(i). Although no stay is imposed automatically in a case filed by or against such an individual debtor, any party in interest (including the debtor) may request that the court impose a stay as to any or all creditors by motion filed within 30 days after the filing of the latest case. The party seeking imposition of a stay must demonstrate "that the filing of the later case is in good faith as to the creditors to be stayed." § 362(c)(4)(B).

The statute creates a presumption, applicable to all creditors, that the most recently-filed case of such a debtor is not filed in good faith if any of three factors is present. § 362(c)(4)(D)(i). First, the presumption arises if the individual debtor was the subject of two or more previous cases pending within the one-year period prior to the filing of the current case. Second, the presumption arises if the individual debtor had a prior case dismissed within the one-year period prior to the filing of the current case for the debtor's failure to file or amend the petition or required documents without substantial excuse or failed to provide adequate protection ordered by the court, or failed to perform a confirmed plan. Third, the presumption arises if "there has not been a substantial change in the financial or personal affairs of the debtor" since the most recent case of that debtor was dismissed, or there is any other reason to believe that the current case will not be successfully concluded. As to any individual creditor that brought a motion for relief from the stay under § 362(d) in a prior case of the individual debtor, a presumption that the most recent case was not filed in good faith arises if that motion was still pending when the prior case was dismissed or had been resolved by terminating, conditioning, or limiting the stay with respect to action by such creditor. § 362(c)(4)(D)(ii).

If the presumption that the current case was not filed in good faith arises, the party in interest seeking imposition of the stay may rebut the presumption by "clear and convincing evidence to the contrary," that is, by demonstrating that the current case was filed in good faith as to the creditors to be stayed. § 362(c)(4)(D). If such a showing is made and a stay is imposed, it becomes effective upon entry of an order to that effect. § 362(c)(4)(C). If no stay has been imposed, the court must enter an order so stating upon the request of any party in interest. § 362(c)(4)(A)(ii).

A visualization of the provisions denying the stay to serial filers follows:

DENIAL OF STAY TO SERIAL FILERS § 362(c)(4)

TO WHOM IT APPLIES	SANCTION	COURT IMPOSITION OF STAY			WHEN PRESUMPTION OF LACK OF GOOD FAITH IS CREATED	
		REQUEST	REQUIRED SHOWING	OVERCOMING PRESUMPTION	AS TO ALL CREDITORS	AS TO ANY CREDITOR WHO FILED § 362(d)
INDIVIDUAL DEBTOR WHO HAD TWO OR MORE SINGLE OR JOINT CASES PENDING WITHIN PREVIOUS YEAR THAT WERE DISMISSED (OTHER THAN UNDER § 707(b))	STAY UNDER § 362(a) DOES NOT GO INTO EFFECT UPON FILING OF LATEST CASE	ANY PARTY IN INTEREST MAY REQUEST THAT COURT IMPOSE STAY AS TO ANY OR ALL CREDITORS	FILING OF LATEST CASE IS IN GOOD FAITH AS TO CREDITORS TO BE STAYED	CLEAR AND CONVINCING EVIDENCE THAT CASE WAS NOT FILED WITH LACK OF GOOD FAITH	1) DEBTOR HAD 2 OR MORE CASES PENDING WITHIN PRIOR YEAR, 2) PREVIOUS CASE WAS DISMISSED WITHIN PRIOR YEAR FOR • FAILURE TO FILE OR AMEND PETITION OR REQUIRED DOCUMENTS WITHOUT SUBSTANTIAL EXCUSE, • FAILURE TO PROVIDE REQUIRED ADEQUATE PROTECTION, OR • FAILURE TO PERFORM CONFIRMED PLAN, OR 3) NO SUBSTANTIAL CHANGE IN FINANCIAL OR PERSONAL AFFAIRS OF DEBTOR SINCE MOST RECENT CASE DISMISSED OR CURRENT CASE NOT LIKELY TO BE SUCCESSFULLY CONCLUDED	§ 362(d) ACTION WAS PENDING WHEN PRIOR CASE WAS DISMISSED OR WAS RESOLVED IN CREDITOR'S FAVOR

The automatic stay also does not apply with respect to serial filers in cases which meet any of four requirements. First, the debtor is a debtor in a "small business case" (§ 101(51C)) at the time of the filing (meaning the debtor has two cases pending concurrently). Second, the debtor was a debtor in a small business case that was dismissed within the two-year period prior to the current filing. Third, the debtor was a debtor in a small business case in which a plan was confirmed within the two-year period prior to the current filing. Fourth, the debtor is an entity that acquired substantially all the assets or business of a small business debtor who was the subject of a bankruptcy case in the two-year period prior to the current filing (unless the assets and business were acquired in good faith and not for purposes of evading the exception to the stay). § 362(n)(1). Exceptions to this rule include involuntary cases in which the debtor did not collude with the filing creditors, and cases in which the debtor establishes by a preponderance of the evidence that the filing was a result of circumstances beyond the debtor's control and not foreseeable at the time the prior case was filed and confirmation of a feasible nonliquidating plan in the current case within a reasonable period of time is more likely than not. § 362(n)(2). The small business case exception to the automatic stay is visualized below:

SMALL BUSINESS CASE EXCEPTION TO AUTOMATIC STAY § 362(n)	
WHEN EXCEPTION IS APPLICABLE § 362(n)(1)	WHEN EXCEPTION IS NOT APPLICABLE § 362(n)(2)
1) DEBTOR IS DEBTOR IN SMALL BUSINESS CASE (§ 101(51C)) PENDING WHEN PETITION IS FILED, OR 2) DEBTOR WAS DEBTOR IN SMALL BUSINESS CASE DISMISSED IN 2-YEAR PERIOD PRIOR TO CURRENT FILING, OR 3) DEBTOR WAS DEBTOR IN SMALL BUSINESS CASE IN WHICH PLAN CONFIRMED IN 2-YEAR PERIOD PRIOR TO CURRENT FILING, OR 4) DEBTOR IS ENTITY THAT ACQUIRED SUBSTANTIALLY ALL ASSETS OR BUSINESS OF SMALL BUSINESS DEBTOR DESCRIBED ABOVE UNLESS ENTITY ACQUIRED ASSETS OR BUSINESS IN GOOD FAITH AND NOT FOR PURPOSE OF EVADING EXCEPTION TO THE STAY	1) INVOLUNTARY CASE WITH NO COLLUSION BETWEEN DEBTOR AND CREDITORS, OR 2) DEBTOR PROVES BY PREPONDERANCE OF EVIDENCE THAT FILING WAS DUE TO CIRCUMSTANCES BEYOND DEBTOR'S CONTROL AND WAS NOT FORESEEABLE, AND MORE LIKELY THAN NOT COURT WILL CONFIRM FEASIBLE NONLIQUIDATING PLAN WITHIN A REASONABLE PERIOD OF TIME

4. When Stay Terminates Automatically

When the stay comes into effect under § 362(a) (whether upon the filing of the bankruptcy petition, or upon court order under § 362(c)(4) upon petition by a party in interest), it terminates thereafter automatically in four situations.

First, as to actions against property of the estate, the stay terminates when the property ceases to be property of the estate. § 362(c)(1). The ways in which property may cease to be property of the estate are discussed in Section 2[A][3], *supra*.

Second, as to all other actions stayed by § 362(a), the stay terminates upon the earliest of the time the case is closed, the time the case is dismissed, and the time discharge is granted or denied. § 362(c)(2).

Third, under another provision of the 2005 BAPCPA amendments designed to discourage serial filers, the stay "with respect to any action taken with respect to a debtor or property securing such debt or with respect to any lease" terminates "with respect to the debtor" 30 days after a bankruptcy filing by or against an individual debtor in a single or joint case under chapter 7, 11 or 13 if the debtor had a single or joint case pending in the preceding year that was dismissed (other than under § 707(b)). § 362(c)(3)(A). The meaning of this provision is somewhat obscure. Some courts, in reliance on the legislative history, have interpreted the language to provide for a complete termination of the stay described in § 362(a) with respect to the debtor, the debtor's property and property of the estate. *See, e.g., In re Curry*, 362 B.R. 394 (Bankr. N.D. Ill. 2007); *In re Jupiter*, 344 B.R. 754 (Bankr. D.S.C. 2006). However, most courts believe that, in order to give meaning to the phrase "with respect to the debtor" in § 362(c)(3)(A), the stay must terminate only insofar as § 362(a) bars actions against the debtor or the debtor's property, not with respect to actions against property of the estate. *See, e.g., In re Holcomb*, 380 B.R. 813 (10th Cir. BAP 2008); *In re Jumpp*, 356 B.R. 789 (1st Cir. BAP 2006); *In re Alvarez*, 432 B.R. 839 (Bankr. S.D. Cal. 2010); *In re Jones*, 339 B.R. 360 (Bankr. E.D.N.C. 2006).

Whatever the scope of the stay that terminates at the end of the 30-day period, a party in interest (including the debtor) may seek continuation of the stay as to any or all creditors by motion. The hearing on any such motion must be completed before the end of the 30-day period. To prevail on such motion, the party in interest must demonstrate that the filing of the latest case was in good faith as to the creditors to be stayed. § 362(c)(3)(B).

The statute creates a presumption, applicable to all creditors, that the most recently-filed case of such a debtor is not filed in good faith if any of three factors is present. § 362(c)(3)(C)(i). First, the presumption arises if the individual debtor was the subject more than one previous case under chapter 7, 11 or 13 pending within the one-year period prior to the filing of the current case. Second, the presumption arises if the individual debtor had a prior case under chapter 7, 11 or 13 dismissed within the one-year period prior to the filing of the current case for the debtor's failure to file or amend the petition or required documents without substantial excuse, or failed to provide adequate protection ordered by the court, or failed to perform a confirmed plan. Third, the presumption arises if "there has not been a substantial change in the financial or personal affairs of the debtor" since the most recent chapter 7, 11, or 13 case of that debtor was dismissed, or there is any other reason to believe that the current case will not be successfully concluded. As to any individual creditor that brought a motion for relief from the stay under § 362(d) in a prior case of the individual debtor, a presumption that the most recent case was not filed in good faith arises if that motion was still pending when the prior case was dismissed or had been resolved by terminating, conditioning, or limiting the stay as to actions of such creditor. § 362(c)(3)(C)(ii).

If the presumption that the current case was not filed in good faith arises, the party in interest seeking imposition of the stay may rebut the presumption by "clear and convincing evidence to the contrary," that is, by demonstrating that the current case was filed in good faith as to the creditors to be stayed. § 362(c)(3)(C).

A visualization of the termination of the stay for certain serial filers under § 362(c)(3) follows.

TERMINATION OF STAY FOR SERIAL FILERS § 362(c)(3)

TO WHOM IT APPLIES	SANCTION	COURT CONTINUATION OF STAY			WHEN PRESUMPTION OF LACK OF GOOD FAITH IS CREATED	
		REQUEST AND HEARING	REQUIRED SHOWING	OVERCOMING PRESUMPTION	AS TO ALL CREDITORS	AS TO ANY CREDITOR WHO FILED § 362(d) ACTION IN PRIOR CASE
INDIVIDUAL DEBTOR WHO HAD A SINGLE OR JOINT CASE UNDER CHAPTER 7, 11 OR 13 PENDING WITHIN PREVIOUS YEAR THAT WAS DISMISSED (OTHER THAN UNDER § 707(b))	STAY UNDER § 362(a) WITH RESPECT TO ACTION TAKEN WITH RESPECT TO A DEBT OR PROPERTY SECURING SUCH DEBT OR WITH RESPECT TO ANY LEASE TERMINATES WITH RESPECT TO DEBTOR ON 30TH DAY AFTER FILING OF LATEST CASE	ANY PARTY IN INTEREST MAY REQUEST THAT STAY CONTINUE AS TO ANY OR ALL CREDITORS, AND HEARING MUST BE HELD WITHIN 30 DAYS AFTER FILING OF LATEST CASE	FILING OF LATEST CASE IS IN GOOD FAITH AS TO CREDITORS TO BE STAYED	CLEAR AND CONVINCING EVIDENCE THAT CASE WAS NOT FILED WITH LACK OF GOOD FAITH	1) DEBTOR HAD MORE THAN 1 CASE UNDER CHAPTER 7, 11 OR 13 PENDING WITHIN PRIOR YEAR, 2) PREVIOUS CASE WAS DISMISSED WITHIN PRIOR YEAR FOR • FAILURE TO FILE OR AMEND PETITION OR REQUIRED DOCUMENTS WITHOUT SUBSTANTIAL EXCUSE, • FAILURE TO PROVIDE REQUIRED ADEQUATE PROTECTION, OR • FAILURE TO PERFORM CONFIRMED PLAN, OR 3) NO SUBSTANTIAL CHANGE IN FINANCIAL OR PERSONAL AFFAIRS OF DEBTOR SINCE MOST RECENT CASE DISMISSED OR CURRENT CASE NOT LIKELY TO BE SUCCESSFULLY CONCLUDED	§ 362(d) ACTION WAS PENDING WHEN PRIOR CASE WAS DISMISSED OR WAS RESOLVED IN CREDITOR'S FAVOR

Fourth, the stay terminates as to personal property collateral or personal property subject to a lease if an individual debtor fails to file his or her statement of intention required by § 521(a)(2) with respect to personal property securing a claim or subject to an unexpired lease, or fails to surrender or redeem the property, reaffirm the debt or assume the lease (as specified in such statement of intention) within the period required by § 521(a)(2) (unless the debtor seems to affirm the debt on the original terms and the creditor refuses). For a discussion of § 521(a)(2), *see* Chapter 1[F][2], *supra*. The stay does not terminate with respect to such personal property if, on motion of the trustee filed before the expiration of the period specified in § 521(a)(2), the court determinates that the personal property is of "consequential value or benefit to the estate" and orders that the creditor's interest in such personal property in the debtor's possession be adequately protected. § 362(h)(2).

The court must issue an order under § 362(c) upon request by a party in interest confirming that the automatic stay has terminated. § 362(j).

A visualization of the circumstances under which the stay terminates automatically and not on motion of a party in interest follows:

AUTOMATIC TERMINATION OF STAY			
ACTIONS AGAINST PROPERTY OF ESTATE § 362(c)(1)	OTHER ACTIONS STAYED BY § 362(a) § 362(c)(2)	PRIOR DISMISSED BANKRUPTCY CASE IN PRECEDING 1-YEAR PERIOD § 362(c)(3)	FAILURE TO ABIDE BY § 521(a)(2) § 362(h)
STAY TERMINATES WHEN PROPERTY CEASES TO BE PROPERTY OF THE ESTATE	STAY TERMINATES UPON EARLIEST OF: 1) CASE IS CLOSED 2) CASE IS DISMISSED 3) DISCHARGE IS GRANTED	STAY TERMINATES WITH RESPECT TO DEBTOR ON 30TH DAY AFTER FILING OF SECOND CASE WITH RESPECT TO ACTIONS TAKEN WITH RESPECT TO A DEBT OR PROPERTY SECURING A DEBT OR WITH RESPECT TO ANY LEASE UNLESS COURT EXTENDS DURING 30-DAY PERIOD UPON SHOWING THAT SECOND CASE WAS FILED IN GOOD FAITH (WITH PRESUMPTION THAT IT WAS NOT)	STAY TERMINATES WITH RESPECT TO PERSONAL PROPERTY SECURING A CLAIM IF INDIVIDUAL DEBTOR FAILS WITHIN TIME PERIOD SPECIFIED IN § 521(a)(2) TO: 1) FILE STATEMENT OF INTENTION OR INDICATE INTENT TO SURRENDER PROPERTY, REDEEM PROPERTY, OR REAFFIRM DEBT, AND 2) TAKE ACTION SPECIFIED IN SUCH STATEMENT OF INTENTION (OTHER THAN PROPOSED REAFFIRMATION OF DEBT ON ORIGINAL TERMS WHICH IS REJECTED BY CREDITOR)

5. Termination of Stay on Motion

Relief from the stay is generally sought by a secured creditor who wishes to take possession of its collateral and sell it to satisfy the debt. Although such relief may certainly be sought in a chapter 7 case, it is likely to be more hotly contested in a chapter 11 or chapter 13 case than in a chapter 7 case, because in a chapter 7 case, the debtor is liquidating the estate and eventually distributing the collateral to the secured creditor anyway.

To seek relief from the stay, the secured creditor files a motion (sometimes called a "lift-stay motion") under § 362(d) and Fed. R. Bankr. P. 4001(a), serving it on representatives of all parties in interest. The court must schedule a hearing on the motion within the next 30 days because, pursuant to § 362(e), the stay is lifted automatically with respect to property of the estate 30 days after the motion is filed unless the court, after notice and a hearing, orders its continuation pending conclusion of a final hearing. The court may order continuation of the stay only if "there is a reasonable likelihood that the party opposing relief from such stay will prevail" at the final hearing.

If the hearing within the first 30 days after a lift-stay motion is filed is only a preliminary hearing, the final hearing must be concluded within another 30 days thereafter unless the parties consent to extend the period or the court finds extension for a specific period is required "by compelling circumstances." § 362(e)(1).

In addition, under § 362(e)(2), the stay is lifted automatically 60 days after a motion for relief from the stay is filed in a case under chapter 7, 11, or 13 of an individual debtor unless the court reaches a final decision within 60 days after the motion is filed or the 60-day period is extended by agreement of all parties in interest or by the court for a specific period for good cause.

The court may grant relief from the stay to a party in interest without a hearing to the extent such relief is "necessary to prevent irreparable damage" to that party's interest in property if the damage will occur before a hearing can be held. § 362(f).

A visualization of the timing rules of § 362(e) follows.

TIMING RULES ON LIFT-STAY MOTIONS § 362(e)		
30 DAYS AFTER MOTION	60 DAYS AFTER MOTION	30 DAYS AFTER PRELIMINARY HEARING
ALL DEBTORS § 362(e)(1)	INDIVIDUAL DEBTORS § 362(e)(2)	ALL DEBTORS § 362(e)(1)
STAY OF ACTIONS AGAINST PROPERTY OF ESTATE LIFTED WITH RESPECT TO MOVING PARTY UNLESS COURT, AFTER NOTICE AND HEARING, ORDERS STAY CONTINUED, AND MAY DO SO AT PRELIMINARY HEARING ONLY IF OPPOSING PARTY IS REASONABLY LIKELY TO PREVAIL AT FINAL HEARING	STAY LIFTED IN CHAPTER 7, 11 OR 13 CASE UNLESS FINAL DECISION RENDERED PRIOR THERETO DENYING MOTION, OR PERIOD IS EXTENDED 1) BY AGREEMENT OF ALL PARTIES IN INTEREST, OR 2) BY COURT FOR SPECIFIC PERIOD FOR GOOD CAUSE	FINAL HEARING MUST BE CONCLUDED UNLESS PERIOD IS EXTENDED 1) BY CONSENT OF PARTIES, OR 2) BY COURT FOR SPECIFIC PERIOD BECAUSE OF COMPELLING CIRCUMSTANCES

Section 362(d) sets forth four bases for obtaining relief from the automatic stay. The first, described in § 362(d)(1), is "for cause, including the lack of adequate protection of an interest in property" of the moving party. A movant has an interest in specific property of the debtor only if the movant has a lien or security interest or mortgage on the property, and even then its interest is generally limited to the portion of its claim that is a secured claim under § 506(a). *See* discussion of secured claims in Chapter 4[A][1], *infra*. The value of that interest which is entitled to adequate protection is the value that is being harmed by the automatic stay, *i.e.*, the value of the creditor's interest in property as of the date the petition is filed and the stay goes into effect. It does not include the right of an undersecured creditor to take immediate possession of its collateral. *See United Sav. Ass'n v. Timbers*, 484 U.S. 365 (1988).

Three illustrations of what might constitute adequate protection of an interest of an entity in property are provided by § 361. The first is by requiring the debtor to make a cash payment or periodic cash payments to the creditor in an amount equal to the decrease in value of the property while the stay is in effect. The second is by providing the creditor an additional or replacement lien to the extent of any decrease in value of the collateral while the stay is in effect. The final type of adequate protection described by § 361 is by granting the creditor such other relief (other than giving the creditor an administrative expense priority claim for the decrease in value of its collateral) as would result in the "realization by such entity of the indubitable equivalent of such entity's interest in such property." The phrase "indubitable equivalent" was based on a phrase used in an opinion by Judge Learned Hand, *In re Murel Holding Corp.*, 75 F.2d 941 (2d Cir. 1935), and is used to permit adequate protection in forms other than cash payments or liens. The existence of an "equity cushion" (the value of the collateral in excess of the creditor's debt) may be found to provide adequate protection of the creditor's interest in property under this third clause. A visualization of the definition of "adequate protection" in § 361 follows:

ADEQUATE PROTECTION
§ 361

---

1)   CASH PAYMENT OR PERIODIC CASH PAYMENTS TO EXTENT OF DECREASE IN VALUE OF INTEREST IN PROPERTY, OR

2)   ADDITIONAL OR REPLACEMENT LIEN TO EXTENT OF DECREASE IN VALUE OF INTEREST IN PROPERTY, OR

3)   OTHER RELIEF RESULTING IN REALIZATION OF "INDUBITABLE EQUIVALENT" OF INTEREST IN PROPERTY

The second basis for a lift-stay motion is described in § 362(d)(2). The court must grant relief from the stay with respect to property if two conditions are met. The debtor must not have an equity in such property, and the property must not be necessary to an effective reorganization.

The debtor has equity in the property only if the value of the property exceeds the amount of all debt secured by the property. Because the debtor generally seeks to retain property subject to a motion for relief from the stay, and § 506(a)(1) states that the value of property securing a claim "shall be determined in light of . . . the proposed disposition or use of such property," most courts employ a fair market value standard in determining whether the debtor has equity in the property. Congress has required that a "replacement value" (without deduction for costs of sale or marketing) be used for personal property of individual debtors in chapter 7 and chapter 13 cases. *See* discussion of § 506(a) in Chapter 4[A][1], *infra*. The party seeking relief from the stay has the burden of proving the debtor has no equity in the property. § 362(g)(1).

In deciding whether the property is necessary to an effective reorganization, the court must first conclude that a successful reorganization is likely to take place (*i.e.*, that there is a "reasonable possibility of a successful reorganization within a reasonable time," *see United Sav. Ass'n v. Timbers*, 484 U.S. 365, 376 (1988)). Only then does the court consider whether the property at issue in the lift-stay motion will be necessary to that reorganization. The debtor bears the burden of proof on the feasibility of a successful reorganization, as well as the debtor's need for the property in that reorganization. § 362(g)(2).

The third basis for seeking relief from the stay under § 362(d)(3) applies only when the collateral is single asset real estate. "Single asset real estate" is defined in § 101(51B) as real property which meets three requirements. It must constitute "a single property or project," it must generate "substantially all of the gross income of a debtor who is not a family farmer," and there can be "no substantial business" conducted on the property by the debtor "other than the business of operating the real property and activities incidental thereto." Excluded from the definition are residential properties with fewer than four residential units. A visualization of the definition of "single asset real estate" follows:

SINGLE ASSET REAL ESTATE § 101(51B)	
REQUIREMENTS	EXCEPTION
SINGLE PROPERTY OR PROJECT GENERATES SUBSTANTIALLY ALL GROSS INCOME OF DEBTOR OTHER THAN FAMILY FARMER NO SUBSTANTIAL BUSINESS CONDUCTED BY DEBTOR OTHER THAN BUSINESS OF OPERATING REAL PROPERTY AND ACTIVITIES INCIDENTAL THERETO	RESIDENTIAL REAL PROPERTY WITH FEWER THAN 4 RESIDENTIAL UNITS

If the collateral constitutes single asset real estate, a motion for relief from the stay will be granted under § 362(d)(3) if, not later than 90 days after filing (or such later date as the court for cause determines during that 90-day period), debtor has not either filed a plan of reorganization that has a reasonable possibility of being confirmed within a reasonable time, or begun making monthly payments to the creditor equal to interest at the applicable nondefault contract rate of interest. This provision was enacted in 1994 to counter abuses by debtors holding only one major asset, a piece of real estate, who would file for bankruptcy on the eve of foreclosure by the secured creditor and thus delay the foreclosure for a lengthy period of time despite their total inability to reorganize.

The final basis for relief from the stay, § 362(d)(4), was included in the 2005 BAPCPA amendments. It permits the stay to be lifted with respect to real property by a secured creditor if the court finds that the filing of the petition was part of a scheme to delay, hinder or defraud creditors involving either transfer of that property without the consent of the secured creditor or the court, or multiple bankruptcy filings affecting the property. An order lifting the stay under this new section is binding in other subsequently filed bankruptcy cases for up to 2 years after the entry of the order, subject to debtor's right to seek modification based on changed circumstances or for good cause shown. § 362(d)(4). As discussed in Section 2[B][2], *supra*, one of the new exceptions from the stay, § 362(b)(20), would explicitly exclude from the stay acts to enforce liens against or security interests in real property within two years after the entry of an order granting relief from the stay under § 362(d)(4) in a prior bankruptcy case.

The grounds for obtaining relief from the automatic stay under § 362(d) are visualized below.

RELIEF FROM THE AUTOMATIC STAY § 362(d)			
§ 362(d)(1)	§ 362(d)(2)	§ 362(d)(3)	§ 362(d)(4)
FOR CAUSE, INCLUDING LACK OF ADEQUATE PROTECTION OF INTEREST IN PROPERTY	IF: 1) DEBTOR DOES NOT HAVE ANY EQUITY IN PROPERTY, AND 2) PROPERTY IS NOT NECESSARY TO AN EFFECTIVE REORGANIZATION	IF PROPERTY IS SINGLE ASSET REAL ESTATE, UNLESS WITHIN 90 DAYS AFTER ORDER FOR RELIEF (OR LATER DATE AS COURT FOR CAUSE DETERMINES) DEBTOR HAS: 1) FILED PLAN WITH REASONABLE POSSIBILITY OF CONFIRMATION WITHIN REASONABLE TIME, OR 2) COMMENCED MONTHLY PAYMENTS (WHICH MAY BE OUT OF PREPETITION OR POSTPETTION RENTS OR INCOME) AT NONDEFAULT CONTRACT RATE OF INTEREST ON CLAIM	IF FILING OF PETITION WAS PART OF SCHEME TO DELAY, HINDER, OR DEFRAUD CREDITORS SECURED BY REAL PROPERTY BY 1) TRANSFERRING INTEREST IN SUCH REAL PROPERTY WITHOUT CONSENT OF CREDITOR OR COURT, OR 2) MAKING MULTIPLE BANKRUPTCY FILINGS

If a court denies relief from the automatic stay because the trustee provides adequate protection of a secured creditor's interest in property under § 362(d)(1), and that adequate protection proves inadequate (meaning that notwithstanding the adequate protection, the secured creditor has an administrative expense claim arising from the stay), then the creditor's claim is given priority over all other administrative expense claims. § 507(b).

In a chapter 13 case, the court may grant relief from the stay of actions to collect all or any part of a consumer debt of the debtor from an individual liable on such debt with the debtor (a "codebtor") imposed by § 1301(a) on request of a party in interest. There are three grounds for relief from the stay. First, the stay may be lifted if the codebtor (rather than the debtor) received the consideration for the creditor's claim. Second, the creditor may receive relief from the stay if the debtor's chapter 13 plan does not propose to pay the creditor's claim. Third, the court may order relief from the stay if the creditor's interest would be irreparably harmed by continuation of the stay (as, for example, if there is reasonable cause to believe that the codebtor is about to dispose of property in the possession of the codebtor which could be used to satisfy the claim, or if such property is depreciating rapidly). A visualization of these grounds follows.

GROUNDS FOR RELIEF FROM § 1301(a) STAY AGAINST INDIVIDUAL CODEBTOR ON CONSUMER DEBT OF CHAPTER 13 DEBTOR § 1301(b)
1) CODEBTOR (RATHER THAN DEBTOR) RECEIVED CONSIDERATION FOR CLAIM,
2) DEBTOR'S PLAN PROPOSES NOT TO PAY CLAIM, OR
3) CREDITOR'S INTEREST WOULD BE IRREPARABLY HARMED BY CONTINUATION OF STAY

The stay imposed by § 1301(a) is terminated with respect to any party in interest requesting relief from the stay 20 days after the request unless the debtor or any codebtor on the debt files and serves a written objection. § 1301(d).

6. Sanctions for Violation of Stay

Conduct that violates the stay is legally ineffective, no matter how innocently it occurs or who is involved and no matter how difficult it is to "unscramble the eggs." Therefore, the first consequence of violating the stay is that the court will require that the violation be undone and the debtor returned to the status quo ante.

If the debtor is an individual, and if the violation of the stay was "willful," the debtor is entitled to recover damages (both actual and, in appropriate cases, punitive). § 362(k)(1). The court may award only actual damages (not punitive) if the entity violated the stay in the good faith belief that the stay was not applicable to the entity's actions by reason of its termination pursuant to § 362(h). *See* discussion of § 362(h) in Section 2[B][4], *supra*. Most courts also conclude that a violation of the stay is equivalent to a violation of an injunction, and is punishable by contempt sanctions pursuant to the court's inherent powers under § 105(a).

However, under § 342(g)(2), the court may not impose a monetary penalty for a violation of the stay (including under § 362(k)) unless the action violating the stay occurred after the creditor received notice of the bankruptcy that was effective under § 342. Section 342(c) requires that notices to a creditor must contain the name, address and last four digits of the taxpayer identification number of the debtor, and be sent to the appropriate address. The appropriate address is the address of which the creditor gives the debtor notice in at least two communications sent to the debtor prior to the bankruptcy filing, or the address the creditor files with the court in a particular chapter 7 or chapter 13 case or files with the court for use in all cases under chapter 7 or 13 filed in that court. § 342(c)(2) and (f). A notice sent to the creditor at any other address is not effective "until such notice is brought to the attention of such creditor." § 342(g)(1). If the creditor specifies a person or subdivision to receive bankruptcy notices and has established reasonable procedures to ensure that bankruptcy notices are delivered to such person or subdivision, a notice to the creditor is not effective until the notice is received by the designated person or subdivision. § 342(g)(1). These notice provisions, added by the 2005 BAPCPA amendments, make imposition of sanctions for violations of the stay more difficult.

A visualization of the provisions for sanctions for violation of the automatic stay follows.

SANCTIONS FOR VIOLATION OF AUTOMATIC STAY	
TYPES OF SANCTIONS AVAILABLE	EXCEPTIONS
FOR WILLFUL VIOLATION OF STAY IN CASE OF INDIVIDUAL DEBTOR, ACTUAL DAMAGES, COSTS AND ATTORNEYS' FEES AND, IN APPROPRIATE CASES, PUNITIVE DAMAGES § 362(k)(1) SANCTIONS FOR CONTEMPT § 105(a)	ONLY ACTUAL DAMAGES AVAILABLE IF CREDITOR ACTED IN GOOD FAITH BELIEF THAT § 362(h) WAS APPLICABLE § 362(k)(2) NO MONETARY PENALTY FOR VIOLATION UNLESS ACTION OCCURRED AFTER CREDITOR RECEIVED NOTICE OF BANKRUPTCY EFFECTIVE UNDER § 342 § 342(g)(2)

Chapter 3

EXEMPTIONS

Absent constitutional or statutory protection, all property of a debtor would be available to creditors to satisfy debts by attachment or garnishment. Each state has enacted laws establishing its own set of exemptions applicable outside of bankruptcy that protect certain property from process to satisfy claims. Some states have also enacted a second set of exemptions applicable only when their debtors file for bankruptcy, the constitutionality of which is unsettled. The Code has its own set of exemptions in § 522(d). For an individual debtor, the ability to claim certain property as exempt provides a small cushion to prevent destitution and begin the debtor on his or her fresh start. In considering the topic of exemptions, we will look at what law determines the applicable exemptions, what state and federal exemptions are available, how a debtor claims that property is exempt and how to object to claimed exemptions, and avoidance of liens impairing exemptions.

A. CHOICE OF EXEMPTIONS

1. The Opt-Out Provision

Under the Bankruptcy Act of 1898, a debtor could exempt any property that was exempt under his or her state law. When the Bankruptcy Code of 1978 was being negotiated, there was considerable support for replacing the non-uniform state exemptions with a single set of federal exemptions, but that approach was not politically feasible. States with more generous exemptions opposed limiting their citizens to less generous exemptions in bankruptcy, and those with less generous exemptions opposed sheltering more of the debtors' property from creditors when the debtors filed. Therefore, Congress determined that the decision on whether federal exemptions should be available to a debtor should be left to the state whose law would otherwise be applicable to that debtor.

It accomplished this goal in § 522(b)(2), the so-called "opt-out provision." Under § 522(b)(1), an individual debtor is allowed to exempt property listed in either § 522(b)(3) (which provides for application of the applicable state exemptions, as well as certain additional exemptions) or § 522(b)(2) (which provides for application of the federal exemptions). However, the debtor may not elect the federal exemptions under § 522(b)(2) if "the State law that is applicable to the debtor . . . specifically does not so authorize." Most states have enacted laws to specifically deny their debtors the ability to elect the federal exemptions. Only in those few states that have not opted out may debtors elect to apply the federal exemptions.

If such an election is permitted under the law of the jurisdiction in which a joint case is filed, the husband and wife must both elect either the federal exemptions or the state exemptions (*i.e.*, they are not permitted to "stack" exemptions). If they cannot agree on which exemptions to elect, they are deemed to have elected the federal exemptions. § 522(b)(1). However, each of the joint debtors is entitled to claim his or her own property as exempt, within the limitations of the applicable exemption statute. § 522(m).

2. State Choice of Law

If the Code had allowed a debtor to elect the state exemptions applicable where the debtor resided at the time of the filing, a debtor would have a strong incentive to move to a state with more generous exemptions immediately before filing for bankruptcy. To discourage this type of forum-shopping, Congress specified that a debtor may elect only the state exemptions applicable to the place where the debtor's domicile was located for the 730 days immediately prior to the filing date. § 522(b)(3)(A). If the debtor's domicile was not in a single state during that 730-day period, the state whose exemption laws are applicable is the state in which the debtor's domicile was located for the 180 days immediately preceding that 730-day period (or the longer portion of that 180-day period than any other place). *Id.*

The state choice of law provision of § 522(b)(3)(A) may purport to make applicable state law exemptions to debtors who do not reside in the state. But the state law exemptions by their terms may apply only to that state's residents or domiciliaries, or may apply only to property located within the state. Under § 522(b)(3), if the effect of § 522(b)(3)(A) is to "render the debtor ineligible for any exemption," the debtor may elect the federal exemptions.

As mentioned above, some states have enacted exemptions applicable only to debtors who have filed for bankruptcy and who either must (because of the opt-out) or may by election select state exemptions. Some of these statutes have been challenged on the grounds that they unconstitutionally infringe on federal power to establish exemptions in a federal bankruptcy case. The results of these challenges have been mixed. *Compare Kulp v. Zeman*, 949 F.3d 1106 (10th Cir. 1991); *In re Applebaum*, 422 B.R. 684 (9th Cir. BAP 2009); *In re Morrell*, 394 B.R. 405 (Bankr. N.D. W. Va. 2008), *aff'd, Sheehan v. Peveich (In re Peveich)*, 574 F.3d 248 (4th Cir. 2009); *In re Brown*, 2007 Bankr. LEXIS 2486 (Bankr. N.D.N.Y. July 23, 2007), *aff'd*, 2007 U.S. Dist. LEXIS 98999 (N.D.N.Y. 2007); *In re Shumaker*, 124 B.R. 820 (Bankr. D. Mont. 1991); *In re Vasko*, 6 B.R. 317 (Bankr. N.D. Ohio 1980) (upholding bankruptcy-specific exemptions), *with In re Kanter*, 505 F.2d 228 (9th Cir. 1974); *In re Schafer*, 2011 Bankr. LEXIS 564 (6th Cir. BAP Feb. 24, 2011); *In re Regevig*, 389 B.R. 736 (Bankr. D. Ariz. 2008); *In re Mata*, 115 B.R. 288 (Bankr. D. Colo. 1990); *In re Lennen*, 71 B.R. 80 (Bankr. N.D. Cal. 1987); *In re Reynolds*, 24 B.R. 344 (Bankr. S.D. Ohio 1982); *In re Cross*, 255 B.R. 25 (Bankr. N.D. Ind. 2000) (striking down bankruptcy-specific exemptions).

A visualization of the choice of exemption provisions in § 522 follows.

CHOICE OF EXEMPTIONS § 522(b)(1)		
FEDERAL EXEMPTIONS § 522(b)(2)	STATE EXEMPTIONS § 522(b)(3)(A)	
DEBTOR MAY ELECT TO EXEMPT PROPERTY LISTED IN § 522(d) UNLESS STATE LAW APPLICABLE TO DEBTOR SPECIFICALLY DOES NOT SO AUTHORIZE	ELECTION OF STATE EXEMPTIONS	EXCEPTION
	DEBTOR MAY ELECT STATE EXEMPTIONS APPLICABLE TO PLACE OF DOMICILE DURING 730 DAYS PRIOR TO FILING, OR IF DEBTOR WAS NOT DOMICILED IN SINGLE STATE DURING THAT PERIOD, DURING 180 DAYS PRIOR TO THAT PERIOD (OR LONGER PORTION OF THAT 180-DAY PERIOD THAN ANYWHERE ELSE)	IF APPLICABLE STATE EXEMPTION LAW IS NOT AVAILABLE TO DEBTOR, FEDERAL EXEMPTIONS APPLY

B.   CONTENT OF EXEMPTIONS

1.   State Exemptions

Examination of 50 state exemption laws is beyond the scope of this volume. However, the Code both limits state exemption law in some circumstances, and expands the exemptions available even when state law is selected by the debtor.

If the debtor or joint debtors elect state exemptions, in addition to the property exempt pursuant to the applicable state law, § 522(b)(3) provides for exemptions for three additional categories of property, whether or not they would be exempt under state law. The first is for property that is exempt under federal law other than § 522(d) of the Code. § 522(b)(3)(A). Various types of property are exempt under federal non-bankruptcy law, including foreign service retirement and disability payments, 22 U.S.C. § 4060; social security payments, 42 U.S.C. § 407; civil service retirement benefits, 5 U.S.C. § 8346; veterans benefits, 38 U.S.C. § 5301; military survivors' benefits, 10 U.S.C. § 1450(i); and federally insured or guaranteed student loans, grants, and work assistance, 20 U.S.C. § 1095a(d).

The second exemption applicable when state law exemptions apply is for an interest held by the debtor as a tenant by the entirety or joint tenant immediately before the case commenced to the extent that such interest would be exempt from process under applicable nonbankruptcy law. § 522(b)(3)(B). Most states find a tenancy by the entirety interest to be exempt from process by individual creditors of one spouse, but available to creditors of the spouses jointly. Therefore, a debtor's interest in property held as tenants by the entirety with the debtor's spouse is generally exempt. Joint tenancy interests are reachable by creditors of the individual joint tenant, and are therefore unaffected by § 522(b)(3)(B) despite the language referring to such interests.

The final type of property exempt as a matter of federal law even when state exemptions are applicable is retirement funds held in a fund or account that is tax-exempt under specified provisions of the Internal Revenue Code. This exemption is typically used to protect individual retirement accounts. However, under § 522(n), the aggregate value of assets in such individual retirement accounts (without regard to amounts attributable to rollover contributions) that may be exempted under § 522(b)(3)(C) is limited to $1,171,650.*

The property presumptively qualifies for the § 522(b)(3)(C) exemption if it is in a retirement fund that has received a favorable determination of tax-exempt status by the Internal Revenue Service which is in effect when the bankruptcy case begins. If the retirement fund has not received such a determination, the debtor must demonstrate that no contrary determination has been made with respect to the retirement fund, and either the retirement fund is in substantial compliance with the applicable requirements of the Internal Revenue Code or if not, the debtor is not materially responsible for that failure. § 522(b)(4)(A) & (B). Direct transfers of funds from trustee to trustee, and eligible rollover distributions between tax-exempt funds (distributions disbursed from an account exempt from taxation and, within sixty days, rolled over into another tax-exempt account), do not affect the exempt status of the property. § 522(b)(4)(C) & (D).

A visualization of the federal additions to state exemptions follows:

---

* This dollar figure, like many of the dollar figures in the Code, is subject to adjustment every three years under § 104(b) of the Code to reflect change in the Consumer Price Index for the most recent three years, and was most recently adjusted effective April 1, 2010 and will be adjusted again in 2013.

FEDERAL ADDITIONS TO STATE EXEMPTIONS § 522(b)(3)			
FEDERAL NON-BANKRUPTCY EXEMPTIONS § 522(b)(3)(A)	TENANCY BY THE ENTIRETY § 522(b)(3)(B)	RETIREMENT FUNDS § 522(b)(3)(C)	
DEBTOR MAY CLAIM AS EXEMPT ANY PROPERTY THAT IS EXEMPT UNDER FEDERAL LAW OTHER THAN § 522(d) OF CODE	DEBTOR MAY CLAIM AS EXEMPT INTEREST AS TENANT BY THE ENTIRETY OR JOINT TENANT TO EXTENT INTEREST IS EXEMPT UNDER APPLICABLE NONBANKRUPTCY LAW	EXEMPT PROPERTY	LIMITATION ON IRA FUNDS § 522(n)
		DEBTOR MAY CLAIM AS EXEMPT RETIREMENT FUNDS IN TAX-EXEMPT FUND OR ACCOUNT UNDER § 401, 403, 408, 408A, 414, 457 OR 501(a) OF INTERNAL REVENUE CODE	EXEMPTION FOR IRA ASSETS (WITHOUT REGARD TO ROLLOVER ASSETS) LIMITED TO $1,171,650.*
		DETERMINATION OF TAX-EXEMPT STATUS OF FUND OR ACCOUNT § 522(b)(4)(A)-(B)	TRANSFERS AND ROLLOVER DISTRIBUTIONS § 522(b)(4)(C)-(D)
		IF FUND HAS RECEIVED FAVORABLE DETERMINATION BY IRS, FUNDS ARE PRESUMED TO BE EXEMPT IF FUND HAS NOT RECEIVED FAVORABLE DETERMINATION BY IRS, DEBTOR MUST SHOW 1) NO PRIOR UNFAVORABLE DETERMINATION, AND 2) FUND IS IN SUBSTANTIAL COMPLIANCE WITH INTERNAL REVENUE CODE OR, IF NOT, DEBTOR IS NOT MATERIALLY RESPONSIBLE FOR FAILURE	DIRECT TRANSFER OF RETIREMENT FUNDS FROM TRUSTEE TO TRUSTEE DOES NOT AFFECT EXEMPTION ELIGIBLE ROLLOVER DISTRIBUTIONS REMAIN EXEMPT

---

* This dollar figure, like many of the dollar figures in the Code, is subject to adjustment every three years under § 104(b) of the Code to reflect change in the Consumer Price Index for the most recent three years, and was most recently adjusted effective April 1, 2010 and will be adjusted again in 2013.

In the 2005 BAPCPA amendments, Congress also adopted limitations on the state homestead exemption in three different circumstances. First, if the debtor claims as exempt an interest in any of four types of homestead property (property used as a residence by debtor or a dependent, a cooperative that owns property used as a residence by debtor or a dependent, a burial plot for debtor or a dependent, or property claimed as a homestead by debtor or a dependent), debtor's interest in that property is not exempt to the extent that the value of the interest was attributable to proceeds of non-exempt property the debtor disposed of within 10 years prior to the date of filing with intent to hinder, delay or defraud a creditor. This provision would allow the trustee to challenge the acquisition of an exempt homestead, payments made to reduce a mortgage on an exempt homestead (thereby creating more exempt equity), or capital improvements made to an exempt homestead, each with the proceeds of non-exempt property up to ten years prior to the bankruptcy filing.

Second, if the debtor claims as exempt an interest in any of the four types of homestead property described above, the debtor may not exempt any amount of interest that was acquired during the 1215-day period prior to filing exceeding $146,450.* § 522(p)(1). This limitation does not apply to an exemption claimed by a family farmer for the principal residence of such farmer. § 522(p)(2)(A). The limitation is not applicable to an interest transferred from a debtor's previous principal residence into the debtor's current principal residence during the 1215-day period, so long as the previous principal residence was acquired prior to the beginning of that period and both residences are located in the same state. § 522(p)(2)(B).

Third, the debtor may not claim as exempt an interest in any of the four types of homestead property described above in excess of $146,450* (without regard to when such interest was acquired) if either the court determines that the debtor has been convicted of a felony under circumstances demonstrating that the filing of the bankruptcy petition was abusive, or the debtor owes a debt arising from securities laws violations, fraud or deceit or manipulation in a fiduciary capacity or in connection with the purchase or sale of a registered security, a civil remedy under the Racketeer Influenced and Corrupt Organizations Act, or any criminal act or intentional tort or willful or reckless misconduct that caused serious physical injury or death to another individual in the preceding five years. § 522(q)(1). This homestead limitation does not apply to the extent the claimed exempt interest "is reasonably necessary for the support of the debtor and any dependent of the debtor." § 522(q)(2).

A visualization of the federal limitations on state homestead exemptions follows:

---

* This dollar figure, like many of the dollar figures in the Code, is subject to adjustment every three years under § 104(b) of the Code to reflect change in the Consumer Price Index for the most recent three years, and was most recently adjusted effective April 1, 2010 and will be adjusted again in 2013.

FEDERAL LIMITATIONS ON STATE HOMESTEAD EXEMPTION
§§ 522(o), (p) & (q)

PROPERTY CLAIMED AS EXEMPT	LIMITATION ON CLAIMED EXEMPTION	APPLICABLE PERIOD	EXCEPTIONS
REAL OR PERSONAL PROPERTY THAT DEBTOR OR A DEPENDENT USES AS A RESIDENCE, OR COOPERATIVE THAT OWNS PROPERTY THAT DEBTOR OR DEPENDENT USES AS A RESIDENCE, OR BURIAL PLOT FOR DEBTOR OR DEPENDENT, OR	VALUE ATTRIBUTABLE TO PROCEEDS OF DISPOSITION OF NON-EXEMPT PROPERTY WITH INTENT TO HINDER, DELAY OR DEFRAUD CREDITORS § 522(o)	10 YEARS PRIOR TO FILING	NONE
	INTEREST ACQUIRED BY DEBTOR EXCEEDING $146,450* § 522(p)	1215-DAY PERIOD PRIOR TO FILING	INTEREST IN PRINCIPAL RESIDENCE ACQUIRED BY FAMILY FARMER INTEREST TRANSFERRED FROM DEBTOR'S PREVIOUS PRINCIPAL RESIDENCE INTO DEBTOR'S CURRENT PRINCIPAL RESIDENCE IF: 1) PREVIOUS PRINCIPAL RESIDENCE WAS ACQUIRED PRIOR TO 1215-DAY PERIOD, AND 2) BOTH RESIDENCES IN THE SAME STATE
REAL OR PERSONAL PROPERTY THAT DEBTOR OR DEPENDENT CLAIMS AS HOMESTEAD	ANY INTEREST EXCEEDING $146,450** IF: 1) COURT DETERMINES DEBTOR IS GUILTY OF FELONY DEMONSTRATING THAT BANKRUPTCY FILING WAS ABUSE, OR 2) DEBT FOR SECURITIES LAW VIOLATION, FIDUCIARY FRAUD, RICO VIOLATION OR PERSONAL INJURY OR DEATH IN PRECEDING 5 YEARS § 522(q)	NONE	AMOUNT REASONABLY NECESSARY FOR SUPPORT OF DEBTOR AND ANY DEPENDENT

* This dollar figure, like many of the dollar figures in the Code, is subject to adjustment every three years under § 104(b) of the Code to reflect change in the Consumer Price Index for the most recent three years, and was most recently adjusted effective April 1, 2010 and will be adjusted again in 2013.

2. Federal Exemptions

As you look at § 522(d), the list of property that may be exempted if the debtor elects the federal exemptions under § 522(b)(2), you will see that certain categories of property are described as exempt, and some categories provide dollar limits on how much property within that category can be exempted. This is typical of state exemption statutes as well. As a result, disputes about exemptions tend to be of two types: one, whether the property claimed as exempt fits within the described category, and two, for those categories in which only a certain dollar value of property may be exempted, whether the property the debtor claims as exempt has the value that the debtor claims for it.

The dollar limitations are for each debtor; therefore, when debtors file jointly, each debtor is entitled to a separate exemption amount for his or her property (although some state exemption statutes provide a married couple a single homestead limitation). No debtor may claim as exempt property owned solely by his or her spouse, although joint debtors may allocate the value of jointly-owned exempt property to their separate exemptions in any way they wish.

If property claimed as exempt falls within a category with a dollar limitation, and the property has a value not exceeding the amount allowed, the debtor can exempt all of the property and it will be removed from the estate. If the property claimed as exempt is valued at an amount in excess of the amount allowed for that category, the debtor can still claim an exemption, but only for the exempt portion of the property (that is, the property is "partially exempt"). If the debtor cannot find another category by which the remaining portion of the property can be claimed as exempt, either the debtor must buy the property from the trustee for the non-exempt portion of its value, or the trustee will sell the property. The debtor then receives the proceeds of the sale equal to the exempt amount, and the trustee retains the excess for the benefit of the creditors.

Obviously, when property can be exempted only up to a dollar limitation, valuation becomes very important; the debtor will always be arguing for a low valuation of potentially exempt property, and the trustee and creditors may claim that the property has been undervalued.

Section 522(a)(2) defines "value" as "fair market value as of the date of the filing of the petition." A fair market valuation, as opposed to a liquidation value, tends to increase the value of the property for purposes of the exemption limitations.

The federal exemptions listed in § 522(d) allow the debtor to claim as exempt twelve types of property. First, the debtor may claim as exempt the debtor's interest in real property or personal property that the debtor or a dependent uses as a residence, in a cooperative that owns property that the debtor or a dependent of the debtor uses as a residence, or in a burial plot for the debtor or a dependent of the debtor. The exemption is subject to an aggregate limitation of $21,625.* § 522(d)(1).

---

* This dollar figure, like many of the dollar figures in the Code, are subject to adjustment every three years under § 104(b) of the Code to reflect change in the Consumer Price Index for the most recent three years, and were most recently adjusted effective April 1, 2010 and will be adjusted again in 2013.

This provision is familiarly known as the "homestead" exemption. If the debtor does not use the full amount of the homestead exemption (perhaps because the debtor rents a home rather than owning one), the debtor is entitled to use up to $10,825[*] of that unused amount to shield other property (called the "spillover" amount). This additional unused amount is added to the "wild card" exemption in § 522(d)(5) described below.

The second category is for debtor's interest in one motor vehicle with a value not to exceed $3,450.[*] § 522(d)(2). This category protects automobiles, buses, motorcycles, or any other motorized vehicle.

Third, the debtor may exempt an interest in household furnishings, household goods, wearing apparel, appliances, books, animals, crops, or musical instruments held primarily for personal, family or household use by the debtor or a dependent. § 522(d)(3). There are two dollar limitations in this provision. First, any individual item is exempt only to the extent of $550.[*] Second, the aggregate value of all items exempted under this provision may not exceed $11,525.[*]

The fourth category covers the debtor's interest in jewelry held primarily for personal, family or household use by the debtor or a dependent. § 522(d)(4). There is no per item limitation, but the aggregate value of jewelry exempted under this category may not exceed $1,450.[*]

The fifth category is the so-called "wild card." It permits the debtor to exempt an interest in any property at all, without regard to the type, so long as the aggregate value of property exempted under the wild card does not exceed $1,150.[*] § 522(d)(5). The value cap is increased by any spillover of unused homestead exemption, up to $10,825,[*] from § 522(d)(1). Therefore, if the full amount of the spillover is added to the wild card amount, the debtor could exempt property having a value of up to $11,975.[*]

Sixth, the debtor may exempt an interest in implements, professional books, or tools of the trade of the debtor or a dependent. This exemption is subject to an aggregate limit of $2,175.[*] § 522(d)(6).

Any unmatured life insurance contract owned by the debtor (other than a credit life insurance contract) is exempt under § 522(d)(7) without limitation. If the debtor owned any unmatured life insurance contract under which the insured is the debtor or an individual of whom the debtor is a dependent, the debtor's aggregate interest in any accrued dividend or interest under such a contract, or any loan value of such a contract, not to exceed $11,525,[*] can be exempted. § 522(d)(8).

The ninth category allows the debtor to exempt any professionally prescribed health aids for the debtor or a dependent without limitation. § 522(d)(9).

Under the tenth category, the debtor may exempt a right to certain future earnings equivalents — social security benefits, unemployment compensation, loan public assistance benefits, veterans' benefits, disability or illness or unemployment

---

[*] These dollar figures, like many of the dollar figures in the Code, are subject to adjustment every three years under § 104(b) of the Code to reflect change in the Consumer Price Index for the most recent three years, and were most recently adjusted effective April 1, 2010 and will be adjusted again in 2013.

benefits, alimony or support or maintenance payments to the extent reasonably necessary for the support of the debtor and any dependent, and payments under stock bonus, pension, profit-sharing, annuity or similar plans or contracts to the extent reasonably necessary for the support of the debtor and any dependent. § 522(d)(10). Although there is no limitation on the amount of the payments entitled to exemption, pension payments are not eligible for exemption if the pension plan or contract was established by debtor's employer who was an insider (§ 101(31)) when debtor's rights arose, the payment is on account of age or length of service, and the plan or contract does not qualify under § 401(a), 403(a), 403(b), or 408 of the Internal Revenue Code.

The eleventh category is for certain compensatory payments — crime victim's reparations, payment for wrongful death of an individual of whom the debtor was a dependent to the extent reasonably necessary for the support of the debtor or a dependent, payment as beneficiary of life insurance policy on the life of someone of whom debtor was dependent to the extent reasonably necessary for the support of the debtor or a dependent, up to $21,625[*] of personal bodily injury payments, and payments for loss of future earnings of the debtor or an individual of whom the debtor is or was a dependent, to the extent reasonably necessary for the support of the debtor or a dependent. § 522(d)(11).

The final category is for retirement funds to the extent they are in a fund or account that is exempt from tax under § 401, 403, 408, 408A, 414, 457, or 501(a) of the Internal Revenue Code. § 522(d)(12). As for the comparable exemption applicable when the debtor uses state law exemptions under § 522(b)(3), any assets in individual retirement accounts claimed as exempt under this provision are subject to a $1,171,650[*] cap, although that amount may be increased "if the interests of justice so require." § 522(n).

A visualization of the federal exemptions under § 522(d) follows:

---

[*] These dollar figures, like many of the dollar figures in the Code, are subject to adjustment every three years under § 104(b) of the Code to reflect change in the Consumer Price Index for the most recent three years, and were most recently adjusted effective April 1, 2010 and will be adjusted again in 2013.

FEDERAL EXEMPTIONS § 522(d)		
SECTION	PROPERTY	LIMIT (IF ANY)*
§ 522(d)(1)	RESIDENCE (INCLUDING COOPERATIVE) OR BURIAL PLOT	$21,625
§ 522(d)(2)	1 MOTOR VEHICLE	$3,450
§ 522(d)(3)	HOUSEHOLD FURNISHINGS, HOUSEHOLD GOODS, CLOTHING, APPLIANCES, BOOKS, ANIMALS, CROPS, MUSICAL INSTRUMENTS HELD PRIMARILY FOR PERSONAL, FAMILY OR HOUSEHOLD USE	$550 PER ITEM $11,525 AGGREGATE
§ 522(d)(4)	JEWELRY HELD PRIMARILY FOR PERSONAL, FAMILY OR HOUSEHOLD USE	$1,450 AGGREGATE
§ 522(d)(5)	ANY PROPERTY ("WILD CARD")	$1,150 PLUS UP TO $10,825 OF UNUSED AMOUNT ("SPILLOVER") FROM § 522(d)(1)
§ 522(d)(6)	IMPLEMENTS, PROFESSIONAL BOOKS, OR TOOLS OR THE TRADE	$2,175
§ 522(d)(7)	UNMATURED LIFE INSURANCE CONTRACT	NONE
§ 522(d)(8)	ACCRUED DIVIDENDS OR INTEREST OR LOAN VALUE OF UNMATURED LIFE INSURANCE CONTRACT UNDER WHICH DEBTOR OR INDIVIDUAL OF WHOM DEBTOR IS DEPENDENT IS INSURED	$11,525
§ 522(d)(9)	PROFESSIONALLY PRESCRIBED HEALTH AIDS	NONE
§ 522(d)(10)	FUTURE EARNINGS EQUIVALENTS — SOCIAL SECURITY, UNEMPLOYMENT, PUBLIC ASSISTANCE, VETERANS, DISABILITY, ALIMONY, SUPPORT, MAINTENANCE, STOCK BONUS, PENSION OR SIMILAR PLAN	PAYMENTS UNDER CERTAIN STOCK BONUS, PENSION OR SIMILAR PLANS ESTABLISHED BY INSIDER EMPLOYER ARE NOT ELIGIBLE
§ 522(d)(11)	COMPENSATION FOR LOSSES — CRIME VICTIM, WRONGFUL DEATH, LIFE INSURANCE, PERSONAL BODILY INJURY, LOSS OF FUTURE EARNINGS	FOR PERSONAL BODILY INJURY RECOVERY — $21,625
§ 522(d)(12)	RETIREMENT FUNDS	FOR IRAS, $1,171,650 AGGREGATE PER § 522(n)

---

* These dollar figures, like many of the dollar figures in the Code, are subject to adjustment every three years under § 104(b) of the Code to reflect change in the Consumer Price Index for the most recent three years, and were most recently adjusted effective April 1, 2010 and will be adjusted again in 2013.

C. CLAIMING EXEMPTIONS AND MAKING OBJECTIONS

A debtor claims exempt property on one of the schedules, Schedule C, filed at the beginning of the case under § 521(a)(1) and Fed. R. Bankr. P. 1007(b). § 522(l) and Fed. R. Bankr. P. 4003(a). A party in interest may file an objection to the list of claimed exemptions within 30 days after the § 341 meeting of creditors is concluded (or within such additional time as the court provides before the period for objecting expires). Fed. R. Bankr. P. 4003(b)(1). Failure to file an objection within the specified period bars all parties in interest from contesting the exemption, even if the debtor has no colorable basis for asserting it. § 522(l). *See Taylor v. Freeland & Kronz*, 503 U.S. 638 (1992). An objection may be filed either because the objector asserts that the property claimed as exempt does not fall within one of the categories listed, or because the value of property listed as exempt exceeds the permissible exempt value of that category of property.

For those categories in which only a limited value of property may be claimed as exempt, the debtor is asked to state the current value of the property claimed as exempt. If the debtor fails to specify a value, the trustee must object to the claimed exemption in order to preserve any claim to the value of the property in excess of the limitation set forth in the statute for that category. Failure to object results in the removal of the property from the estate as exempt, no matter what its value. However, if the debtor claims an exemption in property and specifies a value for the property that is no greater than the amount allowed for that category by statute, the trustee may retain any amount in excess of the value so specified by the debtor, even if the trustee does not object to the claimed exemption. *Schwab v. Reilly*, 130 S. Ct. 2652 (2010).

If there is an objection to a claimed exemption, the party objecting has the burden of showing that the exemption is not properly claimed. Fed. R. Bankr. P. 4003(c).

The following chart visualizes the procedural requirements for claiming and objecting to claimed exemptions.

PROCEDURE FOR CLAIMING AND OBJECTING TO EXEMPTIONS						
CLAIMING EXEMPTIONS FED. R. BANKR. P. 4003(a)		OBJECTING TO CLAIMED EXEMPTION FED. R. BANKR. P. 4003(b)-(c)				
WHEN	HOW	HOW	WHEN	EXCEPTIONS	BURDEN	RESULT
WHEN FILING SCHEDULES UNDER RULE 1007(b)	COMPLETE OFFICIAL FORM 6C	BY FILING OBJECTION	WITHIN 30 DAYS AFTER COMPLETION OF § 341 MEETING (OR EXTENSION GRANTED DURING THAT PERIOD)	TRUSTEE MAY OBJECT PRIOR TO ONE YEAR AFTER CASE CLOSED IF DEBTOR FRAUDULENTLY ASSERTED EXEMPTION OBJECTION BASED ON § 522(q) MAY BE FILED BEFORE CASE IS CLOSED	BURDEN IS ON OBJECTING PARTY	IF NO OBJECTION IS FILED, CLAIMED PROPERTY WITH CLAIMED VALUE IS EXEMPT

D. EXEMPTIONS AND LIEN AVOIDANCE

A debtor is free to give a creditor a lien on property that falls within a category listed as exempt under federal or state law; exemptions operate to protect a debtor's property only from nonconsensual execution, not from consensual security interests or mortgages. If there is a lien on exempt property at the time the debtor files for bankruptcy protection, generally that lien remains enforceable in bankruptcy and the debtor can claim as exempt only the value of the property in excess of the debt secured by the lien (if there is any) (the debtor's "equity" in that property).

However, under § 522(f), the debtor is allowed to avoid certain liens on exempt property if four things are true: it is the right type of lien, the right type of property, the debtor has an interest in that property and the lien impairs an exemption the debtor could otherwise claim.

The first requirement is that the lien be the right type. Two types of lien are subject to avoidance under § 522(f). One is judicial liens on property (such as a judgment lien or lien of garnishment) other than liens securing a domestic support obligation (§ 101(14A)). The second is a nonpossessory, non-purchase-money security interest. "Nonpossessory" is a security interest in property that is not in the possession of the secured creditor. A "purchase-money security interest" is defined in § 9-103 of the Uniform Commercial Code, and refers to a security interest taken by a seller of the collateral to secure a purchaser's obligation to pay the purchase price, or taken by a financer who gives value to the debtor to enable the debtor to acquire the collateral. Nonpossessory, non-purchase-money security interests are therefore security interests that do not secure an enabling loan (credit extended to enable the debtor to acquire the collateral) and for which the creditor is not in possession of the collateral.

The second requirement for § 522(f) to apply is that the property in which the creditor has a lien is the right type of property. When the debtor seeks to take advantage of § 522(f) to avoid a judicial lien, there is no limitation on the type of exempt property for the statute to be available. However, for nonpossessory, non-purchase-money security interests, § 522(f) is available to the debtor to avoid the lien only if the exempt property falls within one of the three categories listed in § 522(f)(1)(B)(i)-(iii). These three categories are, first, household furnishings, household goods, and other itemized consumer goods used primarily for personal, family or household use of the debtor or a dependent; second, tools of the trade and professional books of the debtor or a dependent; and three, professionally prescribed health aids for the debtor or a dependent.

In order to further limit the scope of § 522(f), Congress itemized in § 522(f)(4) what items are included in and excluded from the definition of "household goods" for purposes of § 522(f)(1)(B)(i). Expressly excluded are most works of art, electronic entertainment equipment with a fair market value of more than $600* (except one television, one radio, and one VCR), antiques with a fair market value of more than $600,* jewelry with a fair market value of more than $600* (except wedding rings), and most computers, motor vehicles, watercraft and aircraft. A visualization of these limitations on the definition of "household goods" follows:

---

* This dollar figure, like many of the dollar figures in the Code, is subject to adjustment every three years under § 104(b) of the Code to reflect change in the Consumer Price Index for the most recent three years, and was most recently adjusted effective April 1, 2010 and will be adjusted again in 2013.

HOUSEHOLD GOODS UNDER § 522(f)(1)(B)	
INCLUDED § 522(f)(4)(A)	EXCLUDED § 522(f)(4)(B)
1) CLOTHING 2) FURNITURE 3) APPLIANCES 4) 1 RADIO 5) 1 TELEVISION 6) 1 VCR 7) LINENS 8) CHINA 9) CROCKERY 10) KITCHENWARE 11) EDUCATIONAL MATERIALS AND EQUIPMENT PRIMARILY FOR USE OF MINOR DEPENDENT CHILDREN 12) MEDICAL EQUIPMENT AND SUPPLIES 13) FURNITURE EXCLUSIVELY FOR USE OF MINOR CHILDREN OR ELDERLY OR DISABLED DEPENDENTS 14) PERSONAL EFFECTS OF DEBTOR AND DEPENDENTS 15) 1 PERSONAL COMPUTER AND RELATED EQUIPMENT	1) WORKS OF ART NOT BY DEBTOR OR RELATIVE 2) ELECTRONIC ENTERTAINMENT EQUIPMENT WITH FMV > $600* NOT LISTED AS INCLUDED IN § 522(f)(4)(A) 3) ITEMS ACQUIRED AS ANTIQUES WITH FMV > $600* IN AGGREGATE 4) JEWELRY WITH FMV > $600* IN AGGREGATE EXCEPT WEDDING RINGS 5) COMPUTER NOT LISTED AS INCLUDED IN § 522(f)(4)(A), MOTOR VEHICLE (INCLUDING TRACTOR OR LAWN TRACTOR), BOAT, MOTORIZED RECREATIONAL VEHICLE, CONVEYANCE, VEHICLE, WATERCRAFT OR AIRCRAFT

---

* This dollar figure, like many of the dollar figures in the Code, is subject to adjustment every three years under § 104(b) of the Code to reflect change in the Consumer Price Index for the most recent three years, and was most recently adjusted effective April 1, 2010 and will be adjusted again in 2013.

The third requirement for avoidance of liens under § 522(f) is that the debtor has an interest in the property. The debtor must have had an interest in the property before the lien attached to it (because the statute permits avoidance of the "fixing" of a lien on that interest of the debtor). And of course, the debtor must continue to have an interest in the property to which the lien remains attached, *e.g.*, the debtor has not disposed of the property, or there would be no benefit to the debtor if the lien is avoided.

The final requirement for the debtor to use § 522(f) to avoid the fixing of a lien is that the lien must impair the exemption (*i.e.*, prevent the debtor from claiming it and keeping the property). Section 522(f)(2)(A) explains how to tell if the lien impairs an exemption. First, you add together the amount of challenged lien, the amount of all other liens on property, and the amount of the exemption that would be available to the debtor for that property in the absence of all liens. Then you compare that sum to the total value of debtor's interest in the property if there were no liens. If the sum of the liens and the exemption exceeds the value of debtor's interest in the property were it unencumbered, the challenged lien is avoided to that extent (or to the full extent of the challenged lien, if less). A visualization of this computation follows:

IMPAIRMENT § 522(f)(2)(A)	
IMPAIRMENT = X - Y	
X = SUM OF (1) AMOUNT OF CHALLENGED LIEN (2) AMOUNT OF ALL OTHER LIENS (3) AMOUNT OF EXEMPTION	Y = INTEREST OF DEBTOR IN PROPERTY WITHOUT ANY LIENS

The following chart summarizes the requirements for avoiding liens that impair exemptions under § 522(f).

DEBTOR'S AVOIDANCE OF LIENS
§ 522(f)

TYPE OF LIEN	EXEMPT PROPERTY	DEBTOR HAS INTEREST IN PROPERTY	LIEN IMPAIRS EXEMPTION (FEDERAL OR STATE)
JUDICIAL LIEN NOT SECURING DOMESTIC SUPPORT OBLIGATION, OR	FOR JUDICIAL LIEN: ANY TYPE OF PROPERTY	• BEFORE LIEN IS "FIXED"	DEBTOR IS ENTITLED TO EXEMPTION
NON-POSSESSORY NON-PURCHASE-MONEY SECURITY INTEREST	FOR NONPOSSESSORY NON-PURCHASE-MONEY SECURITY INTEREST: 1) HOUSEHOLD FURNISHINGS, HOUSEHOLD GOODS (§ 522(f)(4)), WEARING APPAREL, APPLIANCES, BOOKS, ANIMALS, CROPS, MUSICAL INSTRUMENTS, JEWELRY HELD PRIMARILY FOR PERSONAL, FAMILY OR HOUSEHOLD USE OF DEBTOR OR DEPENDENT, 2) IMPLEMENTS, PROFESSIONAL BOOKS, OR TOOLS, OF THE TRADE OF DEBTOR OR DEPENDENT, OR 3) PROFESSIONALLY PRESCRIBED HEALTH AIDS FOR DEBTOR OR DEPENDENT	• AT TIME AVOIDANCE IS SOUGHT	LIEN IMPAIRS EXEMPTION UNDER § 522(f)(2)(A)

In one situation, the debtor is limited in avoiding a lien that impairs an exemption under § 522(f)(1). Under § 522(f)(3), if state exemptions are applicable to the debtor and state law either permits an exemption unlimited in amount except to the extent the property is encumbered by a consensual lien, or prohibits avoidance of consensual liens on exempt property, then the debtor may not avoid a nonpossessory, non-purchase-money security interest in implements, professional books, or tools of the trade of the debtor or a dependent, or farm animals or cops of the debtor or a dependent, to the extent the value of such implements, professional books, tools of the trade, animals, and crops exceeds $5,850."* Although the provision is not a model of clarity, it has been interpreted to mean that the amount by which the lien would otherwise be avoided under § 522(f)(1) is reduced by the excess of the actual value of the property over the specified figure. A visualization of this section follows:

LIMITATION ON AVOIDANCE OF LIENS IMPAIRING EXEMPTIONS § 522(f)(3)				
STATE EXEMPTIONS APPLICABLE	STATE EXEMPTION LAW	TYPE OF PROPERTY	TYPE OF LIEN	LIMITATION ON AVOIDANCE
EITHER DEBTOR HAS ELECTED STATE EXEMPTIONS OR STATE PROHIBITS DEBTORS FROM USING FEDERAL EXEMPTIONS	STATE EXEMPTION IS UNLIMITED IN AMOUNT EXCEPT FOR CONSENSUAL LIENS, OR STATE LAW PROHIBITS AVOIDANCE OF CONSENSUAL LIENS ON EXEMPT PROPERTY	IMPLEMENTS, PROFESSIONAL BOOKS, TOOLS OF THE TRADE, FARM ANIMALS, OR CROPS OF DEBTOR OR DEPENDENT	NONPOSSESSORY NON-PURCHASE-MONEY SECURITY INTEREST	AMOUNT OF LIEN OTHERWISE AVOIDABLE (COMPUTED UNDER § 522(f)(1)) IS REDUCED BY EXCESS OF VALUE OF PROPERTY OVER $5,850*

---

* This dollar figure, like many of the dollar figures in the Code, is subject to adjustment every three years under § 104(b) of the Code to reflect change in the Consumer Price Index for the most recent three years, and was most recently adjusted effective April 1, 2010 and will be adjusted again in 2013.

Chapter 4

CLAIMS

A. TYPES OF CLAIMS

A "claim" is defined as "a right to payment, whether or not such right is reduced to judgment, liquidated, unliquidated, fixed, contingent, matured, unmatured, disputed, undisputed, legal, equitable, secured, or unsecured" or "a right to an equitable remedy for breach of performance" that gives rise to a right to payment. § 101(5). The definition is a broad one, and was intended to permit the bankruptcy case to deal with all legal obligations of the debtor, even those that are remote or contingent at the time of filing. A "creditor" is an entity with a claim against the debtor that arises at or before the order for relief. § 101(10).

Claims are categorized by their priority against the estate. Generally, claims fall into one of two basic categories, secured or unsecured. Some unsecured claims may be so-called priority claims, entitled to preferential treatment in a chapter 7 distribution. In addition, parties in interest may assert a right to payment of administrative expenses from the estate, and some claims (either secured or unsecured) may be subordinated to others. We will look at these types of claims in turn.

1. Secured Claims

Under § 506(a)(1), if a creditor has a lien on estate property, or has a right of setoff against such property, that creditor has a secured claim "to the extent of the value of such creditor's interest in the estate's interest in such property, or to the extent of the amount subject to setoff, as the case may be." This phrase means that if the creditor's claim is for an amount in excess of the value of the property on which the creditor has a lien or against which it has a right of setoff, its claim is secured onto to the extent of the value of the property and is unsecured to the extent of any claim in excess of that amount. This is familiarly knows as "bifurcating" a claim into a secured and unsecured portion.

In determining which portion of a claim secured by collateral or subject to a setoff is secured, valuation of the property subject to the lien or setoff is key. Section 506(a)(1) states that the value of the property "shall be determined in light of the purpose of the valuation and of the proposed disposition or use of such property."

In one situation, § 506(a) is more explicit. For personal property securing an allowed claim in a chapter 7 or chapter 13 case of an individual debtor, value is to be determined "based on the replacement value of such property as of the date of the filing of the petition without deduction for costs of sale or marketing." It continues, "[w]ith respect to property acquired for personal, family, or household purposes, replacement value shall mean the price a retail merchant would charge for property of that kind considering the age and condition of the property at the time value is determined." § 506(b)(2). This provision was intended to codify, in a slightly modified form, the holding of the Supreme Court in Associates Commercial Corp. v. Rash, 520 U.S. 953 (1997), in which the Court set out a standard for valuation of collateral a chapter 13 debtor proposed to retain under his plan.

In two situations, an undersecured claim is not bifurcated as contemplated by § 506(a). First, claims described in the so-called "hanging paragraph" in § 1325 are not subject to § 506(a) and therefore must be treated as secured claims to the full extent of the obligation owing to the secured creditor under the chapter 13 plan. See Chapter 8[D], *infra*.

Second, in a chapter 11 case, the claims of nonrecourse secured creditors (i.e., creditors that have a security interest in or mortgage on specified property of the debtor but by contract are limited to recourse against the collateral and cannot sue the debtor individually) are generally treated as if they were recourse claims against the debtor and are entitled to the same treatment under § 506(a) as other recourse secured claims (meaning they get a secured claim for the value of their collateral and an unsecured claim for the excess amount of the claim). § 1111(b)(1).

However, both nonrecourse and recourse undersecured creditors may elect (by class vote, requiring approval by at least 2/3 in amount and more than half in number of allowed claims of such class) to be treated under § 1111(b)(2) instead of bifurcating their claims. § 1111(b)(1). They cannot make that election if the property in which they have a lien is of inconsequential value or is sold during the bankruptcy case or is to be sold pursuant to the plan. If they make the § 1111(b)(2) election, their entire claim (not merely the portion representing the value of the property by which they are secured) must be treated as a secured claim under a chapter 11 plan. See Chapter 9[E][1], *infra*.

The following chart visualizes the provisions of § 1111(b).

NONRECOURSE AND UNDERSECURED CLAIMS § 1111(b)				
NONRECOURSE SECURED CREDITORS		UNDERSECURED CREDITORS		
RULE § 1111(b)(1)	EXCEPTION	VOTING FOR § 1111(b)(2) TREATMENT	WHEN ELECTION IS NOT ALLOWED	CONSEQUENCES OF ELECTION § 1111(b)(2)
CLAIMS TREATED AS RECOURSE AND BIFURCATED UNDER § 506(a)	CLASS MAKES § 1111(b)(2) ELECTION	AT LEAST 2/3 IN AMOUNT AND A MAJORITY IN NUMBER OF ALLOWED CLAIMS IN CLASS	PROPERTY IS SOLD UNDER § 363 OR UNDER PLAN PROPERTY IS OF INCONSEQUENTIAL VALUE	UNSECURED PORTION OF CLAIM IS WAIVED, AND FULL CLAIM IS ALLOWED AS SECURED CLAIM

2. Unsecured Claims and Priority Claims

Unsecured claims are claims that do not qualify as secured claims under § 506(a)(1). There are two types of unsecured claims, priority claims and general unsecured claims. Priority claims are those unsecured claims and expenses that Congress has decided should by paid before other unsecured claims. Priority claims and expenses are listed, in order of priority, in § 507(a). There are ten categories of priority claims and expenses.

First are allowed unsecured claims for "domestic support obligations." In addition, if a trustee is appointed in the bankruptcy case, the administrative expenses of the trustee must be paid before those domestic support obligations to the extent the trustee administers assets that are otherwise available to pay the domestic support obligations. § 507(a)(1).

"Domestic support obligations" are defined in § 101(14A). A domestic support obligation is a prepetition debt (including interest on that debt provided under applicable nonbankruptcy law) that meets four requirements. First, it must be owed to either a spouse, former spouse, or child of the debtor or the child's parent, legal guardian or responsible relative, or to a governmental unit (§ 101(27)). Second, it must be in the nature of alimony, maintenance, or support of such spouse, former spouse, or child of the debtor or such child's parent (even if the debt is not so designated). Third, it must be established or subject to establishment prepetition under a separation agreement, divorce decree, or property settlement agreement or by court order, or by a governmental unit determination in accordance with applicable nonbankruptcy law. Fourth, it may not be assigned to a nongovernmental entity other than voluntarily for purposes of collection. A visualization of the definition of "domestic support obligation" follows:

DOMESTIC SUPPORT OBLIGATIONS
§ 101(14A)

PAYMENT TO SPOUSE, FORMER SPOUSE OR CHILD OF DEBTOR OR CHILD'S PARENT, LEGAL GUARDIAN OR RESPONSIBLE RELATIVE, OR GOVERNMENTAL UNIT,
IN NATURE OF ALIMONY, MAINTENANCE OR SUPPORT,
ESTABLISHED PURSUANT TO SEPARATION AGREEMENT, DIVORCE DECREE, PROPERTY SETTLEMENT AGREEMENT OR OTHER COURT ORDER OR DETERMINATION BY GOVERNMENTAL UNIT, AND
NOT ASSIGNED TO NONGOVERNMENTAL ENTITY UNLESS ASSIGNED VOLUNTARILY FOR PURPOSES OF COLLECTION

After domestic support obligations come allowed "administrative expenses." § 507(a)(2). Administrative expenses are itemized in § 503(b) and are discussed in Section 4[A][3], *infra*. If a court denies relief from the automatic stay because the trustee provides adequate protection of a secured creditor's interest in property under § 362(d)(1), or allows the trustee to use, sell or lease property because the trustee provides adequate protection to the holder of a lien on that property under § 363, or allows the trustee to incur debt having an equal or senior lien on the collateral under § 364(d)(1) because the trustee provides the secured creditor adequate protection of its interest in the collateral, and in any such case that adequate protection proves inadequate (meaning that notwithstanding the adequate protection, the secured creditor has an administrative expense claim arising from the stay or from the use, sale or lease of the property or from the incurrence of debt), then the creditor's claim is given priority over all other administrative expense claims. § 507(b).

Third priority is granted to claims allowed under § 502(f) arising in the ordinary course of the debtor's business or financial affairs in an involuntary case (§ 303) during the period after the commencement of the case but before the earlier of the appointment of a trustee and the order for relief. § 507(a)(3).

Fourth come allowed unsecured claims earned within 180 days before the fling date (or if earlier, the date the debtor's business ceased) for an individual's wages, salaries or commissions, including vacation, severance and sick leave pay. § 507(a)(4). The priority afforded to these wage claims is limited in amount to $11,725* per individual. A fifth priority is granted to allowed unsecured claims for contributions to employee benefit plans arising from services rendered within 180 days prior to the filing date (or if earlier, the date the debtor's business ceased). § 507(a)(5). This priority is also limited for each plan to $11,725* times the number of covered employees, less the aggregate amount paid to those employees under the fourth priority plus the aggregate amount paid on behalf of those employees to any other plan.

---

* These dollar figures, like many of the dollar figures in the Code, are subject to adjustment every three years under § 104(b) of the Code to reflect change in the Consumer Price Index for the most recent three years, and were most recently adjusted effective April 1, 2010 and will be adjusted again in 2013.

Sixth, allowed unsecured claims of persons engaged in the production or raising of grain against grain storage facilities or United States fishermen against operators of fish produce storage or processing facilities, to the extent of $5,775* per individual, are administrative expenses. § 507(a)(6).

Seventh, if an individual purchases, leases, or rents property from the debtor, or purchases services from the debtor, for that individual's personal, family, or household purposes, and gives the debtor a deposit before the commencement of the case, the individual has an administrative expense for the property or services that were not delivered or provided, but limited to an amount of $2,600.* § 507(a)(8).

The eighth priority relates to various types of allowed unsecured claims of governmental units for taxes. § 507(a)(8). Different taxes are entitled to different priorities. The most favored tax claim is that for taxes on income or gross receipts for a taxable year ending before the filing date if the last due date for a return for that year (taking into account any extensions that have been granted) occurred not more than three years immediately before the filing date, or the taxes were assessed within 240 days before the filing date. Next come property taxes incurred prepetition and payable without penalty within one year before filing. Taxes which the debtor was required to collect or withhold from others (so-called "trust fund" taxes, such as those withheld by employers from employee wages) receive the next priority. Then come employment taxes on wages, salaries or commissions (such as social security taxes and required employer payments on unemployment insurance) if the last due date for a return (taking into account any extensions) occurred not more than three years immediately before the filing date.

The fifth tax priority is for excise taxes on transactions occurring before the filing for which a return, if required, is last due not more than three years immediately before the filing date. If a return is not required, the transaction must occur during that three-year period. The next priority is for certain customs duties arising out the importation of merchandise that have not grown unreasonable stale. The final tax priority is for penalties relating to any priority tax claim if the penalty is "in compensation for actual pecuniary loss." Under § 507(c), a claim of a governmental unit arising from an erroneous refund or credit of a tax has the same priority as a claim for the tax with respect to which the refund or credit was made.

The ninth priority claim relates to allowed unsecured claims based on any commitment by the debtor to a Federal depository institutions regulatory agency to maintain the capital of an insured depository institution. § 507(a)(9).

The final priority is for allowed claims for death or personal injury arising from the unlawful operation of a motor vehicle or vessel while the debtor was under the influence of alcohol, a drug, or another substance. § 507(a)(10).

Priority claims can be visualized as follow:

---

* This dollar figure, like many of the dollar figures in the Code, are subject to adjustment every three years under § 104(b) of the Code to reflect change in the Consumer Price Index for the most recent three years, and were most recently adjusted effective April 1, 2010 and will be adjusted again in 2013.

PRIORITY CLAIMS § 507		
SECTION	**CLAIM OR EXPENSE**	**LIMIT ON PRIORITY**
507(a)(1)	DOMESTIC SUPPORT OBLIGATIONS AND RELATED TRUSTEE ADMINISTRATIVE EXPENSES	NONE
507(a)(2)	ADMINISTRATIVE EXPENSES § 503(b)	NONE
507(a)(3)	ORDINARY COURSE UNSECURED CLAIMS ARISING BETWEEN FILING OF INVOLUNTARY PETITION AND ORDER FOR RELIEF § 502(f)	NONE
507(a)(4)	CLAIMS FOR EMPLOYEE WAGES, SALARIES OR COMMISSIONS EARNED WITHIN 180 DAYS OF EARLIER OF FILING OR CESSATION OF DEBTOR'S BUSINESS	$11,725* PER INDIVIDUAL
507(a)(5)	CLAIMS FOR CONTRIBUTIONS TO EMPLOYEE BENEFIT PLAN ARISING FROM SERVICES WITHIN 180 DAYS BEFORE EARLIER OF FILING OR CESSATION OF DEBTOR'S BUSINESS	$11,725* PER EMPLOYEE LESS AMOUNTS PAID UNDER PRIORITY (4) AND AMOUNTS PAID TO ANOTHER PLAN
507(a)(6)	CLAIMS OF GRAIN PRODUCER AGAINST GRAIN STORAGE FACILITY OR OF FISHERMAN AGAINST FISH PRODUCE STORAGE OR PROCESSING FACILITY	$5,775* PER PERSON
507(a)(7)	CLAIMS OF INDIVIDUALS FOR DEPOSITS FOR PURCHASE, LEASE OR RENTAL OF PROPERTY OR PURCHASE OF SERVICES FOR PERSONAL, FAMILY OR HOUSEHOLD USE NOT DELIVERED OR PROVIDED	$2,600* PER PERSON
507(a)(8)	CLAIMS FOR INCOME TAXES AND CERTAIN OTHER TAXES AND PENALTIES	VARIOUS PERIODS
507(a)(9)	CLAIMS TO MAINTAIN CAPITAL OF FEDERAL DEPOSITORY INSTITUTION	NONE
507(a)(10)	CLAIMS FOR DEATH OR PERSONAL INJURY WHILE OPERATING VEHICLE OR VESSEL WHILE UNDER INFLUENCE OF ALCOHOL OR DRUGS	NONE

---

* These dollar figures, like many of the dollar figures in the Code, are subject to adjustment every three years under § 104(b) of the Code to reflect change in the Consumer Price Index for the most recent three years, and were most recently adjusted effective April 1, 2010 and will be adjusted again in 2013.

3.   Administrative Expenses

There are nine types of administrative expenses itemized in § 503(b). The first, and most important, is the "actual, necessary costs and expenses of preserving the estate." § 503(b)(1)(A). These include amounts paid for services rendered to the estate after the commencement of the case. Also included are taxes incurred by the estate.

The second type of administrative expense is compensation and reimbursement awarded to a trustee, consumer privacy ombudsman (§ 332), an examiner, a patient care ombudsman (§ 333), or a professional person employed under § 327 or § 1103. § 503(b)(2). The priority treatment given these fees and expenses enables a debtor to retain professional persons who would not otherwise be willing to serve. It also ensures that, after a conversion of a case to chapter 7, a trustee can be appointed to liquidate the estate.

The expenses of specified creditors and custodians are entitled to administrative expense treatment under § 503(b)(3). These include creditors who file an involuntary petition under § 303, creditors that recover property transferred or concealed by the debtor for the benefit of the estate, creditors involved in the prosecution of a criminal offense relating to the case or property of or business of the debtor, creditors or equity security holders or an indenture trustee or a committee "in making a substantial contribution" in a chapter 9 or chapter 11 case, a custodian superseded by the trustee under § 543, and members of an official committee for expenses incurred in connection with performing their duties as committee members. The reasonable compensation of attorneys and accountants to all of these creditors and custodians (other than members of an official committee, whose professional persons are covered by the second type of administrative expense) is an administrative expense under § 503(b)(4). Reasonable compensation for services rendered by an indenture trustee in making "a substantial contribution" in a chapter 9 or chapter 11 case is also an administrative expense. § 503(b)(5).

A sixth type of administrative expense is the fees and mileage payable to witnesses under 28 U.S.C. § 1821 *et seq.* § 503(b)(6).

The final three types of administrative expenses were added by the 2005 BAPCPA amendments. Under § 503(b)(7), if the debtor assumes a lease of nonresidential real property under § 365 and later rejects it, monetary obligations for the next two years (or two years after the date the property is turned over to the lessor, if later) becomes administrative expenses. Any remaining obligations are treated as general unsecured claims subject to the cap described in § 502(b)(6) (see Section 4[B], *infra*). Section 503(b)(8) gives administrative expense status to the actual, necessary costs and expenses of closing a health care business (§ 101(27A)). And under § 503(b)(9), if goods are sold to the debtor in the ordinary course of the debtor's business and are received by the debtor within 20 days before the commencement of the case, the value of those goods is an administrative expense.

A visualization of administrative expenses follows:

ADMINISTRATIVE EXPENSES
§ 503(b)

1)	ACTUAL, NECESSARY COSTS AND EXPENSES OF PRESERVING THE ESTATE (INCLUDING POSTPETITION WAGES) AND TAXES INCURRED BY ESTATE
2)	COMPENSATION TO A TRUSTEE, CONSUMER PRIVACY OMBUDSMAN, PATIENT CARE OMBUDSMAN, EXAMINER, OR PROFESSIONAL PERSON EMPLOYED UNDER § 327 OR § 1103
3)	ACTUAL, NECESSARY EXPENSES INCURRED BY —
	(A) CREDITOR FILING INVOLUNTARY PETITION
	(B) CREDITOR RECOVERING PROPERTY TRANSFERRED OR CONCEALED BY DEBTOR
	(C) CREDITOR IN CONNECTION WITH CRIMINAL PROSECUTION RELATING TO CASE
	(D) CREDITOR, INDENTURE TRUSTEE, EQUITY SECURITY HOLDER OR COMMITTEE MAKING SUBSTANTIAL CONTRIBUTION TO CHAPTER 9 OR 11 CASE
	(E) CUSTODIAN SUPERSEDED BY TRUSTEE
	(F) MEMBER OF CREDITORS' COMMITTEE IN CONNECTION WITH DUTIES
4)	ATTORNEYS' OR ACCOUNTANTS' FEES FOR THOSE IN 3) ABOVE
5)	COMPENSATION FOR INDENTURE TRUSTEE MAKING SUBSTANTIAL CONTRIBUTION IN CHAPTER 9 OR 11 CASE
6)	FEES AND MILEAGE OF WITNESSES UNDER 28 U.S.C. § 1821 ET SEQ.
7)	MONETARY OBLIGATIONS DUE UNDER ASSUMED, THEN REJECTED, NONRESIDENTIAL REAL PROPERTY LEASES FOR TWO YEARS FOLLOWING LATER OF REJECTION AND TURNOVER OF PROPERTY
8)	COSTS OF CLOSING HEALTH CARE BUSINESS
9)	VALUE OF GOODS RECEIVED BY DEBTOR WITHIN 20 DAYS BEFORE DATE CASE COMMENCED SOLD TO DEBTOR IN ORDINARY COURSE OF DEBTOR'S BUSINESS

4.   Subordinated Claims

Bankruptcy does not affect the enforceability of a subordination agreement. § 510(a). Therefore, if one creditor, whether secured or unsecured, has contractually agreed that another creditor will get paid in full before the first creditor receives any amount in respect of its claim, that agreement will be respected in connection with any distribution from the bankruptcy estate.

Section 510 also provides for subordination of claims under two other circumstances. First, a claim arising from rescission of a purchase or sale of a security of the debtor or an affiliate of the debtor, or for damages arising from such a purchase or sale or reimbursement or contribution in respect thereof, is subordinated to all claims or interests that are senior to the claim or interest represented by the security at issue. § 510(b). If the security is common stock, the claim is treated as having the same priority as common stock. Id.

Second, the court has the power, under principles of equitable subordination, to subordinate all or part of any allowed claim or interest to all or any part of another allowed claim or interest. § 510(c). Equitable subordination is a judicially-created doctrine that may be invoked when the holder of the claim or interest has engaged in inequitable conduct (generally fraudulent or illegal), often by undercapitalizing the debtor or by using the debtor as an alter ego or mere instrumentality, as a result of which the debtor or other creditors were injured or the holder obtained an unfair advantage. The doctrine is most likely to be used when the holder is an insider (such as a director, officer or controlling shareholder), or someone else exercising control over the debtor.

The three types of subordination are visualized below:

SUBORDINATION § 510		
CONTRACTUAL SUBORDINATION § 510(a)	SUBORDINATION OF SECURITY CLAIMS § 510(b)	EQUITABLE SUBORDINATION § 510(c)
SUBORDINATION AGREEMENTS ENFORCEABLE IN BANKRUPTCY TO THE SAME EXTENT AS UNDER APPLICABLE NONBANKRUPTCY LAW	CLAIMS FOR RESCISSION OF PURCHASE OR SALE OF SECURITY OF DEBTOR OR AFFILIATE, OR FOR DAMAGES FROM PURCHASE OR SALE, OR FOR REIMBURSEMENT OR CONTRIBUTION IN RESPECT OF PURCHASE OR SALE, ARE TREATED AS SUBORDINATE TO SECURITY (OR AS COMMON STOCK IF SECURITY IS COMMON STOCK)	COURT MAY SUBORDINATE ALL OR PART OF ALLOWED CLAIM TO ALL OR PART OF ANOTHER ALLOWED CLAIM AND ALL OR PART OF ALLOWED INTEREST TO ALL OR PART OF ANOTHER ALLOWED INTEREST USING PRINCIPLES OF EQUITABLE SUBORDINATION COURT MAY TRANSFER LIEN SECURING SUBORDINATED CLAIM TO ESTATE

B. FILING, ALLOWANCE AND ESTIMATION OF CLAIMS

After a debtor files a petition for bankruptcy under chapter 7, 12, or 13, the clerk of court sends out a notice of the commencement of the case on Official Form 9. This form not only notifies creditors of the § 341 meeting, but also either sets forth the deadline for filing proofs of claim, see Official Form 9C, or informs the creditors that the case appears to be a "no-asset" case in which nothing will be available for distribution to creditors, and thus they should not file proofs of claim, see Official Form 9A. In a case that has assets for distribution, the notice will also give creditors the deadline for filing proofs of claim, which is in most situations a date not later than 90 days after the first date set for the § 341 meeting. Fed. R. Bankr. P. 3002(c). (A governmental unit usually has up to 180 days after the order for relief to file a proof of claim.) A creditor or equity security holder in a chapter 7, 12 or 13 case must generally file a proof of claim or interest for the claim or interest to be allowed. Fed. R. Bankr. P. 3002(a).

In a chapter 11 case, the schedule of liabilities filed by the debtor pursuant to § 521(a)(1) constitutes "prima facie" evidence of the validity and amount of the claims set forth on the schedule, unless the schedule states they are disputed, contingent or unliquidated. Therefore, only creditors whose claims were not scheduled, or whose claims were listed as disputed, contingent or unliquidated need to file proofs of claim in a chapter 11 case. § 1111(a) and Fed. R. Bankr. P. 3003(b)(1) and (c). The court establishes the time within which proofs of claim must be filed. Fed. R. Bankr. P. 3003(c)(3).

Under § 501(a), a creditor may file a "proof of claim" (and an entity holder of an equity security may file a proof of interest). A proof of claim is simply "a written statement setting forth a creditor's claim," Fed. R. Bankr. P. 3001(a), but must substantially conform to Official Form 10 and in most cases must be executed by the creditor or the creditor's authorized agent, Fed. R. Bankr. P. 3001(b). If the claim is based on a writing (like a contract or promissory note), the original or a duplicate of that writing must be filed with the proof of claim, Fed. R. Bankr. P. 3001(c). If the creditor claims a security interest, the proof of claim must be accompanied by evidence that the security interest has been perfected (such as a copy of a stamped UCC-1 or filed mortgage). Fed. R. Bankr. P. 3001(d).

If a proof of claim is filed, under § 502(a) the claim is deemed allowed, meaning it will be allowed unless a party in interest objects to it. An objection to a claim is made by a filed writing, Fed. R. Bankr. P. 3007(a), and a single objection to multiple claims (so-called "omnibus objections") may be filed under some circumstances. Fed. R. Bankr. P. 3007(d)-(e). A properly filed proof of claim "constitutes prima facie evidence of the validity and amount of the claim." Fed. R. Bankr. P. 3001(f). This means that the burden of production (of coming up with some evidence to rebut the presumption of validity created by Rule 3001(f)) rests with the party objecting to the claim. If the burden of coming forward with evidence is met, the ultimate burden of proof rests with the claimant to substantiate the claim by a preponderance of the evidence.

A party in interest may object to a claim on various grounds. Because only a "creditor" or indenture trustee may file proof of claim under § 501(a), and "creditor" is defined in § 101(10) as an entity with a claim that arose on or before the order for relief, if a proof of claim describes a claim that did not arise before the order for relief, it is not properly filed. (The holder of the claim may be entitled to request payment of an administrative expense under § 503(a) if the obligation qualifies as one, but the proofs of claim relate only to prepetition obligations.)

There are three circumstances in which a claim arising after the order for relief is treated as a prepetition claim for purposes of allowance. First, claims arising from the rejection of an executory contract or unexpired lease under § 365 not previously assumed are treated as prepetition claims. See discussion in Chapter 6[D][1], *infra.* § 502(g). The same treatment is afforded damage claims for rejected swap agreements, securities contracts, forward contracts, commodity contracts, repurchase agreements, or master netting agreements under § 562. Second, a claim arising from the recovery of property under § 522, 550 or 553 is treated as a prepetition claim. § 502(h). Third, a claim for a priority tax that arises after commencement of the case is treated as a prepetition claim. § 502(i).

Section 502(b) provides nine grounds for disallowance of a claim. First, the claim must be disallowed if the claim is not enforceable outside of bankruptcy. § 502(b)(1). The estate succeeds to any defense available to the debtor against other entities, including statute of limitations, statute of frauds, usury, and other personal defenses. § 558. The fact that the claim is unmatured or contingent does not constitute grounds for disallowance, even if it could not be enforced outside of bankruptcy until it became mature and noncontingent.

Second, the claim must be disallowed if it is a claim for "unmatured interest." § 502(b)(2). Agreements extending credit to the debtor frequently specify that unpaid amounts bear interest until paid in full. When bankruptcy is filed and the debtor has not paid the full amount, interest will have accrued to the date of bankruptcy, and under the contract will continue to accrue after that date until the full amount was paid. The amount that has already accrued but is unpaid at the time of the bankruptcy filing is called "matured" interest; the amount that is going to accrue after the petition is filed until payment is made is "unmatured" interest. This claim for "unmatured" interest is not allowed, consistent with the theory that a claim is quantified as of the time the petition is filed.

However, there are two exceptions to this rule. If the creditor is a secured creditor (see Section 4[A][1], supra) with an interest in property with a value sufficient to cover the post-petition interest (i.e., the creditor is "oversecured"), the creditor may claim post-petition interest to the extent of the value of the collateral (as well as attorneys' fees and any other costs provided for by the creditor's contract with the debtor). § 506(b). In addition, in a chapter 7 case if there are sufficient assets in the debtor's estate to pay all creditors in full (meaning the debtor is solvent), the creditors get post-petition interest on their claims before money goes back to the debtor. § 726(a)(5).

Third, a property tax claim against property of the estate must be disallowed to the extent that it exceeds the value of the estate's interest in the property. § 502(b)(3).

Fourth, a claim for services of an insider or attorney of the debtor is disallowed to the extent that it exceeds the reasonable value of such services. § 502(b)(4). The provision is intended to avoid overreaching by those who were in a position to further their own economic interests before the bankruptcy filing.

Fifth, an unmatured claim for domestic support obligations must be disallowed. § 502(b)(5). These claims are nondischargeable under § 523(a)(5), and are intended to be paid out of postpetition property.

Sixth, claims by lessors for damages caused by termination of a lease of real property are subject to a cap, and any claim for an amount in excess of the cap is disallowed. § 502(b)(6). Congress capped landlord damages to avoid their claims (particularly on long-term leases) from overwhelming all others, leaving little for other general unsecured creditors. The amount of the allowable capped claim is the sum of rent for one year after the filing date (or if earlier, the date the lessor repossessed or the lessee surrendered the property), or 15% of the rent due for the remaining lease term (not to exceed three years), whichever is greater, plus any unpaid rent as of such date. The landlord may also be entitled to payment of administrative expenses for use of the property after the filing date, which are not affected by the statutory cap.

Seventh, similar to the cap on landlord claims, claims for termination of an employment agreement are capped at the sum of the compensation payable under that agreement for one year after the filing date (or the date on which the employee's services were terminated) plus any accrued unpaid compensation as of such date. § 502(b)(7).

Eighth, if the debtor makes a late payment of an employment tax on wages, salaries or commissions, and as a result an applicable credit due to the debtor should be reduced, the claim for such reduction is disallowed. § 502(b)(8).

Ninth, a claim must be disallowed if proof of such claim is not timely filed. § 502(b)(9). As described above, a proof of claim must generally be filed on a date not later than 90 days after the first date set for the § 341 meeting in a chapter 7, 12 or 13 case, Fed. R. Bankr. P. 3002(c), or during the period set by the court in a chapter 9 or 11 case, Fed. R. Bankr. P. 3003(c)(3).

Two other types of claims are disallowed. The court must disallow claims of entities from whom property is recovered under § 542, 543, 550 or 553 (because of the turnover obligations, the avoiding powers or improper setoffs) or transferees of avoidable transfers if those entities have retained the amount or property for which they are liable to the estate. § 502(d). In addition, reimbursement and contribution claims by entities who are co-obligors with the debtor or who have provided security for a claim against the debtor are disallowed to the extent that the creditor's claim against the debtor is disallowed, or the claim for reimbursement or contribution is contingent at the time the claim is being allowed or disallowed, or such entity asserts a right of subrogation to the rights of the creditor under § 509. § 502(e).

A visualization of allowance of claims follows:

FILING AND ALLOWANCE OF CLAIMS § 502(a) & (b)

FILING PROOFS OF CLAIM		TIMING		EFFECT OF FILING	GROUNDS FOR DISALLOWING CLAIMS § 502(b), (d), (e)
CHAPTER 7, 12 & 13	CHAPTER 9 & 11	CHAPTER 7, 12 & 13	CHAPTER 9 & 11		
UNSECURED CREDITORS MUST FILE FOR CLAIM TO BE ALLOWED IN ASSET CASE	CREDITORS HOLDING UNSCHEDULED, DISPUTED, CONTINGENT, OR UNLIQUIDATED CLAIM MUST FILE FOR CLAIM TO BE ALLOWED	DATE NOT LATER THAN 90 DAYS AFTER THE FIRST DATE SET FOR THE § 341 MEETING RULE 3002(c)	DATE SET BY COURT RULE 3003(c)(3)	FILED CLAIM IS DEEMED ALLOWED UNLESS OBJECTION FILED	1) UNENFORCEABLE 2) UNMATURED INTEREST 3) PROPERTY TAX IN AMOUNT EXCEEDING PROPERTY VALUE 4) SERVICES OF INSIDER OR ATTORNEY FOR DEBTOR EXCEEDING REASONABLE VALUE OF SERVICES 5) UNMATURED DOMESTIC SUPPORT OBLIGATIONS 6) LESSOR CLAIM IN EXCESS OF CAP 7) EMPLOYEE CLAIM FOR TERMINATION UNDER EMPLOYMENT AGREEMENT IN EXCESS OF CAP 8) REDUCTION IN CREDIT FOR LATE PAYMENT OF EMPLOYMENT TAX 9) UNTIMELY FILED CLAIM 10) CLAIM BY ENTITY RETAINING PROPERTY SUBJECT TO TURNOVER OR AVOIDABLE TRANSFER 11) CERTAIN CLAIMS FOR REIMBURSEMENT OR CONTRIBUTION

The fixing of a contingent claim, or liquidation of an unliquidated claim, may require litigation before the bankruptcy judge or another court, which could delay the bankruptcy process were all claims required to be fixed and liquidated before they could be allowed. To avoid such a delay, § 502(c) allows the court to estimate contingent or unliquidated claims to the extent necessary to avoid an undue delay in administration of the case, as well as rights to payment arising from a right to an equitable remedy for breach of performance. The estimated amount may be used for purposes of voting in a chapter 11 case, for purposes of determining whether the requirements for confirmation of a plan are satisfied, and even for purposes of distributions.

Chapter 5

AVOIDING POWERS

The Code confers on the trustee in bankruptcy the ability to undo certain prepetition transactions between the debtor and others because they were detrimental to the debtor or because they unfairly benefitted one creditor at the expense of others who were similarly situated. Familiarly known as the "avoiding powers," these provisions provide the trustee a powerful weapon in dealing with creditors, even those against whom no avoidance action is brought. We will look at seven different situations in which the trustee may avoid a transaction, and will then look at some procedural matters relating to those actions.

A. STRONG-ARM POWER

Under § 544(a), commonly known as the strong-arm clause, the trustee is given, as of the commencement of the case, without regard to any knowledge of the trustee or any creditor, the ability to avoid any transfer of property of the debtor or any obligation incurred by the debtor, that could be avoided by any of three types of creditors — a judgment lien creditor who extends credit as of the commencement of the case and obtained a judgment lien at that moment with respect to all property of the estate; an execution creditor who extends credit as of the commencement of the case and obtains an execution against the debtor at that time that is returned unsatisfied; and a bona fide purchaser of real property from the debtor who obtains that status and has perfected its transfer at the time of the commencement of the case.

The definition of "transfer" in § 101(54) includes any disposition of property or an interest in property, including retention of title as security. Therefore, under the strong-arm clause, the trustee may avoid not only outright conveyances of title to property, but also the creation of security interests or liens on property the title to which remains in the debtor. An obligation is incurred by the debtor whenever the debtor becomes liable to another.

Having the status of a hypothetical judgment lien creditor under § 544(a)(1) allows the trustee to avoid a security interest that is not perfected as of the commencement of the case. The concept of perfection of a security interest is described in Article 9 of the Uniform Commercial Code, and generally requires both the existence of a security interest in specific collateral that is valid between the debtor and the secured creditor, and public notification of that interest either by the secured creditor taking possession of tangible collateral or by the filing of a financing statement with the appropriate state office. By exercise of the strong-arm power, the trustee can strip the unperfected secured creditor of its collateral, rendering its claim a general unsecured claim for all purposes in the bankruptcy case.

The right to stand in the shoes of a hypothetical unsatisfied execution creditor under § 544(a)(2) is only valuable if state law gives such creditors greater rights than the normal judicial lien creditor, which is not generally the case.

The position of a hypothetical bona fide purchaser of real property is determined by state real property law, in particular, state recording laws. Generally if there is an interest in real property that is not properly filed in the real estate records (recorded), a later purchaser of that same real property without knowledge of the prior interest takes free of it automatically (under a notice system) or takes free of it if the subsequent purchaser records first (under a race/notice system). In those few states with a race system of recording, the subsequent purchaser can prevail over a prior interest holder who has not recorded simply by recording first. Under § 544(a)(3), the trustee is given the status of such a bona fide purchaser who has properly recorded as of the commencement of the case, and thereby defeats the unrecorded prior interest in the property.

Section 544(a) focuses on the rights of these hypothetical creditors as of the commencement of the bankruptcy case, the very moment the bankruptcy petition is filed. Therefore, if a creditor's security interest was perfected, or real estate interest was recorded, immediately prior to the bankruptcy filing, the creditor may have problems under other avoiding powers, but the strong-arm power is not available to avoid the transfer.

Various limitations on the strong-arm clause (and the other avoiding powers) are discussed in Section 5[H][1], *infra*. A visualization of the strong-arm power follows:

STRONG-ARM CLAUSE § 544(a)		
TRUSTEE HAS, AS OF COMMENCEMENT OF THE CASE, AND WITHOUT REGARD TO ANY KNOWLEDGE OF THE TRUSTEE OR ANY CREDITOR, RIGHTS AND POWERS OF, AND MAY AVOID ANY TRANSFER OF PROPERTY OF THE DEBTOR OR ANY OBLIGATION INCURRED BY THE DEBTOR THAT IS VOIDABLE BY:		
JUDICIAL LIEN CREDITOR WITH LIEN ON ALL NONEXEMPT PROPERTY OF DEBTOR	EXECUTION CREDITOR WITH UNSATISFIED EXECUTION AGAINST DEBTOR	BONA FIDE PURCHASER OF REAL PROPERTY FROM DEBTOR WHO HAS RECORDED ITS INTEREST

B. STATUTORY LIENS

A "statutory lien" is defined in § 101(53) to mean one of two types of liens, only one of which is "statutory" in the usual sense of the word. First, it relates to a lien "arising solely by force of a statute on specified circumstances or conditions." Second, it includes a "lien of distress for rent," whether or not statutory. At common law, "distress" was the taking of a personal chattel from the possession of a wrongdoer by a person injured by the wrongdoer to compensate the injured party for the wrong.

Therefore, a lien of distress for rent would be a landlord's lien in the tenant's personal property to secure the tenant's obligation to pay rent.

Two types of lien that might otherwise fall within the definition are explicitly excluded. First, a statutory lien does not include a security interest or judicial lien. A security interest is defined in § 101(51) as a "lien created by an agreement" (consensual lien), and a judicial lien is defined in § 101(36) as a "lien obtained by judgment, levy, sequestration, or other legal or equitable process or proceeding."

Generally, "statutory liens" are respected in bankruptcy — they are valid unless the fixing of such liens on property of the debtor is "avoided" by the trustee under § 545. That section allows the trustee to avoid the fixing of a statutory lien on property of the debtor in three situations.

First, the trustee can avoid the lien if it first becomes effective against the debtor at a time when the debtor is in financial difficulty, as evidenced by one of six events having occurred with respect to the debtor — a bankruptcy case is commenced, another type of insolvency proceeding is commenced, a custodian is appointed or authorized to take possession, insolvency, debtor's financial condition fails to meet a specified standard, or upon execution against property of the debtor by someone other than the holder of the statutory lien. § 545(1). This avoiding power is often described as a means of attacking disguised state priorities.

The order in which assets of a bankrupt estate are distributed is a matter of federal law, exclusively within the jurisdiction of Congress. But state law determines whether a creditor has a lien on property of a debtor. If state law could confer on certain preferred classes of creditors a lien that operates only when the debtor is in bankruptcy or other financial difficulty, the states could subvert the federal priority scheme. In order to avoid this result, state statutory liens that are triggered solely by the debtor's financial difficulties are avoidable under § 545(1).

Second, statutory liens may be avoided if they would not be enforceable at the time of the commencement of the case against a bona fide purchaser of property. § 545(2). Unlike the strong-arm clause of § 544(a) which gives the trustee the hypothetical status of a bona fide purchaser of real property, § 545(2) allows the trustee to avoid a statutory lien that could be avoided by a bona fide purchaser of personal property as well. In addition, unlike § 544(a) which allows the trustee to avoid a transfer only if a party benefitting from that transfer could have taken action to make it perfected against a bona fide purchaser (as by filing or recording its interest), § 545(2) also allows avoidance if the statutory lien is simply not enforceable against a bona fide purchaser without regard to any action or inaction by the holder. The state law creating the statutory lien determines whether the lien is effective against a bona fide purchaser, and what steps (if any) must be taken to make it so.

Previously, § 545(2) was used to avoid certain federal tax liens, but the 2005 BAPCPA amendments specifically eliminated this application of the statute.

The final two types of statutory liens that are avoidable are liens for rent or liens of distress of rent. § 545(3) & (4). These provisions render all statutory and common law liens for rent avoidable by the trustee. As was true for the cap on landlord damage claims in § 502(b)(6), these clauses reflect the fear of Congress that rent claims would exhaust a debtor's estate, leaving too little for other creditors. Therefore, any statutory lien that would give such claims priority over other unsecured claims should be avoidable. These clauses do not, however, permit the trustee to avoid a warehouse-man's lien for storage, transportation, or other costs incidental to the storage and handling of goods. § 546(i).

Various other limitations on the trustee's avoidance power under § 545 (and the other avoiding powers) are discussed in Section 5[H][1], *infra*. A visualization of the avoidance of statutory liens follows.

STATUTORY LIENS § 545		
DEFINITION § 101(53)	RULE	EXCEPTIONS
LIEN ARISING SOLELY BY FORCE OF STATUTE LIEN OF DISTRESS FOR RENT NOT SECURITY INTEREST (§ 101(51)) OR JUDICIAL LIEN (§ 101(36))	STATUTORY LIENS ARE ENFORCEABLE IN BANKRUPTCY	DISGUISED PRIORITIES § 545(1) NOT ENFORCEABLE AGAINST BONA FIDE PURCHASER OF PROPERTY AT COMMENCEMENT OF CASE § 545(2) LIENS FOR RENT OR LIEN OF DISTRESS FOR RENT § 545(3) & (4)

C. PREFERENCES

The preferential transfer, as its name implies, is a transfer that prefers one creditor over another. Congress bars these transfers if they take place too close to the date of the bankruptcy filing both because they violate the equality principle underlying bankruptcy (the idea that similarly situated creditors should be treated equally with respect to their claims) and to discourage creditors from pressing a troubled debtor for payment at a time when such pressure could cause the debtor to file for bankruptcy protection.

1. Definition

The definition of the transactions that can be avoided by the trustee as preferences is set forth in § 547(b). In all cases, for § 547(b) to operate, there must have been a transfer of an interest of the debtor in property. Recall that the definition of "transfer" in § 101(54) includes all dispositions of property or an interest therein, including retention of title as a security interest. Therefore, under § 547(b), the trustee can avoid a payment of money, a transfer of property, or the grant of a security interest. The transfer must be of an interest in the debtor's property; if the debtor transfers property in which the debtor has no interest (as when the debtor is a mere conduit of funds belonging to someone else), there can be no preferential transfer. Similarly, under the "earmarking" doctrine, no transfer of an interest of the debtor in property is deemed to have occurred if the debtor is provided funds that are by agreement to be used solely to pay off an existing debt, the funds are in fact used for that purpose and there is no diminution of the estate as a result.

For the trustee to avoid a transfer of an interest of the debtor in property, it must meet five requirements. First, the transfer must be "to or for the benefit of a creditor." § 547(b)(1). A "creditor" is an entity with a "claim" that arose at or prior to bankruptcy. § 101(10). The language "for the benefit of a creditor" picks up situations in which a transfer by the debtor to one entity advantages another, such as when the debtor pays a debt that is guaranteed by a third party whose contingent obligation is reduced by the payment. These types of transfers give rise to what are labelled "indirect preferences."

The second requirement for an avoidable preference is that the transfer must be "for or on account of an antecedent debt owed by the debtor before such transfer was made. § 547(b)(2). Thus, the transfer cannot be a gift, but rather is intended to pay or secure an existing debt.

The third requirement is that the transfer be "made while the debtor is insolvent." § 547(b)(3). A debtor (other than a partnership or municipality, for which there are specific definitions) is "insolvent" if its financial condition is such that "the sum of such entity's debts is greater than all of such entity's property, at a fair valuation" after excluding certain property. § 101(32)(A). Although this requirement seems to suggest that the trustee seeking to avoid a transfer will be required to engage in a lengthy and expense valuation hearing, under § 547(f), the debtor is "presumed to have been insolvent on and during the 90 days immediately precedent" the date of the bankruptcy filing. Because of this presumption, the trustee need not put on any evidence to establish debtor's insolvency if the challenged transfer occurs during the 90 days prior to bankruptcy. If the trustee seeks to avoid a transfer that took place before that 90th day, the trustee will have to establish the debtor's insolvency at the time of the transfer. The creditor may, of course, put on evidence in an effort to rebut the presumption when it exists.

The fourth element of an avoidable preference is that the transfer was made during the appropriate period of time before the date of the filing the petition. If the transfer was not made to an "insider," § 101(31), the trustee may avoid the transfer only if it was made on or within 90 days before the filing date. If the transfer was made to someone who was an "insider," the trustee may avoid the transfer if it was made on or within one year before the filing date. § 547(b)(4). The theory behind the extended "look-back" period for insiders is that insiders are both more likely to know of financial difficulties of a debtor earlier than others, and more capable of compelling the troubled debtor to make transfers on account of debts owed to them through their control or other intimate relationship.

In order to apply this timing requirement, we must be able to determine when a transfer is "made." If the debtor has physically transferred property to a creditor (as by paying cash or delivering tangible goods), the time the transfer is made is self-evident. But if the transfer is of an "interest in" property rather than the property itself, the time of the transfer is not as clear. Therefore, § 547(e)(2) provides guidance on when a transfer is made. The time of the transfer turns on when (if ever) the transfer was perfected. For real property, that means the time "when a bona fide purchaser of such property from the debtor . . . cannot acquire an interest that is superior to the interest of the transferee." § 547(e)(1)(A). Under state real property law, this moment should occur when the transferee records its interest in the property. For personal property and fixtures, the transfer is deemed perfected "when a creditor on a simple contract cannot acquire a judicial lien that is superior to the interest of the transferee." § 547(e)(1)(B). Under the Uniform Commercial Code, a lien creditor cannot prevail against a transferee's interest in the property when that interest is perfected by the filing of a financing statement or otherwise.

If the transferee of the interest in debtor's property has perfected that interest at the time the transfer takes effect as a contractual matter between the transferor and the transferee or within 30 days after that time, under § 547(e)(2)(A), the transfer is deemed to have been made at the time it takes effect between the transferor and the transferee. If perfection occurred subsequent to the 30-day period following the time the transfer took effect between the transferor and transferee, the transfer is deemed to have been made only when perfection occurred. § 547(e)(2)(B). If the transferee did not perfect its interest before the later of 30 days following the time the transfer took effect between the transferor and the transferee and the date of the bankruptcy filing, the transfer is deemed to occur immediately before the bankruptcy filing. § 547(e)(2)(C). The 30-day period was increased from 10 days in the 2005 BAPCPA amendments to the Code. A visualization of these rules follows:

TIME OF TRANSFER OF INTEREST IN DEBTOR'S PROPERTY § 547(e)(2)		
INTEREST PERFECTED (§ 547(e)(1)) AT TIME TRANSFER IS EFFECTIVE BETWEEN PARTIES OR WITHIN 30 DAYS THEREAFTER	INTEREST PERFECTED LATER THAN 30 DAYS AFTER TIME TRANSFER IS EFFECTIVE BETWEEN PARTIES	TRANSFER NOT PERFECTED BY LATER OF 30 DAYS AFTER TIME TRANSFER IS EFFECTIVE BETWEEN PARTIES AND BANKRUPTCY FILING
TRANSFER OCCURS AT TIME TRANSFER IS EFFECTIVE BETWEEN PARTIES § 547(e)(2)(A)	TRANSFER OCCURS AT TIME OF PERFECTION § 547(e)(2)(B)	TRANSFER OCCURS IMMEDIATELY PRIOR TO BANKRUPTCY § 547(e)(2)(C)

The final requirement for a voidable preference is that the transfer must enable the creditor "to receive more than such creditor would receive if" the transfer had not been made and instead the creditor had received whatever that creditor would have been entitled to if the debtor had been liquidated in a chapter 7 case. § 547(b)(5). This is familiarly called "preferential effect," meaning the transfer gave the creditor more than it would have received as a pro rata participant in a distribution to those of similar priority in the debtor's hypothetical liquidation. If the creditor would have received the same amount in such a chapter 7 case (for example, because the creditor holds a claim that is secured by collateral having a value in excess of the claim), there is no preferential effect as a result of the transfer and the trustee cannot avoid it.

Various limitations on the trustee's avoidance power under § 547 (and the other avoiding powers) are discussed in Section 5[H][1], *infra*. The following chart summarizes the elements of a voidable preference.

DEFINITION OF VOIDABLE PREFERENCE § 547(b)
TRUSTEE MAY AVOID A TRANSFER OF AN INTEREST OF THE DEBTOR IN PROPERTY IF: 1) TO OR FOR THE BENEFIT OF A CREDITOR, 2) FOR OR ON ACCOUNT OF ANTECEDENT DEBT, 3) MADE WHILE THE DEBTOR WAS INSOLVENT, 4) MADE DURING PREFERENCE PERIOD (ON OR WITHIN 90 DAYS PRIOR TO FILING FOR NON-INSIDER/ON OR WITHIN ONE YEAR PRIOR TO FILING FOR INSIDER), AND 5) PREFERENTIAL EFFECT AS COMPARED TO HYPOTHETICAL CHAPTER 7 LIQUIDATION WITHOUT TRANSFER BEING MADE

2. Exceptions

In nine situations, Congress has determined that the trustee should not be able to avoid a transfer that meets the definitional requirements of a voidable preference in § 547(b). These exceptions to the trustee's power to avoid preferential transfers are set forth in § 547(c). The first is a transfer to the extent it was both intended by the debtor and creditor to be a contemporaneous exchange for new value given to the debtor, and was in fact a substantially contemporaneous exchange. § 547(c)(1). This exception is intended to exclude transfers that are part of a single transaction in which the debtor is obtaining a benefit equal to the value of the transfer, even if there are minor delays in creditor's receipt of that value, *e.g.*, creditor sells goods for "cash" with payment by check, even if the transfer of funds upon presentation of the check is technically a transfer of an interest in debtor's property to the creditor on account of antecedent debt during the preference period that has preferential effect. How long the delay may be to qualify as "substantially contemporaneous" is a matter for judicial interpretation. Former debates over whether this exception could be used to protect from avoidance the grant of a security interest if perfection occurred later than the period permitted by § 547(e)(2) should be minimized by the change of the period in § 547(e)(2) from 10 days to 30 days. A visualization of the exception follows:

SUBSTANTIALLY CONTEMPORANEOUS EXCHANGE FOR NEW VALUE § 547(c)(1)
1)   INTENDED TO BE CONTEMPORANEOUS EXCHANGE FOR NEW VALUE, AND
2)   IN FACT WAS SUBSTANTIALLY CONTEMPORANEOUS

The second exception is for payments of debts "incurred by the debtor in the ordinary course of business or financial affairs of the debtor and the transferee." These ordinary course payments may not be avoided if the transfer satisfies one of two requirements. Either the transfer was made in the ordinary course of business or financial affairs of the debtor and the transferee, or alternatively, the transfer was made "according to ordinary business terms." § 547(c)(2). In enacting this exception, Congress intended to encourage creditors who deal with a troubled debtor on ordinary business terms to continue to do so without fear that they would have to disgorge payments.

The exception first focuses on the nature of the debt in respect of which the payment was made. Because the debt must be incurred in the ordinary course of business or financial affairs of both the debtor and transferee, incurring debt of this nature must have been in ordinary course of business for debtor and lending money or extending credit of this type must have been in ordinary course of business for the creditor. The payment must then satisfy either a subjective test or an objective test. It is not avoidable if it is made in the ordinary course of business for the debtor and the transferee (a subjective test, looking at whether the attributes of this payment — the form it took, the timing of the payment, etc. — was consistent with the way these specific parties dealt with each other when payments were made on the debt, even if their prior practice was aberrational compared to others in the same industry). Alternatively, the payment is protected if it is made according to ordinary business terms (an objective test, asking whether the payment was within the range of what is normal for the industry in which they operate). A visualization of the exception follows:

ORDINARY COURSE OF BUSINESS PAYMENTS § 547(c)(2)
1)   DEBT INCURRED IN ORDINARY COURSE OF BUSINESS OF BOTH PARTIES, AND
2)   EITHER   • PAYMENT MADE IN ORDINARY COURSE OF BUSINESS OF BOTH PARTIES, OR   • PAYMENT MADE ACCORDING TO ORDINARY BUSINESS TERMS

The third exception protects a security interest granted to a creditor providing value that enables the debtor to acquire the collateral — in the language of Article 9 of the Uniform Commercial Code, a purchase-money security interest or PMSI. § 547(c)(3). Under § 9-317(e) of the Uniform Commercial Code, a PMSI has priority over a lien creditor (including the trustee in bankruptcy) if the holder of the security interest files a financing statement within 20 days after the debtor receives delivery of the collateral. When § 547(e)(2) provided that the transfer of the security interest was made at the time it became effective between the debtor and creditor only if perfection occurred within 10 days of that time, this exception was necessary to give the holder of the PMSI the full 20 days allowed under state law to file a financing statement. Because under amended § 547(e)(2) all secured creditors are given 30 days after the security interest becomes effective to perfect the security interest without the transfer of that security interest being deemed on account of antecedent debt, a specific exception for purchase-money security interests is no longer necessary. In fact, § 547(e)(3) now protects purchase-money security interests that do not prevail against lien creditors under state law.

The exception requires that new value be given by or on behalf of the secured creditor at or after the signing of a security agreement containing a description of the collateral, that the new value be given to enable the debtor to acquire the collateral, and that the new value in fact be used for that purpose. The security interest securing that new value must be perfected within 30 days after the debtor receives possession of the collateral. A visualization of the exception follows:

PMSI EXCEPTION § 547(c)(3)

1)   SECURITY INTEREST SECURES NEW VALUE
 	
    • GIVEN AT OR AFTER SIGNING OF SECURITY AGREEMENT DESCRIBING COLLATERAL,
 	
    • GIVEN BY SECURED PARTY AT OR AFTER SIGNING OF SECURITY AGREEMENT,
 	
    • GIVEN TO ENABLE DEBTOR TO ACQUIRE COLLATERAL, AND
 	
    • USED TO ACQUIRE COLLATERAL
 	
AND
 	
2)   SECURITY INTEREST IS PERFECTED WITHIN 30 DAYS AFTER DEBTOR RECEIVES POSSESSION OF COLLATERAL

The fourth exception protects transfers to the extent that, after the transfer, the creditor gave new value to or for the benefit of the debtor. § 547(c)(4). This exception is intended to give a creditor who has received a preferential transfer credit for any portion of the transfer that the creditor later permanently returns to the debtor in the form of new unsecured value, because the actual detrimental impact on the debtor's estate (and thus on other creditors) is diminished by the new value provided. To qualify for the credit against the original transfer, the new value must be given after the transfer was made, and must not be secured by an unavoidable security interest or be subsequently repaid by an unavoidable transfer from the debtor back to the creditor.

The new value exception can be visualized as follows:

NEW VALUE EXCEPTION § 547(c)(4)

1)   PREFERENTIAL TRANSFER FROM DEBTOR TO CREDITOR,
 	
2)   LATER NEW VALUE GIVEN BY CREDITOR TO DEBTOR, AND
 	
3)   NEW VALUE IS NOT
 	
      •   SECURED BY UNAVOIDABLE SECURITY INTEREST, OR
 	
      •   SUBJECT OF SUBSEQUENT UNAVOIDABLE TRANSFER BY DEBTOR TO CREDITOR

The fifth exception deals with the so-called "floating lien." A "floating lien" type of financing is one under which a creditor's security interest attaches not only to the collateral that exists on the date the financing is consummated, but "floats" over after-acquired collateral of the same type. Although the Uniform Commercial Code explicitly validates liens in after-acquired collateral under § 9-204(a), their position in bankruptcy is more problematic. When the security interest securing preexisting debt attaches to the new after-acquired collateral, we have a transfer of an interest in the debtor's property to or for the benefit of a creditor on account of antecedent debt potentially made while the debtor was insolvent during the preference period which has a preferential effect. This suggests that a security interest in collateral the debtor acquires within 90 days of bankruptcy may be an avoidable preference. But if a secured creditor had to relinquish its security interest in all collateral that the debtor acquired within 90 days of bankruptcy, no one would be willing to finance inventory or accounts receivable, because that type of collateral "turns" rapidly (is sold or collected in the ordinary course of business and is replaced by other collateral of the same type), and there may be no collateral left at the date of bankruptcy that existed more than 90 days prior thereto.

When Congress enacted the Code, it was unwilling to carve out from preference attack all security interests in after-acquired collateral, for fear that a secured creditor might exert pressure on a troubled debtor to acquire more collateral on the eve of bankruptcy in order to increase the secured position of the secured creditor at the expense of the general unsecured creditors. In fact, Congress specifically provided under § 547(e)(3) that a transfer cannot be made until the debtor has rights in the collateral, meaning that a transfer of a security interest in after-acquired collateral is not made until the debtor acquires that collateral, perhaps during the 90 days prior to bankruptcy.

But Congress then inserted an exception, § 547(c)(5), which was intended to protect from avoidance certain security interests in after-acquired property to the extent necessary to promote inventory and accounts receivable financing, and so long as the policies underlying the preference statute were not violated. In order to qualify for the exception, the transfer must be one that creates a perfected security interest in inventory, receivables or their proceeds (proceeds being what is received upon the disposition of the inventory or receivables by the debtor). Next, the transfer must not harm other creditors by reducing the estate value available to them during the preference period. If the value of the after-acquired collateral does not exceed the value of the original collateral it replaced, no one has been disadvantaged and the transfers cannot be avoided. But to the extent that the secured creditor gets an improved position on the eve of bankruptcy by using free assets to increase the amount of collateral, other creditors are being harmed, and the secured creditor should have to turn over the improvement in position.

The exception is applied through a mathematical calculation at two points in time to see if the position of the secured creditor has improved during that period. (The exception is sometimes called the "two point net improvement test.") You begin by comparing the value of the collateral (the sum of all inventory, receivables, and proceeds in which the creditor has a perfected security interest) to the amount of the secured debt at the beginning of the preference period (90 days prior to filing if the creditor is not an insider, and one year prior to filing if the creditor is an insider) or, if the financing occurred after that date, the first date on which there was a secured loan. If the value of the collateral at least equals the amount of the secured debt, the creditor was fully secured on that date and there is no deficiency in collateral coverage. If the value of the collateral was less than the amount of the secured debt, the creditor was undersecured and there was a deficiency in collateral coverage on that date.

You then do the same comparison between the value of the collateral and the amount of the secured debt at the date of the bankruptcy filing. Again, either the secured creditor will be fully secured because the value of the collateral at least equals the amount of the secured debt, or the creditor will be undersecured because there is a deficiency between collateral value and the amount of the debt.

To determine whether any security interest in after-acquired collateral can be avoided by the trustee, we compare the deficiencies (if any) at these two points in time. There are four possibilities. One, at the first point in time there was no deficiency, and on the date of bankruptcy there was no deficiency. In this situation, the secured creditor has not improved its position vis-à-vis the general unsecured creditors, and the trustee may not avoid any preference. Two, at the first point in time there was no deficiency, and on the date of bankruptcy there is a deficiency. In this situation, the secured creditor's position has deteriorated, not improved, and against the trustee may not avoid any preference. Third, at the first point in time there was a deficiency, but on the date of bankruptcy there is no deficiency. Here the secured creditor has improved its position, and the trustee may avoid the security interest in after-acquired collateral as necessary to return the creditor to the deficiency position it had at the first point in time. Fourth, there may be deficiencies at both points in time. If the deficiency has increased from the first point in time to the date of bankruptcy, the creditor has not improved its position and the trustee may not avoid any preferential transfer. If the deficiency has declined during that period, the trustee may avoid the security interest in after-acquired collateral to the extent necessary to return the creditor to the deficiency position it had at the beginning of the period. A visualization of these four scenarios follows:

TWO POINT NET IMPROVEMENT TEST § 547(c)(5)		
	NO DEFICIENCY AT BANKRUPTCY	DEFICIENCY AT BANKRUPTCY
NO DEFICIENCY AT BEGINNING OF PREFERENCE PERIOD OR FIRST DATE ON WHICH THERE WAS SECURED LOAN	NO PREFERENCE (FULLY-SECURED)	NO PREFERENCE (NO IMPROVEMENT IN POSITION)
DEFICIENCY AT BEGINNING OF PREFERENCE PERIOD OR FIRST DATE ON WHICH THERE WAS SECURED LOAN	PREFERENCE TO EXTENT OF IMPROVEMENT IN POSITION	1) DEFICIENCY IS GREATER AT BEGINNING OF PREFERENCE PERIOD OR FIRST DATE ON WHICH THERE WAS SECURED LOAN — PREFERENCE TO EXTENT OF IMPROVEMENT IN POSITION 2) DEFICIENCY IS GREATER AT BANKRUPTCY — NO PREFERENCE (NO IMPROVEMENT IN POSITION)

If a floating lien creditor has an improvement in position other than by a transfer (*e.g.*, the collateral simply improves in value because of market forces), this improved value is not a preference and is not avoidable. Section 547 allows the trustee to avoid only transfers of an interest of the debtor in property, not changes in collateral value through other means.

Notice that the computations involved in § 547(c)(5) take into account both the value of the collateral and the amount of the secured debt. Even if the value of the collateral increases during the preference period, if there is no improvement in position because of an increase in the debt amount (due to new loans or accrued interest and late fees), there is no preference.

The sixth exception revisits the concept of "statutory liens" (§ 101(53)) which we discussed under § 545 (see Section 5[B], *supra*). Under § 545, we saw statutory liens are avoidable by the trustee if they fall in one of the three categories listed there. Section 547(c)(6) simply tells us that all other statutory liens (those not avoidable under § 545) are not avoidable as preferential transfers. Section 545 is intended to be the exclusive means of attacking statutory liens. The exception is visualized below:

STATUTORY LIENS § 547(c)(6)

STATUTORY LIENS (§ 101(53)) OTHER THAN THE FOLLOWING § 545 AVOIDABLE LIENS
 	
1)   DISGUISED PRIORITIES
    § 545(1)
 	
2)   NOT ENFORCEABLE AGAINST BONA FIDE PURCHASER OF PROPERTY AT
    COMMENCEMENT OF CASE
    § 545(2)
 	
3)   LIENS FOR RENT OR LIEN OF DISTRESS FOR RENT
    § 545(3) & (4)

Section 547(c)(7) is intended to protect child support and alimony claimants. It excludes from preference attack bona fide payments of debts for domestic support obligations (§ 101(14A)). The definition of "domestic support obligation" is visualized in Chapter 4[A][2], *supra*.

The final two exceptions are intended to exclude from the trustee's avoiding powers transfers that, although qualifying as voidable preferences, are sufficiently small in amount that Congress thought the trustee should not spend the time and money necessary to pursue them. Section 547(c)(8) deals with cases filed by an individual debtor whose debts are primarily consumer debts. A transfer may not be avoided by the trustee if the value of all property involved in such transfer is less than $600. In a case filed by a debtor whose debts are not primarily consumer debts, a transfer may not be avoided by the trustee if the value of all property "that constitutes or is affected by such transfer" is less than $5,850.* § 547(c)(9).

A visualization of the small transfer exceptions follows:

---

* This dollar figure, like many of the dollar figures in the Code, is subject to adjustment every three years under § 104(b) of the Code to reflect change in the Consumer Price Index for the most recent three years, and was most recently adjusted effective April 1, 2010 and will be adjusted again in 2013. The figure for consumer cases is not subject to adjustment.

SMALL TRANSFER EXCEPTIONS	
CONSUMER CASES § 547(c)(8)	NONCONSUMER CASES § 547(c)(9)

1) INDIVIDUAL DEBTOR
 	
2) DEBTS OF DEBTOR ARE PRIMARILY
     CONSUMER DEBTS
 	
3) AGGREGATE VALUE OF ALL PROPERTY
     INVOLVED IN TRANSFER IS LESS THAN
     $600
	1) DEBTS OF DEBTOR ARE NOT
	     PRIMARILY CONSUMER DEBTS
	
	2) AGGREGATE VALUE OF ALL PROPERTY
	     INVOLVED IN TRANSFER IS LESS THAN
	     $5,850*

---

* This dollar figure, like many of the dollar figures in the Code, is subject to adjustment every three years under § 104(b) of the Code to reflect change in the Consumer Price Index for the most recent three years, and was most recently adjusted effective April 1, 2010 and will be adjusted again in 2013. The figure for consumer cases is not subject to adjustment.

A summary of all preferences exceptions appears below:

EXCEPTIONS TO PREFERENCES § 547(c)	
§ 547(c)(1)	SUBSTANTIALLY CONTEMPORANEOUS EXCHANGE FOR NEW VALUE
§ 547(c)(2)	ORDINARY COURSE OF BUSINESS PAYMENTS
§ 547(c)(3)	PMSI PERFECTED WITHIN 30 DAYS OF DEBTOR'S POSSESSION OF COLLATERAL
§ 547(c)(4)	NEW VALUE EXCEPTION
§ 547(c)(5)	TWO-POINT NET IMPROVEMENT IN POSITION TEST
§ 547(c)(6)	STATUTORY LIENS UNAVOIDABLE UNDER § 545
§ 547(c)(7)	BONA FIDE PAYMENTS OF DOMESTIC SUPPORT OBLIGATIONS
§ 547(c)(8)	SMALL CONSUMER TRANSFERS < $600
§ 547(c)(9)	SMALL NON-CONSUMER TRANSFERS < $5,850*

---

* This dollar figure, like many of the dollar figures in the Code, is subject to adjustment every three years under § 104(b) of the Code to reflect change in the Consumer Price Index for the most recent three years, and was most recently adjusted effective April 1, 2010 and will be adjusted again in 2013. The figure for consumer cases is not subject to adjustment.

D.   FRAUDULENT TRANSFERS

The goal of fraudulent conveyance law is to maximize the estate for the benefit of all creditors by undoing prepetition transactions between the debtor and another entity that were inherently unfair to creditors because they diminished the debtor's assets. The prohibition on fraudulent conveyances or fraudulent transfers is embodied in statute, both state and federal. Most states have enacted the Uniform Fraudulent Transfer Act, and in a bankruptcy case, the trustee can pursue a fraudulent conveyance under state law by use of its powers under § 544(b) (*see* Section 5[E], *infra*).

The trustee may avoid a transfer of an interest of the debtor in property or any obligation incurred by the debtor as fraudulent under § 548 of the Code. As previously discussed with respect to the other avoiding powers, a "transfer" under § 101(54) includes any method, "voluntary or involuntary, of disposing of or parting with . . . property; or . . . an interest in property." It includes the creation of a security interest or lien, or retention of title as security. Incurrence of an obligation includes the borrowing of money, or obtaining credit in any other way as a result of which something is owed to another entity. The incurrence of an obligation by the debtor adversely affects creditors by increasing claims against the debtor's estate, while a transfer of an interest in debtor's property adversely affects creditors by reducing the estate against which claims can be asserted.

To be avoidable under § 548(a), such a transfer or incurrence of an obligation must meet two requirements. First, it must have been made or incurred within two years before the date of the filing of the petition. Under § 548(d)(1), a transfer is made when it has been perfected in such a way that applicable nonbankruptcy law permits the recipient thereof to defeat a bona fide purchaser. If the transfer was not so perfected prior to bankruptcy, it is deemed to have been made immediately prior to the filing of the petition.

The two-year period is a requirement of voidability, not a statute of limitations. The statute of limitations applicable to avoidance actions under § 548 is set forth in § 546(a) (see Section 5[H][1], *infra*). If the transfer was made or obligation incurred more than two years prior to the filing date, § 548 is not available to the trustee without regard to any statute of limitations.

The second requirement for a transfer or obligation to be avoidable under § 548 is that it be fraudulent in one of two ways. The first type of fraud is actual fraud, which is present when the transfer is made or the obligation incurred with actual intent to hinder, delay or defraud any entity to which the debtor was indebted or became indebted after the transfer or incurrence of the obligation. § 548(a)(1)(A). To prove actual fraud, the trustee must establish the subjective intention of the debtor in making the transfer or incurring the obligation, which can be difficult. Barring an admission of fraudulent intent by the debtor, the trustee must rely on so-called "badges of fraud," a judicially-created concept dating back to an early seventeenth century fraudulent conveyance case, to provide circumstantial evidence of such intent. These badges of fraud (which are codified in § 4(b) of the Uniform Fraudulent Transfer Act) include such suspicious circumstances as the fact that the transfer was to a family member or close relation, the absence or inadequacy of consideration, the transaction taking place in secrecy, the debtor retaining possession of the property after transfer, or the fact that the transfer was made at a time when a creditor was threatening to take action against the debtor.

The second type of fraud is constructive fraud. This is the label given to the transfer of property or incurrence of an obligation with respect to which two elements are satisfied. First, the debtor must have received less than a reasonably equivalent value in exchange for the transfer or the obligation, § 548(a)(1)(B)(i), and second, one of four different tests must be met (three of which are financial in nature), § 548(a)(1)(B)(ii).

"Reasonably equivalent value" is not defined in the Code, but "value" is defined in § 548(d)(2)(A) to be "property, or satisfaction or securing of a present or antecedent debt of the debtor," but excluding an unperformed promise to furnish support. Value is clearly obtained when debtor receives something in exchange for the transfer or obligation which increases the estate or reduces the debtor's liabilities. Reasonably equivalent value need not be equal to the value of the interest in property transferred or obligation incurred, but it must be a fair economic bargain from the debtor's standpoint. If the estate has received a fair amount in exchange for the loss of an interest in property or the incurrence of an obligation, there is no justification for avoiding the transaction. The equivalence of the value is determined at the time of the transfer, not in light of subsequent events affecting the value of what was transferred or what was received in exchange. The transfer or obligation may withstand fraudulent transfer challenge even if the direct value received in exchange was given to someone other that the debtor (such as a subsidiary corporation) so long as the benefit to the debtor is clear.

If the debtor received reasonably equivalent value for the transfer or the obligation, it is not avoidable under § 548(a)(1)(B) as constructively fraudulent. If the debtor did not receive reasonably equivalent value, then the transfer or obligation can be avoided only if one of four additional factors is present.

First, the debtor must have been insolvent on the date the transfer was made or the obligation incurred, or became insolvent as a result of the transfer or incurrence of the obligation. § 548(a)(1)(B)(ii)(I). "Insolvent" is defined for non-partnership, non-municipal entities in § 101(32)(A) as a balance sheet test. The debtor is insolvent if the sum of the debtor's debts is greater than all of the debtor's property at a "fair valuation." The asset side of the equation excludes any property that was "transferred, concealed, or removed with intent to hinder, delay, or defraud" creditors and, for individual debtors, exempt property (which is not available to satisfy claims). "Fair valuation" has been interpreted to mean the amount a willing buyer would pay a willing seller within a commercially reasonable period of time for the property in question. On the liability side, because "debt" is defined as "liability on a claim," § 101(12), and "claim" includes rights to payment that are liquidated, unliquidated, fixed, contingent, matured, unmatured, disputed, undisputed, secured and unsecured, § 101(5), even off-balance-sheet items must be included and valued in making the solvency determination.

The trustee challenging a transaction as fraudulent on this basis has the burden of proof on insolvency at the time of transfer, and unlike for preferences under § 547(f), there is no presumption of insolvency for the 90 days prior to the bankruptcy filing.

The second alternative establishing constructive fraud for a transfer made or obligation incurred without reasonably equivalent value being given in exchange is if the debtor was engaged in business or a transaction, or was about to do so, for which any property remaining with the debtor was an "unreasonably small capital." § 548(a)(1)(B)(ii)(II). The third is that the debtor intended to incur, or believed that it would incur, debts "beyond the debtor's ability to pay as such debts matured." § 548(a)(1)(B)(ii)(III). These two financial tests are generally raised in conjunction with a claim of insolvency, rather than as alternatives, although each would suffice to justify avoidance of a transfer or obligation.

The 2005 BAPCPA amendments to the Code added a fourth alternative, permitting the trustee to avoid a transfer made or obligation incurred in the absence of reasonably equivalent value if the transfer was made or obligation incurred to or for the benefit of an insider under an employment contract and not in the ordinary course of business. § 548(a)(1)(B)(ii)(IV). This provision is intended to prevent the masking of an otherwise fraudulent transfer as employment compensation.

An additional type of fraudulent transfer is avoidable under § 548(e). If a debtor makes a transfer of an interest of the debtor in property to a self-settled trust or similar device of which the debtor is a beneficiary, and that transfer was made with actual intent to hinder, delay, or defraud an entity to which the debtor was indebted or to which the debtor thereafter became indebted, the trustee may avoid the transfer if it was made on or within 10 years before the filing date.

One type of transfer that would otherwise be avoidable is expressly excluded from attack under § 548(a)(2). The trustee may not avoid a transfer of a "charitable contribution" to a "qualified religious or charitable entity or organization" if it satisfies one of two tests. First, it cannot be avoided if "the amount of that contribution does not exceed 15 percent of the gross annual income of the debtor for the year in which the transfer of the contribution is made." Second, it cannot be avoided if the contribution "was consistent with the practices of the debtor in making charitable contributions." The term "charitable contribution" is defined in § 548(d)(3) and is limited to contributions by an individual debtor of cash or financial instruments.

If a transfer or obligation is avoided solely under § 548, the transferee or obligee who took for value and in good faith is given a lien on or may retain any interest transferred, or may enforce any obligation incurred, to the extent the transferee or obligee gave value to the debtor in exchange. § 548(c).

Various limitations on the trustee's avoidance power under § 548 (and the other avoiding powers) are discussed in Section 5[H][1], *infra*. A visualization of the provisions relating to fraudulent transfers follows:

FRAUDULENT TRANSFERS § 548			
FRAUDULENT TRANSFERS AND OBLIGATIONS § 548(a)(1)	ADDITIONAL FRAUDULENT TRANSFERS § 548(e)	EXCEPTION § 548(a)(2)	DEFENSE § 548(c)
TRUSTEE MAY AVOID TRANSFER MADE OR OBLIGATION INCURRED WITHIN 2 YEARS OF BANKRUPTCY FILING IF:	TRUSTEE MAY AVOID TRANSFER MADE WITHIN 10 YEARS OF BANKRUPTCY FILING IF: 1) MADE TO SELF-SETTLED TRUST OR SIMILAR DEVICE, 2) MADE BY DEBTOR, 3) DEBTOR IS BENEFICIARY, AND 4) MADE WITH ACTUAL INTENT TO HINDER, DELAY, OR DEFRAUD ANY CREDITOR	TRUSTEE MAY NOT AVOID TRANSFER OF "CHARITABLE CONTRIBUTION" (§ 548(d)(3)) TO "QUALIFIED RELIGIOUS OR CHARITABLE ENTITY OR ORGANIZATION" (§ 548(d)(4)) IF EITHER: 1) AMOUNT DOES NOT EXCEED 15% OF GROSS ANNUAL INCOME OF DEBTOR FOR THAT YEAR, OR 2) TRANSFER WAS CONSISTENT WITH PRACTICES OF DEBTOR IN MAKING CHARITABLE CONTRIBUTIONS	TRANSFEREE OR OBLIGEE WHO TOOK TRANSFER OR OBLIGATION FOR VALUE IN GOOD FAITH RETAINS PROPERTY OR LIEN ON PROPERTY OR MAY ENFORCE OBLIGATION TO EXTENT OF VALUE GIVEN

Detail of first column (§ 548(a)(1)):

ACTUAL FRAUD	CONSTRUCTIVE FRAUD
MADE OR INCURRED WITH ACTUAL INTENT TO HINDER, DELAY, OR DEFRAUD ANY CREDITOR	DEBTOR RECEIVED LESS THAN REASONABLY EQUIVALENT VALUE IN EXCHANGE AND: 1) WAS INSOLVENT OR WAS RENDERED INSOLVENT, 2) WAS ENGAGED IN BUSINESS OR TRANSACTION FOR WHICH REMAINING PROPERTY WAS UNREASONABLY SMALL CAPITAL, 3) INTENDED OR EXPECTED TO INCUR DEBTS BEYOND ABILITY TO PAY, OR 4) TRANSFER OR OBLIGATION WAS TO INSIDER UNDER EMPLOYMENT CONTRACT NOT IN ORDINARY COURSE OF BUSINESS

E. SUBROGATION

Section 544(b) allows the trustee to avoid any obligation of the debtor or transfer of an interest in the debtor's property that is "voidable under applicable law" by a creditor holding an allowable unsecured claim. Unlike § 544(a) (the strong-arm clause), under which the trustee exercises the rights of a hypothetical lien creditor, execution creditor or bona fide purchaser of real property to avoid certain unperfected transfers, § 544(b) requires that there be an actual creditor holding an unsecured claim that is allowable under § 502 to whose avoidance rights under nonbankruptcy law the trustee is subrogated.

Section 544(b) is most often used by a trustee to take advantage of the ability of an actual unsecured creditor to avoid a transaction pursuant to state fraudulent transfer law. The trustee may be forced to use its right of subrogation under § 544(b) rather than its own avoiding power under § 548 because the transaction occurred more than two years prior to the bankruptcy filing, the temporal extent of the trustee's powers under § 548. The Uniform Fraudulent Transfer Act (UFTA), in effect in most states, generally permits avoidance up to four years after the transfer is made or obligation incurred.

In addition to allowing the avoidance of fraudulent transfers having most of the same attributes as those avoidable under § 548(a), the UFTA makes a transfer fraudulent as to a creditor whose claim arose before the transfer if it was made to an insider for an antecedent debt, the debtor was insolvent at the time, and the insider had reasonable cause to believe that the debtor was insolvent. § 5(b) of UFTA. This special preference section is broader than any similar provision in the Code, and may be a valuable weapon in the hands of the trustee. A visualization of this provision, available to the trustee by reason of § 544(b), follows:

PREFERENTIAL TRANSFERS TO INSIDERS UFTA § 5(b)		
CREDITORS WHO MAY AVOID TRANSFERS	TRANSFEREE OF AVOIDABLE TRANSFER	REQUIREMENTS FOR AVOIDING TRANSFER
CREDITOR WHOSE CLAIM AROSE BEFORE TRANSFER	INSIDER (UFTA § 1(7)) FOR AN ANTECEDENT DEBT	1) DEBTOR WAS INSOLVENT, (UFTA § 2), AND 2) INSIDER HAD REASONABLE CAUSE TO BELIEVE DEBTOR WAS INSOLVENT

Like § 548, § 544(b) provides an exception protecting from avoidance a transfer of a "charitable contribution" that would not be subject to avoidance under § 548(a)(1). § 544(b)(2).

Various limitations on the trustee's avoidance power under § 544 (and the other avoiding powers) are discussed in Section 5[H][1], *infra*. A visualization of the right of subrogation under § 544(b) follows:

RIGHT OF SUBROGATON § 544(b)	
TRUSTEE'S AVOIDANCE POWER	EXCEPTION
TRUSTEE MAY AVOID ANY TRANSFER OF AN INTEREST OF THE DEBTOR IN PROPERTY OR ANY OBLIGATION INCURRED BY DEBTOR THAT COULD BE AVOIDED UNDER APPLICABLE LAW BY HOLDER OF ALLOWED UNSECURED CLAIM	TRUSTEE MAY NOT AVOID TRANSFER OF "CHARITABLE CONTRIBUTION" (§ 548(c)(3)) THAT WOULD NOT BE AVOIDABLE UNDER § 548(a)(1)(B) BECAUSE OF § 548(a)(2)

F.　POSTPETITION TRANSACTIONS

Once a bankruptcy petition is filed, the debtor (as opposed to the trustee or the debtor in possession acting in that capacity) is precluded from transferring property of the estate. The trustee may avoid these postpetition transfers under § 549(a) if they were unauthorized, or were authorized only by reason of § 303(f) (which allows a debtor subject to an involuntary petition to continue to operate its business and use, acquire or dispose of property until an order for relief is entered) or § 542(c) (which allows an entity without notice or knowledge of the bankruptcy case to transfer property of the estate in good faith).

There are two exceptions to this avoidance power. First, if the trustee seeks to avoid a transfer made in an involuntary case between the filing of the petition and the date of the order for relief, the involuntary gap transferee is protected to the extent of any value (including services, but not included the satisfaction or securing of a prepetition debt) given after the filing of the petition in exchange for the transfer. § 549(b).

Second, the trustee may not avoid a transfer of an interest in real property to a good faith purchaser without knowledge of the commencement of the case and for present fair equivalent value unless a copy or notice of the petition was filed in the real property recording records before the transfer was perfected so as to be protected from a subsequent bona fide purchaser (as by recording in a jurisdiction with a race/notice recording statute). § 549(c). If the trustee avoids a transfer of an interest in real property to a good faith purchaser without knowledge of the commencement of the case but who provided less than present fair equivalent value, that purchaser has a lien on the property transferred to the extent of any present value given unless a copy or notice of the petition was filed in the real property recording records before the transfer was so perfected.

The trustee may bring an avoidance action under § 549 only within the shorter of two years after the date the transfer was made, and the time the case is closed or dismissed.

Various limitations on the trustee's avoidance power under § 549 (and the other avoiding powers) are discussed in Section 5[H][1], *infra*. The following chart visualizes the provisions of § 549.

POSTPETITION TRANSACTIONS § 549		
AVOIDING POWER § 549(a)	EXCEPTIONS § 549(b) & (c)	STATUTE OF LIMITATIONS § 549(d)
TRUSTEE MAY AVOID TRANSFER OCCURRING AFTER COMMENCEMENT OF CASE THAT IS 1) NOT AUTHORIZED, OR 2) AUTHORIZED ONLY UNDER § 303(f) OR § 542(c)	IN INVOLUNTARY CASE, TRUSTEE MAY NOT AVOID TRANSFER DURING PERIOD BETWEEN FILING AND ORDER FOR RELIEF TO EXTENT TRANSFEREE PROVIDED POSTPETITION VALUE TRANSFER OF INTEREST IN REAL PROPERTY TO GOOD FAITH PURCHASER WITHOUT KNOWLEDGE OF CASE AND FOR PRESENT FAIR EQUIVALENT VALUE MAY NOT BE AVOIDED UNLESS NOTICE OF PETITION WAS FILED IN REAL ESTATE RECORDS BEFORE TRANSFER WAS PERFECTED GOOD FAITH PURCHASER OF REAL PROPERTY WITHOUT KNOWLEDGE OF CASE AND FOR LESS THAN PRESENT FAIR EQUIVALENT VALUE HAS LIEN ON PROPERTY FOR VALUE GIVEN UNLESS NOTICE OF PETITION WAS FILED IN REAL ESTATE RECORDS BEFORE TRANSFER WAS PERFECTED	TRUSTEE MUST COMMENCE ACTION BY EARLIER OF: 1) TWO YEARS AFTER DATE OF TRANSFER, AND 2) DATE CASE IS CLOSED OR DISMISSED

G. SETOFFS

Under § 553(a), nothing in the Code (other than the provisions of § 553 and the automatic stay provisions of § 362 and the limitations on the use, sale and lease of property in § 363) affects the ability of debtors and creditors to offset their mutual debts against each other as long as the debts were both created prior to bankruptcy. The most likely holder of a right of setoff is a depositary bank holding a bank account of the debtor (representing a debt of the bank to the depositor) which is also a creditor of the debtor because it made the debtor a loan.

Section 553(a) sets forth three exceptions to the ability of a creditor to set off a mutual debt owing to the debtor against a claim against the debtor, even when the creditor obtains relief from the stay. These exceptions are designed to prevent the bank from obtaining preferential treatment not available to other creditors.

The first exception is when the creditor's claim against debtor is disallowed (in which case there is no claim against which to set off). § 553(a)(1).

The second exception precludes setoff if the creditor obtained the claim against the debtor from another entity either after the case began, or during the 90 days before filing and while the debtor was insolvent. § 553(a)(2). This provision prevents creditors from buying up claims at a discount and getting full value for them by setoff.

Third, setoff is not permitted if the debt of the creditor to the debtor was incurred within 90 days before filing while debtor was insolvent and for the purpose of obtaining a right of setoff. § 553(a)(3). This exception prevents a bank who is owed money by a debtor from demanding that the debtor make deposits at the bank on the eve of bankruptcy so that the bank will be able to exercise the right of setoff and get paid in full while other creditors are getting cents on the dollar for their debts.

For purposes of both § 553(a)(2) and § 553(a)(3), the debtor is presumed to be insolvent for the 90 day period preceding the bankruptcy filing. § 553(c).

The exceptions to setoff can be visualized as follows:

RECOGNITION OF RIGHT OF SETOFF § 553(a)	
RULE	**EXCEPTIONS**

CODE DOES NOT AFFECT RIGHT OF CREDITOR TO OFFSET
 	
1) DEBT OWING BY CREDITOR TO DEBTOR THAT AROSE PRIOR TO BANKRUPTCY
 	
AGAINST
 	
2) CLAIM OF CREDITOR AGAINST DEBTOR THAT AROSE PRIOR TO BANKRUPTCY
	SETOFF NOT ALLOWED TO THE EXTENT THAT:
	
	1) CLAIM OF CREDITOR AGAINST DEBTOR IS DISALLOWED
	
	2) CLAIM OF CREDITOR AGAINST DEBTOR WAS TRANSFERRED TO CREDITOR BY ANOTHER ENTITY EITHER
	
	    (A) AFTER CASE BEGAN, OR
	
	    (B) WITHIN 90 DAYS BEFORE FILING AND WHILE DEBTOR WAS INSOLVENT
	
	3) DEBT OWED TO DEBTOR BY CREDITOR WAS INCURRED BY CREDITOR
	
	    (A) WITHIN 90 DAYS BEFORE FILING,
	
	    (B) WHILE DEBTOR WAS INSOLVENT, AND
	
	    (C) FOR PURPOSE OF OBTAINING RIGHT OF SETOFF
	
	DEBTOR IS PRESUMED TO BE INSOLVENT DURING 90 DAYS PRIOR TO FILING § 553(c)

In addition to these three situations in which the right of setoff is barred, § 553(b) provides a limitation on the right of setoff by allowing the trustee to avoid it to the extent the creditor who sets off a debt owing to the debtor against a claim has improved its position during the 90 days prior to bankruptcy. This provision is similar to the preference exception for inventory and accounts financing in § 547(c)(5) discussed in Section 5[C][2], *supra*.

As in § 547(c)(2), § 553(b) uses a mathematical computation at two points in time to determine whether the creditor has improperly benefitted to the detriment of unsecured creditors during the preference period. The first point is the date 90 days prior to bankruptcy or, if no "insufficiency" existed on that date, the first date thereafter on which there is an "insufficiency." An insufficiency is equivalent to a deficiency or undercollateralization under § 547(c)(5), that is, it is the amount by which the creditor's claim against the debtor exceeds the debt owed by the creditor to the debtor. If there is an insufficiency, the creditor is not fully protected by its right of setoff because, if a setoff occurred, the creditor would still have a claim against the debtor.

The second point in time is the date of the setoff (after giving effect to it). The amount of the setoff that can be recovered is the amount by which the insufficiency of the creditor at point two is less than the insufficiency of the creditor at point one, meaning that the creditor has improved its position by virtue of the setoff. The avoidance action returns the creditor to the insufficiency position it had at the beginning of the preference period (or when the loan was made, if later).

Various limitations on the trustee's avoidance power under § 553 (and the other avoiding powers) are discussed in Section 5[H][1], *infra*. A visualization of this avoiding power is set forth below:

PREFERENTIAL SET-OFFS § 553(b)		
INSUFFICIENCY	TWO POINTS	AMOUNT OF AVOIDANCE
CLAIM OWING BY DEBTOR TO CREDITOR IS GREATER THAN MUTUAL DEBT OWING BY CREDITOR TO DEBTOR	POINT 1: LATER OF 1) 90 DAYS PRIOR TO BANKRUPTCY, AND 2) FIRST DATE THEREAFTER ON WHICH THERE IS AN INSUFFICIENCY POINT 2: DATE OF SETOFF	AMOUNT BY WHICH INSUFFICIENCY AT POINT 2 IS LESS THAN INSUFFICIENCY AT POINT 1

H. PROCEDURAL MATTERS

1. Limitations on Avoiding Powers

An avoidance action under § 544, 545, 547, 548 or 553 must be brought within the period specified in § 546(a). This statute of limitations gives the trustee until the later of two years after the order for relief or, if a trustee is appointed or elected during that period, one year after the trustee's election or appointment, but in any event, such action must be brought prior to the time the case is closed or dismissed.

The power of the trustee to avoid transactions under § 544, 545 and 549 are subject to an additional limitation. Under § 546(b)(1), the trustee's powers are subject to any applicable law that permits perfection of a security interest, or acts taken to continue that perfection, to be effective against an entity (such as the trustee) that acquires an interest in the property prior to perfection or continuation. Thus, if a secured creditor would still have the right under applicable nonbankruptcy law to perfect its security interest and prevail over a prior lien creditor (as, for example, under § 9-317(e) of the Uniform Commercial Code for the holder of a purchase-money security interest who files a financing statement within 20 days after the debtor receives delivery of the collateral), the holder of that security interest may perfect its security interest and prevail against the trustee in the same way. If perfection would require seizure of property to accomplish that perfection, § 546(b)(2) permits the secured creditor to give notice to the trustee in lieu of seizure. As discussed in Chapter 2[B][2], § 362(b)(3) allows the secured party to take any action to perfect or to continue the perfection of a security interest without violating the automatic stay to the extent the trustee's avoiding powers are subject to that perfection or continuation under § 546(b) or the perfection is accomplished within the 30-day period described in § 547(e)(2)(A) (which is 30 days after the security interest becomes effective between the debtor and the secured party).

The trustee's avoiding powers under § 544(a), 545, 547 and 549 are also subject to the right of a seller of goods to reclaim the goods from the debtor under certain circumstances. § 546(c). In order to prevail with respect to its reclamation right, the seller of goods must establish that four requirements are met. First, the goods must have been sold to the debtor in the ordinary course of the seller's business. Second, the goods must have been received while the debtor was insolvent (§ 101(32)). Third, the debtor must have received the goods within 45 days before the case commenced. Fourth, the seller must have made a written demand for reclamation not later than 45 days after the debtor received the goods of, if the bankruptcy filing occurred during that period, not later than 20 days after the filing (if later). The seller's reclamation rights are subject to the prior rights of a holder of a security interest in the goods or their proceeds.

The trustee's powers are also subject to a right of reclamation with respect to sellers of grain to debtor's grain storage facility or fishermen selling fish to debtor's fish processing facility. § 546(d).

In a chapter 11 case, the trustee may also seek the return of goods to a creditor who has not sought reclamation. If the trustee makes a motion not later than 120 days after the order for relief in a chapter 11 case and the court determines that a return is in the best interests of the estate and the debtor, and the creditor consents, goods shipped to the debtor prior to the commencement of the case may be returned to the creditor and the creditor may offset the purchase price against any prepetition claim the creditor has against the debtor. § 546(h). The right to return goods is also subject to the prior rights of holders of security interests in the goods or their proceeds.

As discussed in Section 5[B], *supra*, the trustee may not use § 545 to avoid a warehouseman's lien for storage, transportation or other costs incidental to the storage and handling of goods. § 546(i). Certain margin payments and other payments in connection with repurchase agreements, swap agreements, and master netting agreements are also immune from avoidance. § 546(e), (f), (g) & (j).

A visualization of the limitations on the avoiding powers follows:

LIMITATIONS ON AVOIDING POWERS
§ 546

STATUTE OF LIMITATIONS	PERFECTION OR CONTINUATION OF SECURITY INTEREST	RIGHTS OF RECLAMATION	WAREHOUSE-MAN'S LIENS	FINANCIAL INSTRUMENTS	RETURN OF GOODS
ACTION UNDER § 544, 545, 547, 548 OR 553 MUST BE BROUGHT BEFORE LATER OF 1) 2 YEARS AFTER ORDER FOR RELIEF, OR 2) IF TRUSTEE IS APPOINTED OR ELECTED DURING THAT PERIOD, 1 YEAR AFTER TRUSTEE IS APPOINTED OR ELECTED AND BEFORE CASE IS CLOSED OR DISMISSED	TRUSTEE'S POWERS UNDER § 544, 545 AND 549 ARE SUBJECT TO ANY GENERALLY APPLICABLE LAW PERMITTING PERFECTION OR CONTINUATION OF SECURITY INTEREST TO BE EFFECTIVE AGAINST ENTITY ACQUIRING RIGHTS IN COLLATERAL BEFORE DATE OF PERFECTION OR CONTINUATION	TRUSTEE'S POWERS UNDER § 544(a), 545, 547 AND 549 ARE SUBJECT TO RIGHT OF SELLER OF GOODS TO RECLAIM FROM DEBTOR (SUBJECT TO PRIOR RIGHTS OF SECURED CREDITORS) IF 1) GOODS SOLD IN ORDINARY COURSE OF SELLER'S BUSINESS, 2) GOODS SOLD WITHIN 45 DAYS BEFORE CASE COMMENCED, 3) DEBTOR RECEIVED GOODS WHILE INSOLVENT, AND 4) SELLER MAKES WRITTEN DEMAND FOR RECLAMATION NOT LATER THAN 45 DAYS AFTER DEBTOR RECEIVED GOODS OR, IF BANKRUPTCY INTERVENES, NOT LATER THAN 20 DAYS AFTER CASE COMMENCES	TRUSTEE MAY NOT AVOID WAREHOUSE-MAN'S LIEN FOR STORAGE, TRANSPORTATION, OR OTHER COSTS INCIDENTAL TO STORAGE AND HANDLING OF GOODS UNDER § 545	TRUSTEE MAY NOT AVOID CERTAIN MARGIN PAYMENTS, SETTLEMENT PAYMENTS, OR TRANSFERS IN CONNECTION WITH REPURCHASE AGREEMENTS, SWAP AGREEMENTS, OR MASTER NETTING AGREEMENTS	COURT MAY ORDER RETURN TO CREDITOR OF GOODS SHIPPED TO DEBTOR PREPETITION ON MOTION OF TRUSTEE MADE NOT LATER THAN 120 DAYS AFTER ORDER FOR RELIEF IN CHAPTER 11 CASE IF RETURN IS IN BEST INTERESTS OF ESTATE AND DEBTOR, AND CREDITOR CONSENTS, SUBJECT TO PRIOR RIGHTS OF SECURED CREDITORS, AND CREDITOR MAY OFFSET PURCHASE PRICE AGAINST PREPETITION CLAIM AGAINST DEBTOR

2. Liability of Transferees

If a transfer is avoided under § 544, 545, 547, 548, 549, 553(b) or 724(a) (which allows the trustee to avoid liens securing claims for fines, penalties, forfeitures or punitive damages that are not compensatory in nature), the trustee may seek to recover the property so transferred or, if the court so orders, the value of such property, from any of three targets. First, the trustee may seek to recover from the "initial transferee" who received the property directly from the debtor. Second, the trustee may seek to recover from "the entity for whose benefit such transfer was made" if other than the initial transferee (*e.g.*, the guarantor of a debt paid by a debtor, or the primary obligor when a payment is made by a guarantor/debtor). Third, if the initial transferee has not retained the property, the trustee may seek to recover from any "immediate or mediate transferee of such initial transferee," meaning anyone who subsequently receives the property from the initial transferee or from a subsequent transferee. § 550(a). If the transfer from the debtor was made for the benefit of a creditor who was an insider between 90 days and one year before the filing of the bankruptcy petition and is avoided as a preference under § 547(b), the trustee may not recover the transfer from a transferee who was not an insider, even if that transferee received the property directly from the debtor. § 550(c). This might happen if the debtor paid a debt guaranteed by an insider to a non-insider creditor during the extended preference period for insiders. Under § 550(c), such a preferential transfer could be recovered only from the insider, not from the creditor who received the payment.

The trustee may not recover from a subsequent transferee who took the property for value, in good faith, and without knowledge of the voidability of the transfer, or an immediate or mediate transferee of such a subsequent transferee. § 550(b).

An action to avoid the transfer and an action seeking its recovery are separate actions. A recovery action must be brought no later than one year after the avoidance of the transfer with respect to which recovery is sought, and in any event before the case is closed or dismissed. § 550(f). The trustee may seek recovery from any or all relevant entities, but may recover from only one. § 550(d).

If a good faith transferee of a voidable transfer has made improvements to the property, meaning physical additions or changes, repairs, payments of taxes, payments of debts secured by liens that are not subordinate to the rights of the trustee, or payments to preserve the property, § 550(e)(2), the transferee is entitled to a lien on the property recovered by the trustee. Such a lien secures the lesser of (x) the cost to the transferee of any improvement made after the transfer less any profit realized by the transferee, and (y) the increase in value to the property as a result of the improvement. § 550(e)(1).

A visualization of the provisions relating to the liability of transferees for avoided transfers follows:

LIABILITY OF TRANSFEREES OF AVOIDED TRANSFERS §550			
WHO MAY BE LIABLE	FOR WHAT ARE THEY LIABLE	EXCEPTIONS TO LIABILITY	LIEN FOR IMPROVEMENTS
INITIAL TRANSFEREE, ANY ENTITY FOR WHOSE BENEFIT THE TRANSFER WAS MADE, OR ANY IMMEDIATE OR MEDIATE TRANSFEREE OF THE INITIAL TRANSFEREE	TRANSFERRED PROPERTY OR, IF COURT SO ORDERS, ITS VALUE	TRUSTEE MAY NOT RECOVER FROM ANY IMMEDIATE OR MEDIATE TRANSFEREE OF THE INITIAL TRANSFEREE WHO TOOK FOR VALUE IN GOOD FAITH AND WITHOUT KNOWLEDGE OF THE VOIDABILITY OF THE TRANSFER, OR ANY IMMEDIATE OR MEDIATE TRANSFEREE OF SUCH TRANSFEREE AVOIDED TRANSFER UNDER § 547(b) MADE BETWEEN 90 DAYS AND 1 YEAR BEFORE FILING FOR THE BENEFIT OF AN INSIDER MAY NOT BE RECOVERED FROM A NON-INSIDER	GOOD FAITH TRANSFEREE WHO HAS MADE IMPROVEMENTS TO TRANSFERRED PROPERTY HAS LIEN ON PROPERTY TO SECURE LESSER OF 1) TRANSFEREE'S COST OF IMPROVEMENTS LESS AMOUNT OF REALIZED PROFITS, AND 2) INCREASE IN VALUE TO PROPERTY BY REASON OF IMPROVEMENTS

3. Preservation of Avoided Transfer

To the extent that an avoided transfer has any value as against other creditors of the debtor, any transfer avoided under § 522, 544, 545, 547, 548, 549 or 724(a) (which allows the trustee to avoid liens securing claims for fines, penalties, forfeitures or punitive damages that are not compensatory in nature) is automatically preserved for the benefit of the estate rather than simply undone. § 551. This means that if property was transferred, the property comes back to the estate. If an interest in property was transferred (such as a security interest), that interest is recovered from the transferee and is held by the trustee for the benefit of the estate. Any value attributable to that interest will benefit the estate rather than any creditor with a subordinate interest to the original transferee but superior to unsecured creditors.

Section 551 can be visualized as follows:

PRESERVATION OF AVOIDED TRANSFER
§ 551

TRANSFER AVOIDED UNDER § 522, 544, 546, 547,548, 549 OR 724(a) IS PRESERVED FOR BENEFIT OF THE ESTATE WITH RESPECT TO PROPERTY OF THE ESTATE

Chapter 6

OPERATING THE BUSINESS

A. AUTHORIZATION TO OPERATE BUSINESS

When a debtor files for bankruptcy under chapter 7, the property of the debtor's business (if any) will be liquidated for the benefit of creditors. However, if operation of the business for a short time is "in the best interest of the estate and consistent with the orderly liquidation of the estate," the court may authorize the trustee to operate the business of the chapter 7 debtor "for a limited period." § 721. If the court provides such authorization, the trustee is required to provide periodic reports and summaries of the operation of the business, including a statement of receipts and disbursements, and other information required by the U.S. trustee or the court. § 704(a)(8).

The situation in a chapter 11 or chapter 13 bankruptcy is different. If the debtor files for bankruptcy under chapter 11, the goal of the case is generally a reorganization of the debtor and the debtor's business. The trustee in a chapter 11 (whose functions are in most cases performed by the debtor in possession under § 1107(a)) is always authorized to operate the chapter 11 debtor's business unless the court, upon the request by a party in interest, orders otherwise. § 1108. The trustee, or debtor in possession performing the functions of the trustee, has the same reporting duties with respect to the business as would a chapter 7 trustee. § 1106(a)(1).

In a chapter 13 case, although there is an appointed or standing trustee who performs certain administrative functions and advises the debtor with respect to his or her chapter 13 plan under § 1302, the debtor continues to hold the property of the estate and may use it, sell it, or lease it subject to judicial oversight. § 1303. A chapter 13 debtor who is engaged in business may continue to operate that business unless the court orders otherwise. § 1304(b). A debtor is deemed to be "engaged in business" if the debtor is self-employed and incurs trade credit in the production of employment income. § 1304(a). If the debtor is engaged in business, the debtor has the same reporting duties with respect to the business as would a chapter 7 trustee. § 1304(c).

The circumstances under which the trustee or the debtor may operate the debtor's business are visualized below:

AUTHORIZATION TO OPERATE DEBTOR'S BUSINESS		
CHAPTER 7 § 721	CHAPTER 11 § 1108	CHAPTER 13 § 1304(b)
COURT MAY AUTHORIZE THE TRUSTEE TO OPERATE BUSINESS OF DEBTOR FOR LIMITED PERIOD IF IN THE BEST INTEREST OF THE ESTATE AND CONSISTENT WITH ORDERLY LIQUIDATION OF ESTATE	TRUSTEE MAY OPERATE BUSINESS OF THE DEBTOR UNLESS COURT, ON REQUEST OF PARTY, ORDERS OTHERWISE	DEBTOR ENGAGED IN BUSINESS MAY OPERATE BUSINESS OF THE DEBTOR UNLESS COURT ORDERS OTHERWISE

B. USE, SALE OR LEASE OF PROPERTY

In recent years, one of the major functions of a chapter 11 bankruptcy case has been to facilitate the disposition of property of the debtor, sometimes all or substantially all of such property. Such a sale is subject to the provisions of § 363 rather than the requirements of a plan of reorganization, and can be accomplished in less time and with less expense. But the major attraction of a § 363 sale is that no creditor approval is required; although creditors may object to the sale, the ultimate decision rests in the hands of the court.

Under § 363, the trustee has broad powers to use, sell, or lease property of the estate. If the trustee is authorized to operate the business of the debtor, the trustee may use, sell or lease such property in the ordinary course of business without notice or a hearing unless the court orders otherwise. § 363(c)(1). The trustee may use, sell or lease property of the estate other than in the ordinary course of business after notice and a hearing (subject to certain protections for personally identifiable information (§ 101(41A)). § 363(b)(1). The trustee may use, sell or lease property notwithstanding any contractual or legal provision conditioned on the debtor's insolvency or financial condition or filing for bankruptcy or appointment of a trustee that provides for forfeiture, modification or termination of the debtor's interest in the property. § 363(l). Procedural rules relating to motions to use, sell or lease property are set out in Fed. R. Bankr. P. 6004.

The trustee is also given certain protections with respect to sales or leases of estate property. If the sale price of property of the estate was controlled by collusion between potential bidders, the trustee may either avoid the sale, or may recover from one of the bidders the amount by which the value of the sold property exceeded the purchase price. The court may also award costs, attorneys' fees and expenses, as well as punitive damages against any party that entered into a bidding agreement "in willful disregard" of the requirements of the Code. § 363(n).

In addition, even if an order authorizing the sale or lease of estate property is reversed or modified on appeal, the sale or lease remains valid if the purchaser or lessee acquired the property in good faith, unless the party challenging the authorization obtained a stay pending appeal. § 363(m).

A visualization of these powers of the trustee to use, sell or lease property follows.

USE, SALE OR LEASE OF PROPERTY OF THE ESTATE § 363				
POWERS OF TRUSTEE WITH RESPECT TO PROPERTY OF THE ESTATE		PROTECTIONS FOR TRUSTEE		
ORDINARY COURSE OF BUSINESS § 363(c)(1)	NOT IN ORDINARY COURSE OF BUSINESS § 363(b)(1)	IPSO FACTO CLAUSES § 363(l)	SAFE HARBOR § 363(m)	AVOIDANCE OF COLLUSIVE SALES § 363(n)
IF TRUSTEE IS AUTHORIZED TO ENGAGE IN BUSINESS, TRUSTEE MAY USE, SELL OR LEASE PROPERTY IN THE ORDINARY COURSE OF BUSINESS WITHOUT NOTICE OR HEARING	TRUSTEE MAY USE, SELL OR LEASE PROPERTY OUTSIDE ORDINARY COURSE OF BUSINESS WITH NOTICE AND HEARING	TRUSTEE MAY USE, SELL OR LEASE PROPERTY NOTWITHSTANDING CONTRACTUAL OR LEGAL PROVISION CONDITIONED ON DEBTOR'S INSOLVENCY, FINANCIAL CONDITION, BANKRUPTCY, OR APPOINTMENT OF TRUSTEE THAT TRIGGERS FORFEITURE, MODIFICATION OR TERMINATION OF DEBTOR'S INTEREST IN PROPERTY	SALE OR LEASE TO GOOD FAITH ENTITY REMAINS VALID DESPITE MODIFICATION OR REVERSAL OF AUTHORIZATION ORDER ON APPEAL UNLESS AUTHORIZATION WAS STAYED PENDING APPEAL	TRUSTEE MAY AVOID COLLUSIVE SALE OR MAY RECOVER EXCESS OF PROPERTY'S VALUE OVER PURCHASE PRICE, PLUS COSTS, FEES AND EXPENSES AND PUNITIVE DAMAGES

However, the trustee's broad powers under § 363(b) and (c) are restricted when the trustee seeks to use, sell or lease "cash collateral," defined broadly in § 363(a) as "cash, negotiable instruments, documents of title, securities, deposit accounts, or other cash equivalents" in which someone other than the estate has an interest. The trustee may not use, sell, or lease cash collateral unless it gets consent from the entity with an interest in the cash collateral or the court authorizes such action after notice and a hearing. § 363(c)(2). The trustee must segregate and account for all cash collateral in the trustee's possession. § 363(c)(4).

A hearing on a request to use, sell or lease cash collateral must be made in compliance with Fed. R. Bankr. P. 4001(b) and scheduled in accordance with the needs of the debtor. If it is a preliminary hearing, the court may still authorize the use, sale or lease of the cash collateral, but only if there is a reasonable likelihood that the trustee will prevail at the final hearing. The court is required to act promptly on a request for permission to use, sell or lease cash collateral. § 363(c)(3). If the secured party so requests, the court will condition such use, sale or lease on provision of adequate protection of the secured party's interest in the cash collateral, § 363(e), and may combine the adequate protection hearing with the hearing seeking authorization to use, sell or lease the cash collateral, § 363(c)(3). For a discussion of adequate protection, see Chapter 2[B][5], *supra*. Frequently the secured party and the trustee enter into a cash collateral agreement under which the secured party consents to the use of cash collateral and the parties stipulate to the adequate protection to be provided by the trustee, usually current payments of interest. *See* Fed. R. Bankr. P. 4001(d).

A visualization of the provisions relating to use, sale or lease of cash collateral follows:

USE, SALE OR LEASE OF CASH COLLATERAL § 363			
DEFINITION § 363(a)	LIMITATIONS ON TRUSTEE § 363(c)(2) & (4)	ADEQUATE PROTECTION § 363(e)	HEARING § 363(c)(3)
PROPERTY OF THE FOLLOWING TYPES IN WHICH ESTATE AND ANOTHER ENTITY HAS AN INTEREST: 1) CASH, 2) NEGOTIABLE INSTRUMENTS, 3) DOCUMENTS OF TITLE, 4) SECURITIES, 5) DEPOSIT ACCOUNTS, OR 6) OTHER CASH EQUIVALENTS INCLUDING PROCEEDS, PRODUCTS, OFFSPRING, RENTS OR PROFITS	TRUSTEE MAY USE, SELL OR LEASE CASH COLLATERAL ONLY IF 1) CREDITOR CONSENTS, OR 2) COURT APPROVES TRUSTEE MUST SEGREGATE AND ACCOUNT FOR CASH COLLATERAL IN TRUSTEE'S POSSESSION	USE, SALE OR LEASE MAY BE PROHIBITED OR CONDITIONED ON PROVISION OF ADEQUATE PROTECTION	HEARING MUST BE SCHEDULED ACCORDING TO NEEDS OF DEBTOR IF HEARING IS PRELIMINARY, COURT MAY AUTHORIZE USE, SALE OR LEASE ONLY IF THERE IS REASONABLE LIKELIHOOD THAT TRUSTEE WILL PREVAIL AT FINAL HEARING COURT MUST ACT PROMPTLY ON REQUEST FOR AUTHORIZATION

For property in which an entity other than the estate has an interest, the trustee may use, sell or lease such property as permitted by § 363(b) or (c), but on request of the entity with an interest in such property, the court may prohibit its use, sale or lease by the trustee, or may condition such use, sale or lease on provision of adequate protection of the interest of such entity. § 363(e). The entity asserting an interest in the property has the burden of proof as to the validity, priority or extent of its interest, but the trustee has the burden of proof on the issue of adequate protection. § 363(p). If the trustee provides adequate protection of a secured creditor's interest in property under § 363(e), and that adequate protection proves inadequate (meaning that notwithstanding the adequate protection, the secured creditor has an administrative expense claim arising from the use, sale or lease of property), then the creditor's claim is given priority over all other administrative expense claims. § 507(b). *See* Chapter 4[A][2], *supra.*

If the trustee seeks to sell the property in which an entity other than the estate has an interest, the entity has additional protections. First, at any sale of such property, if the property is subject to a lien, unless the court for cause orders otherwise, the holder of the claim secured by such lien is entitled to bid at such sale (called a "credit bid") and, if successful, offset the amount of its purchase price against its allowed claim. § 363(k).

Second, any sale of such property may be made free and clear of the entity's interest in the property only if one of five conditions is satisfied. § 363(f). First, such sale may occur if applicable nonbankruptcy law would permit a sale of such property free and clear of the interest. An example of a sale covered by this exception would be a sale of inventory to a buyer in the ordinary course of business. Second, such sale may occur if the entity with the interest in the property consents to the sale free and clear of such interest. Third, the sale is permitted if the entity's interest in the property is a lien and the purchase price to be received for the property is sufficient to satisfy all liens. Fourth, the sale may occur if the interest of the entity is in bona fide dispute. Finally, the trustee may sell the property free and clear of the interest if the entity holding the interest could be compelled in a legal or equitable proceeding to accept a money satisfaction of its interest.

Third, if an entity is a co-owner of the property (*i.e.,* the debtor and such entity hold the property as tenants in common, joint tenants or tenants by the entirety), the trustee may sell not only the estate's interest in the property but also the co-owner's interest only if partition in kind of the property is impracticable, sale of only the estate's interest would realize substantially less for the estate than its interest in the proceeds of a sale of the whole property, the benefit to the estate of selling the whole property outweighs the detriment to the co-owner, and the property is not used in the production, transmission or distribution for sale of electric energy or gas. § 363(h). Property of the estate may always be sold free and clear of any right of dower or curtesy. § 363(g). Before any sale of property in which an entity other than the estate has a co-ownership or dower or curtesy interest, or property that was community property before commencement of the case, the other entity with an interest in the property may purchase the property at the sale price. § 363(i). If a sale to someone other than such entity occurs, the trustee must distribute to the estate and to such entity the proceeds of the sale, less the costs and expenses of the sale, in accordance with their respective interests. § 363(j).

A visualization of the provisions protecting entities with an interest in estate property when such property is sold or leased follows:

PROTECTIONS FOR ENTITIES WITH INTEREST IN PROPERTY OF THE ESTATE WHEN PROPERTY IS USED, SOLD OR LEASED § 363			
ADEQUATE PROTECTION § 363(e)	SALE FREE AND CLEAR § 363(f)	CO-OWNERSHIP INTERESTS § 363(g)-(j)	CREDIT BID § 363(k)
USE, SALE OR LEASE MAY BE PROHIBITED OR CONDITIONED ON PROVISION OF ADEQUATE PROTECTION	PROPERTY MAY NOT BE SOLD FREE AND CLEAR OF INTEREST UNLESS: 1) APPLICABLE NONBANKRUPTCY LAW WOULD PERMIT SUCH SALE, 2) SUCH ENTITY CONSENTS, 3) THE INTEREST IS A LIEN AND THE PURCHASE PRICE IS HIGHER THAN ALL LIENS, 4) INTEREST IS IN BONA FIDE DISPUTE, OR 5) ENTITY COULD BE COMPELLED TO ACCEPT MONEY	PROPERTY MAY BE SOLD FREE OF DOWER OR CURTESY INTEREST PROPERTY MAY NOT BE SOLD FREE OF CO-OWNERSHIP INTEREST UNLESS 1) PARTITION IN KIND NOT PRACTICABLE, 2) SALE OF WHOLE WOULD REALIZE SIGNIFICANTLY MORE THAN SALE OF ESTATE'S INTEREST, 3) BENEFIT TO ESTATE OF SALE OF WHOLE OUTWEIGHS DETRIMENT TO CO-OWNERS, AND 4) PROPERTY IS NOT USED IN ENERGY OR GAS PRODUCTION CO-OWNERS OR HOLDERS OF DOWER, CURTESY OR COMMUNITY PROPERTY INTEREST HAVE RIGHT TO BUY PROPERTY AT SALE PRICE TRUSTEE MUST PAY CO-OWNERS OR SPOUSE THEIR SHARE OF PROCEEDS LESS COSTS OF SALE	HOLDER OF LIEN SECURING ALLOWED CLAIM MAY BID FOR PROPERTY AND OFFSET ITS CLAIM AGAINST PURCHASE PRICE UNLESS COURT FOR CAUSE ORDERS OTHERWISE

C. OBTAINING CREDIT

When a debtor files for bankruptcy protection, unless it is liquidating (and perhaps even then), it will continue to need cash to finance its operations and pay for goods and services. Any cash in which the debtor had an interest on the date of the filing becomes property of the estate under § 541(a) and will be available for such use. In addition, any cash generated by estate assets after the filing, like any other property acquired by the estate postpetition, is also an asset of the estate under § 541(a)(7) and is available for use.

But if the cash is subject to a security interest, it constitutes cash collateral and the trustee cannot use it without either the consent of the secured lender or court order (which will be conditioned upon providing the secured lender adequate protection) under § 363(c)(2). *See* Section 6[B], *supra*.

Even if the trustee can use cash collateral, its unencumbered cash and cash collateral may not be sufficient to fund the debtor's operations; the trustee may need to bring in new money to the business from outside sources. Because the trustee cannot assume a prepetition contract to make a loan or other financial accommodations to the debtor, § 365(c)(2), *see* Section 6[D], *infra*, the most likely source for this new money is a new financing arrangement (often called "DIP financing" because it is generally provided to a debtor in possession in a chapter 11 case). Under § 364, the trustee is authorized to obtain credit or incur debt, but must attempt to do so on a basis that is less intrusive to existing creditors in terms of security and priority before moving to a more intrusive means. Any motion to obtain credit must comply with Fed. R. Bankr. P. 4001(c).

Under § 364(a), if the trustee is authorized to operate the business of the debtor, the trustee may obtain unsecured credit and incur unsecured debt in the ordinary course of business without notice or a hearing unless the court orders otherwise. Any obligation of the estate with respect to such credit or debt constitutes an administrative expense under § 503(b)(1). *See* Chapter 4[A][3], *supra*.

If the trustee needs to obtain unsecured credit or incur unsecured debt other than in the ordinary course of business, it may do so with court authorization after notice and a hearing. § 364(b). This obligation would also constitute an administrative expense under § 503(b)(1).

Financers are often unwilling to extend credit or make loans to a debtor relying solely on an administrative expense priority. If the trustee is not able to obtain unsecured credit under § 364(b), after notice and a hearing, the court may authorize the debtor to obtain credit or incur debt that has priority over other administrative expenses under § 503(b) and § 507(b), or that is secured by a lien on unencumbered estate property, or that is secured by a junior lien on encumbered estate property. § 364(c).

Even with such benefits, new credit may not be available to the trustee. In that case, the court may authorize the trustee to obtain credit or incur debt that has an equal or superior lien on already encumbered assets, a so-called "priming lien" (because it comes ahead of an existing secured creditor). § 364(d)(1). Because such an order affects existing property rights of the secured creditor, § 364(d)(1)(B) requires that the existing creditor's interest in the property be given adequate protection. For a discussion of adequate protection, see Chapter 2[B][5], *supra*. The trustee has the burden of proof on the issue of whether the existing creditor's interest is adequately protected. § 364(d)(2). If the court allows the incurrence of new debt with a priming lien because the trustee provides adequate protection of the secured creditor's interest in the collateral, and that adequate protection proves inadequate (meaning that notwithstanding the adequate protection, the secured creditor has an administrative expense claim arising from the incurrence of the debt), then the creditor's claim is given priority over all other administrative expense claims. § 507(b). *See* Chapter 4[A][2], *supra*.

A visualization of options for obtaining credit under § 364 follows:

OBTAINING CREDIT § 364			
ORDINARY COURSE, UNSECURED § 364(a)	NON-ORDINARY COURSE, UNSECURED § 364(b)	SUPERPRIORITY OR SECURED BY UNENCUMBERED ASSETS OR JUNIOR LIEN § 364(c)	SECURED BY SENIOR OR EQUAL LIEN § 364(d)
IF TRUSTEE IS AUTHORIZED TO OPERATE BUSINESS, TRUSTEE MAY OBTAIN UNSECURED CREDIT OR INCUR UNSECURED DEBT IN ORDINARY COURSE OF BUSINESS UNLESS COURT ORDERS OTHERWISE	COURT MAY AUTHORIZE TRUSTEE TO OBTAIN UNSECURED CREDIT OR INCUR UNSECURED DEBT OTHER THAN IN ORDINARY COURSE OF BUSINESS	IF UNSECURED CREDIT NOT AVAILABLE, COURT MAY AUTHORIZE TRUSTEE TO OBTAIN CREDIT OR INCUR DEBT 1) WITH PRIORITY OVER ALL ADMINISTRATIVE EXPENSES UNDER § 503(b) OR § 507(b), 2) WITH LIEN ON UNENCUMBERED ESTATE PROPERTY, OR 3) WITH JUNIOR LIEN ON ESTATE PROPERTY	IF TRUSTEE IS UNABLE TO OBTAIN CREDIT OTHERWISE, COURT MAY AUTHORIZE TRUSTEE TO OBTAIN CREDIT OR INCUR DEBT SECURED BY SENIOR OR EQUAL LIEN IF TRUSTEE PROVIDES ADEQUATE PROTECTION OF INTEREST OF HOLDER OF EXISTING LIEN TRUSTEE HAS BURDEN OF PROOF ON ISSUE OF ADEQUATE PROTECTION

The new postpetition financer is given one additional protection, the so-called "safe harbor clause" of § 364(e). Even if an order authorizing the obtaining of credit under § 364 is reversed or modified on appeal, as long as the entity extending the credit did so in good faith, the debt and the liens (if any) securing the debt remain valid, unless the authorization and incurrence of debt were stayed pending appeal.

D. EXECUTORY CONTRACTS AND UNEXPIRED LEASES

Under § 365(a), the trustee may assume or reject any executory contract or unexpired lease of the debtor. Either action requires court approval; with the exception of deemed rejections for failure to assume within the time provided by § 365, the trustee cannot assume or reject an executory contract or unexpired lease merely by conduct. *See* Fed. R. Bankr. P. 6006. To understand this provision, we have to look at the words Congress used, none of which are defined.

First, we have to understand what executory contracts and unexpired leases are. An unexpired lease is a lease on which the debtor is either the lessor or lessee and which has not expired in accordance with its terms at the time the trustee seeks to assume or reject the lease.

An executory contract is a type of contract to which the debtor is a party. The dictionary definition of "executory" refers to future performance, and the legislative history of § 365 suggested that the concept was intended to embrace "contracts on which performance remains due to some extent on both sides." If one party has completely performed its obligations under a contract, that party has a claim against the other party but the contract is no longer executory. The Code provides no guidance on what happens to contracts in bankruptcy other than executory contracts.

The two options given to the trustee with respect to executory contracts and unexpired leases are the options to "assume" or "reject." As we will see, in fact, the option to assume encompasses two sub-options — the option to assume and retain, or the option to assume and assign. The following chart visualizes these options:

OPTIONS FOR EXECUTORY CONTRACTS AND UNEXPIRED LEASES § 365(a)	
ASSUMPTION	REJECTION
1) ASSUME AND RETAIN 2) ASSUME AND ASSIGN	

1. Rejection

"Rejection" of an executory contract or unexpired lease is a decision by the trustee to dishonor the contract or lease, leaving it behind with all other prepetition obligations of the debtor. Rejection of an executory contract or unexpired lease "constitutes a breach of such contract or lease" which (unless the contract or lease had previously been assumed by the trustee) is deemed to have occurred immediately before the filing of the petition and thus be a prepetition claim for purposes of the bankruptcy case. § 365(g)(1). A claim arising from such rejection is determined, and allowed or disallowed, "the same as if such claim had arisen before the date of the filing of the petition." § 502(g)(1). If a lease of personal property is rejected or deemed rejected, the leased property "is no longer property of the estate and the stay under section 362(a) is automatically terminated." § 365(p)(1).

The consequences of rejection to the parties to an executory contract or unexpired lease are visualized as follows:

CONSEQUENCES OF REJECTION § 365(g)(1) & (p)	
ESTATE	NONDEBTOR
BREACH OF EXECUTORY CONTRACT OR LEASE PERSONAL PROPERTY SUBJECT TO REJECTED LEASE IS NO LONGER PROPERTY OF THE ESTATE AND THE AUTOMATIC STAY IS TERMINATED	RECEIVES PREPETITION UNSECURED CLAIM FOR BREACH OF EXECUTORY CONTRACT OR LEASE § 502(g)(1)

Despite the rejection of an executory contract or unexpired lease, Congress provided the nondebtor party to certain types of contracts and leases protection from the consequences of rejection. The first protected class is the class of lessees in possession of real property under rejected unexpired leases. Such lessee is given the option to treat the lease as terminated, or alternatively to retain its rights under the lease for the balance of the lease term and for any renewal or extension of the term to the same extent as under applicable nonbankruptcy law. § 365(h). If the lessee retains its rights under the unexpired lease after its rejection, the lessee may offset against the rent the value of any damage caused by the trustee's nonperformance of the debtor's obligations after the date of the rejection to the exclusion of any other remedy for such nonperformance.

The second protected class is composed of purchasers of real property or timeshare interests under a timeshare plan, which purchasers are in possession of the property. Such purchasers are entitled to elect to treat the contract as terminated or instead may remain in possession, continue to make all payments due under the contract (offsetting against such payments any damages caused by the trustee's nonperformance of the debtor's postpetition obligations to the exclusion of any other remedy for such nonperformance), and the trustee is obligated to deliver title to the purchaser in accordance with the contract. § 365(i). If the purchaser treats the contract as terminated, or the purchaser is not in possession of the property when the executory contract is rejected, the purchaser is given a lien on the property for any portion of the purchase price already paid. § 365(j).

Licensees of rights to intellectual property are protected under § 365(n). If the trustee rejects such a license, the licensee is given the option to treat the license as terminated or to retain its rights under the contract and any supplementary agreements to the intellectual property covered thereby for the duration of the contract and any period for which the contract may be extended by the licensee under applicable nonbankruptcy law. If the licensee elects to retain its rights under the license agreement, the trustee must allow the licensee to exercise those rights, the licensee must make all required royalty payments to the trustee, and the licensee is deemed to waive any right of setoff or claim with respect to the license agreement. The trustee must also provide the intellectual property to a licensee electing to retain its rights under the license, and must not interfere with the licensee's rights to the intellectual property.

A visualization of the parties protected upon rejection of an executory contract or unexpired lease follows:

PARTIES PROTECTED UPON REJECTION § 365(h), (i), (j) & (n)		
LEASE OF REAL PROPERTY	EXECUTORY CONTRACT FOR SALE OF REAL PROPERTY OR TIMESHARE INTEREST	LICENSE OF INTELLECTUAL PROPERTY
LESSEE MAY TREAT LEASE AS TERMINATED OR RETAIN ITS RIGHTS UNDER LEASE FOR REMAINING LEASE TERM AND ANY RENEWAL OR EXTENSION TO WHICH IT IS ENTITLED UNDER APPLICABLE NONBANKRUPTCY LAW LESSEE MAY OFFSET AGAINST RENT DAMAGES CAUSED BY TRUSTEE'S NONPERFORMANCE TO EXCLUSION OF OTHER REMEDIES	PURCHASER IN POSSESSION MAY TREAT CONTRACT AS TERMINATED OR REMAIN IN POSSESSION IF PURCHASER REMAINS IN POSSESSION, PURCHASER MUST CONTINUE TO MAKE PAYMENTS DUE UNDER CONTRACT (BUT MAY OFFSET DAMAGES CAUSED BY TRUSTEE'S NONPERFORMANCE TO EXCLUSION OF OTHER REMEDIES) AND TRUSTEE MUST DELIVER TITLE IF PURCHASER TREATS CONTRACT AS TERMINATED, OR PURCHASER IS NOT IN POSSESSION, PURCHASER HAS LIEN ON PROPERTY FOR RECOVERY OF PURCHASE PRICE	LICENSEE MAY TREAT LICENSE AS TERMINATED OR MAY RETAIN ITS RIGHTS UNDER THE LICENSE TO THE INTELLECTUAL PROPERTY FOR DURATION OF CONTRACT AND ANY ADDITIONAL PERIOD FOR WHICH LICENSEE MAY EXTEND LICENSE UNDER APPLICABLE NONBANKRUPTPCY LAW IF LICENSEE RETAINS ITS RIGHTS, TRUSTEE MUST ALLOW LICENSEE TO EXERCISE RIGHTS, PROVIDE THE INTELLECTUAL PROPERTY, AND NOT INTERFERE WITH LICENSEE'S RIGHTS IF LICENSEE RETAINS ITS RIGHTS, LICENSEE MUST MAKE ALL ROYALTY PAYMENTS, AND WAIVES ANY RIGHT OF SETOFF OR OTHER CLAIM UNDER LICENSE

If the trustee in a chapter 7 case of an individual debtor rejects a lease of personal property, the debtor may notify the lessor in writing that the debtor wishes to assume such lease. § 365(p)(2)(A). The lessor may then, at its option, notify the debtor that it is willing to permit such assumption and may condition the assumption on cure of any outstanding default on the terms specified in the contract. *Id.* If the debtor then notifies the lessor in writing within 30 days after the notice from the lessor that the lease is assumed, the debtor assumes the liability under the lease. § 365(p)(2)(B). Notification to the debtor and negotiation of cure in effectuating such an assumption do not violate the automatic stay under § 362 or the permanent injunction of § 524(a)(2). § 365(p)(2)(C). The consequences of such an assumption are unclear. *Compare In re Thompson,* 440 B.R. 130 (Bankr. W.D. Mich. 2010) (holding that debtor's obligations under assumed lease are post-petition and not subject to discharge), *with In re Eader,* 426 B.R. 164 (Bankr. D. Md. 2010) (holding that debtor's obligations under assumed lease are subject to discharge unless debtor enters into reaffirmation agreement under § 524(c)).

2. Assumption

"Assumption" of an executory contract or unexpired lease is a decision on the part of the trustee that such contract or lease should remain in full force and effect and be valid against the trustee. Assumption results in the estate replacing the debtor as the party entitled to performance from the other party under the contract or lease, and the party who is required to perform the debtor's obligations. Because the debtor's obligations (both prepetition and postpetition) under an assumed contract or lease become obligations of the estate, they are given administrative expense priority under § 503(b)(1)(A), and are therefore priority claims under § 507(a). *See* Chapter 4[A][2] & [3], *supra.* These obligations remain priority claims even if the trustee subsequently rejects the assumed contract or lease, with the exception for the limit on priority claims under a nonresidential real property lease rejected after assumption under § 503(b)(7).

The consequences of assumption are visualized below:

CONSEQUENCES OF ASSUMPTION	
ESTATE	NONDEBTOR PARTY
DEBTOR'S OBLIGATIONS BECOME OBLIGATIONS OF ESTATE, AND ESTATE OBTAINS BENEFIT OF EXECUTORY CONTRACT OR UNEXPIRED LEASE	BECOMES OBLIGATED TO PERFORM FOR BENEFIT OF ESTATE, AND OBTAINS ADMINISTRATIVE EXPENSE PRIORITY FOR OBLIGATIONS OF ESTATE

Before the trustee may assume an executory contract or lease, there must be a contract or lease to assume which is in existence when the trustee acts to assume it. Therefore, if the contract or lease has validly terminated in accordance with nonbankruptcy law before the bankruptcy filing, the trustee cannot resurrect the contract or lease simply by filing for bankruptcy protection. This general principle is codified for nonresidential real property leases in § 365(c)(3), but is equally applicable to other executory contracts and unexpired leases.

Once the debtor has filed for bankruptcy, the nondebtor party to an executory contract or unexpired lease may not terminate or modify that contract or lease, even if the contract or lease so provides, solely because of the insolvency or financial condition of the debtor, the commencement of a bankruptcy case, or the appointment of a trustee or a custodian. § 365(e)(1). These "ipso facto" clauses are rendered unenforceable in all cases except when applicable law excuses the nondebtor party from accepting performance from or rendering performance to the trustee or to an assignee, and the nondebtor party does not consent to that assumption or assignment. The clauses are also enforceable with respect to contracts to make a loan or extend other financial accommodations to the debtor. § 365(e)(2).

Two types of contracts cannot by their nature be assumed or assigned. The first is a contract or lease as to which applicable law excuses the nondebtor party from accepting performance from or rendering performance to anyone other than the debtor or debtor in possession, and the nondebtor party does not consent to the assumption or assignment. § 365(c)(1). This provision generally applies to personal services contracts, although some cases have expanded its scope to include situations in which applicable law requires approval by a governmental agency of assignment of a contract. Courts are divided over whether this provision bars assumption of a contract when no assignment is contemplated. *Compare In re Catapult Entertainment, Inc.*, 165 F.3d 747 (9th Cir. 1999); *In re Sunterra Corp.*, 361 F.3d 257 (4th Cir. 2004); *In re James Cable Partners, L.P.*, 27 F.3d 534 (11th Cir. 1994) *(per curiam); In re West Electronics, Inc.*, 852 F.2d 79 (3d Cir. 1988) (holding that assumption is not permitted), *with Institut Pasteur v. Cambridge Biotech Corp.*, 104 F.3d 489, 493 (1st Cir. 1997) (holding assumption is permitted). Second, § 365(c)(2) precludes the trustee from assuming contracts to lend money (so-called financial accommodations) — the only way to finance the debtor is through the mechanisms provided in § 364. *See* Section 6[C], *supra*.

If there has been any default under the executory contract or unexpired lease, the trustee may not assume the contract or lease unless the trustee takes three actions at the time of assumption. First, the trustee must cure any existing defaults under the contract, or provide adequate assurance that the trustee will promptly cure such defaults (other than nonmonetary defaults under an unexpired lease of real property — excluding defaults caused by failure to operate in accordance with the lease — if cure is impossible at the time of assumption). § 365(b)(1)(A). Second, the trustee must compensate the other party for any actual pecuniary loss resulting from prior defaults, or provide adequate assurance of prompt compensation. § 365(b)(1)(B). Third, the trustee must provide adequate assurance of future performance under such contract or lease. § 365(b)(1)(C).

Adequate assurance of future performance has a distinct meaning for the assumption of shopping center leases. Under § 365(b)(3), the trustee must provide adequate assurance of four things. One, the trustee must provide adequate assurance of the source of rent and other consideration due under the lease. Two, the trustee must provide adequate assurance that any percentage rent due under the lease will not dramatically decline. Three, the trustee must provide adequate assurance that assumption of the lease is subject to all provisions of the lease (including any provisions relating to radius, location, use or exclusivity) and will not breach any such provision relating to such shopping center contained in any other agreement. Four, the trustee must provide adequate assurance that assumption of the lease will not disrupt any tenant mix or balance in the shopping center.

The conditions to assumption are visualized below:

CONDITIONS TO ASSUMPTION		
CONTRACT EXISTS	DEFAULTS ARE ADDRESSED	CONTRACT IS ASSUMABLE
CONTRACT HAS NOT VALIDLY TERMINATED PREPETITION, AND IPSO FACTO CLAUSES ARE NOT ENFORCEABLE § 365(e)	CURE OR PROVIDE ADEQUATE ASSURANCE OF PROMPT CURE OF EXISTING DEFAULTS OTHER THAN NONMONETARY OBLIGATIONS UNDER UNEXPIRED LEASE OF REAL PROPERTY § 365(b)(1)(A) COMPENSATE, OR PROVIDE ADEQUATE ASSURANCE OF PROMPT COMPENSATION, FOR ACTUAL PECUNIARY LOSSES § 365(b)(1)(B) PROVIDE ADEQUATE ASSURANCE OF FUTURE PERFORMANCE, § 365(b)(1)(C), INCLUDING (FOR SHOPPING CENTER LEASES, § 365(b)(3)) OF 1) THE SOURCE OF AGREED RENT AND OTHER CONSIDERATION DUE UNDER THE LEASE, 2) THAT ANY PERCENTAGE RENT DUE WILL NOT DECLINE SUBSTANTIALLY, 3) THAT ASSUMPTION IS SUBJECT TO ALL PROVISIONS OF THE LEASE, INCLUDING RADIUS, LOCATION, USE OR EXCLUSIVITY, AND WILL NOT BREACH SUCH PROVISIONS IN ANOTHER AGREEMENT, AND 4) THAT ASSUMPTION WILL NOT DISRUPT ANY TENANT MIX OR BALANCE IN THE SHOPPING CENTER	CONTRACTS CANNOT BE ASSUMED IF NON-ASSUMABLE UNDER APPLICABLE NON-BANKRUPTCY LAW § 365(c)(1) CONTRACTS TO MAKE FINANCIAL ACCOMMODATION CANNOT BE ASSUMED § 365(c)(2)

In connection with an assumption of the contract or lease, the trustee can choose to retain the benefits of the executory contract or unexpired lease, or assign the contract or lease to someone else for present consideration, thereby relieving itself of this administrative liability. Section 365(f) permits the trustee to assume the contract, but assign it to a third party, notwithstanding any provision in the contract or lease or in applicable law that prohibits, restricts or conditions such assignment. § 365(f)(1). Section 365(f)(3) also prevents the nondebtor party from terminating or modifying an executory contract or lease based on its assignment despite a provision in the contract or lease, or in applicable law, that would permit such action.

If the executory contract or unexpired lease is assigned to a third party after assumption, the estate and the trustee are relieved from any liability on the contract or lease, including for any breach that occurs after the assignment. § 365(k). The third party assumes all liabilities, and receives the benefit of performance by the nondebtor party, under the assigned contract or lease.

The consequences of assignment are visualized below:

CONSEQUENCES OF ASSIGNMENT	
ESTATE	ASSIGNEE
IS RELIEVED FROM ALL OBLIGATIONS ON CONTRACT OR LEASE, INCLUDING LIABILITY FOR SUBSEQUENT BREACH § 365(k)	BECOMES OBLIGATED TO PERFORM, AND OBTAINS ALL BENEFITS OF, EXECUTORY CONTRACT OR UNEXPIRED LEASE

The trustee cannot assign an executory contract or unexpired lease without assuming it first. § 365(f)(2)(A). Therefore, all the conditions to assumption must first be satisfied. In addition, § 365(f)(2)(B) requires that adequate assurance of future performance by the assignee must be provided, whether or not there has been a default in the contract or lease. Adequate assurance of future performance must be demonstrated as a condition for assumption of an executory contract or unexpired lease only if there was a default. § 365(b)(1)(C). The meaning of the phrase is the same in this context, and the special rules dealing with adequate assurance in the case of shopping center leases in § 365(b)(3) are applicable.

The conditions to assignment are visualized below.

CONDITIONS TO ASSIGNMENT	
CONTRACT HAS BEEN ASSUMED § 365(f)(2)(A)	ASSIGNEE PROVIDES ADEQUATE ASSURANCE OF FUTURE PERFORMANCE § 365(f)(2)(B)
CONTRACT EXISTS DEFAULTS ADDRESSED CONTRACT IS ASSUMABLE	ADEQUATE ASSURANCE OF FUTURE PERFORMANCE BY ASSIGNEE IS PROVIDED, WHETHER OR NOT THERE HAS BEEN DEFAULT, INCLUDING (FOR SHOPPING CENTER LEASES, § 365(c)(3)) OF 1) THE SOURCE OF AGREED RENT AND OTHER CONSIDERATION DUE UNDER THE LEASE AND THAT THE FINANCIAL CONDITION AND OPERATING PERFORMANCE OF THE PROPOSED ASSIGNEE AND ITS GUARANTORS IS SIMILAR TO FINANCIAL CONDITION AND OPERATING PERFORMANCE OF DEBTOR AND ITS GUARANTORS AT THE TIME THE DEBTOR LEASED THE PREMISES, 2) THAT ANY PERCENTAGE RENT DUE WILL NOT DECLINE SUBSTANTIALLY, 3) THAT ASSUMPTION AND ASSIGNMENT IS SUBJECT TO ALL PROVISIONS OF THE LEASE, INCLUDING RADIUS, LOCATION, USE OR EXCLUSIVITY, AND WILL NOT BREACH SUCH PROVISIONS IN ANOTHER AGREEMENT, AND 4) THAT ASSUMPTION OR ASSIGNMENT WILL NOT DISRUPT ANY TENANT MIX OR BALANCE IN THE SHOPPING CENTER

3. Timing of Decision

The trustee, and the unsecured creditors represented by the trustee, will ordinarily be in no hurry to assume or reject executory contracts and unexpired leases. Assumption requires that the trustee immediately cure defaults or provide reasonable assurance of prompt cure, which may require payments to the nondebtor parties to those contracts or leases. In addition, once a contract or lease is assumed, the obligations of the estate under that contract or lease become administrative expense obligations, even if the trustee later decides that the assumption was imprudent and rejects the contract or lease.

Premature rejection is also potentially harmful to the estate. The trustee may need to develop a business plan to figure out its needs on a reorganized basis before it can decide what contracts and leases it requires; if it rejects too soon, it loses the benefit of that contract or lease forever.

On the other hand, the nondebtor party to the executory contract or unexpired lease will usually want an early decision so it can either know that its contract or lease will be honored, or make alternative arrangements.

Section 365 provides some statutory limits on how long the trustee may take to assume or reject executory contracts or leases, depending on whether the case is a chapter 7 liquidation or not, and on the nature of the contract or lease involved.

In a chapter 7 case, the trustee has 60 days after the petition is filed to assume or reject an executory contract or unexpired lease of residential real property or of personal property. If the trustee fails to take action (or get an extension from the court for cause) during that 60-day period, the contract is deemed rejected. § 365(d)(1).

In a case under chapter 11 or 13, § 365(d)(2) allows the trustee to assume or reject an executory contract or unexpired lease of residential real property or of personal property at any time before confirmation of a plan. However, the court, upon request by a party to the contract or lease, may order the trustee to assume or reject within a specified period of time.

In any bankruptcy case, if the debtor is a lessee under a lease of nonresidential real property, the trustee must assume or reject such lease by the earlier of 120 days after the petition is filed or the date of plan confirmation. If the trustee does not do so, the lease is deemed rejected. § 365(d)(4)(A). The 120-day period can be extended for cause only upon a motion of the trustee or lessor made during the 120-day period, and only for one additional period of 90 days; any extension after that requires the prior written consent of the lessor. § 365(d)(4)(B).

If a lease of personal property is not timely assumed, the leased property is removed from property of the estate and the automatic stay is automatically lifted § 365(p)(1).

The timing rules for assumption or rejections are visualized below:

TIMING OF DECISION TO ASSUME OR REJECT § 365(d)		
EXECUTORY CONTRACTS, LEASES OF RESIDENTIAL REAL PROPERTY AND PERSONAL PROPERTY		LEASES OF NONRESIDENTIAL REAL PROPERTY IF DEBTOR IS LESSEE § 365(d)(4)
CHAPTER 7 § 365(d)(1)	CHAPTER 11 § 365(d)(2)	EARLIER OF 120 DAYS AFTER ORDER FOR RELIEF OR DATE OF CONFIRMATION, OR DEEMED REJECTED
60 DAYS AFTER ORDER FOR RELIEF, OR DEEMED REJECTED COURT MAY GRANT ADDITIONAL TIME FOR CAUSE UPON REQUEST MADE DURING 60-DAY PERIOD	UNTIL CONFIRMATION OF PLAN UNLESS OTHERWISE ORDERED ON REQUEST OF PARTY TO CONTRACT OR LEASE	COURT MAY GRANT ADDITIONAL TIME UP TO 90 DAYS FOR CAUSE UPON REQUEST MADE DURING 120-DAY PERIOD SUBSEQUENT EXTENSIONS MAY BE GRANTED ONLY WITH PRIOR WRITTEN CONSENT OF LESSOR

4. Period Before Decision

Upon the filing of a petition in bankruptcy, an executory contract or unexpired lease is no longer immediately enforceable against the debtor or the estate — this is a natural consequence of the automatic stay under § 362. But the contract remains in existence, and can be enforced against the nondebtor party even while it is not enforceable against the debtor or the estate.

Congress has modified this imbalance in performance obligation for certain types of executory contracts and unexpired leases. Under § 365(d)(3), the trustee must timely perform all obligations of the debtor under any unexpired lease of nonresidential real property (other than under ipso facto clauses) until the lease is assumed or rejected. The court may postpone the time for performance of obligations arising with 60 days after the order for relief for cause for a period not to exceed that 60-day period.

In addition, for unexpired leases of personal property (other than leases to an individual for personal, family or household purposes) on which a chapter 11 debtor is the lessee, under § 365(d)(5), the trustee must timely perform all obligations of the debtor under the lease (other than under ipso facto clauses) first arising from and after 60 days after the order for relief until the lease is assumed or rejected unless the court orders otherwise based on the equities of the case.

These special rules requiring performance by the trustee prior to assumption or rejection are visualized below.

PERIOD PRIOR TO ASSUMPTION OR REJECTION OF EXECUTORY CONTRACT AND LEASE		
GENERAL RULE	EXCEPTIONS	
EXECUTORY CONTRACT OR LEASE IS NOT ENFORCEABLE AGAINST DEBTOR OR TRUSTEE BUT IS ENFORCEABLE AGAINST NONDEBTOR PARTY	NONRESIDENTIAL REAL PROPERTY LEASES § 365(d)(3)	COMMERCIAL PERSONAL PROPERTY LEASES § 365(d)(5)
	TRUSTEE MUST TIMELY PERFORM ALL OBLIGATIONS OF DEBTOR ARISING FROM AND AFTER ORDER FOR RELIEF COURT FOR CAUSE MAY POSTPONE TIME FOR PERFORMANCE OF OBLIGATIONS ARISING WITHIN 60 DAYS OF ORDER FOR RELIEF BUT NOT BEYOND THAT 60-DAY PERIOD	TRUSTEE IN CHAPTER 11 CASE MUST TIMELY PERFORM OBLIGATIONS OF DEBTOR FIRST ARISING FROM AND AFTER 60 DAYS AFTER ORDER FOR RELIEF COURT MAY ORDER OTHERWISE BASED ON EQUITIES OF THE CASE

E. COLLECTIVE BARGAINING AGREEMENTS AND RETIREE BENEFITS

For unionized companies, perhaps the most important executory contracts (those that are materially unperformed on both sides) are the collective bargaining agreement and related agreements providing retiree benefits, and § 365 on its face treats all executory contracts the same — the trustee has the option of assuming or rejecting.

But other federal policies come into play for labor contracts; the National Labor Relations Act sets forth detailed obligations of employers with respect to such contracts, including a prohibition on unfair labor practices.

For some years, courts tried to reconcile the policies of the bankruptcy laws with those of the labor laws. The tension between the two has led to two major Supreme Court cases, and the enactment of special provisions dealing with such contracts in chapter 11 cases. These are discussed below.

1. Collective Bargaining Agreements

Labor costs are often a precipitating factor in a chapter 11 debtor's financial difficulties. After the debtor files for bankruptcy, the trustee may seek to avoid the collective bargaining agreement as an executory contract under § 365. In the early years after the enactment of the Code, courts were divided about whether the trustee could do so. Some courts treated collective bargaining agreements just like any other executory contract, and allowed the trustee to reject them if, as a matter of its business judgment, rejection was in the best interest of the estate. Other courts permitted rejection of labor contracts, but only if a higher showing was made than the ordinary business judgment demanded of the routine executory contract (some requiring a showing that the reorganization would fail absent rejection).

In *NLRB v. Bildisco & Bildisco*, 465 U.S. 513 (1984), the Supreme Court unanimously agreed that that labor contracts are subject to rejection under § 365, but only if two additional tests not required for other executory contracts were met. First, the court must apply a balancing of the equities test — not only must the contract be burdensome to the estate, but the equities must balance in favor of rejection. Second, before approving the trustee's motion to reject, the bankruptcy court must be persuaded that the trustee has made reasonable efforts to negotiate a voluntary modification to the agreement with the affected employees, and that such negotiations are not likely to produce a prompt and satisfactory solution to the financial burdens imposed by the agreement. But the Supreme Court rejected the contention of the union that by making unilateral modifications to the collective bargaining agreement pending rejection, the trustee had committed an unfair labor practice barred by the National Labor Relations Act. The Court held that, until an executory contract is assumed, it is not enforceable against the bankrupt debtor and the trustee may modify it without breaching it.

In response to *Bildisco*, Congress enacted a new provision to the Code dealing specifically with labor agreements. Section 1113 essentially codifies the Supreme Court's decision on the first two issues. Under § 1113(a), the debtor in possession or the trustee may assume or reject a collective bargaining agreement. The court may approve a motion to reject only if the court finds that "the balance of the equities clearly favors rejection." § 1113(c)(3). In addition, the court may not authorize rejection until attempted negotiations between the trustee and the union have occurred. § 1113(c)(1) & (2).

First, after the bankruptcy filing but before seeking to reject the collective bargaining agreement, the trustee must make a proposal to the authorized representative of the employees covered by the agreement. The proposal must be based on the most complete and reliable information available, and must provide for those "necessary modifications" to the existing agreement that are "necessary to permit the reorganization of the debtor." § 1113(b)(1)(A). Although some courts interpret this language to limit the proposal to those specific modifications that are essential to the debtor's reorganization, *see Wheeling-Pittsburgh Steel Corp. v. United Steelworkers*, 791 F.2d 1074, 1088 (3d Cir. 1986), most courts conclude that the proposal may include nonessential concessions as well, and it is the duty of the employees to negotiate about those individual issues in the proposal that are not really "necessary," *see, e.g., In re Mile Hi Metal Systems, Inc.*, 899 F.2d 887, 893 (10th Cir. 1990); *Truck Drivers Local 807 v. Carey Transportation*, 816 F.2d 82, 90 (2d Cir. 1988).

In addition, the proposal must assure that "all creditors, the debtor and all of the affected parties are treated fairly and equitably." *Id*. This requirement precludes imposing a disproportionate burden on the covered employees.

The trustee must also provide the representative of the employees "with such relevant information as is necessary to evaluate the proposal." § 1113(b)(1)(B). The court may enter protective orders with respect to the information provided to the employee representative when necessary to prevent disclosure of that information to competitors. § 1113(d)(3).

As soon as the trustee has made its proposal and provided the relevant information to the employee representative, the trustee may file an application to reject the collective bargaining agreement. Between the time the trustee makes its proposal and the time a hearing is scheduled on its application to reject, the trustee must "meet, at reasonable times," with the authorized representative of the employees to negotiate in good faith to try "to reach mutually satisfactory modifications" to the agreement. § 1113(b)(2).

The time for such negotiations is limited. The court must schedule a hearing on an application for rejection not later than fourteen days after the application is filed. § 1113(d)(1). The date for the hearing may be extended for a period not exceeding seven days "where the circumstances of the case, and the interests of justice require such extension." Any further extensions require the consent of the trustee and the employee representative. *Id.*

If the parties cannot agree on modifications, § 1113(c)(2) imposes three conditions to rejection. First, the trustee must show that a qualifying proposal was made to the union under § 1113(b)(1)(A). Second, the union must have refused to accept the trustee's proposal "without good cause." If the union representatives negotiating the modifications recommend them to the union membership, and the union membership rejects them, the court is likely to find the rejection to be without good cause. The final requirement for rejection is that the balance of the equities clearly favors rejection of the agreement. § 1113(c)(3). In balancing the equities, courts consider such factors as the likelihood and consequences of liquidation if rejection is not permitted, the likely reduction in value of creditors' claims if the collective bargaining agreement remains in force, the likelihood and consequences of a strike if the bargaining agreement is voided, the possibility and likely effect of employee claims for breach of contract if rejection is approved, the cost-spreading abilities of various parties (taking into account the number of employees covered by the bargaining agreement and how various employees' wages and benefits compare to those of others in the industry), and the good or bad faith of the parties in dealing with the debtor's financial dilemma.

The court must reach a decision on the application to reject the collective bargaining agreement within 30 days after the commencement of the hearing. § 1113(d)(2). Any extensions of the 30 day period require the agreement of the trustee and the employee representative. *Id.* If the court fails to rule within that period, the debtor is allowed to "terminate or alter any provisions of the collective bargaining agreement pending the ruling of the court on such application." *Id.*

These provisions are consistent with the opinion of the Supreme Court in *Bildisco*. However, in § 1113(f) Congress prohibited the trustee from unilaterally terminating or altering any provisions of the collective bargaining agreement prior to a court-approved rejection, reversing the Supreme Court's holding on the unfair labor practices issue. In only one situation may the trustee make changes to the agreement prior to approval of its rejection. If such interim changes are "essential to the continuation of the debtor's business, or in order to avoid irreparable damage to the estate," interim changes to the "terms, conditions, wages, benefits, or work rules" provided by the contract may be made with court approval. § 1113(e). The statute does not require that an application to reject the collective bargaining agreement have been filed at the time interim changes are sought.

The provisions of § 1113 are visualized below.

REJECTION OF LABOR CONTRACTS § 1113			
LIMBO PERIOD § 1113(e) & (f)	OBLIGATIONS PRIOR TO REJECTION § 1113(b)	STANDARD FOR REJECTION § 1113(c)	TIMING OF DECISION § 1113(d)
COURT MAY AUTHORIZE INTERIM CHANGES IF ESSENTIAL TO CONTINUATION OF DEBTOR'S BUSINESS OR TO AVOID IRREPARABLE DAMAGE TO ESTATE TRUSTEE MAY NOT UNILATERALLY TERMINATE OR ALTER AGREEMENT	TRUSTEE MAKES A PROPOSAL FOR NECESSARY MODIFICATIONS NECESSARY TO PERMIT REORGANIZATION AND FAIR AND EQUITABLE TREATMENT OF ALL PARTIES TRUSTEE PROVIDES EMPLOYEE REPRESENTATIVE WITH RELEVANT INFORMATION TRUSTEE MEETS WITH EMPLOYEE REPRESENTATIVE AT REASONABLE TIMES TO NEGOTIATE IN GOOD FAITH OVER MODIFICATIONS	TRUSTEE HAS MADE PROPOSAL, PROPOSAL REJECTED BY EMPLOYEES WITHOUT GOOD CAUSE, AND BALANCE OF EQUITIES FAVOR REJECTION	HEARING WITHIN 14 DAYS AFTER APPLICATION FOR REJECTION FILED, SUBJECT TO EXTENSION BY NOT MORE THAN 7 DAYS WHERE CIRCUMSTANCES OF CASE AND INTERESTS OF JUSTICE REQUIRES, OR MORE THAN 7 DAYS WITH AGREEMENT OF PARTIES DECISION WITHIN 30 DAYS AFTER HEARING COMMENCED, SUBJECT TO EXTENSION WITH AGREEMENT OF PARTIES

2. Retiree Benefits

LTV Steel filed for bankruptcy in 1986 in order to restructure its pension obligations under three defined benefit plans, two of which were established for union employees under collective bargaining agreements, and one of which was for nonunion salaried employees; all the plans were underfunded to the extent of $2.3 billion in the aggregate. The Pension Benefit Guaranty Corporation, which guaranteed $2.1 billion of this underfunding, terminated the plans to avoid incremental liabilities, triggering the guaranteed benefits. In response to litigation over the termination, the union and the company then negotiated an agreement to protect the workers by using the payments guaranteed by the PBGC as a base, and then topping up those payments to reach 75% of the prior levels for some benefits, and 100% of the prior levels for others, including retirees (thus substituting the PBGC for LTV to the extent of its guaranteed minimum payments). The PBGC objected to this agreement, calling it an impermissible "follow-on plan," and after considering the improved economic situation in the steel industry in general and LTV in particular, responded by restoring the terminated plans, thereby eliminating its guaranteed payments. LTV refused to comply with the restoration order, and the PBGC sued to enforce it in district court. After the PBGC lost in the lower courts, the Supreme Court held in *Pension Benefit Guaranty Corporation v. LTV Corp.*, 496 U.S. 633 (1990), that the PBGC did not act improperly in restoring the terminated plans.

Congress responded with the enactment of § 1114, which is modeled closely after § 1113 and is intended to protect certain employee benefits when a company files for bankruptcy under chapter 11. The statute applies to modifications of "retiree benefits," which are defined to mean payments to retired employees and their spouses and dependents for "medical, surgical, or hospital care benefits, or benefits in the event of sickness, accident, disability, or death" under an employer-maintained plan or program. A retiree (or the spouse or dependent of a retiree) may not claim the protection of § 1114 if the retiree's gross income for the twelve months preceding the bankruptcy filing was not less than $250,000, unless the retiree can demonstrate that the retiree is unable to obtain coverage comparable to the coverage provided by the employer immediately prior to the bankruptcy filing. § 1114(m).

As was true for collective bargaining agreements under § 1113(f), the trustee is required to timely pay, and is barred from unilaterally (without the consent of the authorized representative for the recipients) modifying, retiree benefits. § 1114(e)(1). Retiree benefits payable during the bankruptcy case are afforded administrative expense priority, § 1114(e)(2), without limitation under § 502(b)(7), § 1114(j), and may not be offset against an employee's claim for unpaid benefits, § 1114(i). If modifications to retiree benefits are "essential to the continuation of the debtor's business, or in order to avoid irreparable damage to the estate," the court may authorize the trustee to implement interim modifications in retiree benefits before the court authorizes permanent modifications. § 1114(h)(1).

If the trustee wishes to modify retiree benefits on a permanent basis, after the bankruptcy filing and before filing an application with the court for approval of such modifications, the trustee must make a proposal to the authorized representative for retirees, and must provide such representative with "such relevant information as is necessary to evaluate the proposal." § 1114(f)(1). The court may enter protective orders with respect to any information provided to the retiree representative necessary to prevent disclosure to competitors. § 1114(k)(3). For purposes of this provision, the "authorized representative" of the retirees is a labor organization (*i.e.*, union) if the retiree benefits are covered by a collective bargaining agreement unless the labor organization elects not to serve in that role or a party in interest brings a motion for different representation and the court determines that someone else should serve. § 1114(c)(1). If a labor organization is not serving as authorized representative, the court, upon motion by any party in interest, must appoint or order the appointment of a committee of retired employees to serve as the authorized representative. § 1114(c)(2) and § 1114(d).

The proposal must be based on the most complete and reliable information available, and provide for those "necessary modifications" that are "necessary to permit the reorganization" and that treat all affected parties "fairly and equitably." § 1114(f)(1)(A). As soon as the trustee makes its proposal, it may file an application to modify the retiree benefits.

Between the date it makes its proposal and the date of the hearing on its application to modify retiree benefits, the trustee must meet with the authorized representative, at reasonable times, to negotiate in good faith with the aim of agreeing on mutually satisfactory modifications to the retiree benefits. § 1114(f)(2).

The court must schedule a hearing on the application to modify retiree benefits within fourteen days after the application is filed (subject to extension for up to seven additional days where the circumstances of the case and the interests of justice require the extension, or longer if the parties agree). § 1114(k)(1). After the hearing, the court must rule on the application within 90 days after the date of the commencement of the hearing or such additional time to which the parties agree; if no ruling is made within that time, the trustee may act unilaterally to modify benefits pending the court's ruling. § 1114(k)(2).

The court may approve the application to modify retiree benefits if three conditions are met. First, the trustee must have made a proposal that complies with the requirements of § 1114(f)(1). Second, the authorized representative of the retirees must have refused to accept that proposal "without good cause." Third, the modifications sought must be "necessary to permit the reorganization of the debtor" and assure that "all creditors, the debtor, and all of the affected parties are treated fairly and equitably" and must be "clearly favored by the balance of the equities." § 1114(g). The court may not authorize any modification to a level lower than that proposed by the trustee to the authorized representative of the retirees, although subsequent applications to modify retiree benefits are permitted. *Id.*

If the debtor made any modification to retiree benefits during the 180-day period prior to the bankruptcy filing at a time when the debtor was insolvent, the court, on motion of a party in interest, must issue an order undoing any such modification and reinstating the pre-existing benefits unless the court "finds that the balance of equities clearly favors such modification." § 1114(l).

A visualization of the provisions of § 1114 protecting retiree benefits from modification follows.

MODIFICATION OF RETIREE BENEFITS
§ 1114

RETIREE BENEFITS § 1114(a)	LIMBO PERIOD § 1114(e) & (h)	PREFILING MODIFICATIONS § 1114(l)	OBLIGATIONS PRIOR TO MODIFICATION § 1114(f)	STANDARD FOR MODIFICATION § 1114(g)	TIMING OF DECISION § 1114(k)
"RETIREE BENEFITS" MEANS PAYMENTS TO RETIRED EMPLOYEES AND THEIR SPOUSES AND DEPENDENTS FOR MEDICAL, SURGICAL, OR HOSPITAL CARE BENEFITS OR BENEFITS FOR SICKNESS, ACCIDENT, DISABILITY, OR DEATH UNDER ANY EMPLOYER-SPONSORED PLAN OR PROGRAM	TRUSTEE MUST TIMELY PAY AND MAY NOT UNILATERALLY MODIFY ANY RETIREE BENEFITS COURT MAY AUTHORIZE INTERIM CHANGES IF ESSENTIAL TO CONTINUATION OF DEBTOR'S BUSINESS OR TO AVOID IRREPARABLE DAMAGE TO ESTATE	IF DEBTOR MADE MODIFICATION TO RETIREE BENEFITS WITHIN 180 DAYS PRIOR TO BANKRUPTCY FILING WHILE INSOLVENT, COURT, ON MOTION OF PARTY IN INTEREST, MUST ISSUE AN ORDER REINSTATING PRIOR BENEFITS UNLESS COURT FINDS BALANCE OF EQUITIES CLEARLY FAVORS MODIFICATION	1) TRUSTEE MAKES A PROPOSAL FOR NECESSARY MODIFICATIONS NECESSARY TO PERMIT REORGANIZATION AND FAIR AND EQUITABLE TREATMENT OF ALL PARTIES 2) TRUSTEE PROVIDES RETIREE REPRESENTATIVE WITH RELEVANT INFORMATION 3) TRUSTEE MEETS WITH RETIREE REPRESENTATIVE TO NEGOTIATE IN GOOD FAITH OVER MODIFICATIONS	1) TRUSTEE HAS MADE PROPOSAL, 2) PROPOSAL REJECTED BY AUTHORIZED REPRESENTATIVE OF RETIREES WITHOUT GOOD CAUSE, AND 3) MODIFICATION IS NECESSARY TO PERMIT REORGANIZATION, ASSURES ALL PARTIES ARE TREATED FAIRLY AND EQUITABLY, AND IS CLEARLY FAVORED BY BALANCE OF EQUITIES	HEARING WITHIN 14 DAYS AFTER APPLICATION FOR MODIFICATION FILED, SUBJECT TO EXTENSION BY NOT MORE THAN 7 DAYS WHERE CIRCUMSTANCES OF CASE AND INTERESTS OF JUSTICE REQUIRES, OR MORE THAN 7 DAYS WITH AGREEMENT OF PARTIES DECISION WITHIN 30 DAYS AFTER HEARING COMMENCED, SUBJECT TO EXTENSION WITH AGREEMENT OF PARTIES

F. UTILITY SERVICE

Under § 366, when a debtor files for bankruptcy protection, a utility is precluded from taking certain actions against a trustee or debtor solely on the basis of the commencement of a bankruptcy case or on the basis that the debtor has not paid when due a prepetition debt to the utility. The utility is barred from altering, refusing, or discontinuing service to the trustee or debtor, and from discriminating against the trustee or debtor. § 366(a).

However, the restrictions on the utility terminate unless the utility receives, within 20 days after the date of the order for relief, "adequate assurance of payment, in the form of a deposit or other security," for service after that date. § 366(b). Although the court does not specify the terms of the adequate assurance to be provided by the debtor or trustee, if a party in interest so requests, the court may order reasonable modification of the amount of the deposit or other security required by § 366(b).

In a chapter 11 case, the permissible forms of adequate assurance are specified. They include a cash deposit, letter of credit, certificate of deposit, surety bond, prepayment or another form of security the utility and the debtor or trustee find mutually agreeable. § 366(c)(1)(A). An administrative expense priority does not constitute adequate assurance. § 366(c)(1)(B). A utility may alter, refuse, or discontinue utility service to a chapter 11 debtor or trustee if, during the 30-day period following the filing date, the utility does not receive adequate assurance of payment for utility service "that is satisfactory to the utility." § 366(c)(2). The court may, on request of a party in interest, order modification of the amount of the assurance of payment, but in doing so, the court is barred from considering the absence of security before the filing date, debtor's payment of utility charges in a timely manner before the filing date, or the availability of an administrative expense priority. § 366(c)(3).

Utilities are expressly authorized to set off amounts owed by a chapter 11 debtor against a prepetition security deposit provided by the debtor "without notice or order of the court." § 366(c)(4).

A visualization of the § 366 provisions relating to utility service follows.

**UTILITY SERVICE
§ 366**

	ALL CASES			CHAPTER 11 CASES		
	LIMITS ON UTILITY ACTION	ADEQUATE ASSURANCE EXCEPTION	MODIFICATION BY COURT	LIMITS ON UTILITY ACTION	ADEQUATE ASSURANCE EXCEPTION	MODIFICATION BY COURT
	UTILITY MAY NOT ALTER, REFUSE, OR DISCONTINUE SERVICE TO, OR DISCRIMINATE AGAINST, TRUSTEE OR DEBTOR SOLELY ON BASIS OF CASE OR NONPAYMENT OF PREPETITION DEBT FOR UTILITY SERVICES	BAR ON UTILITY ACTION IS LIFTED UNLESS TRUSTEE OR DEBTOR FURNISHES, WITHIN 20 DAYS AFTER ORDER FOR RELIEF, ADEQUATE ASSURANCE OF PAYMENT, IN THE FORM OF A DEPOSIT OR OTHER SECURITY, FOR SERVICES AFTER THAT DATE	ON REQUEST OF PARTY IN INTEREST, COURT MAY ORDER REASONABLE MODIFICATION OF AMOUNT OF DEPOSIT OR OTHER SECURITY NECESSARY TO PROVIDE ADEQUATE ASSURANCE OF PAYMENT	UTILITY MAY NOT ALTER, REFUSE, OR DISCONTINUE SERVICE TO, OR DISCRIMINATE AGAINST, TRUSTEE OR DEBTOR SOLELY ON BASIS OF CASE OR NONPAYMENT OF PREPETITION DEBT FOR UTILITY SERVICES	BAR ON UTILITY ACTION IS LIFTED UNLESS TRUSTEE OR DEBTOR FURNISHES, WITHIN 30 DAYS AFTER FILING, ADEQUATE ASSURANCE OF PAYMENT THAT IS SATISFACTORY TO THE UTILITY IN THE FORM OF: 1) CASH DEPOSIT, 2) LETTER OF CREDIT, 3) CERTIFICATE OF DEPOSIT, 4) SURETY BOND, 5) PREPAYMENT OF USAGE, OR 6) ANOTHER MUTUALLY AGREEABLE FORM OF SECURITY	ON REQUEST OF PARTY IN INTEREST, COURT MAY ORDER MODIFICATION OF AMOUNT OF ASSURANCE OR PAYMENT, BUT MAY NOT CONSIDER 1) ABSENCE OF SECURITY BEFORE FILING DATE, 2) TIMELY PAYMENT BY DEBTOR BEFORE FILING DATE, OR 3) AVAILABILITY OF ADMINISTRATIVE EXPENSE PRIORITY

Chapter 7

TREATMENT OF CLAIMS IN CHAPTER 7

A. PRIORITY IN DISTRIBUTION

The filing of a proof of claim is primarily important in order to enable the creditor to share in the distribution of estate assets. In chapter 7, the trustee is directed to "collect and reduce to money the property of the estate" under § 704. The trustee must also dispose of any property "in which an entity other than the estate has an interest" that has not otherwise been disposed of (as by sale under § 363, abandonment under § 554, or foreclosure after obtaining relief from the stay under § 362) before final distribution of the estate. § 725. This would include property in which a creditor has a lien or security interest, or property that is co-owned with a non-debtor. This provision allows secured creditors to be paid in full the allowed amount of their secured claims before unsecured creditors receive any distribution.

The order in which remaining estate assets are distributed is specified in § 726. Only if a higher priority claim is satisfied in full can a distribution be made to a lower priority. Payment of claims within the same priority level is made pro rata among claims of that kind. There is only one exception to that general principle. If a case is converted to chapter 7 from chapter 11, 12 or 13, administrative expenses incurred in the converted chapter 7 case have priority over administrative expenses incurred prior to the conversion. § 726(b). This super-priority provision is necessary to ensure that there are adequate resources to permit final liquidation and distribution of the debtor's assets.

Assets are distributed first to satisfy priority claims and expenses specified in § 507, in the order provided in that section. *See* Chapter 4[A][2], *supra*. To share in this distribution, the party to whom the claim or expense is owing must file a proof of that claim or expense on or before the earlier of the date that is 10 days after the trustee mails a final report to creditors, or the date on which the trustee commences the final distribution of estate assets. § 726(a)(1).

After priority claims and expenses are satisfied in full, distributions may be made to allowed unsecured claims (other than claims explicitly given a different priority under § 726) proof of which was filed on a timely basis, or tardily filed if the creditor did not have notice or actual knowledge of the case in time to file timely and if proof of claim is filed in time to permit its payment. § 726(a)(2).

If all unsecured claims meeting those requirements are paid in full, distributions may next be made to other allowed unsecured claims for which proofs of claim were tardily filed. § 726(a)(3).

The fourth distribution goes to allowed claims (secured or unsecured) for a fine, penalty, or forfeiture, or for punitive damages, to the extent those punitive penalties are not compensation for actual pecuniary loss suffered by the holder (which are treated under § 726(a)(2)). § 726(a)(4). This provision subordinates non-compensatory penalties to other unsecured claims, allowing them to receive distributions only to the extent that the estate has excess funds after paying all other obligations of the debtor. The trustee may avoid any lien securing such a claim under § 724(a).

If there are still assets in the estate after these distributions, prepetition claims are entitled to receive postpetition interest at the legal rate before any property is returned to the debtor. § 726(a)(5). Any property remaining after these payments goes to the debtor. § 726(a)(6).

There is a special distribution section relating to community property. § 726(c).

A visualization of the distribution scheme for a chapter 7 case follows:

DISTRIBUTION OF ESTATE § 725 & § 726
1) ESTATE PROPERTY IN WHICH ENTITY OTHER THAN ESTATE HAS AN INTEREST § 725
2) PRIORITY CLAIMS (§ 507)
3) NONPRIORITY UNSECURED CLAIMS FOR WHICH TIMELY PROOF OF CLAIM WAS FILED, OR UNTIMELY PROOF OF CLAIM FILED IF • CREDITOR DID NOT HAVE NOTICE OR KNOWLEDGE OF CASE IN TIME TO MAKE TIMELY FILING, AND • PROOF OF CLAIM IS FILED IN TIME TO PERMIT PAYMENT
4) OTHER NONPRIORITY UNSECURED CLAIMS FOR WHICH UNTIMELY PROOF OF CLAIM WAS FILED
5) ALLOWED SECURED AND UNSECURED CLAIMS FOR FINE, PENALTY, FORFEITURE OR PUNITIVE DAMAGES TO THE EXTENT NOT COMPENSATION FOR ACTUAL PECUNIARY LOSS SUFFERED BY HOLDER
6) INTEREST ON PRIORITY AND NONPRIORITY UNSECURED CLAIMS
7) DEBTOR RECEIVES REMAINING PROPERTY

B. REDEMPTION

The distribution scheme of chapter 7 assumes that any property constituting collateral for a secured claim must be distributed to the creditor (if the collateral has no value in excess of the secured claim) or sold (if the value of the collateral exceeds the secured claim) so that the creditor can receive the value of its interest in the collateral. If the debtor wishes to retain the property in which a secured creditor has an interest, § 722 provides the debtor a right to redeem the collateral from the secured creditor under certain circumstances.

Redemption is available only to individual debtors. The only type of collateral subject to redemption is tangible personal property (which would exclude real property, and intangible personal property, like copyrights or accounts). Only a limited category of tangible personal property is eligible for redemption; the property must be intended primarily for personal, family or household use, often called "consumer goods." The debt secured by these consumer goods must be a dischargeable consumer debt. Finally, the consumer goods must be claimed as exempt under § 522, or abandoned by the trustee under § 554.

To redeem the property, the debtor must pay the secured creditor the amount of the allowed secured claim that is secured by the property in full at the time of redemption. The allowed secured claim may be less than the full amount of the debt owing to the creditor because of the provisions of § 506(a). The creditor need not consent to the redemption; the debtor has an absolute right to redeem qualifying property by making the specified payment.

If redemption is unavailable to the debtor (either because the legal requirements are not satisfied or the debtor cannot obtain the funds necessary to make the required payment), the only way the debtor can retain collateral that would otherwise be surrendered or sold is by reaffirmation, discussed in Chapter 10[B][3]).

A visualization of the provisions relating to redemption follows:

REDEMPTION § 722				
WHO	TYPE OF COLLATERAL	TYPE OF SECURED DEBT	STATUS OF COLLATERAL	PAYMENT TO REDEEM
INDIVIDUAL DEBTOR	TANGIBLE PERSONAL PROPERTY INTENDED FOR PERSONAL, FAMILY OR HOUSEHOLD USE	DISCHARGEABLE CONSUMER DEBT	EXEMPT UNDER § 522 OR ABANDONED UNDER § 554	AMOUNT OF ALLOWED SECURED CLAIM IN FULL AT TIME OF REDEMPTION

Chapter 8

TREATMENT OF CLAIMS IN CHAPTER 13

A. FILING OF THE PLAN

Concurrently with the filing of the bankruptcy petition, and in any event within 14 days thereafter (unless the court grants an extension for cause), Fed. R. Bankr. P. 3015(b), the chapter 13 debtor must file a plan that specifies how the debtor intends to satisfy claims. Only the chapter 13 debtor may file a plan in a chapter 13 case. § 1321.

B. CONTENTS OF THE PLAN

A chapter 13 plan must satisfy three requirements under § 1322(a). First, it must provide for the submission to the supervision of the trustee of whatever portion of the debtor's future earnings or other future income is necessary to carry out the plan. § 1322(a)(1). Second, the plan must provide for full payment, in deferred cash payments, of all priority claims under § 507. § 1322(a)(2). There are two exceptions to this requirement. One, the holder of a priority claim may agree to other treatment. § 1322(a)(2). Two, a plan may provide for less than full payment of priority claims consisting of domestic support obligations that that have been assigned to or are owed to a government unit, but only if the plan dedicates all the debtor's projected disposable income for a five-year period to make payments under the plan. § 1322(a)(4). The concept of "projected disposable income" will be discussed in Section 8[D], *infra*. The third requirement for the chapter 13 plan is that, if the plan classifies claims, the plan must treat each claim within a particular class the same. § 1322(a)(3). Classification of claims is discussed in Chapter 9[B], *infra*.

The mandatory provisions of a chapter 13 plan are visualized below.

REQUIRED PROVISIONS FOR CHAPTER 13 PLAN § 1322(a)	
MANDATORY PROVISIONS	EXCEPTIONS
PLAN MUST PROVIDE FOR SUBMISSION TO SUPERVISION AND CONTROL OF TRUSTEE OF DEBTOR'S FUTURE EARNINGS OR INCOME NECESSARY FOR EXECUTION OF PLAN	NONE
PLAN MUST PROVIDE FOR FULL PAYMENT IN DEFERRED CASH PAYMENTS OF ALL § 507 PRIORITY CLAIMS	1) HOLDER OF CLAIM AGREES TO DIFFERENT TREATMENT, OR 2) PLAN MAY PROVIDE FOR LESS THAN FULL PAYMENT OF DOMESTIC SUPPORT OBLIGATION OWING TO GOVERNMENTAL UNIT IF PLAN DEDICATES ALL DEBTOR'S PROJECTED DISPOSABLE INCOME FOR 5 YEARS TO MAKE PAYMENTS UNDER PLAN
IF PLAN CLASSIFIES CLAIMS, PLAN MUST PROVIDE SAME TREATMENT TO ALL CLAIMS IN CLASS	NONE

With the exception of these mandatory provisions, the chapter 13 plan may incorporate various permissive provisions described in § 1322(b), some of which have limitations or exceptions.

First, the plan may create a class or classes of unsecured claims. § 1322(b)(1). As discussed above, classification of claims in a chapter 13 plan is not mandatory, but if claims are classified, all claims within a class must be treated the same. § 1322(a)(3). In addition, if the debtor chooses to designate classes of claims, the debtor may not "discriminate unfairly against any class so designated," but may treat claims for a consumer debt on which an individual is a codebtor differently from other unsecured claims. § 1322(b)(1). The only reason for the debtor to designate classes of claims is to enable the debtor to afford different treatment to different classes. However, different treatment is not necessarily unfair discrimination. In determining whether unfair discrimination exists, courts look at such factors as whether the disparate treatment has a reasonable basis, whether it is necessary to enable the debtor to complete the plan, whether it is proposed in good faith, and whether the extent of the different treatment is directly related to the rationale for it.

Second, the plan may modify the rights of secured or unsecured creditors, or leave their rights unaffected. § 1322(b)(2). Modifications could include changes to the principal amount, interest rate, term, or (for secured claims) collateral for the debt.

The provision permitting such modifications is subject to both two exceptions and a limitation.

The plan may not modify a claim secured only by a security interest in real property that is the debtor's principal residence, often called the "home mortgage exception." § 1322(b)(2). However, if the last payment on the debt secured by the debtor's principal residence is due before the date on which the final payment is due under the plan, the prohibition on modification does not apply. § 1322(c)(2). The holder's rights may not be modified if any portion of its claim is so secured. *Nobelman v. American Savings Bank*, 508 U.S. 324 (1993). But most courts conclude that this provision is inapplicable to a debt for which the creditor has a junior mortgage on the debtor's principal residence if the value of the residence is insufficient to satisfy the senior mortgage in full so that the debt is not "secured" within the meaning of § 506(a)(1). *See, e.g., In re Zimmer*, 313 F.3d 1220 (9th Cir. 2002); *In re Lane*, 280 F.3d 663 (6th Cir. 2002); *In re Pond*, 252 F.3d 122 (2d Cir. 2001); *In re Dickerson*, 222 F.3d 924 (11th Cir. 2000); *In re Bartee*, 212 F.3d 277 (5th Cir. 2000); *In re McDonald*, 205 F.3d 606 (3d Cir. 2000). The plan may also not "materially alter" the terms of a loan from certain pension and thrift savings plans described in § 362(b)(19). § 1322(f). The extent to which a chapter 13 plan may modify claims is limited by the confirmation requirements for chapter 13 plans, which are discussed in Section 8[D], *infra*.

Third, the plan may provide for the curing or waiving of any default. § 1322(b)(3). If the debtor has failed to make a payment, this provision allows the plan to provide for that default to be cured by a payment under the plan. The cure amount is determined in accordance with the underlying agreement and nonbankruptcy law pursuant to § 1322(e), and may include postpetition interest if the agreement so provides. If the creditor has accelerated the debt on the basis of the default, the debtor may "de-accelerate" the debt, returning the parties to their respective positions prior to the default. If the debt is secured solely by the debtor's principal residence, the plan may provide for the curing of any default with respect to such a debt only until the residence securing the debt is sold at a regularly-conducted foreclosure sale. § 1322(c)(1).

Fourth, the plan may provide for payments on any unsecured claim to be made at the same time as payments on any secured claim or any other unsecured claim. § 1322(b)(4). There is no requirement in a chapter 13 that secured creditors be paid before unsecured creditors, or that priority claims be paid before general unsecured claims.

Fifth, the plan may provide for any default to be cured "within a reasonable time" and for "maintenance of payments while the case is pending" on any secured or unsecured claim if the last payment on such claim is due after the due date for the final plan payment. § 1322(b)(5). As was true under § 1322(b)(3), the cure of a default may include "de-accelerating" debt as to which the creditor took action on the basis of the default. "Maintenance of payments" means meeting the current obligations on the debt as they come due, essentially reinstating the pre-default payment schedule. The right to "cure and maintain" is applicable only to long-term secured or unsecured debt, that is debt with respect to which the final payment is due after the plan is scheduled to be completed. This would include most home mortgage debt the modification of which is precluded by § 1322(b)(2).

Sixth, the plan may provide for the payment of all or any part of claims for taxes that become payable to a governmental until while the case is pending, or claims for consumer debts arising after the order for relief for property or services necessary for the debtor's performance under the plan. § 1322(b)(6). These postpetition claims may be allowed under § 1305 to the same extent as if they had arisen prepetition.

Seventh, the plan may provide for the assumption, rejection, or assignment of any executory contract or unexpired lease not previously rejected consistent with the requirements of § 365. § 1322(b)(7). *See* Chapter 6[D], *supra*.

Eighth, the plan may provide for payment of a claim from property of the estate or property of the debtor. § 1322(b)(8). Property of the debtor includes property that would be exempt under § 522.

Ninth, the plan may vest property of the estate in the debtor or in any other entity upon confirmation or the plan or at any later time. § 1322(b)(9). Unless the plan provides otherwise, confirmation of a chapter 13 plan vests all property of the estate in the debtor, free and clear of any claim or interest of any creditor provided for by the plan. § 1327(b) & (c).

Tenth, the plan may provide for payment of postpetition interest on unsecured claims that are nondischargeable under § 1328(a) to the extent debtor has disposable income available to pay such interest after all allowed claims are paid in full. § 1322(b)(10).

A chapter 13 plan may also include any other provision that is not inconsistent with the requirements of the Code. § 1322(b)(11).

A visualization of the permitted provisions of a chapter 13 plan follows:

PERMITTED PROVISIONS IN CHAPTER 13 PLAN § 1322(b)		
§ 1322(b)(1)	DESIGNATE CLASSES OF UNSECURED CLAIMS	MAY NOT DISCRIMINATE AGAINST ANY DESIGNED CLASS, BUT MAY TREAT CLAIMS FOR CONSUMER DEBT ON WHICH INDIVIDUAL IS CODEBTOR DIFFERENTLY FROM OTHER UNSECURED CLAIMS
§ 1322(b)(2)	MODIFY RIGHTS OF HOLDERS OF SECURED OR UNSECURED CLAIMS	MAY NOT MODIFY RIGHTS OF SECURED CREDITOR SECURED ONLY BY DEBTOR'S PRINCIPAL RESIDENCE, § 1322(b)(2), OTHER THAN DEBT FOR WHICH LAST PAYMENT IS DUE BEFORE LAST PAYMENT UNDER PLAN (§ 1322(c)(2)) MAY NOT MATERIALLY ALTER TERMS OF LOAN FROM PENSION OR THRIFT SAVING PLAN UNDER § 362(b)(19) (§ 1322(f))
§ 1322(b)(3)	CURE OR WAIVE DEFAULTS	
§ 1322(b)(4)	PAYMENTS ON ANY UNSECURED CLAIM MADE CONCURRENTLY WITH PAYMENTS ON ANY OTHER UNSECURED OR SECURED CLAIM	
§ 1322(b)(5)	CURE OF DEFAULTS AND MAINTENANCE OF PAYMENTS ON DEBT FOR WHICH LAST PAYMENT IS DUE AFTER LAST PAYMENT UNDER PLAN	
§ 1322(b)(6)	PAYMENT OF ALL OR PART OF POSTPETITION CLAIMS UNDER § 1305	
§ 1322(b)(7)	ASSUME, REJECT OR ASSIGN EXECUTORY CONTRACTS OR UNEXPIRED LEASES UNDER § 365	
§ 1322(b)(8)	PAYMENT OF CLAIMS FROM PROPERTY OF ESTATE OR PROPERTY OF DEBTOR	
§ 1322(b)(9)	VESTING OF PROPERTY IN DEBTOR OR ANY OTHER ENTITY UPON CONFIRMATION OF PLAN	
§ 1322(b)(10)	PAYMENT OF POSTPETITION INTEREST ON NONDISCHARGEABLE CLAIMS TO EXTENT OF DISPOSABLE INCOME REMAINING AFTER PAYMENT OF ALLOWED CLAIMS IN FULL	
§ 1322(b)(11)	ANY OTHER APPROPRIATE PROVISION NOT INCONSISTENT WITH CODE	

Section 1322(d) limits the duration of a chapter 13 plan. The permissible duration depends on whether the "current monthly income" of the debtor and the debtor's spouse combined, multiplied by 12, is less than the highest median family income of the applicable state for a household having the same number of family members. "Current monthly income" is discussed in Chapter 1[D], *supra*. If the debtor is such a below-median debtor, the chapter 13 plan may not provide for payments over a period longer than three years, "unless the court, for cause, approves a longer period" not to exceed five years. § 1322(d)(2). A longer period might be necessary, for example, to enable the debtor to meet the requirements for confirmation of the plan, as by paying priority claims in full and curing arrearages on debt. If the debtor is not a below-median debtor, the chapter 13 plan may not provide for payments over a period longer than five years. § 1322(d)(1). The permissible length of a chapter 13 plan is visualized below:

LIMITATIONS ON LENGTH OF CHAPTER 13 PLAN § 1322(d)			
BELOW-MEDIAN DEBTOR		NOT BELOW-MEDIAN DEBTOR	
WHEN APPLICABLE	DURATION OF PLAN	WHEN APPLICABLE	DURATION OF PLAN
CURRENT MONTHLY INCOME (§ 101(10A)) OF DEBTOR AND DEBTOR'S SPOUSE COMBINED, MULTIPLIED BY 12, IS LESS THAN HIGHEST MEDIAN FAMILY INCOME OF APPLICABLE STATE FOR HOUSEHOLD OF SAME SIZE	NOT LONGER THAN 3 YEARS UNLESS COURT, FOR CAUSE, APPROVES LONGER PERIOD NOT IN EXCESS OF 5 YEARS	CURRENT MONTHLY INCOME (§ 101(10A)) OF DEBTOR AND DEBTOR'S SPOUSE COMBINED, MULTIPLIED BY 12, IS NOT LESS THAN HIGHEST MEDIAN FAMILY INCOME OF APPLICABLE STATE FOR HOUSEHOLD OF SAME SIZE	NOT LONGER THAN 5 YEARS

C. PRECONFIRMATION MODIFICATION OF THE PLAN

The debtor may need to modify the plan originally filed because it becomes apparent that the original plan cannot be confirmed, or because the debtor's circumstances have changed since the plan was filed. Before confirmation, the debtor has an absolute right to modify the plan (so long as the modified plan still complies with § 1322). § 1323(a). After the debtor files the modification, the plan as modified becomes the "plan" for all purposes of future proceedings in the case without the need for any approval by the court or creditors. However, any secured creditor that previously accepted or rejected the plan may change its prior acceptance or rejection if its rights under the modified plan have changed from under the original plan. § 1323(b) & (c).

A visualization of the provisions relating to preconfirmation modification of a chapter 13 plan follows.

PRECONFIRMATION MODIFICATION OF CHAPTER 13 PLAN § 1323			
WHO	WHEN	LIMITS	RESULTS
DEBTOR	AT ANY TIME BEFORE CONFIRMED	MODIFIED PLAN MUST MEET REQUIREMENTS OF § 1322	MODIFIED PLAN BECOMES THE CHAPTER 13 PLAN HOLDERS OF SECURED CLAIMS WHO ACCEPTED OR REJECTED UNMODIFIED PLAN ARE DEEMED TO HAVE ACCEPTED OR REJECTED MODIFIED PLAN UNLESS THEIR RIGHTS WERE CHANGED AND THEY CHANGE THEIR ACCEPTANCE OR REJECTION

D.   CONFIRMATION OF THE PLAN

The court must hold a hearing on confirmation of the chapter 13 plan not earlier than 20 days or later than 45 days after the § 341(a) meeting of creditors. The court may hold the confirmation hearing earlier than that period if it determines that would be in the best interests of the creditors and there is no objection. § 1324(b). Some courts combine the § 341 meeting and the confirmation hearing. An objection to confirmation must be filed and served before the confirmation hearing under Fed. R. Bankr. P. 3015(f). Local bankruptcy rules may require that an objection be filed and served several days before the hearing.

When neither the trustee nor the holder of an allowed unsecured claim objects to the chapter 13 plan, there are nine conditions to confirmation. § 1325(a). The first is that the plan complies with all provisions of chapter 13 and other applicable provisions of the Code. § 1325(a)(1). This provision allows enforcement of the requirements of § 1322 with respect to the content of the chapter 13 plan.

Second, all filing fees in connection with the case under 28 U.S.C. § 1930, and all fees required by the plan to be paid prior to confirmation, must be paid. § 1325(a)(2).

Third, the plan must be proposed in good faith and not by any means forbidden by law. § 1325(a)(3). In determining whether the plan was proposed in good faith, most courts apply a "totality of the circumstances" test. Under this test, the court may considers such factors as "(1) the debtor's income; (2) the debtor's living expenses; (3) the debtor's attorney's fees; (4) the expected duration of the Chapter 13 plan; (5) the sincerity with which the debtor has petitioned for relief under Chapter 13; (6) the debtor's potential for future earning; (7) any special circumstances, such as unusually high medical expenses; (8) the frequency with which the debtor has sought relief before in bankruptcy; (9) the circumstances under which the debt was incurred; (10) the amount of payment offered by debtor as indicative of the debtor's sincerity to repay the debt; (11) the burden which administration would place on the trustee; (12)

the statutorily-mandated policy that bankruptcy provisions be construed liberally in favor of the debtor." *In re Alt*, 305 F.3d 413, 419 (6th Cir. 2002).

Under § 1325(a)(4) a chapter 13 plan must provide property to each holder of an unsecured claim having a "value, as of the effective date of the plan," of not less than the amount that would be paid on such claim if the debtor's estate were liquidated under chapter 7 on that date. This requirement, familiarly known as the "best interest of the creditors" or "best interests" test, provides a statutory floor on distributions to unsecured creditors after giving effect to any modifications made to their rights under § 1322(b)(2). The floor is pretty low — most chapter 7 bankruptcies are "no asset" cases; unsecured creditors receive nothing after payment of priority claims, satisfaction of secured claims, and removal of exempt property by the debtor. Therefore, the best interests test in chapter 13 may be met easily in most cases.

The phrase "as of the effective date of the plan" means that any value to be received by unsecured creditors after the effective date of the plan must be discounted to present value when it is compared with the single lump-sum amount that would be paid in a chapter 7 liquidation. In other words, interest must be paid on the deferred payments to compensate the creditors for the lost value of money received in the future rather than on the effective date of the plan. Courts differ on the appropriate interest rate to use for this computation. *Compare In re Hoskins*, 405 B.R. 576 (Bankr. N.D. W. Va. 2009) (using rate of interest used under § 1325(a)(5), *see* discussion below), *with In re Smith*, 431 B.R. 607 (Bankr. E.D.N.C. 2010) (using federal judgment rate of interest).

In order to get a chapter 13 plan confirmed under § 1325, the plan must deal with secured debt in one of three specified ways under § 1325(a)(5). First, the holder of the secured claim must have accepted the plan (*i.e.*, agreed with the debtor's proposed means of satisfying the claim). § 1325(a)(5)(A). Second, the debtor can surrender the collateral to the holder of the secured claim. § 1325(a)(5)(C).

The third method, and the one most frequently employed, allows the secured creditor to retain its lien until the underlying debt is paid in full or discharged, and receive property under the plan with value, as of the effective date of the plan, of not less than the allowed amount of the secured claim. § 1325(a)(5)(B). If the debtor distributes property to the secured creditor in the form of periodic payments, those payments must be in equal monthly amounts. § 1325(a)(5)(B)(iii)(I). If the collateral consists of personal property, the payments made to the secured creditor must not be less than the amount necessary to provide the creditor adequate protection for the duration of the plan. § 1325(a)(5)(B)(iii)(II).

There are two concepts in this requirement that require further examination. First, the value of property to which the secured creditor is entitled under the plan is measured by the allowed amount of its "secured claim." Generally the allowed amount of a secured claim is determined under § 506(a)(1) and is limited to the value of the collateral securing such claim. If the total claim exceeds the value of the collateral, the secured claim is "stripped down" to the value of the collateral, and the excess of the total claim over that amount is treated as unsecured. *See* Chapter 4[A][1], *supra*.

Section 506(a) states that the value of collateral should be determined "in light of the purpose of the valuation and of the proposed disposition or use of such property." In the context of a chapter 13 plan under which the debtor proposes to retain the collateral, the Supreme Court decided in *Associates Commercial Corp. v. Rash*, 520 U.S. 953 (1997), that the property retained in a chapter 13 plan should be valued at its replacement cost (the price a willing buyer in debtor's place would pay to obtain like property from a willing seller, but without warranties, inventory storage or reconditioning charges) rather than its liquidation value. Congress codified *Rash* (with certain modifications) in § 506(a)(2).

Under the 2005 BAPCPA amendments, Congress made two types of debt ineligible for strip-down by providing that § 506 does not apply to them. The new provision in § 1325(a) (commonly called the "hanging paragraph" because it hangs at the end of § 1325(a) without being attached to any subsection) singles out debt for which the creditor has a purchase money security interest (PSMI) if either the debt was incurred within 910 days preceding the filing and the collateral for that debt consists of a motor vehicle acquired for personal use of the debtor, or the debt was incurred within one year preceding the filing and the collateral consists of any other thing of value. For these types of debts, the debtor who keeps the collateral under a chapter 13 plan must treat the entire debt secured by the collateral as an allowed secured claim, even if the collateral is worth less than the debt, and the creditor must receive property having a value as of the effective date of the plan of not less than the entire debt.

The second key concept in § 1325(a)(5)(B)(ii) is the requirement that property to be distributed under the plan to the secured creditor in respect of the creditor's secured claim must be valued as of the effective date of the plan (meaning on a present value basis). As was true in applying the "best interests" test of § 1325(a)(4), this means that if payments are to be received over time, interest must be paid on those payments to compensate the creditor for the time-value of money.

A plurality of the Supreme Court decided in *Till v. SCS Credit Corp.*, 541 U.S. 465 (2004), that the appropriate interest rate under § 1325(a)(5) is a "prime-plus" or "formula" rate under which you begin with the prime rate and then adjust it upward (perhaps by 1–3%) to reflect the risk of non-payment by this bankrupt debtor. Four dissenting Justices would have used the rate specified in the agreement between the secured creditor and the debtor as a presumptive rate; Justice Thomas would have used the prime rate alone (with no risk adjustment).

A visualization of the confirmation requirements with respect to treatment of secured debt in a chapter 13 case follows:

REQUIRED TREATMENT OF SECURED DEBT IN CHAPTER 13 § 1325(a)(5)		
SECURED CREDITOR ACCEPTS PLAN	SECURED CREDITOR KEEPS LIEN UNTIL DEBT PAID OR DISCHARGED, AND RECEIVES PROPERTY WITH VALUE, AS OF EFFECTIVE DATE OF PLAN, OF NOT LESS THAN AMOUNT OF ALLOWED SECURED CLAIM THE FOLLOWING DEBT IS NOT SUBJECT TO § 506 AND FULL AMOUNT OF DEBT CONSTITUTES SECURED CLAIM: 1) DEBT INCURRED WITHIN 910 DAY PERIOD PRIOR TO FILING SECURED BY PMSI IN MOTOR VEHICLE ACQUIRED FOR PERSONAL USE OF DEBTOR 2) DEBT INCURRED WITHIN 1 YEAR PRIOR TO FILING SECURED BY PMSI IN ANY OTHER THING OF VALUE	DEBTOR SURRENDERS COLLATERAL TO SECURED CREDITOR

The sixth confirmation requirement is that the debtor will be able to perform all requirements of the chapter 13 plan, often referred to as the "feasibility" requirement. § 1325(a)(6). In deciding whether the feasibility requirement is met, the court will consider the information included on Official Form 6, Schedule I (current income) and Schedule J (current expenditures), Official Form 7 (Statement of Financial Affairs), and the testimony of the debtor at the § 341 meeting, as well as the advice of the chapter 13 trustee. Courts tend to be lenient in interpreting this provision and allow willing debtors to sign on to overly ambitious plans.

Seventh, the action of the debtor in filing the petition must be in good faith. § 1325(a)(7). This new provision is intended to deny confirmation to serial filers.

Eighth, the debtor must be current in paying any required domestic support obligations for the period after the filing date. § 1325(a)(8).

Finally, the debtor must have filed all applicable tax returns for the four years preceding filing as required by § 1308. § 1325(a)(9).

If the trustee or the holder of an allowed unsecured claim objects to the chapter 13 plan, the court may not confirm the plan unless it satisfies one of two additional requirements. § 1325(b)(1). First, the plan can be confirmed if the value of property to be distributed under the plan on account of such claim is not less than the amount of such claim (meaning the unsecured claim will be paid in full under the plan). This is not a likely scenario. Alternatively, the plan may be confirmed if it provides that all of the debtor's "projected disposable income" to be received during the "applicable commitment period" be applied to make payments to unsecured creditors.

"Disposable income" is defined in § 1325(b)(2). It is computed by beginning with "current monthly income" (§ 101(10A)), discussed in Chapter 1[D], *supra*, other than certain payments to dependent children (including child support payments, foster care payments, or disability payments made in accordance with applicable nonbankruptcy law to the extent reasonably necessary). Next, deductions are made for "amounts reasonably necessary to be expended" for three purposes: postpetition maintenance or support of debtor or a dependent of the debtor or postpetition "domestic support obligations" (§ 101(14A)); charitable contributions to a qualified religious or charitable entity or organization (§ 548(d)(4)) not to exceed 15% of debtor's gross income for the year in which the contributions are made; and if the debtor is engaged in business, expenditures necessary for the continuation, preservation and operation of the business.

"Amounts reasonably necessary to be expended" for the three purposes described in the definition of "disposable income" are determined by the court if the debtor's current monthly income (§ 101(10A)), multiplied by 12, is less than the highest median family income of the applicable state for a household having the same number of family members. But if debtor's current monthly income, multiplied by 12, is not less than such state median income, under § 1325(b)(3), the "amounts reasonably necessary to be expended" for purposes of the definition of disposable income in § 1325(b)(2) (other than for charitable contributions) are to be determined in accordance with the new detailed means-testing provisions in § 707(b)(2)(A) & (B)* (using the IRS-specified amounts for expenses, with certain adjustments) which we examined in Chapter 1[D], *supra.*

A visualization of the methodology for determining the "amounts reasonably necessary to be expended" for purposes of the "disposable income" definition follows.

AMOUNTS REASONABLY NECESSARY TO BE EXPENDED § 1325(b)(3)			
BELOW-MEDIAN DEBTOR		ABOVE-MEDIAN DEBTOR	
WHEN APPLICABLE	METHOD OF COMPUTATION	WHEN APPLICABLE	METHOD OF COMPUTATION
DEBTOR HAS CURRENT MONTHLY INCOME TIMES 12 LESS THAN HIGHEST STATE MEDIAN FAMILY INCOME FOR HOUSEHOLD OF SAME SIZE	COURT DETERMINES WHAT IS REASONABLY NECESSARY	DEBTOR HAS CURRENT MONTHLY INCOME TIMES 12 NOT LESS THAN HIGHEST STATE MEDIAN FAMILY INCOME FOR HOUSEHOLD OF SAME SIZE	AMOUNTS REASONABLY NECESSARY (OTHER THAN FOR CHARITABLE CONTRIBUTIONS) DETERMINED UNDER § 707(b)(2)(A) & (B)

The above-median debtor's "applicable monthly expense amounts specified under the National Standards and Local Standards" (*see* Chapter 1[D], *supra*) within the

---

* The reference to § 707(b)(2)(B) is probably superfluous; that paragraph deals with rebutting a presumption of abuse created under § 707(b)(2)(A), which is not relevant to § 1325(b). It is also unclear whether Congress intended to preclude deduction of expenses for the continuation, preservation and operation of the debtor's business described in § 1325(b)(2)(B) if the debtor is an above-median debtor; § 707(b)(2)(A) does not include such expenses, and § 1325(b)(3) states that amounts reasonably necessary to be expended "under paragraph 2" with the exception of charitable contributions under § 1325(b)(2)(ii) are to be "determined in accordance with" § 707(b)(2)(A). Most likely Congress intended the § 707(b)(2)(A) expenses to be used only to determine the amounts "reasonably necessary to be expended" for the purposes described in § 1325(b)(2)(A)(i), that is, maintenance and support of the debtor or a dependent of the debtor or domestic support obligations.

meaning of § 707(b)(2) used in computing "disposable income" under § 1325(b)(2) do not include transportation ownership expenses if the debtor does not have debt or lease payments on his automobile. *Ransom v. FIA Card Services, N.A.*, 131 S. Ct. 716 (2011). Whether *Ransom* is applicable to other expenses listed in the IRS National Standards and Local Standards is currently unsettled. Also yet to be determined is whether the chapter 13 debtor may deduct the full amount specified in the IRS National Standards and Local Standards if the debtor's actual expenses are less. *Id.* at 727 n.8.

To be included in the test for confirmation, the "disposable income" must be "projected . . . to be received" during the "applicable commitment period." "Applicable commitment period" is also a defined phrase and its meaning, like the computation method for "amounts reasonably necessary to be expended," turns on whether the debtor is an above-median or below-median debtor. If the current monthly income of the debtor and the debtor's spouse combined, multiplied by 12, is less than the highest state median family income for a household of the same size, the applicable commitment period is three years. If the current monthly income of the debtor and the debtor's spouse combined, multiplied by 12, is not less than such highest state median family income, the applicable commitment period is not less than five years. § 1326(b)(4)(A). In either case, the applicable commitment period may be less than the required length, but only if the plan provides for payment of allowed unsecured claims in full over the shorter period. § 1325(b)(4)(B). A visualization of the definition of "applicable commitment period" follows:

APPLICABLE COMMITMENT PERIOD § 1325(b)(4)		
3 YEARS IF:	5 YEARS IF:	LESS THAN 3 OR 5 YEARS IF:
CURRENT MONTHLY INCOME OF DEBTOR AND DEBTOR'S SPOUSE TIMES 12 IS LESS THAN HIGHEST STATE MEDIAN FAMILY INCOME (§ 101(39A)) FOR HOUSEHOLD OF SAME SIZE	CURRENT MONTHLY INCOME OF DEBTOR AND DEBTOR'S SPOUSE TIMES 12 IS NOT LESS THAN HIGHEST STATE MEDIAN FAMILY INCOME (§ 101(39A)) FOR HOUSEHOLD OF SAME SIZE	PLAN PROVIDES FOR PAYMENT IN FULL OF ALL ALLOWED UNSECURED CLAIMS OVER SHORTER PERIOD

Some courts had interpreted the phrase "all of the debtor's projected disposable income to be received in the applicable commitment period" to mandate a mathematical computation. They would take the debtor's disposable income, computed in accordance with § 1325(b)(2), and multiply it by the applicable commitment period (either three or five years), and label the resulting figure the debtor's projected disposable income to be received in the applicable commitment period. The Supreme Court rejected this "mechanical" approach in *Hamilton v. Lanning*, 130 S. Ct. 2464 (2010). Although the Court agreed that computation of debtor's projected disposable income to be received in the applicable commitment period begin with the multiplication of disposable income by the applicable commitment period, the resulting figure may be adjusted by the bankruptcy court to "account for changes in the debtor's income or expenses that are known or virtually certain at the time of confirmation." *Id.* at 2478. A summary of the methodology for computing debtor's projected disposable income to be received in the applicable commitment period follows:

PROJECTED DISPOSABLE INCOME § 1325(b)(2)	
1)	COMPUTE DEBTOR'S CURRENT MONTHLY INCOME § 101(10A)
2)	DEDUCT CHILD SUPPORT PAYMENTS, FOSTER CARE PAYMENTS OR DISABILITY PAYMENTS FOR DEPENDENT CHILD REQUIRED UNDER APPLICABLE NONBANKRUPTCY LAW TO THE EXTENT REASONABLY NECESSARY
3)	DEDUCT AMOUNTS REASONABLY NECESSARY TO BE EXPENDED (§ 1325(b)(3)) FOR: • MAINTENANCE OR SUPPORT OF DEBTOR OR DEPENDENT OR FOR DOMESTIC SUPPORT OBLIGATION FIRST PAYABLE AFTER FILING OF PETITION, • CHARITABLE CONTRIBUTIONS NOT EXCEEDING 15% OF GROSS INCOME FOR SUCH YEAR, AND • IF DEBTOR IS IN BUSINESS, FOR CONTINUATION, PRESERVATION AND OPERATION OF BUSINESS
4)	DETERMINE DEBTOR'S APPLICABLE COMMITMENT PERIOD § 1325(b)(4)
5)	MULTIPLY DEBTOR'S CURRENT MONTHLY INCOME, TIMES 12, BY APPLICABLE COMMITMENT PERIOD
6)	ADJUST RESULT TO TAKE ACCOUNT OF CHANGES IN INCOME OR EXPENSES THAT ARE KNOWN OR VIRTUALLY CERTAIN AT TIME OF CONFIRMATION

Every chapter 13 debtor must file a computation of current monthly income, applicable commitment period and disposable income with his or her other schedules. Official Form B22C. These figures are used to compute projected disposable income to be received during the applicable commitment period, so that the debtor can prepare a chapter 13 plan that will satisfy any objection.

The debtor's projected disposable income to be received during the applicable commitment period is the minimum that must be devoted to paying creditors under § 1325(b)(1) in order to confirm the plan over an objection, and is also the maximum that can be devoted to paying creditors under § 1325(a)(6) (to devote more would render the plan not feasible).

The requirements for confirmation of a chapter 13 plan are visualized below:

REQUIREMENTS FOR CONFIRMATION OF CHAPTER 13 PLAN § 1325	
IF NO OBJECTION BY TRUSTEE OR UNSECURED CREDITOR § 1325(a)	IF OBJECTION BY TRUSTEE OR UNSECURED CREDITOR § 1325(b)
1) COMPLIANCE WITH PROVISIONS OF CHAPTER 13 AND CODE, 2) FILING FEES PAID, 3) PROPOSED IN GOOD FAITH, 4) MEETS BEST INTEREST OF THE CREDITORS TEST, 5) TREATS SECURED CREDITORS AS REQUIRED BY § 1325(a)(5), 6) PLAN IS FEASIBLE, 7) DEBTOR FILED PETITION IN GOOD FAITH, 8) DEBTOR HAS PAID ALL DOMESTIC SUPPORT OBLIGATIONS PAYABLE AFTER FILING, AND 9) DEBTOR HAS FILED TAX RETURNS FOR 4-YEAR PERIOD PRIOR TO FILING	AS OF EFFECTIVE DATE OF THE PLAN EITHER: 1) VALUE OF PROPERTY TO BE DISTRIBUTED ON ACCOUNT OF OBJECTOR'S UNSECURED CLAIM IS NOT LESS THAN AMOUNT OF CLAIM, OR 2) PLAN COMMITS ALL DEBTOR'S PROJECTED DISPOSABLE INCOME (§ 1325(b)(2)) TO BE RECEIVED IN THE APPLICABLE COMMITMENT PERIOD (§ 1325(b)(4)) TO PAY UNSECURED CREDITORS UNDER PLAN

E. POSTCONFIRMATION ISSUES

Once the court confirms the chapter 13 plan, it becomes binding on the debtor and each creditor, whether or not the plan provides for the creditor's claim, and whether or not the creditor has objected to the plan. § 1327(a). Confirmation of the plan vests all property of the estate in the debtor, free and clear of any claim or interest of any creditor provided for by the plan, except as otherwise provided in the plan or the confirmation order. § 1327(b) & (c).

The debtor must begin making payments proposed by the plan to the trustee (or, in certain cases of leases of personal property or debts secured by personal property, directly to the lessor or secured party) not later than 30 days after the earlier of the order for relief or the date the plan is filed, unless the court orders otherwise. § 1326(a)(1). The trustee retains those payments until confirmation or denial of confirmation; if the court confirms the plan, the trustee distributes the payments in accordance with the plan "as soon as is practicable." § 1326(a)(2). Before, or at the time of, any payment to creditors, the trustee must pay any unpaid administrative expenses (*see* Chapter 4[A][3], *supra*), the percentage fee fixed for any standing chapter 13 trustee under 28 U.S.C. § 586(e)(1)(B), and if the case was converted from chapter 7 or refiled under chapter 13 after dismissal under chapter 7 and some portion of the chapter 7 trustee's compensation remains unpaid, pro rata monthly payments towards the unpaid chapter 7 trustee's compensation. § 1326(b).

If the court confirms a chapter 13 plan, the court may revoke the confirmation order, but only on very limited grounds. § 1330. A party in interest must request revocation of confirmation within 180 days after the date of entry of the confirmation order. The only ground for revoking confirmation is if the confirmation order was procured by fraud. If the court revokes the confirmation order, the court may either convert or dismiss the case under § 1307, unless the debtor proposes a modified plan that the court confirms. A visualization of the provisions for revocation of confirmation of a chapter 13 plan follows.

REVOCATION OF CONFIRMATION § 1330		
WHEN	WHY	RESULT
REQUEST OF PARTY IN INTEREST WITHIN 180 DAYS AFTER DATE OF ENTRY OF CONFIRMATION ORDER	ORDER WAS PROCURED BY FRAUD	COURT MUST CONVERT OR DISMISS CASE UNLESS, WITHIN TIME SPECIFIED, DEBTOR PROPOSES AND COURT CONFIRMS MODIFIED PLAN

After confirmation, the debtor may become unable to meet his or her payment obligations because of a change in circumstances since filing or because the original plan was unduly optimistic. On the other hand, the debtor's circumstances may have improved dramatically, as a result of which the amounts dedicated to creditors under the confirmed plan no longer represent all the debtor's projected disposable income. When the confirmed plan requires changes, under § 1329(a), modification may be sought by the debtor, the trustee or a holder of an allowed unsecured claim. Only four possible modifications to the plan after confirmation are permitted: (1) to increase or reduce the amount of payments on claims of a particular class, (2) to extend or reduce the time for payments on claims of a particular class, (3) to alter the amount of distribution to a creditor to take account of payments outside of the plan, and (4) to reduce amounts to be paid under the plan by the actual, documented amount expended by debtor to purchase health insurance for the debtor and any dependent without health insurance if the expenses were reasonable and necessary, the amount is not materially larger than the cost the debtor previously paid for health insurance (or if the debtor did not previously have health insurance, materially larger than health insurance costs for a comparable uncovered individual), and the amount was not otherwise included in computing "disposable income" under § 1325(b). Other changes to a confirmed plan, such as modifying the amount of secured claims or recharacterizing claims from secured to unsecured, are not permitted.

Any modified plan must still comply with § 1322 and must meet the requirements for confirmation in § 1325. § 1329(b)(1). The modified plan may not exceed the limitations on the length of the plan in § 1322(d) counting from the time payment was first due under the unmodified original plan. § 1329(c). The modified plan becomes the "plan" for all purposes of chapter 13 unless, after notice and a hearing, the court orders otherwise. § 1329(b)(2).

A visualization of the provisions on postconfirmation modifications to a chapter 13 plan follows.

POSTCONFIRMATION MODIFICATION OF CHAPTER 13 PLAN § 1329				
WHO	WHEN	LIMITS	PERMITTED MODIFICATIONS	RESULTS
DEBTOR, TRUSTEE, HOLDER OF ALLOWED UNSECURED CLAIM	AT ANY TIME AFTER PLAN CONFIRMED AND BEFORE PAYMENTS COMPLETED	MODIFIED PLAN MUST MEET REQUIREMENTS OF § 1322, 1325 MODIFIED PLAN MAY NOT PROVIDE FOR PAYMENTS BEYOND END OF APPLICABLE COMMITMENT PERIOD FROM TIME OF FIRST PAYMENT UNDER ORIGINAL PLAN UNLESS COURT FOR CAUSE APPROVES LONGER PERIOD NOT TO EXCEED 5 YEARS	INCREASE OR REDUCE PAYMENTS EXTEND OR REDUCE TIME FOR PAYMENT ALTER AMOUNT OF DISTRIBUTION TO CREDITOR PAID OUTSIDE PLAN REDUCE AMOUNTS TO BE PAID BY ACTUAL AMOUNT SPENT TO PURCHASE REASONABLE AND NECESSARY HEALTH INSURANCE	MODIFIED PLAN BECOMES THE CHAPTER 13 PLAN UNLESS DISAPPROVED BY COURT HOLDERS OF SECURED CLAIMS WHO ACCEPTED OR REJECTED UNMODIFIED PLAN ARE DEEMED TO HAVE ACCEPTED OR REJECTED MODIFIED PLAN UNLESS THEIR RIGHTS WERE CHANGED AND THEY CHANGE THEIR ACCEPTANCE OR REJECTION

Chapter 9

TREATMENT OF CLAIMS IN CHAPTER 11

A. FILING OF THE PLAN

The chapter 11 process is geared toward the confirmation of something called a *"plan of reorganization,"* which specifies how the debtor intends to treat allowed claims and interests. The plan becomes binding when "confirmed" by the bankruptcy judge.

In chapter 13, only the debtor may draft a plan. § 1301. The question of who should have the right to draft and file a plan of reorganization in chapter 11 was an issue that was hotly debated in connection with the enactment of the Code in 1978. The result of this debate was § 1121.

Unlike under chapter 13, the debtor is not required to file a plan with the chapter 11 petition (although it may do so, and generally does in connection with a pre-packaged chapter 11, *i.e.*, one that has been negotiated prior to the bankruptcy filing). § 1121(a). Instead, the debtor is given the exclusive right to file a plan for a period of 120 days after the date of the order for relief. § 1121(b). If the debtor has not filed a plan within that period of "exclusivity," or has filed the plan but has failed to get it accepted by each class of claims or interests that is impaired under the plan within 180 days after date of the order for relief, or a trustee has been appointed, then any party in interest, including the debtor but also including any creditor, equity holder, committee, or even the trustee, or more than one of those parties, may file a plan of reorganization and attempt to obtain support to get it confirmed. § 1121(c).

The court may, for cause, shorten or lengthen the debtor's exclusive period for filing a plan or for obtaining acceptance of a filed plan on motion by a party in interest made before the prior period has expired. § 1121(d)(1). However, in no event may the court extend the debtor's exclusive period for filing a plan beyond a date that is 18 months after the date of the order for relief, nor may the court extend the debtor's exclusive period for obtaining acceptance of a filed plan beyond the date that is 20 months after the date of the order for relief. § 1121(d)(2). The exclusivity period is visualized below.

EXCLUSIVITY $\S 1121$	
DEBTOR'S EXCLUSIVE PERIODS $\S 1121(b) \& (c)$	MODIFICATIONS $\S 1121(d)$
120 DAYS AFTER ORDER FOR RELIEF TO FILE A PLAN 180 DAYS AFTER ORDER FOR RELIEF TO GET ACCEPTANCE BY EACH CLASS OF IMPAIRED CLAIMS AND INTERESTS	EXCLUSIVE PERIODS MAY BE REDUCED OR INCREASED ON MOTION AFTER NOTICE AND HEARING FOR CAUSE, BUT NO EXTENSION BEYOND 18 MONTHS TO FILE A PLAN AND 20 MONTHS TO GET ACCEPTANCE OF A FILED PLAN

B. CONTENTS OF THE PLAN

Section 1123 sets out the parameters for a plan of reorganization, and as was the case for § 1322 regarding the contents of a chapter 13 plan, there are mandatory provisions and permissive provisions (some of which have exceptions or limitations).

A chapter 11 plan must satisfy the eight requirements of § 1123(a). First, except for certain priority claims, the plan must designate classes of claims and classes of interests in compliance with § 1122. § 1123(a)(1). Classification is critically important because, as discussed below, all claims in the class must be treated the same (unless they otherwise agree to less favorable treatment). § 1123(a)(4). In addition, the approval of the plan is accomplished by class votes under § 1129(a)(8) and § 1126(c), so designation of classes is necessary.

A claim or interest may be placed in a class only if it is "substantially similar" to the others in that class. § 1122(a). Thus, § 1122 implicitly prohibits the inclusion of dissimilar claims or interests in the same class. An analysis of whether claims or interests are substantially similar to each other focuses on the nature of the claim or interest, not the nature of the creditor or interest holder (e.g., a single creditor could have claims in multiple classes). Similarity is judged with respect to the priority of the claim or interest as against the assets of the estate. Therefore, secured claims are not substantially similar to unsecured claims, and unsecured claims are not substantially similar to interests.

But within those general categories, further refinements may be made. Secured claims are not substantially similar to each other if they are secured by different collateral, or if they have different legal or contractual priorities (e.g., first lien, second lien on the same collateral). Unsecured claims are not substantially similar to each other if some have priority under § 507, or are contractually subordinated to other unsecured claims. Holders of interests consisting of preferred stock would have interests that are not substantially similar to holders of common stock.

Beyond these basic distinctions, the plan proponent is permitted to put claims or interests in the same class, but nothing in § 1122 requires the plan proponent to do so.

A plan proponent may choose not to put substantially similar claims or interests in the same class for either or both of two reasons: treatment under the plan, and voting.

One reason for separate classification is that the plan proponent wishes to treat certain creditors holding substantially similar claims or interests more favorably than others, and could not do so were they all in a single class because of § 1123(a)(4). Separate classification to achieve this result is permitted as long as there is a valid business reason for the separate classification and the plan satisfies the requirement for confirmation that it does not "discriminate unfairly" and is "fair and equitable" under § 1129(b)(1) (which we will be discussing in Section 9[E][2], *infra*).

Perhaps the most frequent reason for separately classifying substantially similar claims is to try to put together a class which will support the plan, so-called "gerrymandering" of classes. One of the requirements for confirmation of the plan which we will be discussing in Section 9[E][1], *infra*, is that at least one impaired class must vote in favor of the plan. § 1129(a)(10). A favorable class vote under § 1126(c) requires at least a majority in number and at least 2/3 in amount of claims, *see* Section 9[C], *infra*; separating out creditors who are inclined to vote in favor from those who aren't may create such a favorable impaired class vote.

This issue frequently arises in single-asset real estate cases (SARE), or in other cases in which there is a large and disgruntled undersecured creditor who is left with an unsecured claim because of the operation of § 506(a). If the unsecured portion of this secured creditor's debt is placed in the same class as all other unsecured debt, this creditor can control the vote in the class and may vote the plan down. If the debtor places that secured creditor's unsecured portion of its claim in a separate class, this separate class may reject the plan, but the other unsecured class may accept, satisfying the requirements of § 1129(a)(10) that there be at least one class of impaired claimants supporting the plan.

If the sole reason for the separate classification of substantially similar claims is to gerrymander the voting, most courts will not permit it. However, if the plan proponent offers some other legitimate reason for the separate classification, the plan will be held to meet the requirements of § 1123(a).

In addition, § 1122(b) recognizes one specific situation in which unsecured claims otherwise substantially similar to claims in a different class may be separately classified — when they are so small in amount, or are reduced to such a small amount, that administrative convenience is served by treating them separately (generally by paying them in full so the estate can save the expense of cutting small checks).

A visualization of the classification requirements follows.

CLASSIFICATION § 1122		
MAY BE CLASSIFIED TOGETHER	MAY NOT BE CLASSIFIED TOGETHER	LIMITS ON SEPARATE CLASSIFICATION OF SUBSTANTIALLY SIMILAR CLAIMS
SUBSTANTIALLY SIMILAR CLAIMS § 1122(a) ADMINISTRATIVE CONVENIENCE CLAIMS § 1122(b)	CLAIMS THAT ARE NOT SUBSTANTIALLY SIMILAR § 1122(a)	NO UNFAIR DISCRIMINATION AND FAIR AND EQUITABLE TREATMENT § 1129(b)(1) NO GERRYMANDERING

The second requirement for a chapter 11 plan is that the plan must specify which classes of claims or interests are not "impaired." § 1123(a)(2). A class of claims or interests is impaired under a plan unless one of two situations exists. § 1124. First, a class is not impaired if the plan leaves unaltered the legal, equitable or contractual rights of the holders of the claims or interests in that class. § 1124(a). "Unaltered" is interpreted literally; if the plan alters the rights of the holders at all, even if the change was intended to improve its position, the class is impaired.

Alternatively, the class is deemed unimpaired if the only alteration of the legal, equitable or contractual rights of the holders of claims or interests in the class made by the plan is to undo the consequences of a contractual provision or applicable law that entitled the holder to demand or receive accelerated payment of the claim or interest after the occurrence of a default. § 1124(2). The plan may, without impairing the class, cure any prepetition default (other than ipso facto defaults described in § 365(b)(2)), reinstate the non-accelerated maturity of the claim or interest, compensate the holder of the claim or interest for damages incurred as a result of reasonable reliance on such contractual provision or applicable law, compensate the holder of the claim or interest (other than the debtor or an insider) for actual pecuniary loss incurred as a result of failure to perform a nonmonetary obligation (other than failure to operate a nonresidential real property lease subject to § 365(b)(1)(A)), and not otherwise alter the legal, equitable, or contractual rights of the holders.

A visualization of the circumstances under which a class is not impaired follows.

IMPAIRMENT § 1124	
A CLASS OF CLAIMS OR INTERESTS IS IMPAIRED UNDER A PLAN UNLESS, WITH RESPECT TO EACH CLAIM OR INTEREST IN THE CLASS, EITHER:	
NO ALTERATION § 1124(1)	DEACCELERATION § 1124(2)
PLAN DOES NOT ALTER LEGAL, EQUITABLE OR CONTRACTUAL RIGHTS OF HOLDER	NOTWITHSTANDING HOLDER'S CONTRACTUAL OR LEGAL RIGHT TO ACCELERATE BASED ON OCCURRENCE OF DEFAULT, PLAN 1) CURES DEFAULTS (OTHER THAN IPSO FACTO DEFAULTS), 2) REINSTATES MATURITY OF CLAIM OR INTEREST, 3) COMPENSATES HOLDER FOR DAMAGES INCURRED AS A RESULT OF REASONABLE RELIANCE ON CONTRACT OR LEGAL RIGHT PERMITTING ACCELERATION, 4) COMPENSATES HOLDER FOR PECUNIARY LOSS FROM FAILURE TO PERFORM NONMONETARY OBLIGATIONS, AND 5) DOES NOT OTHERWISE ALTER LEGAL, EQUITABLE OR CONTRACTUAL RIGHTS OF HOLDER

The third requirement for the chapter 11 plan is that it must specify the treatment of any class of claims or interests that is impaired. § 1123(a)(3). Obviously, no description of the treatment of unimpaired classes is required, because their rights will either remain unaltered or they will be entitled to the treatment described in § 1124(2).

Fourth, the plan must provide the same treatment for each claim or interest in a given class, unless the holder of a particular claim or interests agrees to less favorable treatment. § 1123(a)(4).

Fifth, the plan must provide adequate means for the plan's implementation (meaning the debtor must be able to perform its obligations under the plan after emerging from bankruptcy). § 1123(a)(5). There are various permissible methods for ensuring that the plan can be implemented. Those listed in § 1123(a)(5) (which are not intended to be exclusive) are retention by the debtor of property of the estate, transfer of property of the estate to other entities, merger or consolidation of the debtor with one or more other persons, sale of all or part of the property of the estate, satisfaction or modification of liens, cancellation or modification of any indenture, curing or waiving of any default, extension of a maturity date or change in interest rate or other terms of outstanding securities, amendment of the debtor's charter, or issuance of securities. These provisions illustrate the broad discretion given to the plan proponent to craft a plan that will work. If the plan provides for the cure of any default, the amount necessary to cure must be determined in accordance with the underlying agreement and applicable nonbankruptcy law. § 1123(d).

If the debtor is a corporation, or if the plan provides for transfer of all or any part of the property of the estate to a corporation or provides for merger or consolidation of the debtor with a corporation, the plan must provide for the inclusion in the corporate charter of each such corporation of a provision prohibiting the issuance of nonvoting securities, and providing for an appropriate distribution of voting power between the classes of securities having voting power. If any such corporate charter includes a provision for preferred stock entitled to priority in payment of dividends, the charter must include adequate provisions for holders of preferred stock to elect directors representing them if there is an event of default in the payment of dividends. § 1123(a)(6).

Seventh, the plan must include only provisions consistent with the interests of creditors and equity security holders and with public policy relating to selection of officers, directors or trustees under the plan and their successors. § 1123(a)(7).

Finally, for an individual chapter 11 debtor, the plan must provide that the creditors receive all or such portion of postpetition income as is necessary for the execution of the plan, a provision that mirrors the requirement of § 1322(a)(1). § 1123(a)(8).

Beyond these eight mandatory provisions, the plan may include any other appropriate provision not inconsistent with the applicable provisions of chapter 11. § 1123(b)(6). Five such permissive provisions are described in § 1123(b). First, the plan may impair or leave unimpaired any class of claims or interests, including secured claims. Second, the plan may deal with any executory contract or unexpired lease not previously rejected through assumption, assumption and assignment, or rejection in accordance with § 365. *See* Chapter 6[D], *supra*. Third, the plan may provide for settlement or adjustment, or retention and enforcement, of any claim or interest belonging to the debtor or the estate. Fourth, the plan may provide for the sale of all or substantially all of the debtor's property (*i.e.*, a "liquidating chapter 11 plan"). Fifth, the plan may provide for modification of secured or unsecured claims, or leave them unaffected.

An individual debtor's chapter 11 plan may not include two provisions. First, although generally the plan may provide for the modification of secured debt, the plan may not modify the rights of a holder of a secured claim secured only by a security interest in real property that is the debtor's principal residence. § 1123(b)(5). This prohibition on modification of home mortgage debt is consistent with the prohibition in § 1322(b)(2) for chapter 13 cases, but without the distinction between short-term and long-term mortgages because chapter 11 plans are not limited to five years as are chapter 13 plans. Second, if a plan is proposed for an individual debtor by an entity other than the debtor, it may not provide for the sale, use or lease of exempt property without debtor's consent. § 1123(c).

A visualization of the provisions that must, may and may not be included in a chapter 11 plan follows.

CONTENTS OF PLAN § 1123		
MANDATORY	PERMISSIVE	PROHIBITED
1) DESIGNATE CLASSES UNDER § 1122	1) IMPAIR OR LEAVE UNIMPAIRED CLAIMS OR INTERESTS	1) FOR INDIVIDUAL DEBTOR, MODIFICATION OF HOME MORTGAGE DEBT
2) SPECIFY UNIMPAIRED CLASSES	2) ASSUME, REJECT OR ASSIGN EXECUTORY CONTRACTS AND UNEXPIRED LEASES NOT PREVIOUSLY REJECTED	2) IN PLAN PROPOSED FOR INDIVIDUAL DEBTOR BY ENTITY OTHER THAN DEBTOR, SALE, USE OR LEASE OF EXEMPT PROPERTY WITHOUT DEBTOR'S CONSENT
3) DESCRIBE TREATMENT OF IMPAIRED CLASSES		
4) PROVIDE SAME TREATMENT FOR ALL CLAIMS OR INTERESTS WITHIN CLASS UNLESS HOLDER AGREES OTHERWISE	3) SETTLE OR ADJUST CLAIMS OR PROVIDE FOR RETENTION AND ENFORCEMENT OF CLAIMS	
5) PROVIDE ADEQUATE MEANS FOR IMPLEMENTATION	4) PROVIDE FOR SALE OF ALL OR SUBSTANTIALLY ALL OF PROPERTY OF THE ESTATE	
6) INCLUDE CORPORATE VOTING PROVISIONS IN CHARTER(S)		
7) CONTAIN PROVISIONS FOR SELECTION OF OFFICERS, DIRECTORS OR TRUSTEES THAT ARE CONSISTENT WITH INTERESTS OF CREDITORS AND EQUITY HOLDERS	5) MODIFY, OR LEAVE UNAFFFECTED, SECURED OR UNSECURED CLAIMS	
8) FOR INDIVIDUAL DEBTOR, PROVIDE FOR PAYMENTS FROM FUTURE INCOME AS NECESSARY FOR PLAN	6) OTHER APPROPRIATE PROVISIONS NOT INCONSISTENT WITH CHAPTER 11	

C. DISCLOSURE, SOLICITATION AND VOTING

A key part of the confirmation process for a plan of reorganization is voting by the classes of creditors and equity holders. Before they vote, creditors and interest holders must be given adequate information on which to base their decision; no votes may be solicited after the commencement of the case unless at or before the time of the solicitation, the creditors and interest holders have received the plan or a summary of the plan, and a written disclosure statement that has been approved by the court as containing adequate information. § 1125(b). If holders of claims or interests are solicited before the bankruptcy case begins in compliance with applicable nonbankruptcy law, the solicitation is valid under § 1125(g).

"Adequate information" is defined in § 1125(a)(1) to be "information of a kind and in sufficient detail, as far as is reasonably practicable" under the circumstances, to enable "a hypothetical investor of the relevant class to make an informed judgment about the plan." In determining whether the disclosure statement includes adequate information, the court is directed to take into account "the complexity of the case, the benefit of additional information to creditors and other parties in interest, and the cost of providing additional information." In any event, the disclosure statement does not contain adequate information unless it includes a "discussion of the potential material Federal tax consequences of the plan to the debtor, any successor to the debtor, and a hypothetical investor typical of the holders of claims or interests in the case." An "investor typical of holders of claims or interests of the relevant class" is defined to be a investor with a claim or interest of the relevant class, such a relationship with the debtor as the holders of other claims or interests of such class generally have, and such ability to obtain such information from sources other than the disclosure statement as holders of claims or interests in such class generally have. § 1125(a)(2).

Whether a disclosure statement contains adequate information is not governed by otherwise applicable nonbankruptcy law (such as the Securities Act of 1933), but an agency or official responsible for such nonbankruptcy law may be heard on the issue. § 1125(d).

To obtain court approval of the disclosure statement, the plan proponent files the proposed disclosure statement with the court at the same time as the plan or within a time fixed by the court. Fed. R. Bankr. P. 3016(b). All members of a particular class must receive the same disclosure statement, but there may be different disclosure statements for different classes, because different classes may need different information to make an informed decision. § 1125(c).

After the filing of the proposed disclosure statement or statements, and upon at least 28 days' notice to the debtor, creditors, equity security holders and other parties in interest (*see* Official Form 12), the court holds a hearing to consider the disclosure statement and any objections or modifications to it. Fed. R. Bankr. P. 3017(a). Objections must be filed and served prior to the hearing or by the date fixed by the court. Following the hearing, the court will decide whether the disclosure statement contains "adequate information" and thus should be approved. Fed. R. Bankr. P. 3017(b) and Official Form 13. Special provisions apply with respect to disclosure statements in small business cases. § 1125(f) and Fed. R. Bankr. P. 3017.1.

At the same time that the court approves a disclosure statement, the court will specify the date by which ballots must be returned and the date set for a confirmation hearing. Fed. R. Bankr. P. 3017(c). Once the disclosure statement is approved, the plan proponent puts together a package most of which is then sent to each holder of a claim or interest. It will include the plan, or a court-approved summary of the plan; the disclosure statement; a ballot conforming to Official Form 14 for all those entitled to vote; notice of the time for filing ballots; notice of the time for filing objections to confirmation of the plan and the time of the confirmation hearing; and such other information as the court may direct. Fed. R. Bankr. P. 3017(d).

Anyone who solicits acceptances or rejections of a plan, or who participates in the offer, issuance, sale or purchase of a security offered or sold under the plan, in good faith and in compliance with the requirements of § 1125, is immune from liability under any applicable law, rule or regulation governing solicitation of acceptance or rejection of a plan or the offer, issuance, sale or purchase of securities. § 1125(e). This so-called "safe harbor" provision protects a good faith plan proponent who complies with the requirements of the Code from the risk of liability for violation of the federal securities laws.

A visualization of the provisions relating to disclosure and solicitation follows.

DISCLOSURE AND SOLICITATION § 1125		
REQUIREMENTS FOR DISCLOSURE STATEMENT	REQUIREMENTS FOR SOLICITATION § 1125(b), BR 3017(d)	SAFE HARBOR § 1125(e)
ADEQUATE INFORMATION, § 1125(a), DETERMINED WITHOUT REGARD TO OTHERWISE APPLICABLE NONBANKRUPTCY LAW, § 1125(d) MAY BE DIFFERENT DISCLOSURE STATEMENTS FOR DIFFERENT CLASSES § 1125(c)	PLAN OR SUMMARY OF PLAN COURT-APPROVED WRITTEN DISCLOSURE STATEMENT BALLOT (OFFICIAL FORM 14) NOTICE OF TIME FOR FILING BALLOTS NOTICE OF TIME FOR FILING OBJECTIONS TO CONFIRMATION NOTICE OF TIME OF CONFIRMATION HEARING OTHER INFORMATION DIRECTED BY COURT	NO VIOLATION OF SECURITIES LAWS FOR SOLICITING IN COMPLIANCE WITH § 1125 IN GOOD FAITH

On the ballot received by each creditor and interest holder entitled to vote, that party will be asked to vote to accept the plan or reject it. Voting is tabulated by the classes designated in the plan under § 1122 and § 1123(a). Generally speaking, only holders of allowed claims and interests in that class are allowed to accept or reject the plan. § 1126(a). However, the court may temporarily allow a claim or interest solely for purposes of voting under Fed. R. Bankr. P. 3018(a). The court may also estimate a contingent or unliquidated claim for purposes of voting under § 502(c). *See* Chapter 4[B], *supra*.

Only members of classes that are impaired may vote; a class that is unimpaired and each member of such a class is conclusively presumed to accept the plan under § 1126(f). Classes that are totally impaired (*i.e.*, they are getting nothing on account of their claims or interests under the plan) are deemed to have rejected the plan. § 1126(g).

On request of a party in interest, the court may "designate" any holder of a claim or interest whose acceptance or rejection of the plan was "not in good faith, or was not solicited or procured in good faith or in accordance with the provisions" of the Code. § 1126(e). The vote of a holder of a designated claim or interest does not count in determining whether the class to which such claim or interest belongs has accepted or rejected the plan. A claim or interest may be designated if the holder attempts to use its vote for reasons completely unrelated to the proposed distribution to the holder's class, for example, in order to drive the debtor out of business, benefit itself as holder of a different claim or interest, because the holder was bribed, or for other non-economic purposes.

A class of claims accepts the plan if the plan is accepted by creditors (other than designated claims) holding a majority in number of allowed claims in the class, and at least 2/3 in amount of allowed claims in the class, in each case based on the holders of allowed claims in the class (other than designated claims) actually voting to accept or reject the plan. § 1126(c). A class of interests (equity holders) accepts the plan if the plan is accepted by interest holders (other than designed interest holders) holding at least 2/3 in amount of the allowed interests in the class, based on the holders of interests (other than designated interests) actually voting to accept or reject the plan. § 1126(d).

The following visualizes the provisions relating to acceptance of a chapter 13 plan.

ACCEPTANCE OF THE PLAN § 1126			
WHO MAY VOTE?	WHAT CONSTITUTES ACCEPTANCE?		WHAT IS A "DESIGNATED" CLAIM OR INTEREST? § 1126(e)
1) HOLDERS OF ALLOWED CLAIMS OR INTERESTS § 1126(a) 2) CLASS IS IMPAIRED § 1126(f) 3) CLASS IS NOT TOTALLY IMPAIRED § 1126(g)	CLAIMS § 1126(c) MAJORITY IN NUMBER OF ALLOWED CLAIMS (EXCLUDING DESIGNATED CLAIMS) AND AT LEAST 2/3 IN AMOUNT OF ALLOWED CLAIMS (EXCLUDING DESIGNATED CLAIMS) OF TOTAL ALLOWED CLAIMS IN CLASS ACTUALLY VOTING (EXCLUDING DESIGNATED CLAIMS)	INTERESTS § 1126(d) AT LEAST 2/3 IN AMOUNT OF ALLOWED INTERESTS (EXCLUDING DESIGNATED INTERESTS) OF TOTAL ALLOWED INTERESTS IN CLASS ACTUALLY VOTING (EXCLUDING DESIGNATED INTERESTS)	ACCEPTANCE OR REJECTION NOT IN GOOD FAITH ACCEPTANCE OR REJECTION NOT SOLICITED IN GOOD FAITH AND IN COMPLIANCE WITH § 1125

D. PRECONFIRMATION MODIFICATION OF THE PLAN

The filing of a plan of reorganization with the bankruptcy court is often merely the first step in the process of structuring a confirmable plan — the first filed plan may become the basis for negotiations between the debtor and its creditors and interest holders with the goal of modifying it to achieve the greatest degree of consensus possible.

Under § 1127(a), a plan proponent may modify a plan at any time prior to confirmation of the plan, so long as the modification complies with the requirements of § 1122 (classification) and § 1123 (contents of a plan).

If the plan proponent has not yet gotten a disclosure statement approved by the court and sent out to solicit approval of the plan from creditors, the modified plan simply becomes "the plan" and is thus the subject of any hearing on the adequacy of the disclosure statement under § 1125. If a disclosure statement and ballots have already been sent out, the interests of those creditors who have essentially voted on the "wrong" plan must be protected. The court may order a new disclosure statement be circulated. § 1125. Any creditor is allowed to change its vote in light of the amendment within a time fixed by the court under § 1127(d). If the creditor does not act to change its vote, the creditor will be deemed to vote the same way on the modified plan as on the original plan. § 1127(d).

A visualization of the provisions relating to preconfirmation modification of a chapter 11 plan follows.

PRECONFIRMATION MODIFICATION OF PLAN § 1127		
RIGHT TO MODIFY	RESTRICTIONS ON MODIFICATION	PROTECTIONS FOR HOLDERS OF CLAIMS AND INTERESTS
PROPONENT OF PLAN HAS RIGHT TO MODIFY PLAN AT ANY TIME BY FILING MODIFICATION § 1127(a)	MODIFIED PLAN MUST COMPLY WITH §§ 1122 AND 1123 § 1127(a) PROPONENT MUST COMPLY WITH § 1125 § 1127(c)	HOLDERS HAVE RIGHT TO CHANGE VOTES WITHIN TIME SPECIFIED BY COURT, BUT IF THEY DO NOT, ORIGINAL VOTE APPLIES TO MODIFIED PLAN § 1127(d)

E. CONFIRMATION OF THE PLAN

After the period of solicitation of votes, the next step in the process is the confirmation hearing held under § 1128. The confirmation hearing is the time that the court will hear the plan proponent's motion to confirm the plan, and rule on any objections to confirmation made under § 1128(b) and Fed. R. Bankr. P. 3020(b).

At the hearing, the court will be determining whether the plan is entitled to confirmation under the legal standards set forth in § 1129. If it is, the court will enter a confirmation order (Official Form 15) and the plan will become effective. Confirmation can occur either on a consensual basis (which does not mean that each creditor consents to confirmation, but that all classes of impaired claims and interests have accepted the plan pursuant to § 1126) or on a nonconsensual basis (meaning that at least one class of impaired claims or interests has rejected the plan under § 1126). We will look at each.

1. Consensual Confirmation

There are sixteen requirements for confirmation under § 1129(a). The court may not confirm the plan on a consensual basis unless all are met.

The first requirement is that the plan complies with applicable provisions of the Code. § 1129(a)(1). This is the provision that enables the court to enforce, for example, the classification requirements of § 1122, and the mandatory and prohibited provisions of a plan under § 1123.

Second, the plan cannot be confirmed unless the proponent complies with the applicable provisions of the Code. § 1129(a)(2). These applicable provisions would include, for example, the disclosure and solicitation rules of § 1125.

Third, the plan must be proposed in good faith and not by any means forbidden by law. § 1129(a)(3). The goal behind this requirement is to ensure that the chapter 11 plan is used in a way consistent with the policy behind bankruptcy, and not for some improper purpose. It focuses on the sort of conduct that, were it exhibited by a creditor, would result in the creditor's claim being "designated" under § 1126(e).

Fourth, all payments made or to be made for services or costs or expenses in connection with the case must be approved as "reasonable." § 1129(a)(4). Through this provision, the court can police the charges of professionals in the case, preventing excessive fees.

The fifth requirement includes three different requirements relating to management and insiders of the debtor and related entities. Two of the requirements require disclosure. The proponent of the plan must have disclosed the identity and affiliations of any postconfirmation director, officer or voting trustee of the debtor, an affiliate participating in a joint plan with the debtor, or a successor to the debtor. In addition, the plan proponent must have disclosed the identity of any insider that will be employed or retained by the reorganized debtor, and the nature of any proposed compensation for that insider.

Section 1129(a)(5) also imposes a substantive check on the ability of the debtor to name management. The court must find that the appointment of (or continuation in office of) each proposed director, officer, or voting trustee of the debtor, an affiliate participating in a joint plan with the debtor, or a successor to the debtor is "consistent with the interests of creditors and equity security holders and with public policy."

When the debtor is in a regulated industry for which a governmental regulatory commission approves rates (e.g., public utilities), the sixth requirement is that such regulatory commission must have approved any rate changes contemplated by the plan. § 1129(a)(6). Rate changes for such industries may be necessary to enable the debtor to fund the plan.

The seventh requirement is that, with respect to each class of impaired claims or interests, each holder of a claim or interest in that class must either have voted in favor of the plan (in which case that holder is presumably satisfied with its proposed distribution), or the court must conclude that the creditor or interest holder will receive under the chapter 11 plan a value, as of the effective date of the plan, that is not less than the value it would have received in a hypothetical chapter 7 liquidation as of the same date. § 1129(a)(7)(A). This provision, comparable to § 1325(a)(4), is commonly known as the "best interest of the creditors" or "best interests" test.

If any single holder of a claim or interest in an impaired class objects to the plan on this basis, the plan proponent must provide a liquidation analysis, establishing which assets would be available for distribution in a hypothetical chapter 7, what additional claims would be made (such as claims for rejection of contracts that are being assumed in chapter 11, and chapter 7 administrative expenses), what the assets would realize on a liquidation basis, and how much that claimant or interest holder would receive under § 726. That amount is then compared to the distribution the holder is entitled to receive under the chapter 11 plan. No holder of an impaired claim or interest may be compelled to accept in chapter 11 less than that holder would have received in a chapter 7 liquidation.

The comparison between chapter 7 and chapter 11 distributions must be made as of the same time, so any payments proposed to be made under chapter 11 over time must be discounted to present value for purposes of the test (the meaning of the language "a value, as of the effective date of the plan"). The interest rate applicable to chapter 11 distributions is not specified. You recall from Chapter 8[D], *supra*, a plurality of the Supreme Court decided in *Till v. SCS Credit Corp.*, 541 U.S. 465 (2004), that the appropriate interest rate to be used in discounting payments to be made to a secured creditor under § 1325(a)(5) is a "prime-plus" or "formula" rate under which you begin with the prime rate and then adjust it upward (perhaps by 1–3%) to reflect the risk of non-payment by this bankrupt debtor. *Till* includes dictum suggesting that the plurality thought Congress would favor using the same approach when choosing an appropriate interest rate in other sections of the Code requiring a payment stream to be discounted to present value, including § 1129(a)(7). 541 U.S. at 474 & n.10.

The best interests test has a different meaning when applied to undersecured creditors who have made the § 1111(b)(2) election (*see* Chapter 4[A][1], *supra*). If there were no special rule for such creditors, the court would have to compare the distribution the creditors are to receive under the chapter 11 plan with the distribution to which they would have been entitled in a chapter 7 case in which such an election cannot be made. In that hypothetical chapter 7, their claim would have been bifurcated, and they would have not only have been entitled to receive on account of their secured claim the value of their collateral, but would also have received their proportionate share of any distribution made to unsecured creditors in respect of the unsecured portion of their claim. This may well be more than they are receiving under the chapter 11 plan, but was a necessary part of the calculation they made when electing § 1111(b)(2) treatment. Therefore, the chapter 11 plan is deemed to satisfy the best interests test with respect to such creditors as long as they receive property having a value, as of the effective date of the plan, that is not less than the value of their collateral. § 1129(a)(7)(B).

The eighth confirmation requirement is that each class of claims or interests that is impaired has accepted the plan. § 1129(a)(8). As discussed in Section 9[E][2], *infra*, this is the only requirement that need not be met for confirmation of a plan on a nonconsensual, or cramdown, basis.

Ninth, the plan must provide for treatment of priority claims in accordance with § 1129(a)(9) unless the holder of a particular priority claim agrees to less favorable treatment.

Administrative expenses (§ 507(a)(2)) and ordinary course obligations incurred between the filing of an involuntary case and the date of the order for relief or appointment of a trustee (§ 507(a)(3)) must be paid in full in cash on the effective date of the plan. § 1129(a)(9)(A).

Domestic support obligations (§ 507(a)(1)), priority claims for employee wages, salaries, or commissions (§ 507(a)(4)), priority claims for contributions to employee benefit plans (§ 507(a)(5)), priority claims for grain storage facilities and fish produce storage or processing facilities (§ 507(a)(6)) and priority claims of individuals for prepetition deposits in connection with the purchase, lease or rental of property for personal, family or household purposes (§ 507(a)(7)) must be paid in full in cash on the effective date of the plan unless the class to which such claims belong has accepted the plan, in which event they may receive deferred cash payments with a present value equal to the allowed amount of the claim. § 1129(a)(9)(B).

Priority tax claims (whether secured or unsecured) (§ 507(a)(8)) must be paid in regular installment cash payments having a total value as of the effective date of the plan equal to the allowed amount of the claim, over a period of not more than five years after the date of the order for relief, and in a manner not less favorable than the most favored nonpriority unsecured claim under the plan (other than small claims separately classified for administrative convenience under § 1122(b)). § 1129(a)(9)(C)

Section 1129(a)(9)(B) and (C) are both provisions cited by the plurality opinion in *Till v. SCS Credit Corp.*, 541 U.S. 465 (2004), as one for which Congress may have intended the "prime-plus" interest rate to be applied in computing present value. 541 U.S. at 474 & n.10.

Priority claims listed in § 507(a)(9) (dealing with commitments to Federal depository institutions regulatory agencies) or § 507(a)(10) (dealing with claims for death or personal injury resulting from operation of a motor vehicle or vessel under the influence) are not addressed in § 1129(a)(9). Presumably, the plan may be confirmed without regard to the manner in which such priority claims are treated.

Tenth, a chapter 11 plan in which any class of claims is impaired cannot be confirmed unless at least one class of claims that is impaired under the plan has accepted the plan (without giving effect to any acceptance by insiders (§ 101(31)). § 1129(a)(10). Obviously, if § 1129(a)(8) is satisfied (each impaired class has accepted the plan), § 1129(a)(10) will also be satisfied; this provision is only relevant if

§ 1129(a)(8) is not satisfied and the plan can be confirmed only on a non-consensual, or cramdown, basis.

The eleventh condition to confirmation requires the court to conclude that the plan is likely to be effective to solve the debtor's financial woes — that "[c]onfirmation of the plan is not likely to be followed by the liquidation, or the need for further financial reorganization, of the debtor." § 1129(a)(11). The necessary showing to meet this feasibility test is minimal; courts are likely to confirm aspirational plans if the creditors wish to do so and if there is some evidence (even if not persuasive) of the future viability of the debtor. The court will decline to confirm a plan if the debtor's own projections fail to demonstrate that the required payments can be made, or if the plan has contingencies that the court considers unlikely to come to pass.

Twelfth, the plan cannot be confirmed unless all filing fees and quarterly U.S. trustee fees payable under 28 U.S.C. § 1930 have been paid or the plan provides for their payment on the effective date of the plan. § 1129(a)(12).

If the debtor is contractually obligated to provide retiree benefits (§ 1114) at preconfirmation levels, the plan must provide for continuation of those benefits after confirmation. § 1129(a)(13).

If the debtor is required to pay domestic support obligations, the debtor must be current for the period after the filing of the petition. § 1129(a)(14).

If the debtor is an individual and the holder of an allowed unsecured claim objects to the plan, the holder must receive under the plan property having a value, as of the effective date of the plan, of not less than the amount of the holder's claim, or debtor must pay all the debtor's projected disposable income to be received during the 5-year period beginning on the date the first payment is due under the plan, or during the period for which the plan provides payments, whichever is longer. § 1129(a)(15). This provision is intended to discourage debtors from attempting to circumvent the requirements of § 1325(b) by filing under chapter 11. *See* Chapter 8[D], *supra.*

Finally, if the debtor is a corporation or trust that is not a moneyed, business, or commercial corporation or trust, any transfers of property contemplated by the plan must comply with applicable nonbankruptcy law on such transfers. § 1129(a)(16).

A visualization of the confirmation requirements under § 1129(a) follows.

CONFIRMATION REQUIREMENTS § 1129(a)

1)	PLAN COMPLIES WITH CODE
2)	PLAN PROPONENT COMPLIES WITH CODE
3)	PLAN PROPOSED IN GOOD FAITH AND NOT BY MEANS FORBIDDEN BY LAW
4)	PAYMENTS FOR SERVICES, COSTS, EXPENSES APPROVED AS REASONABLE
5)	DISCLOSURE AND APPROVAL OF MANAGEMENT AND INSIDERS
6)	APPROVAL OF RATE CHANGES FOR REGULATED INDUSTRIES
7)	BEST INTERESTS TEST SATISFIED
8)	APPROVAL OF PLAN BY EACH IMPAIRED CLASS
9)	APPROPRIATE PROVISIONS FOR PAYMENT OF PRIORITY CLAIMS
10)	ONE IMPAIRED CLASS ACCEPTED PLAN
11)	FEASIBILITY TEST MET
12)	FILING AND U.S. TRUSTEE FEES PAID
13)	RETIREE BENEFITS CONTINUED
14)	DEBTOR HAS PAID POSTPETITION DOMESTIC SUPPORT OBLIGATIONS
15)	IF DEBTOR IS INDIVIDUAL AND UNSECURED CREDITOR OBJECTS TO PLAN, CREDITOR IS PAID IN FULL OR PROPERTY DISTRIBUTED IS NOT LESS THAN PROJECTED DISPOSABLE INCOME OF DEBTOR FOR LONGER OF FIVE YEARS OR DURATION OF PLAN PAYMENTS
16)	TRANSFERS UNDER PLAN COMPLY WITH APPLICABLE NONBANKRUPTCY LAW GOVERNING TRANSFERS OF PROPERTY BY NON-MONEYED, BUSINESS, OR COMMERCIAL CORPORATION OR TRUST

2. Cramdown

The goal of a chapter 11 plan of reorganization is a consensual allocation of reorganization value among creditor groups; this is reflected in the requirement for confirmation set forth in § 1129(a)(8) that each class accept the plan or be unimpaired. However, creditors cannot always agree with each other and with the debtor on dividing up the bankruptcy pie; indeed some creditors may not want the reorganization to succeed at all, preferring the recovery they would obtain upon immediate liquidation of the bankrupt. Section 1129(b) provides an alternative mechanism for confirming a plan of reorganization in the face of opposition from one or more creditor groups.

A nonconsensual confirmation, familiarly known as a "cramdown," can occur only if all the requirements of § 1129(a) are met other than § 1129(a)(8) (the requirement that each class of impaired claims or interests has accepted the plan). This means that a plan cannot be crammed down on all classes, because § 1129(a)(10) requires that at least one impaired class of claims has accepted the plan.

If a plan proponent seeks to confirm its plan under § 1129(b)(1), the court must confirm the plan if it meets two requirements — it does not discriminate unfairly with respect to each impaired class of claims or interests that has not accepted the plan, and it is fair and equitable with respect to each such class.

The concept of unfair discrimination is also used in § 1322, setting forth the requirements for a chapter 13 plan. Section 1322(b)(1) provides that classification of claims is not required in such a plan, but if a chapter 13 plan creats classes of claims, the plan can not "discriminate unfairly against any class so designated." *See* Chapter 8[B], *supra*. As was true in the chapter 13 context, different treatment between classes is insufficient to establish unfair discrimination, but the court will examine whether there is some reasonable basis for the discrimination, such as whether the particular creditor group has a relationship with the debtor that justifies a different treatment.

Whether the plan is "fair and equitable" with respect to the dissenting impaired classes must be determined by applying the definition of that phrase in § 1129(b)(2). That section describes what "fair and equitable" treatment requires for each of the three types of classes that may be impaired.

Holders of secured claims are treated fairly and equitably if the plan provides for their claims to be treated in one of three ways. § 1129(b)(2)(A). The first approach (and by far the most frequently employed) is for the plan to provide for the holder to retain the lien securing the allowed claim, and for the holder to receive under the plan deferred cash payments in an amount that meets two statutory requirements. § 1129(b)(2)(A)(i). First, the total amount of the payments must at least equal the allowed amount of the secured claim (which is determined under § 506(a) unless the class to which the holder belongs has elected to be treated under § 1111(b)(2), in which event the entire claim is treated as a secured claim). Thus, if the total claim of the secured creditor is $10,000, and the collateral is worth $7,500, the secured creditor must receive deferred cash payments totaling $7,500. Second, the deferred cash payments must have a value as of the effective date of the plan of at least the value of the collateral. So if our secured creditor with the $10,000 claim is receiving deferred cash payments totaling $7,500, the secured creditor will not be treated fairly and equitably unless it receives interest on those payments sufficient to make the present value of the stream of payments no less than $7,500.

The importance of valuation of the collateral in establishing the present value of the required distribution raises all the valuation issues we have seen in other contexts. Under § 506(a), the value should be determined "in light of the purpose of the valuation." The Supreme Court decided in *Associates Commercial Corp. v. Rash*, 520 U.S. 953 (1997), that the property retained in a chapter 13 plan should be valued at its replacement cost (the price a willing buyer in debtor's place would pay to obtain like property from a willing seller, but without warranties, inventory storage or reconditioning charges) rather than its liquidation value. The same standard is probably applicable to property retained in a chapter 11 plan.

Equally important to the secured creditor is the interest rate that must be applied to the deferred cash payments. The Supreme Court held in *Till v. SCS Credit Corp.*, 541 U.S. 465 (2004), that the appropriate interest rate to be used in discounting payments to be made to a secured creditor under § 1325(a)(5) is a "prime-plus" or "formula" rate under which you begin with the prime rate and then adjust it upward (perhaps by 1-3%) to reflect the risk of non-payment by this bankrupt debtor. *Till* includes dictum suggesting that the plurality thought Congress would favor using the same approach when choosing an appropriate interest rate in other sections of the Code requiring a payment stream to be discounted to present value, including § 1129(b). 541 U.S. at 474 & n.10. However, the plurality also noted that, unlike chapter 13, chapter 11 has an active market for loans to chapter 11 debtors and therefore "when picking a cramdown rate in a Chapter 11 case, it might make sense to ask what rate an efficient market would produce." *Id.* at 476 n.14. The Sixth Circuit in *In re American Homepatient Inc.*, 420 F.3d 559 (6th Cir. 2005), has suggested that the *Till* formula rate should be used under § 1129(b)(2)(A)(i) only when there is no efficient market for chapter 11 financing; where there is an efficient market, that market rate should be used.

The second alternative "fair and equitable" treatment of the secured creditor is for the collateral to be sold (allowing the secured creditor to credit bid its debt) and the lien to attach to the proceeds of the sale. Then that lien is treated under one of the other approaches. § 1129(b)(2)(A)(ii).

The final alternative for "fair and equitable" treatment of a secured claim is if the plan provides for the creditor to realize the "indubitable equivalent" of its secured claim. § 1129(b)(2)(A)(iii). Abandonment of collateral to creditor would satisfy this test, as would a plan that provided the creditor a replacement lien on similar collateral. If the creditor is asked to accept something that differs dramatically in nature and/or value from the original collateral, the plan will fail to satisfy the requirement.

Holders of unsecured claims are treated fairly and equitably if either they receive property, having a value as of the effective date of the plan, equal to the allowed amount of their claims, or the plan implements the so-called "absolute priority" rule. The absolute priority rule requires that value be distributed in accordance with the absolute priorities of the respective creditors, allowing those higher up in priority to be paid in full before lower classes get anything. No matter what the plan allocates to the unsecured creditors (if anything), their treatment is fair and equitable if no holder of any claim or interest that is junior to such creditors will receive any property under the plan on account of such claim or interest. § 1129(b)(2)(B).

Section 1129(b)(2)(C) takes a similar approach for holders of interests. A class of interests is treated fairly and equitably if the plan provides that each holder of an interest receive property having a value, as of the effective date of the plan, equal to the greatest of the allowed amount of any fixed liquidation preference, any fixed redemption price, or the value of the interest, or alternatively the holder of any junior interest will not receive any property under the plan on account of such interest.

A visualization of the requirements for confirmation of a chapter 11 plan on a cramdown basis follows.

CRAMDOWN § 1129(b)			
REQUIREMENTS FOR CRAMDOWN § 1129(b)(1)	FAIR AND EQUITABLE § 1129(b)(2)		
	SECURED CLAIMS § 1129(b)(2)(A)	UNSECURED CLAIMS § 1129(b)(2)(B)	EQUITY INTERESTS § 1129(b)(2)(C)
1) ALL REQUIREMENTS OF § 1129(a) ARE MET EXCEPT § 1129(a)(8), 2) REQUEST BY PLAN PROPONENT FOR CRAMDOWN, 3) PLAN "DOES NOT DISCRIMINATE UNFAIRLY" AGAINST ANY DISSENTING IMPAIRED CLASS, AND 4) PLAN IS "FAIR AND EQUITABLE" WITH RESPECT TO EACH DISSENTING IMPAIRED CLASS	1) HOLDER RETAINS LIEN AND RECEIVES PROPERTY DEFERRED CASH ≥ ALLOWED AMOUNT OF CLAIM AND HAVING PRESENT VALUE ≥ VALUE OF COLLATERAL, 2) PROPERTY SOLD AND LIEN ATTACHES TO PROCEEDS, OR 3) HOLDER RECEIVES INDUBITABLE EQUIVALENT OF CLAIM	1) HOLDER RECEIVES PROPERTY WITH PRESENT VALUE ≥ ALLOWED AMOUNT OF CLAIM, OR 2) NO JUNIOR HOLDER RECEIVES ANYTHING ON ACCOUNT OF CLAIM OR INTEREST	1) HOLDER RECEIVES PROPERTY WITH PRESENT VALUE ≥ ALLOWED AMOUNT OF LIQUIDATION PREFERENCE, REDEMPTION PRICE OR VALUE OF INTEREST, OR 2) NO JUNIOR HOLDER RECEIVES ANYTHING ON ACCOUNT OF INTEREST

Notice that both § 1129(b)(2)(B) and (C) implement the absolute priority rule by barring junior claimants or interest holders from receiving any property "on account of" their claims or interests under the plan. Prior to the enactment of the Code, case law had interpreted the absolute priority rule as consistent with the notion that, even if dissenting unsecured creditors were not being paid in full, holders of junior claims or interests could still receive property in the reorganized company so long as it was on account of new value given and not on account of their old claims or interests. Courts had suggested that this "new value" exception to the absolute priority rule would apply only if the holder of the junior claim or interest contributed new, substantial value to the debtor in the form of money or money's worth that was necessary to the success of the reorganization and the property received on account of that contribution was reasonably equivalent to the value given. *See, e.g., In re Bonner Mall Partnership*, 2 F.3d 899, 908 (9th Cir. 1993), *cert. granted*, 510 U.S. 1039, *appeal dismissed as moot*, 513 U.S. 18 (1994). These requirements are visualized below.

NEW VALUE EXCEPTION
1)   NEW CONTRIBUTION OF VALUE,
2)   VALUE MUST BE SUBSTANTIAL,
3)   VALUE MUST BE NECESSARY FOR A SUCCESSFUL REORGANIZATION,
4)   VALUE MUST BE IN THE FORM OF MONEY OR MONEY'S WORTH, AND
5)   PROPERTY RECEIVED UNDER THE PLAN MUST BE REASONABLY EQUIVALENT TO THE VALUE GIVEN

The Code makes no mention of a "new value" exception to the absolute priority rule, and some have questioned whether congressional silence should be seen as a repudiation of the previously-existing doctrine. Although the issue is still not free from doubt, the Supreme Court decided in *Bank of America Nat'l Trust & Savings Assoc. v. 203 North LaSalle Street Partnership*, 526 U.S. 434 (1999), that, "assuming a new value corollary," a plan providing junior interest holders the exclusive opportunity to obtain equity in the new reorganized company (for which they provided no new value) free from competition and without benefit of market valuation violated the absolute priority rule. In so holding, the Court noted, without deciding the issue, that "the possibility [is] apparent in the statutory text, that the absolute priority rule . . . may carry a new value corollary." *Id.* at 449.

F. POSTCONFIRMATION ISSUES

When a chapter 11 plan is confirmed, there are four major consequences described in § 1141. First, the confirmed plan becomes binding on the debtor and its creditors and equity holders, as well as any general partner of the debtor, any entity issuing securities under the plan and any entity acquiring assets under the plan, even if their claims or interests are impaired under the plan and whether or not they accepted it. § 1141(a). Second, all property of the estate is vested in the debtor (except to the extent the plan provides otherwise). § 1141(b). Third, all property dealt with by the plan is free and clear of all claims and interests of creditors, equity holders and general partners in the debtor (except to the extent the plan or confirmation order provides otherwise). § 1141(c). Fourth, the debtor is discharged and equity interests are terminated (except to the extent the plan or confirmation order provides otherwise). § 1141(d). The discharge will be discussed in Chapter 10, *infra*. The effect of confirmation is visualized below.

EFFECT OF CONFIRMATION § 1141

1)	PLAN BINDS DEBTOR, CREDITORS, EQUITY HOLDERS, GENERAL PARTNERS, EQUITY ISSUERS, PROPERTY ACQUIRERS,
2)	ESTATE PROPERTY IS VESTED IN DEBTOR,
3)	PROPERTY IS FREE AND CLEAR OF CLAIMS AND INTERESTS, AND
4)	DEBTOR IS DISCHARGED FROM PRE-CONFIRMATION DEBTS AND EQUITY INTERESTS ARE TERMINATED

After the plan is confirmed, the debtor and any entity organized for purposes of carrying out the plan are directed to carry out the plan and to comply with any orders of the court. § 1142(a). Carrying out the plan will include making any distributions thereunder in the amounts and according to the schedule specified therein. The court may require the debtor or any other necessary party to execute or deliver any instrument required to transfer property under the plan and to perform any other act necessary to consummate the plan. § 1142(b). The Code imposes one restriction on parties seeking to participate in distributions under the plan — if there is a condition to participation in distributions, such as surrender of a security or instrument or any other act, that condition must be satisfied within five years after confirmation or the party is barred from participation. § 1143.

Once the chapter 11 plan is confirmed, the creditors and equity interest holders have few bases for attacking it. Of course, the order confirming the plan is a final order, and like any other final order of a bankruptcy court it can be appealed. A notice of appeal must be filed within 14 days after entry of the confirmation order under Fed. R. Bankr. P. 8002(a). In order to avoid mooting the appeal after substantial consummation of the plan, the party appealing the confirmation order would want to seek a stay of the confirmation order pending appeal under Fed. R. Bankr. P. 8005. The motion for such a stay must be presented to the bankruptcy judge in the first instance, but the bankruptcy judge is under no obligation to grant such a stay. If the bankruptcy judge denies relief, the appellant may seek a stay from the district court or bankruptcy appellate panel (if there is one). Any court granting a stay may condition the granting of the stay on the filing of a bond or other appropriate security to protect all parties against damages caused by the delay of the appeal. Fed. R. Bankr. P. 8005.

A party in interest may also seek revocation of the confirmation order under § 1144. A motion to revoke must be made within 180 days after entry of the confirmation order, and the court may revoke the order only if such order was obtained by fraud. Courts have construed the statute to require a showing of actual fraud (misrepresentation or failure to disclose made with intent to defraud), *e.g.*, intentional failure to disclose assets, misrepresenting value of assets, concealing potential purchasers of assets, presenting false financial statements. The debtor's failure to comply with the requirements of the plan does not constitute grounds for revocation.

If the court revokes the confirmation order, the order of revocation must contain provisions necessary to protect any entity acquiring rights in good faith reliance on the confirmation order, and must revoke the debtor's discharge. § 1144.

A visualization of options to attack a confirmed plan follows.

ATTACKS ON CONFIRMED PLAN		
APPEAL RULES 8002(a), 8005	REVOCATION § 1144	
NOTICE OF APPEAL MUST BE FILED WITHIN 14 DAYS AFTER ENTRY OF ORDER	GROUNDS	TIMING
APPELLANT MAY REQUEST STAY FROM BANKRUPTCY COURT OR, IF DENIED, FROM DISTRICT COURT OR BAP COURT MAY CONDITION GRANT OF STAY PENDING APPEAL ON FILING BOND OR OTHER SECURITY	ACTUAL FRAUD	MUST BE SOUGHT WITHIN 180 DAYS AFTER ENTRY OF CONFIRMATION ORDER

If the debtor believes that an attack on the confirmed plan is meritorious, the debtor may seek to modify the plan to meet the objections on which the appeal or motion to revoke is premised. The plan may be modified after confirmation only prior to "substantial consummation" of the plan. § 1127(b). "Substantial consummation" is defined in § 1101(2) to be the time when three things occur: transfer of all or substantially all property to be transferred under the plan, assumption by debtor or its successor of the business or management of all or substantially all of the property dealt with by the plan, and commencement of distribution under the plan. The modified plan must meet the requirements of § 1122 and § 1123. The modified plan becomes effective only if the court determines that circumstances warrant the modification and, after notice and hearing, confirms the plan as modified under § 1129. § 1127(b).

As was true for preconfirmation modifications of the plan, the plan proponent must circulate a disclosure statement with respect to the modified plan under § 1125, § 1127(c), and holders of claims may change their votes within the time set by the court. § 1127(d).

The following chart visualizes the provisions relating to postconfirmation modification of a chapter 11 plan.

POSTCONFIRMATION MODIFICATION OF PLAN § 1127		
RIGHT TO MODIFY	RESTRICTIONS ON MODIFICATION	PROTECTIONS FOR HOLDERS OF CLAIMS AND INTERESTS
PROPONENT OF PLAN HAS RIGHT TO MODIFY PLAN AT ANY TIME AFTER CONFIRMATION AND BEFORE SUBSTANTIAL CONSUMMATION (§ 1101(2)) OF PLAN § 1127(b)	MODIFIED PLAN MUST COMPLY WITH §§ 1122 & 1123 § 1127(b) PROPONENT MUST COMPLY WITH § 1125 § 1127(c) MODIFIED PLAN BECOMES PLAN ONLY IF CIRCUMSTANCES WARRANT MODIFICATION AND COURT CONFIRMS PLAN AS MODIFIED § 1127(b)	HOLDERS HAVE RIGHT TO CHANGE VOTES WITHIN TIME SPECIFIED BY COURT, BUT IF THEY DO NOT, ORIGINAL VOTE APPLIES TO MODIFIED PLAN § 1127(d)

If modification of the plan is not feasible, the debtor may elect to convert the chapter 11 case to a chapter 7 case, § 1112(a), or the court may dismiss the case or convert it to a chapter 7 on the motion of a party in interest under § 1112(b), for cause. *See* Chapter 11, *infra*.

Chapter 10

DISCHARGE

A. WHEN DISCHARGE IS AVAILABLE

For an individual debtor, the purpose of bankruptcy is to obtain a discharge from all prepetition debts, and in most cases this is exactly what the debtor obtains, whether the debtor files under chapter 7, chapter 13 or chapter 11.

In rare cases, however, the debtor goes through the bankruptcy process to emerge without any discharge at all. If a general discharge is denied, all of the debtor's assets and future income are subject to the claims of all creditors to the same extent as if bankruptcy had not occurred. Because this result destroys any "fresh start" for the debtor, it is invoked very rarely and only because the debtor, through his or her own conduct, has demonstrated that the debtor is not entitled to the protection afforded by discharge.

Any party in interest may object to the debtor's discharge. The objection must be filed no later than 60 days after the first date set for the § 341 meeting in a chapter 7 or 13 case, and no later than the first date set for the confirmation hearing in a chapter 11 case (subject to extension by the court). Fed. R. Bankr. P. 4004(a). The party objecting to discharge has the burden of establishing why discharge should not be granted. Fed. R. Bankr. P. 4005. In any case in which the debtor is an individual, the court may hold a hearing on discharge at which the debtor must appear in person. At the hearing, the court must inform the debtor that a discharge has been granted or explain the reasons why it is being denied. § 524(d).

1. Chapter 7

A discharge under § 727(a) discharges the individual debtor "from all debts [other than those excluded from discharge under § 523, discussed in Section 10[B][1], *infra*] that arose before the date of the order for relief," whether or not a proof of claim was filed with respect to any such debt or whether a filed claim was allowed. § 727(b). The court must grant a discharge in a chapter 7 case unless the debtor does not qualify for discharge for one of the reasons set forth in § 727(a). There are 12 reasons why a discharge might be denied.

First, a chapter 7 discharge is available only if the debtor is an individual (a living, breathing person rather than a corporation or other entity). § 727(a)(1).

Second, the debtor may not receive a discharge if the debtor made certain fraudulent transfers under § 727(a)(2). To disqualify the debtor for discharge, the debtor must have transferred, removed, destroyed, mutilated or concealed property with actual fraudulent intent, *i.e.*, intent to hinder, delay or defraud a creditor or an officer of the estate having custody of estate property. If the property involved was property of the debtor, the action must have been taken within one year prior to the bankruptcy filing; if the property was property of the estate, the action must have been taken after the bankruptcy filing. To determine whether the debtor acted with fraudulent intent, courts look for the same so-called "badges of fraud" that are used in seeking avoidance of fraudulent transfers under § 548(a)(1)(A), such as absence of consideration, transfer to family member, timing of transfer, continued use or possession by debtor, secrecy. *See* Chapter 5[D], *supra*.

Third, the court may deny discharge if the debtor has concealed, destroyed, mutilated, falsified, or failed to keep adequate books and records from which the debtor's financial condition or business transactions can be ascertained. § 727(a)(3). The debtor's actions may be excused if the debtor's conduct was "justified under all of the circumstances of the case."

Fourth, a debtor will be denied a discharge if the debtor has knowingly and fraudulently engaged in conduct that interferes with the operation of the bankruptcy system. § 727(a)(4). The prohibited acts include making a false oath or account; presenting or using a false claim; giving, offering, receiving or attempting to obtain money, property or advantage or a promise thereof for acting or not acting; or withholding from an officer of the estate any recorded information relating to the debtor's property or financial affairs. These actions may also trigger criminal prosecution under 18 U.S.C. § 152.

The fifth basis for denying a chapter 7 discharge is if the debtor has failed to provide a satisfactory explanation of any loss of assets. § 727(a)(5). Discharge will be denied only if the explanation is evasive or vague or incredible or the debtor can provide no evidence that the explanation is true. The debtor is entitled to a discharge even if the debtor used assets in a way that was unwise (speculative investments or gambling) but can fully substantiate those actions.

Sixth, the debtor cannot receive a discharge if the debtor has refused in the case to obey lawful court orders or to respond to material questions or testify. § 727(a)(6). The court might order the debtor to turn over assets to the trustee, to file schedules, to produce documents, or to appear at meetings or hearings, for example. The debtor may refuse to answer questions or testify only by asserting his or her privilege against self-incrimination, and must answer the questions or testify if the court grants the debtor immunity from prosecution with respect to the matter concerning which the privilege was claimed.

Seventh, debtor's acts describe above (§ 727(a)(2)-(6)) that serve as a basis for denial of discharge when they occur in the debtor's own bankruptcy case are also grounds for denial of a discharge when they occur within one year prior to, or during, a bankruptcy case of an insider. § 727(a)(7). An "insider" of an individual debtor includes a relative, relatives of a general partner of the debtor, a general partner of the debtor, or a corporation of which the debtor is a director, officer or person in control (§ 101(31)(A)).

The next two provisions of § 727(a) are intended to prevent serial filers (those who file bankruptcy cases one after another) from obtaining discharges too often. Under § 727(a)(8), a debtor is denied a discharge if the debtor obtained a discharge in another chapter 7 or in a chapter 11 bankruptcy case filed within the eight-year period prior to the filing of the current chapter 7 case. Under § 727(a)(9), the debtor cannot get a discharge in a chapter 7 case if the debtor obtained a discharge in a prior chapter 12 or chapter 13 case filed within the six-year period prior to the filing of the current chapter 7 case, unless the debtor paid all debtor's allowed unsecured claims under the prior chapter 12 or chapter 13 plan (very unlikely), or if the debtor did not do so, the debtor paid at least 70% of those claims and the plan was proposed in good faith and "was the debtor's best effort."

Tenth, the court will not grant a discharge if the debtor executes a written waiver of discharge after the order for relief in the case. § 727(a)(10). Prebankruptcy waivers of discharge are not enforceable.

Under the 2005 BAPCPA amendments, Congress added two more grounds for denying a discharge to a chapter 7 debtor. The first is for failure to complete an instructional course concerning personal financial management after the filing of the bankruptcy petition. § 727(a)(11). This course is distinct from the credit counseling session that is an eligibility requirement for filing the case under § 109(h) (*see* Chapter 1[C], *supra*). The debtor is required to file a statement of completion of such a course on Official Form 23. Fed. R. Bankr. P. 1007(b)(7). The court may not grant a discharge unless such statement has been filed. Fed. R. Bankr. P. 4004(c)(1)(H). The debtor is excused from completing such a course if the debtor would be excused from the prepetition credit counseling requirement under § 109(h)(4), or if the debtor resides in a district for which the U.S. trustee determines that the approved instructional courses are not adequate to provide this service. § 727(a)(11).

The other recent provision, § 727(a)(12), denies the chapter 7 debtor a discharge if the court, after notice and a hearing held not more than 10 days before the date the court enters a discharge order, finds there is "reasonable cause to believe" the § 522(q)(1) limit on the debtor's homestead exemption may be applicable, *see* Chapter 3[B][1], *supra*, and there is pending any proceeding in which the debtor may be convicted of a felony under circumstances demonstrating that the filing of the bankruptcy petition was abusive, or the debtor may owe a debt arising from securities laws violations, fraud or deceit or manipulation in a fiduciary capacity or in connection with the purchase or sale of a registered security, a civil remedy under the Racketeer Influenced and Corrupt Organizations Act, or any criminal act or intentional tort or willful or reckless misconduct that caused serious physical injury or death to another individual in the preceding five years (§ 522(q)(1)).

A visualization of the grounds for denying a chapter 7 discharge follows.

GROUNDS FOR DENIAL OF CHAPTER 7 DISCHARGE
§ 727(a)

SECTION	GROUNDS	EXCEPTIONS OR LIMITATIONS
§ 727(a)(1)	DEBTOR IS NOT AN INDIVIDUAL	NONE
§ 727(a)(2)	DEBTOR TRANSFERRED, REMOVED, DESTROYED, MUTILATED OR CONCEALED PROPERTY OF DEBTOR OR PROPERTY OF ESTATE WITH INTENT TO HINDER, DELAY OR DEFRAUD CREDITOR	ACT WITH RESPECT TO PROPERTY OF DEBTOR MUST HAVE OCCURRED WITHIN ONE YEAR PRIOR TO BANKRUPTCY FILING
§ 727(a)(3)	DEBTOR CONCEALED, DESTROYED, MUTILATED, FALSIFIED OR FAILED TO KEEP RECORDED INFORMATION ABOUT FINANCIAL CONDITION OR BUSINESS	ACTION OR FAILURE TO ACT WAS JUSTIFIED UNDER ALL OF THE CIRCUMSTANCES OF CASE
§ 727(a)(4)	DEBTOR KNOWINGLY OR FRAUDULENTLY MADE FALSE OATH OR ACCOUNT, MADE FALSE CLAIM, ENGAGED IN BRIBERY OR WITHHELD RECORDED INFORMATION	NONE
§ 727(a)(5)	DEBTOR FAILED TO EXPLAIN SATISFACTORILY LOSS OF ASSETS	NONE
§ 727(a)(6)	DEBTOR REFUSED TO OBEY COURT ORDER, RESPOND TO MATERIAL QUESTION OR TESTIFY	DEBTOR MAY REQUIRE IMMUNITY FROM PROSECUTION BEFORE ANSWERING QUESTION OR TESTIFYING IN A WAY THAT WOULD INCRIMINATE DEBTOR
§ 727(a)(7)	DEBTOR HAS COMMITTED ACT UNDER § 727(a)(2)-(6) IN BANKRUPTCY CASE OF INSIDER	SAME AS ABOVE
§ 727(a)(8)	DEBTOR RECEIVED DISCHARGE IN PRIOR CHAPTER 7 OR 11 CASE FILED WITHIN 8 YEARS BEFORE PETITION FILED IN PRESENT CASE	NONE
§ 727(a)(9)	DEBTOR RECEIVED DISCHARGE IN PRIOR CHAPTER 12 OR 13 CASE FILED WITHIN 6 YEARS BEFORE PETITION FILED IN PRESENT CASE	PLAN PAID 100% OF ALLOWED UNSECURED CLAIMS, OR PAID AT LEAST 70% OF ALLOWED UNSECURED CLAIMS AND WAS PROPOSED IN GOOD FAITH AND WAS DEBTOR'S BEST EFFORT
§ 727(a)(10)	WRITTEN WAIVER OF DISCHARGE AFTER ORDER FOR RELIEF	NONE
§ 727(a)(11)	DEBTOR FAILED TO COMPLETE POSTPETITION FINANCIAL INSTRUCTIONAL COURSE	DEBTOR IS EXCUSED UNDER § 109(h), OR U.S. TRUSTEE DETERMINES THAT DISTRICT HAS INSUFFICIENT APPROVED COURSES
§ 727(a)(12)	COURT FINDS REASONABLE CAUSE TO BELIEVE DEBTOR MAY BE SUBJECT TO § 522(q) AND PENDING FELONY PROCEEDING DESCRIBED IN § 522(q)(1)(A) OR POTENTIAL LIABILITY FOR DEBT DESCRIBED IN § 522(q)(1)(B)	NONE

The court may not grant a discharge if certain motions are pending, or if the debtor has not paid the fees required by 28 U.S.C. § 1930 upon the commencement of the case unless the court has waived such fees. Fed. R. Bankr. P. 4004(c).

2. Chapter 13

A discharge under chapter 13 is intended to be granted upon completion of all payments required by the chapter 13 plan, and discharges the debtor from "all debts provided for by the plan or disallowed under section 502," with certain exceptions discussed in the Section 10[B][1], *infra*. § 1328(a). There are five conditions that must be met before a court may grant a chapter 13 discharge if plan payments are completed.

First, if the debtor is required to pay a domestic support obligation under any judicial or administrative order or statute, the debtor must have certified that all such obligations due on or before the date of certification (including prepetition amounts to the extent provided by the plan) have been paid. § 1328(a).

Second, the debtor must not have executed a written waiver of discharge after the order for relief which has been approved by the court. § 1328(a).

Third, the debtor must not have received a discharge in a prior chapter 7, 11 or 12 case filed within four years prior to filing of the current case, or in a prior chapter 13 case filed within two years prior to the fling of the current case. § 1328(f). This provision, added by the 2005 BAPCPA amendments, is intended to discourage serial filers.

Fourth, the debtor must have completed an instructional course concerning personal financial management after the filing of the petition. § 1328(g)(1). This course is distinct from the credit counseling session that is an eligibility requirement for filing the case under § 109(h) (*see* Chapter 1[C], *supra*). The debtor is required to file a statement of completion of such a course on Official Form 23. Fed. R. Bankr. P. 1007(b)(7). The court may not grant a discharge unless such statement has been filed. Fed. R. Bankr. P. 4004(c)(4). The debtor is excused from completing such a course if the debtor would be excused from the prepetition credit counseling requirement under § 109(h)(4), or if the debtor resides in a district for which the U.S. trustee determines that the approved instructional courses are not adequate to provide this service. § 1328(g)(2).

Fifth, no discharge may be granted to the debtor unless after notice and a hearing held not more than 10 days before the date the court enters a discharge order, the court finds there is "no reasonable cause to believe" the § 522(q)(1) limit on the debtor's homestead exemption may be applicable, *see* Chapter 3[B][1], *supra*, and there is pending any proceeding in which the debtor may be convicted of a felony under circumstances demonstrating that the filing of the bankruptcy petition was abusive, or the debtor may owe a debt arising from securities laws violations, fraud or deceit or manipulation in a fiduciary capacity or in connection with the purchase or sale of a registered security, a civil remedy under the Racketeer Influenced and Corrupt Organizations Act, or any criminal act or intentional tort or willful or reckless misconduct that caused serious physical injury or death to another individual in the preceding five years (§ 522(q)(1)). § 1328(h). This new provision is comparable to § 727(a)(12) and § 1141(d)(5)(C), applicable to chapter 7 and chapter 11 cases, respectively.

If the debtor has not completed the plan payments (and the vast majority of chapter 13 debtors fail to do so), the court may grant the debtor a discharge (often called a "hardship discharge"), but only if three additional conditions are met. First, debtor's failure to complete the plan must be "due to circumstances for which the debtor should not justly be held accountable," such as an unexpected change in financial position, illness, divorce or the like. § 1328(b)(1). Second, the "best interests" test must have been satisfied with respect to plan distributions actually made, that is, the value, as of the effective date of the plan, of the property actually distributed to creditors under the plan must not be less than the amount that would have been paid on their claims in a hypothetical chapter 7 liquidation on that date. § 1328(b)(2). Third, modification of the plan under § 1329 must be impracticable. § 1328(b)(3).

The conditions for a discharge in chapter 13 are visualized below.

CONDITIONS TO CHAPTER 13 DISCHARGE § 1328	
ALL DISCHARGES § 1328(a)	ADDITIONAL CONDITIONS TO DISCHARGE IF DEBTOR HAS NOT COMPLETED PLAN PAYMENTS § 1328(b)
DEBTOR WHO IS REQUIRED TO PAY DOMESTIC SUPPORT OBLIGATION BY JUDICIAL OR ADMINISTRATIVE ORDER OR BY STATUTE HAS CERTIFIED THAT ALL AMOUNTS PAYABLE ON OR BEFORE DATE OF CERTIFICATION HAVE BEEN PAID	DEBTOR'S FAILURE TO COMPLETE PLAN WAS DUE TO CIRCUMSTANCES FOR WHICH DEBTOR SHOULD NOT JUSTLY BE HELD ACCOUNTABLE
COURT HAS NOT APPROVED WRITTEN WAIVER OF DISCHARGE EXECUTED BY DEBTOR AFTER ORDER FOR RELIEF	
DEBTOR HAS NOT RECEIVED DISCHARGE 1) IN CHAPTER 7, 11 OR 12 CASE FILED WITHIN 4 YEARS PRIOR TO CURRENT CHAPTER 13 FILING, OR 2) IN CHAPTER 13 CASE FILED WITHIN 2 YEARS PRIOR TO CURRENT CHAPTER 13 FILING	VALUE, AS OF EFFECTIVE DATE, OF PROPERTY CREDITORS ACTUALLY RECEIVED UNDER PLAN WAS NOT LESS THAN AMOUNT THAT THEY WOULD HAVE RECEIVED IN HYPOTHETICAL CHAPTER 7 ON THAT DATE
DEBTOR HAS COMPLETED POSTPETITION A PERSONAL FINANCIAL MANAGEMENT INSTRUCTIONAL COURSE (§ 111) UNLESS: 1) DEBTOR IS PERSON DESCRIBED IN § 109(h), OR 2) DEBTOR RESIDES IN DISTRICT FOR WHICH U.S. TRUSTEE DETERMINES APPROVED INSTRUCTIONAL COURSES ARE NOT ADEQUATE	MODIFICATION OF PLAN UNDER § 1329 IS NOT PRACTICABLE
COURT FINDS NO REASONABLE CAUSE TO BELIEVE THAT DEBTOR MAY BE SUBJECT TO § 522(q) AND PENDING FELONY PROCEEDING DESCRIBED IN § 522(q)(1)(A) OR POTENTIAL LIABILITY FOR DEBT DESCRIBED IN § 522(q)(1)(B)	

3. Chapter 11

For a chapter 11 debtor that is not an individual, confirmation of a chapter 11 plan discharges the debtor from all preconfirmation debts, whether or not a proof of claim is filed or the claim is allowed or the holder of the claim accepts the plan. § 1141(d)(1). An individual debtor in a chapter 11 case does not receive a discharge (unless the court orders otherwise for cause) until the court grants a discharge upon completion of all payments under the chapter 11 plan, and does not receive a discharge of any debt excluded from discharge under § 523 (discussed in Section 10[B][1], *infra*). § 1141(d)(5)(A). This puts the individual chapter 11 debtor in the same position as a debtor seeking a discharge upon completion of plan payments in chapter 13. As was true for a chapter 13 debtor, the individual chapter 11 debtor may request a discharge before all plan payments have been completed. The court, after notice and a hearing, may grant such a discharge if two conditions are met. First, the value, as of the effective date, of payments actually made to holders of allowed secured claims must not be less than the amount they would have received in a hypothetical chapter 7 liquidation on that date. Second, modification of the plan under § 1127 must be impracticable. § 1141(d)(5)(B).

There are only three circumstances under which the debtor is not so discharged. First, confirmation of a plan providing for the liquidation of all or substantially all of the property of the estate does not discharge the debtor if the debtor does not engage in business after consummation of the plan and the debtor would be denied a discharge under § 727(a) were the case a case under chapter 7. § 1141(d)(3). See Section 10[A][1], *supra*, for a discussion of the grounds for denial of a discharge under chapter 7.

Second, a debtor may waive discharge by executing a written waiver of discharge after the order for relief that is approved by the court. § 1141(d)(4).

Third, no discharge may be granted to an individual chapter 11 debtor unless, after notice and a hearing held not more than 10 days before the date the court enters a discharge order, the court finds there is "no reasonable cause to believe" the § 522(q)(1) limit on the debtor's homestead exemption may be applicable, *see* Chapter 3[B][1], *supra*, and there is pending any proceeding in which the debtor may be convicted of a felony under circumstances demonstrating that the filing of the bankruptcy petition was abusive, or the debtor may owe a debt arising from securities laws violations, fraud or deceit or manipulation in a fiduciary capacity or in connection with the purchase or sale of a registered security, a civil remedy under the Racketeer Influenced and Corrupt Organizations Act, or any criminal act or intentional tort or willful or reckless misconduct that caused serious physical injury or death to another individual in the preceding five years (§ 522(q)(1)). § 1141(d)(5)(C). This new provision is comparable to § 727(a)(12) and § 1328(h), applicable to chapter 7 and chapter 13 cases, respectively.

The provisions relating to the grant of a chapter 11 discharges are visualized below.

DISCHARGE UNDER CHAPTER 11 § 1141(d)			
WHEN DISCHARGE IS EFFECTIVE			GROUNDS FOR DENYING DISCHARGE § 1141(d)(3)-(5)
NON-INDIVIDUAL DEBTOR § 1141(d)(1)	INDIVIDUAL DEBTOR § 1141(d)(5)		1) CHAPTER 11 PLAN PROVIDES FOR LIQUIDATION OF ALL OR SUBSTANTIALLY ALL PROPERTY OF ESTATE, DEBTOR DOES NOT ENGAGE IN BUSINESS AFTER CONSUMMATION DATE, AND DEBTOR WOULD BE DENIED DISCHARGE UNDER § 727(a) IF CASE WERE A CHAPTER 7 CASE,
UPON CONFIRMATION OF CHAPTER 11 PLAN	UPON COMPLETION OF PLAN PAYMENTS	PRIOR TO COMPLETION OF PLAY PAYMENTS	
	UNLESS COURT ORDERS OTHERWISE FOR CAUSE, UPON COURT GRANT OF DISCHARGE	IF COURT FINDS: 1) VALUE, AS OF EFFECTIVE DATE, OF PROPERTY CREDITORS ACTUALLY RECEIVED UNDER PLAN WAS NOT LESS THAN AMOUNT THAT THEY WOULD HAVE RECEIVED IN HYPOTHETICAL CHAPTER 7 ON THAT DATE, 2) MODIFICATION OF PLAN UNDER § 1127 IS NOT PRACTICABLE, AND 3) DISCHARGE PERMITTED UNDER § 1141(d)(5)(C)	2) COURT APPROVES WRITTEN WAIVER OF DISCHARGE EXECUTED AFTER ORDER FOR RELIEF, OR 3) FOR INDIVIDUAL CHAPTER 11 DEBTOR, COURT FINDS REASONABLE CAUSE TO BELIEVE THAT DEBTOR MAY BE SUBJECT TO § 522(q) AND PENDING FELONY PROCEEDING DESCRIBED IN § 522(q)(1)(A) OR POTENTIAL LIABILITY FOR DEBT DESCRIBED IN § 522(q)(1)(B)

B.   EFFECT OF DISCHARGE

1.   Exceptions to Discharge

Even if debtor obtains a general discharge, certain debts are not subject to discharge, either because Congress has made a policy judgment that debts of that type should always survive bankruptcy, or because the facts and circumstances of the particular debtor/creditor relationship disqualifies that debt from discharge.

Exceptions to discharge are described in § 523. There are nineteen different types of debts that are nondischargeable in a chapter 7 case, a chapter 11 case, or a chapter 13 case after completion of all plan payments.

Several of the exceptions relate to taxes and other payments due to a governmental unit. Under § 523(a)(1), three tax-related obligations are excluded from discharge. First, taxes entitled to third or eighth priority under § 507(a) are also nondischargeable under § 523(a)(1)(A). Their priority status makes it more likely that these obligations will be paid by the estate and therefore not remain a burden on the debtor after discharge. Second, taxes for which a required return was not filed or was filed late and within two years prior to bankruptcy are not discharged. § 523(a)(1)(B). This exception gives the government time to audit and challenge more recently filed tax returns to see if taxes are due. Third, taxes that were the subject of a fraudulent return or attempted tax evasion are excluded. § 523(a)(1)(C). This exception reflects the general principle that claims arising from debtor's fraudulent or willful misconduct cannot be discharged. A visualization of the nondischargeable taxes follows.

NONDISCHARGEABLE TAXES § 523(a)(1)		
PRIORITY TAXES § 507(a)(3) & § 507(a)(8)	TAXES COVERED BY UNFILED RETURN, OR RETURN FILED LATE WITHIN TWO YEARS BEFORE FILING OF PETITION	TAXES COVERED BY FRAUDULENT RETURN OR SUBJECT OF WILLFUL ATTEMPT TO EVADE TAX

Other provisions excepting obligations to or imposed by governmental units from discharge include § 523(a)(7), which excepts other governmental fines, penalties or forfeitures; § 523(a)(13), which excepts payments of any criminal order of restitution; § 523(a)(14), excepting debts incurred to pay a Federal tax which would be nondischargeable (for example, credit card debt or a family loan); § 523(a)(14A), which excepts similar debts incurred to pay taxes other than Federal taxes; and § 523(a)(14B), excepting debts incurred to pay fines or penalties under Federal election law.

Seven more exceptions from discharge are attributable to some sort of bad conduct by the debtor. Four of those sections provide for exclusions from discharge in all cases. Three others permit an individual creditor to seek a determination of nondischargeability for its debt, but if it does not do so, the debt will be dischargeable.

Under § 523(a)(2), certain debts obtained by fraud may be excepted from discharge upon request by a creditor. A creditor seeking to except its debt from discharge on this basis must file a complaint no later than 60 days after the first date set for the § 341 meeting of creditors (subject to extension by the court before such period expires). Fed. R. Bankr. P. 4007(c). The debt is dischargeable unless the court, after notice and a hearing, determines the debt to be excepted from discharge. § 523(c)(1).

Two different categories of debts may be excluded. First, debts are nondischargeable to the extent they are incurred as a result of common law fraud (false pretenses, a false representation or actual fraud), other than a statement respecting debtor's financial condition. § 523(a)(2)(A). Section 523(a)(2)(C)(i)(I) creates a presumption that debts are nondischargeable under § 523(a)(2)(A) if the debts constitute consumer

debts owed by an individual debtor to a single creditor aggregating more than $600*
for "luxury goods or services" incurred within 90 days prior to the order for relief.
Cash advances to an individual debtor aggregating more than $875* constituting
extensions of consumer credit under an open end credit plan within 70 days before the
order for relief are also presumptively nondischargeable. § 523(a)(2)(C)(i)(II). The
term "luxury goods or services" is defined to exclude goods or services that are
reasonably necessary for the support or maintenance of debtor or the debtor's
dependents. § 523(a)(2)(C)(ii)(II). The second type of fraudulently-incurred debt that
may be excluded from discharge is a debt incurred as a result of the use of a materially
false written statement with respect to debtor's financial condition (generally a
financial statement, but not necessarily) made with intent to deceive on which creditor
reasonably relied. § 523(a)(2)(B). A visualization of these provisions follows.

DEBT OBTAINED BY FRAUD § 523(a)(2)		
COMMON LAW FRAUD	PRESUMPTION	DEBT FOR MONEY, PROPERTY, SERVICES OR CREDIT INCURRED BY USE OF STATEMENT IN WRITING:
DEBT FOR MONEY, PROPERTY, SERVICES OR CREDIT INCURRED BY FALSE PRETENSES, FALSE REPRESENTATION OR ACTUAL FRAUD OTHER THAN STATEMENT RESPECTING DEBTOR'S OR INSIDER'S FINANCIAL CONDITION	1) CONSUMER DEBTS TO SINGLE CREDITOR AGGREGATING MORE THAN $600* FOR LUXURY GOODS OR SERVICES INCURRED WITHIN 90 DAYS OF BANKRUPTCY, OR 2) CASH ADVANCES OF CONSUMER CREDIT AGGREGATING MORE THAN $875* UNDER OPEN END CREDIT PLAN WITHIN 70 DAYS OF BANKRUPTCY PRESUMED TO BE NONDISCHARGEABLE	1) THAT WAS MATERIALLY FALSE, 2) RESPECTING DEBTOR'S OR INSIDER'S FINANCIAL CONDITION, 3) ON WHICH CREDITOR REASONABLY RELIED, AND 4) THAT DEBTOR MADE OR PUBLISHED WITH INTENT TO DECEIVE

If a creditor tries to get a consumer debt excluded from discharge under § 523(a)(2)
and fails, and the position of the creditor in asserting that the debt was nondischargeable was not substantially justified, the court must award the debtor costs and
attorneys' fees unless special circumstances would render the award unjust. § 523(d).

A creditor may also seek to exclude from discharge debts for fraud or defalcation
(misappropriation of, or failure to account for, trust funds) while acting in a fiduciary
capacity, embezzlement, or larceny. § 523(a)(4). As was true for § 523(a)(2), a creditor
seeking to exclude its debt on this basis must file a complaint no later than 60 days

---

* These dollar figures, like many of the dollar figures in the Code, are subject to adjustment every three
years under § 104(b) of the Code to reflect change in the Consumer Price Index for the most recent three
years, and were most recently adjusted effective April 1, 2010 and will be adjusted again in 2013.

after the first date set for the § 341 meeting of creditors (subject to extension by the court before such period expires). Fed. R. Bankr. P. 4007(c). The debt is dischargeable unless the court, after notice and a hearing, determines the debt to be excepted from discharge. § 523(c)(1).

The final type of debt that may be determined nondischargeable on request by a creditor is a debt for willful and malicious injury by the debtor to another entity or to property of another entity. § 523(a)(6). A "willful" act is one that is deliberate or intentional. The requirement that the act be "malicious" means that the debtor's actions must have been intended to cause harm or the debtor must have been substantially certain harm would result. This exception is generally applicable to claims based on intentional torts with aggravating circumstances.

Four types of debts arising by reason of a debtor's bad acts are always excluded from discharge without the need for application by the creditor to whom they are owed. The first is for death or personal injury caused by intoxicated driver. § 523(a)(9). For the debt to be nondischargeable it must be for death or personal injury caused by the debtor's operation of a motor vehicle, vessel or aircraft at a time when the debtor was intoxicated from alcohol, drugs or another substance. The public policy against driving while under the influence of alcohol or drugs militates against providing such drivers a discharge from debts for the harms they cause.

Second, a debtor who is an insured depository institution may not be discharged from debts for the malicious or reckless failure to fulfill any commitment to a Federal depository institutions regulatory agency to maintain its capital. § 523(a)(12). Nor may a debtor be discharged from a debt arising from any act of fraud or defalcation while acting in a fiduciary capacity committed with respect to any depository institution or insured credit union if a final judgment, order or decree has been entered by a court, or by a Federal depository institutions regulatory agency, or if the debtor has entered into a settlement agreement with respect to such debt. § 523(a)(11).

Finally, § 523(a)(19) makes nondischargeable debts embodied in a judicial or administrative judgment, order or decree or a settlement agreement incurred for violations of Federal or state securities laws, regulations or orders, as well as common law causes of action relating to the purchase or sale of securities. This provision was enacted to crack down on securities fraud in the wake of the Enron and Worldcom accounting scandals.

The remaining exceptions from discharge are related less to the debtor's misconduct and more to the legislative assessment that certain debts should survive a bankruptcy case. A debtor is required to file accurate schedules of its debts and creditors at the inception of the case so these creditors can be given notices, including notice of the deadline for filing a proof of claim. Creditors who don't get notice of the deadline for filing proofs of claim because they were not listed on the schedules are not likely to file proofs of claim and receive distributions in respect of their claims. A bankruptcy discharge operates on prepetition debts whether or not the creditors file proofs of claim; it would be unfair (indeed, it would be unconstitutional under the Due Process Clause) to permit discharge to eliminate the claim of someone who didn't have the opportunity to file a proof of claim and participate in the distribution because of lack of notice. Therefore § 523(a)(3) makes nondischargeable debts the debtor did not list in the schedules with the name of the creditor (if known to the debtor) in time to permit the creditor to file a proof of claim and, if the debt is of a type potentially subject to exception from discharge under § 523(a)(2), (4) or (6), in time to seek a determination of nondischargeability unless creditor had notice or actual knowledge of the case in time. A visualization of this exception follows.

NONSCHEDULED DEBTS § 523(a)(3)	
DEBTS EXCLUDED FROM DISCHARGE	EXCEPTION
DEBT NOT LISTED OR SCHEDULED UNDER § 521(a)(1) WITH NAME OF CREDITOR IF KNOWN TO DEBTOR IN TIME TO PERMIT FILING OF PROOF OF CLAIM AND, IF APPLICABLE, TIMELY REQUEST FOR DETERMINATION OF DISCHARGE UNDER § 523(a)(2), (4) OR (6)	CREDITOR HAD NOTICE OR ACTUAL KNOWLEDGE OF CASE IN TIME TO MAKE FILING OR REQUEST

Certain "domestic support obligations" (§ 101(14A)) and other divorce-related obligations are excluded from discharge under § 523(a)(5) and § 523(a)(15). The reason behind these exceptions is that the public policy in favor of meeting family obligations trumps the debtor's interest in a fresh start. Therefore, all debts constituting domestic support obligations (*see* Chapter 4[A][2], *supra*) are nondischargeable. § 523(a)(5).

Sometimes in connection with a divorce, the parties make financial arrangements that do not fall within the definition of a domestic support obligation. The former spouses may simply divide up property and one owes the other an obligation to make payments over time with respect to that property settlement. Or the parties may allocate responsibility for existing debts between them, without regard to the identity of the debtor on the account (*e.g.*, one spouse takes the house mortgage, another takes the credit card debt and the car payments). Before 1994, this sort of debt owing to the other spouse whose name was on the original account was always dischargeable; in 1994, Congress made such obligations nondischargeable unless the debtor did not have the ability to pay, or the benefit to the debtor of discharging this debt outweighed the harm to the former spouse. The 2005 BAPCPA amendments made these debts nondischargeable without regard to ability to pay or benefit of the discharge. § 523(a)(15).

The provisions relating to discharge of familial obligations follows.

DISCHARGEABILITY OF FAMILIAL PAYMENTS §§ 523(a)(5) & 523(a)(15)	
DOMESTIC SUPPORT OBLIGATIONS § 101(14A)	**OTHER DIVORCE OR SEPARATION PAYMENTS**
1) TO A SPOUSE, FORMER SPOUSE, CHILD OF DEBTOR OR CHILD'S PARENT, LEGAL GUARDIAN OR RESPONSIBLE RELATIVE OR GOVERNMENTAL UNIT 2) IN NATURE OF ALIMONY, MAINTENANCE OR SUPPORT 3) ESTABLISHED BY SEPARATION AGREEMENT, DIVORCE DECREE, PROPERTY SETTLEMENT AGREEMENT OR OTHER COURT ORDER OR GOVERNMENTAL DETERMINATION 4) NOT ASSIGNED TO NONGOVERNMENTAL ENTITY UNLESS ASSIGNED VOLUNTARILY FOR PURPOSE OF COLLECTING DEBT	1) TO SPOUSE, FORMER SPOUSE, CHILD OF DEBTOR 2) NOT DOMESTIC SUPPORT OBLIGATION 3) INCURRED IN COURSE OF DIVORCE OR SEPARATION OR IN CONNECTION WITH SEPARATION AGREEMENT, DIVORCE DECREE OR OTHER COURT ORDER OR GOVERNMENTAL DETERMINATION

Most educational loans are nondischargeable under § 523(a)(8). The provision applies to educational benefit overpayments or loans made, insured or guaranteed by a governmental unit, or made under a program funded in whole or in part by a governmental unit or nonprofit institution; an obligation to repay educational benefits or scholarships or stipends; and any other qualified educational loan to an individual under the Internal Revenue Code. The debtor may seek to obtain discharge of such educational loans by filing a complaint under Fed. R. Bankr. P. 4007(a). The court may find the loans dischargeable if excepting the loans from discharge will impose an undue hardship on the debtor and the debtor's dependents. § 523(a)(8).

The showing necessary to make educational loans dischargeable is difficult to meet. Most courts require the debtor to prove that the debtor cannot maintain, based on current income and expenses, a minimal standard of living for the debtor and the debtor's dependents if forced to repay the loan, that additional circumstances exist indicating that this state of affairs is likely to persist for a significant portion of the repayment period of the loan, and that the debtor has made good faith efforts to repay the loan. *See Brunner v. New York State Higher Education Services Corp.*, 831 F.2d 395 (2d Cir. 1987). Other courts apply a "totality of the circumstances" approach that requires the debtor to demonstrate that, considering the debtor's past, present and reasonably reliable future resources, reasonably necessary living expenses and other relevant facts and circumstances prevent debtor from paying the student loans while maintaining a minimal standard of living. *See In re Long*, 322 F.3d 549 (8th Cir. 2003); *In re Bronsdon*, 435 B.R. 791 (1st Cir. BAP 2010).

A visualization of the provisions relating to discharge of educational loans follows.

EDUCATIONAL LOANS § 523(a)(8)		
NONDISCHARGEABLE DEBTS	EXCEPTION	*BRUNNER* TEST
EDUCATIONAL BENEFIT OVERPAYMENT OR LOAN MADE, INSURED OR GUARANTEED BY GOVERNMENTAL UNIT OR MADE UNDER PROGRAM INSURED BY GOVERNMENTAL UNIT OR NONPROFIT INSTITUTION OBLIGATION TO REPAY EDUCATIONAL BENEFIT, SCHOLARSHIP OR STIPEND OTHER QUALIFIED EDUCATION LOAN UNDER INTERNAL REVENUE CODE INCURRED BY INDIVIDUAL DEBTOR	EXCEPTING DEBT FROM DISCHARGE WOULD IMPOSE AN UNDUE HARDSHIP ON THE DEBTOR AND THE DEBTOR'S DEPENDENTS	1) DEBTOR CANNOT MAINTAIN, BASED ON CURRENT INCOME AND EXPENSES, A MINIMAL STANDARD OF LIVING FOR DEBTOR AND DEBTOR'S DEPENDENTS IF FORCED TO REPAY THE LOAN, AND 2) ADDITIONAL CIRCUMSTANCES EXIST INDICATING THAT THIS STATE OF AFFAIRS IS LIKELY TO PERSIST FOR A SIGNIFICANT PORTION OF THE REPAYMENT PERIOD OF THE LOAN, AND 3) DEBTOR HAS MADE GOOD FAITH EFFORTS TO REPAY THE LOAN

If a debt is not discharged in an earlier bankruptcy case because the debtor waived discharge, or if the debtor was denied a discharge under § 727(a)(2)-(7) in a prior chapter 7 case in which the debt could have been scheduled or listed, then that debt cannot be discharged in a subsequent bankruptcy case. § 523(a)(10). This provision is not applicable to debts that were excepted from discharge under § 523 in the prior case, but they are likely excepted from discharge in the current case for the same reasons they were excepted in the prior case.

Postpetition condominium or cooperative or homeowners' association fees are not dischargeable as long as the debtor or the trustee has a legal, equitable or possessory ownership interest in the unit (even if the debtor does not live there or rents it out). § 523(a)(16). Prepetition fees are subject to discharge, as are fees incurred after the order for relief in the current case if they remain unpaid when a subsequent bankruptcy case is filed.

Prisoners have been known to make frequent court filings, incurring obligations for court costs and fees. Under § 523(a)(17), the debts they owe for such filings are not dischargeable even if they claim indigency.

Finally, debts owed to a pension, profit-sharing, stock bonus or other similar benefit plan by reason of a loan permitted under Federal laws governing those plans are nondischargeable under § 523(a)(18).

The exceptions to discharge included in § 523 are visualized below.

CLAIMS EXCEPTED FROM GENERAL DISCHARGE § 523		
AUTOMATIC		**UPON OBJECTION**
§ 523(a)(1)	CERTAIN TAX CLAIMS	§ 523(a)(2) COMMON LAW FRAUD OR MATERIALLY FALSE FINANCIAL STATEMENTS
§ 523(a)(3)	UNSCHEDULED CLAIMS	
§ 523(a)(5)	DOMESTIC SUPPORT OBLIGATIONS	
§ 523(a)(7)	GOVERNMENTAL FINES, PENALTIES AND FORFEITURES	§ 523(a)(4) FIDUCIARY FRAUD OR DEFALCATION, LARCENY, EMBEZZLEMENT
§ 523(a)(8)	EDUCATIONAL LOANS UNLESS UNDUE HARDSHIP	
§ 523(a)(9)	CLAIMS FOR DEATH OR PERSONAL INJURY CAUSED BY DRIVING UNDER INFLUENCE	§ 523(a)(6) WILLFUL AND MALICIOUS INJURY TO PERSON OR PROPERTY
§ 523(a)(10)	PRIOR NONDISCHARGED CLAIMS	
§ 523(a)(11)	FIDUCIARY FRAUD OR DEFALCATION RELATED TO DEPOSITORY INSTITUTION	
§ 523(a)(12)	MALICIOUS OR RECKLESS FAILURE TO MAINTAIN CAPITAL OF INSURED DEPOSITORY INSTITUTION	
§ 523(a)(13)	CRIMINAL RESTITUTION PAYMENTS	
§ 523(a)(14)	DEBT INCURRED TO PAY NONDISCHARGEABLE U.S. TAXES	
§ 523(a)(14A)	DEBT INCURRED TO PAY NONDISCHARGEABLE STATE OR LOCAL TAX	
§ 523(a)(14B)	DEBT INCURRED TO PAY FINES OR PENALTIES UNDER FEDERAL ELECTION LAW	
§ 523(a)(15)	PAYMENTS PURSUANT TO DIVORCE DECREE	
§ 523(a)(16)	POSTPETITION CONDOMINIUM OR COOPERATIVE OR HOMEOWNERS ASSOCIATION COMMON CHARGES	
§ 523(a)(17)	COURT FEES OF PRISONER	
§ 523(a)(18)	LOAN OWED TO PENSION, PROFIT-SHARING, STOCK BONUS OR OTHER PLAN	
§ 523(a)(19)	SECURITIES LAW JUDGMENTS	

These exclusions from discharge are applicable in all individual chapter 7 cases (a non-individual debtor is not entitled to a discharge in chapter 7, *see* Section 10[A][1], *supra*), as well a chapter 11 case of an individual debtor, § 1141(d)(2), and a chapter 13 case in which the debtor seeks a discharge (a "hardship discharge") prior to the payment of all claims under the plan, § 1328(c)(2). For a chapter 13 hardship discharge, the only debts excepted from discharge, other than those listed in § 523(a), are debts that are due after the end of the plan which the debtor has chosen to cure and maintenance under § 1322(b)(5). § 1328(c)(1).

In a chapter 13 case in which the debtor completes all plan payments and seeks a discharge under § 1328(a), the exceptions from discharge are somewhat more limited than all those listed in § 523(a). For this reason, a discharge under § 1328(a) is sometimes called a "superdischarge." In addition to debts that are subject to cure and maintenance under § 1322(b)(5), the debts excepted from the superdischarge include those described in § 523(a)(1)(B), (1)(C), (2), (3), (4), (5), (8) and (9), taxes described in § 507(a)(8)(C), debts for restitution or a criminal fine imposed upon debtor's criminal conviction, and debts for restitution or damages awarded in a civil action for willful or malicious injury by the debtor that caused death or personal injury. The exceptions to the superdischarge in a chapter 13 case are visualized below.

EXCEPTIONS TO CHAPTER 13 SUPERDISCHARGE § 1328(a)
ANY DEBT THAT IS DUE AFTER THE END OF THE PLAN WHICH THE DEBTOR HAS CURED AND MAINTAINED DURING THE PLAN UNDER § 1322(b)(5)
DEBT FOR WITHHOLDING TAXES § 507(a)(8)(C)
DEBT FOR TAXES FOR WHICH RETURN OR REPORT NOT FILED OR GIVEN § 523(a)(1)(B)
DEBT FOR TAXES FOR WHICH DEBTOR MADE FRAUDULENT RETURN OR ATTEMPTED TO EVADE PAYMENT § 523(a)(1)(C)
DEBT OBTAINED BY FRAUD § 523(a)(2)
UNSCHEDULED DEBT § 523(a)(3)
DEBT FOR FRAUD OR DEFALCATION IN FIDUCIARY CAPACITY, EMBEZZLEMENT, LARCENY § 523(a)(4)
DEBT FOR DOMESTIC SUPPORT OBLIGATIONS § 523(a)(5)
DEBT FOR EDUCATIONAL LOANS UNLESS UNDUE HARDSHIP § 523(a)(8)
DEBT FOR PERSONAL INJURY OR DEATH CAUSED BY OPERATING VEHICLE WHILE UNDER INFLUENCE OF ALCOHOL OR DRUGS § 523(a)(9)
DEBT FOR RESTITUTION OR CRIMINAL FINE IMPOSED BY CRIMINAL SENTENCE UPON CONVICTION § 1328(a)(3)
DEBT FOR RESTITUTION OR DAMAGES IN CIVIL ACTION FOR WILLFUL OR MALICIOUS INJURY CAUSING PERSONAL INJURY OR DEATH § 1328(a)(4)

A corporate debtor discharged under § 1141(d) is not discharged from two types of debts. First, the debtor is not discharged from a debt for money, property, services or credit obtained by common law fraud or use of a materially false financial statement under § 523(a)(2) owed to a domestic governmental unit, or owed to a person as a result of an action filed under 31 U.S.C. § 3721 *et seq.* (claims against the U.S. government) or a similar state statute. Second, the debtor is not discharged from any tax or customs duty with respect to which the debtor made a fraudulent return or willfully attempted to evade or defeat the tax or customs duty. § 1141(d)(6). The exceptions from discharge for a corporate chapter 11 debtor are visualized below.

EXCEPTIONS FROM DISCHARGE FOR CHAPTER 11 CORPORATE DEBTOR § 1141(d)(6)	
§ 523(a)(2) DEBTS OBTAINED BY COMMON LAW FRAUD OR MATERIALLY FALSE FINANCIAL STATEMENT OWED TO A DOMESTIC GOVERNMENTAL UNIT, OR OWED AS A RESULT OF AN ACTION FILED UNDER 31 U.S.C. § 3721 ET SEQ. AGAINST THE U.S. GOVERNMENT OR UNDER ANY SIMILAR STATE STATUTE	DEBT FOR A TAX OR CUSTOMS DUTY IF DEBTOR: 1) MADE A FRAUDULENT RETURN, OR 2) WILLFULLY ATTEMPTED TO EVADE OR DEFEAT THE TAX OR CUSTOMS DUTY

2. Effect of Discharge

A discharge under any chapter of the Code has three effects. First, it voids any judgment that determines personal liability of the debtor with respect to a discharged debt, whether or not the debtor has waived discharge with respect to that debt. Second, it operates as an injunction against any attempt to collect, recover or offset any discharged debt as a personal liability of the debtor. Third, with certain exceptions, it operates as an injunction against any attempt to collect, recover or offset any discharged debt against community property of the debtor and the debtor's spouse that is acquired after the commencement of the case on account of any allowable community claim (except those claims excepted from discharge).

A creditor's willful failure to credit payments received under a confirmed plan (other than one for which the confirmation order has been revoked or if the plan is in default or the creditor has not received plan payments in the manner required), constitutes a violation of the injunction imposed by § 524(a)(2) if such failure "caused material injury to the debtor." § 524(i).

The permanent injunction imposed by § 524(a) is not applicable to an act by a holder of a secured claim if three factors are present. First, the creditor must be secured by real property that is the principal residence of the debtor. Second, the creditor's act must be in the ordinary course of business between the creditor and the debtor. Third, the creditor's act must be limited to seeking or obtaining periodic payments on the secured debt in lieu of taking action to enforce the lien against the property itself on an in rem basis.

A visualization of the provisions describing the effect of discharge follows.

EFFECT OF DISCHARGE §524(a)				
§524(a)(1)	§524(a)(2)		§524(a)(3)	
VOIDS JUDGMENT DETERMINING PERSONAL LIABILITY OF DEBTOR ON DISCHARGED DEBT	PROHIBITION §524(a)(2) & (i)	EXCEPTION §524(j)	PROHIBITION §524(a)(3)	EXCEPTION §524(b)
	PERMANENTLY ENJOINS ACTS TO COLLECT, RECOVER, OFFSET DISCHARGED DEBT AS PERSONAL LIABILITY OF DEBTOR, INCLUDING FAILURE TO CREDIT PAYMENTS RECEIVED UNDER PLAN CAUSING MATERIAL INJURY TO DEBTOR	ACT BY SECURED CREDITOR IF: 1) SECURED BY DEBTOR'S PRINCIPAL RESIDENCE, 2) ACT IS IN ORDINARY COURSE OF BUSINESS, AND 3) ACT IS SEEKING OR OBTAINING PERIODIC PAYMENTS IN LIEU OF IN REM ACTION AGAINST PROPERTY	PERMANENTLY ENJOINS ACTS TO COLLECT, RECOVER, OFFSET ALLOWABLE COMMUNITY CLAIMS (OTHER THAN THOSE EXCEPTED FROM DISCHARGE) AGAINST COMMUNITY PROPERTY OF THE DEBTOR AND DEBTOR'S SPOUSE ACQUIRED AFTER COMMENCEMENT OF CASE	1) COURT DENIES DEBTOR'S SPOUSE A DISCHARGE IN BANKRUPTCY CASE FILED BY SPOUSE WITHIN SIX YEARS OF DATE OF FILING BY DEBTOR, OR 2) COURT DENIES DEBTOR'S SPOUSE A DISCHARGE IN CHAPTER 7 CASE COMMENCED ON DATE OF FILING OF DEBTOR'S PETITION WITHIN TIME AND IN MANNER SPECIFIED UNDER §727 IN DEBTOR'S CASE

Discharge of a debt does not affect the liability of any other entity on such debt, or a creditor's interest in property of any other entity that secures such debt. § 524(e). In some chapter 11 plans, enterprising debtors seek to obtain a discharge or release from liability for other entities related to the debtor, such as officers, directors, shareholders, or general partners. With the exception of chapter 11 reorganization cases for debtors liable on claims for asbestos-related injuries or death — for which special provisions in § 524(g) and (h) validate injunctions protecting non-debtor entities that may be liable with the debtor for such claims — some courts have declined to permit third party releases absent unusual circumstances. *See, e.g., In re Pacific Lumber Co.*, 584 F.3d 229 (5th Cir. 2009); *In re Lowenschuss*, 67 F.3d 1394, 1401 (9th Cir. 1995); *In re Western Real Estate*, 922 F.2d 592, 600 (10th Cir. 1990). However, other courts permit nonconsensual releases in a chapter 11 plan, concluding that § 524(e) does not purport to limit the bankruptcy court's inherent powers under § 105(a) to release a non-debtor from a creditor's claims in some circumstances. *See, e.g., In re Airadigm Communications, Inc.*, 519 F.3d 640 (7th Cir. 2008).

3. Reaffirmation

A debtor may voluntarily repay any debt, including one that is subject to discharge in a bankruptcy case. § 524(f). However, in order to make the debtor's undertaking to pay binding, the parties must enter into an agreement that is enforceable under § 524(c). Although such an agreement, called a "reaffirmation agreement," is often used to allow the debtor to retain collateral securing a debt under circumstances where redemption is not possible, a reaffirmation agreement is not limited to secured debt.

The requirements for an enforceable reaffirmation agreement are set forth in § 524(c). Any agreement that does not comply with all requirements is unenforceable, and collection of debt pursuant to such an agreement violates § 524(a)(2). First, the agreement must be made prior to discharge. § 524(c)(1). Second, the debtor must receive detailed disclosures outlined in § 524(k) at or before the time the debtor signs the agreement. § 524(c)(2). These consist of a "disclosure statement" with specified information in it, § 524(k)(3); a reaffirmation agreement in the specified form, § 524(k)(4); a declaration by the debtor's attorney (if he or she has one) in the specified form, § 524(k)(5); a statement by the debtor in support of the reaffirmation agreement signed by the debtor in the specified form, § 524(k)(6); a motion for court approval signed and dated by the movant in the specified form, § 524(k)(7); and a court order to approve any agreement in the specified form, § 524(k)(8). No other disclosures are required. § 524(k)(1). All disclosures are required to be made "clearly and conspicuously and in writing." Special emphasis must be given to the terms "Amount Reaffirmed" and "Annual Percentage Rate." § 524(k)(2). The disclosure requirements are satisfied if the required disclosures are made "in good faith." § 524(l)(3).

Third, the agreement must be filed with the court. § 524(c)(3). If the debtor is represented by counsel, the agreement must be accompanied by a declaration or affidavit of that counsel stating that that agreement represents a fully informed and voluntary agreement by the debtor, does not impose an "undue hardship" on the debtor or debtor's dependents, and the attorney fully informed the debtor of the legal effect and consequences of the agreement and any default thereunder.

Fourth, the debtor must not have rescinded the agreement within 60 days after it was filed, or before discharge (whichever is first). § 524(c)(4).

Fifth, the requirements of § 524(d) must be satisfied. § 524(c)(5). If the debtor is not represented by counsel and a discharge is granted, under § 524(d) the court must hold a hearing at which the debtor appears in person, must inform the debtor that a reaffirmation agreement is not required and of the legal effect and consequences of the agreement and any default thereunder, and must determine whether the agreement meets the requirements for approval under § 524(c)(6) if the agreement relates to a consumer debt that is not secured by real property of the debtor. § 524(d)(1).

Sixth, if the debtor is an individual and wishes to enter into a reaffirmation agreement but was not represented by an attorney while negotiating such an agreement, then unless the reaffirmation agreement relates to a consumer debt secured by real property, the court must approve the agreement as "not imposing an undue hardship" on the debtor or debtor's dependents and "in the best interest of the debtor." § 524(c)(6).

Until 60 days after reaffirmation agreement is filed (or such additional time as the court for cause orders before the 60 days expires), unless the creditor is a credit union, it is presumed that the agreement is an undue hardship if debtor's monthly income less debtor's monthly expenses as shown on debtor's signed statement is less than the scheduled payments on the reaffirmed debt. § 524(m). The debtor may rebut the presumption by showing additional sources of funds to make the agreed payments. If the presumption is not rebutted, the court may disapprove the agreement, § 524(m), and may not grant the debtor a discharge. Fed. R. Bankr. P. 4004(c)(1)(K).

A creditor may accept payments from a debtor before and after the filing of a reaffirmation agreement, and may accept payments from a debtor under a reaffirmation agreement that the creditor believes in good faith to be effective. § 524(l)(1) & (2).

A visualization of the requirements for an enforceable reaffirmation agreement follows.

REAFFIRMATION AGREEMENT § 524(c)

TIMING § 524(c)(1)	DISCLOSURES § 524(c)(2)	FILING WITH COURT § 524(c)(3)	ROLE OF THE COURT § 524(d), (c)(5) & (c)(6), (m)(1)	ABILITY TO RESCIND § 524(c)(4)

AGREEMENT MADE PRIOR TO DISCHARGE	DEBTOR RECEIVES § 524(k) DISCLOSURES AT OR BEFORE SIGNING:
	
	1) DISCLOSURE STATEMENT,
	
	2) REAFFIRMATION AGREEMENT,
	
	3) COUNSEL DECLARATION,
	
	4) SUPPORTING STATEMENT BY DEBTOR,
	
	5) MOTION FOR APPROVAL, AND
	
	6) COURT ORDER OF APPROVAL
		AGREEMENT IS FILED AND, IF DEBTOR IS REPRESENTED BY COUNSEL IN NEGOTIATING AGREEMENT, COUNSEL FILES AFFIDAVIT THAT:
		
		1) AGREEMENT IS INFORMED AND VOLUNTARY,
		
		2) AGREEMENT DOES NOT IMPOSE UNDUE HARDSHIP, AND
		
		3) ATTORNEY FULLY ADVISED DEBTOR OF CONSEQUENCES
			IF DEBTOR IS NOT REPRESENTED BY COUNSEL, COURT MUST HOLD HEARING AT WHICH DEBTOR APPEARS IN PERSON AND COURT MUST:
			
			1) INFORM DEBTOR THAT REAFFIRMATION AGREEMENT IS NOT LEGALLY REQUIRED AND OF THE LEGAL EFFECT AND CONSEQUENCES OF SUCH AN AGREEMENT OR A DEFAULT THEREUNDER, AND
			
			2) APPROVE THE AGREEMENT AS:
			
			  (a) NOT IMPOSING UNDUE HARDSHIP, AND
			
			  (b) IN BEST INTEREST OF DEBTOR
			
			UNLESS AGREEMENT RELATES TO CONSUMER DEBT SECURED BY REAL PROPERTY
			
			IF PRESUMPTION OF UNDUE HARDSHIP IS CREATED UNDER § 524(m)(1), THE COURT MUST HOLD HEARING AND APPROVE REAFFIRMATION AGREEMENT ONLY IF DEBTOR REBUTS PRESUMPTION
				AGREEMENT MAY BE RESCINDED BEFORE LATER OF DATE OF DISCHARGE AND 60 DAYS AFTER FILING WITH COURT

4. Discrimination

The Code not only provides the protection of § 524 with respect to personal liability on discharged debt, but also protects debtors to some extent from other methods of "punishing" them for having filed for bankruptcy. Under § 525, the debtor is protected against three different types of discriminatory treatment based on having been a bankrupt.

First, governmental units are prohibited from discriminating against former or present bankrupts with respect to governmental grants (licenses, permits, charters, franchises) or employment "solely because" of the debtor's bankruptcy or insolvency or failure to pay a dischargeable debt. § 525(a).

Second, private employers are prohibited from discriminating against former or present bankrupts with respect to employment "solely because" of the debtor's bankruptcy or insolvency or failure to pay a dischargeable debt. § 525(b).

Third, governmental units that operate student grant or loan programs or persons engaged in the government-backed student loan business are prohibited from discriminating against former or present bankrupts with respect to student loans or loan guarantees or insurance because of the debtor's bankruptcy or insolvency or failure to pay a dischargeable debt. § 525(c).

These provisions, which are visualized below, tend to be invoked very rarely both because of the difficulty of making the required showing (particularly when the discrimination is prohibited only when it is "solely" attributable to the debtor's financial problems) and because debtors have neither the sophistication nor the resources to bring such complaints.

DISCRIMINATION
§ 525

§ 525(a)			§ 525(b)			§ 525(c)		
WHO	WHAT	WHEN	WHO	WHAT	WHEN	WHO	WHAT	WHEN
GOVERNMENTAL UNITS	LICENSES, PERMITS, CHARTERS, FRANCHISES OR OTHER SIMILAR GRANTS, OR EMPLOYMENT	SOLELY BECAUSE OF DEBTOR'S BANKRUPTCY OR INSOLVENCY OR FAILURE TO PAY DISCHARGEABLE DEBT	PRIVATE EMPLOYERS	EMPLOYMENT	SOLELY BECAUSE OF DEBTOR'S BANKRUPTCY OR INSOLVENCY OR FAILURE TO PAY DISCHARGEABLE DEBT	GOVERNMENTAL UNITS AND OTHER PERSONS ENGAGED IN STUDENT LOAN BUSINESS	STUDENT LOANS, GRANTS, LOAN GUARANTEES OR INSURANCE	BECAUSE OF DEBTOR'S BANKRUPTCY OR INSOLVENCY OR FAILURE TO PAY DISCHARGEABLE DEBT

Chapter 11

CONVERSION OR DISMISSAL

A. CONVERSION

A debtor who has filed for bankruptcy protection under one chapter of the Code has the absolute right to convert the case to one under another chapter for which the debtor is eligible, with limited exceptions. Under § 706(a), the debtor may convert a chapter 7 case to one under chapter 11, 12, or 13 "at any time" if the case was not previously converted from a chapter 11, 12 or 13 case to chapter 7. The right to convert cannot be waived. *Id.* The debtor must be eligible to be a debtor under the chapter to which the case is converted. § 706(d). Although the right to convert under § 706(a) appears to be absolute (if the debtor is eligible for the chapter to which the debtor seeks to convert the case), the Supreme Court has concluded in *Marrama v. Citizens Bank of Massachusetts*, 549 U.S. 365 (2007), that a bankruptcy court may deny a chapter 7 debtor's motion to convert the case to chapter 13 when the court determines that the motion is brought in bad faith.

The individual chapter 7 debtor whose debts are primarily consumer debts may also consent to a conversion of the case to a chapter 12 or chapter 13 case in the event the court, on its own motion or a motion by the U.S. trustee or any party in interest, seeks dismissal of the chapter 7 case under § 707(b)(1) on the grounds that the granting of relief under chapter 7 would be an abuse of that chapter. A presumption of abuse is created under § 707(b)(2), the so-called "means-testing" provisions discussed in Chapter 1[D], *supra*.

Parties in interest other than the debtor may also seek conversion of a case from chapter 7 to another chapter. Under § 706(b), on request of a party in interest, and after notice and a hearing, the court may order conversion of a chapter 7 case to chapter 11 at any time. A chapter 7 case may not be converted to a case under chapter 12 or 13 without the request or consent of the debtor. § 706(c).

A visualization of the provisions dealing with conversion of a chapter 7 case to a case under another chapter follows:

CONVERSION FROM CHAPTER 7 CASE § 706 & § 707(b)(1)			
CONVERSION BY DEBTOR § 706(a) & § 707(b)(1)		CONVERSION BY COURT § 706(b)	
WHEN AVAILABLE	EXCEPTIONS	WHEN AVAILABLE	EXCEPTIONS
AT ANY TIME DEBTOR MAY CONVERT CASE TO CASE UNDER CHAPTER 11, 12 OR 13 IF CASE WAS NOT PREVIOUSLY CONVERTED TO CHAPTER 7 INDIVIDUAL DEBTOR WITH PRIMARILY CONSUMER DEBTS MAY CONSENT TO CONVERSION OF CASE TO CHAPTER 12 OR 13 IF RELIEF UNDER CHAPTER 7 WOULD BE ABUSE	CASE MAY NOT BE CONVERTED UNLESS DEBTOR MAY BE DEBTOR UNDER NEW CHAPTER	AT ANY TIME COURT MAY CONVERT CASE TO CHAPTER 11 ON REQUEST OF PARTY IN INTEREST AFTER NOTICE AND HEARING	COURT MAY NOT CONVERT CASE TO CHAPTER 12 OR 13 WITHOUT DEBTOR REQUEST OR CONSENT CASE MAY NOT BE CONVERTED UNLESS DEBTOR MAY BE DEBTOR UNDER NEW CHAPTER

A chapter 13 debtor may similarly convert a chapter 13 case to a case under chapter 7 "at any time." § 1307(a). The right to convert is not subject to waiver. *Id.* The operative language of § 1307(a) is almost identical to that in § 706(a), and the rationale of *Marrama* (discussed above), holding that the debtor's right to convert a chapter 7 case to a case under chapter 11, 12 or 13 under § 706(a) is qualified by a requirement of good faith, may be equally applicable to these conversions. *See In re Garrett*, Bankr. LEXIS 1673 (Bankr. E.D. Va. May 23, 2008) (dictum). However, unlike conversion of a chapter 7 case under § 706(a) — which requires a motion by the debtor pursuant to Fed. R. Bankr. P. 1017(f)(2) — a chapter 13 case is converted without court order upon the debtor's filing of a notice of conversion under § 1307(a). Fed. R. Bankr. P. 1017(f)(3). This suggests that the court may lack authority to refuse to permit the conversion, although the court could subsequently dismiss the converted case if appropriate.

In addition, a party in interest or the U.S. trustee may request that the case be converted to a case under chapter 7. After notice and a hearing, the court may order such conversion, or may dismiss the case, "whichever is in the best interests of creditors and the estate, for cause." § 1307(c). Examples of events constituting cause include unreasonable delay by the debtor that is prejudicial to creditors, nonpayment of required filing fees and charges, failure to file a plan timely, failure to commence making timely payments, denial of confirmation of a plan and denial of additional time to file a new plan or to modify the plan, material default under the plan requirements, revocation of a confirmation order and denial of confirmation of a modified plan, termination of a confirmed plan, failure to file required information under § 521(a)(1), or failure to pay postpetition domestic support obligations. *Id.* The court must either dismiss the case or convert it to a chapter 7 case, "whichever is in the best interest of the creditors and the estate," if the debtor fails to file a required tax return under § 1308. § 1307(e). The court may convert the chapter 13 case to one under chapter 11 or 12 on request of a party in interest or the U.S. trustee at any time before confirmation of the plan. § 1307(d). The court may not convert the case to a case under chapter 7, 11 or 12 if the debtor is a "farmer" (§ 101(20)) except at the request of the debtor. § 1307(f). In all cases, the case may not be converted to a chapter for which the debtor is ineligible. § 1307(g).

A visualization of the provisions relating to conversion of a chapter 13 case follows.

CONVERSION FROM CHAPTER 13
§ 1307

BY DEBTOR		BY COURT			
WHEN AVAILABLE § 1307(a)	EXCEPTIONS § 1307(g)	TO CHAPTER 7 § 1307(c) & (e)	TO CHAPTER 11 OR 12 § 1307(d)	CAUSE § 1307(c)	EXCEPTIONS § 1307(f) & (g)
AT ANY TIME DEBTOR MAY CONVERT CASE TO CASE UNDER CHAPTER 7	CASE MAY NOT BE CONVERTED UNLESS DEBTOR MAY BE DEBTOR UNDER NEW CHAPTER	ON REQUEST OF PARTY IN INTEREST OR U.S. TRUSTEE, AFTER NOTICE AND HEARING, COURT: 1) MAY CONVERT TO CHAPTER 7 FOR CAUSE, AND 2) MUST CONVERT OR DISMISS FOR FAILURE TO FILE REQUIRED TAX RETURN	ON REQUEST OF PARTY IN INTEREST OR U.S. TRUSTEE, AFTER NOTICE AND HEARING, COURT MAY CONVERT CASE TO CASE UNDER CHAPTER 11 OR 12 AT ANY TIME BEFORE CONFIRMATION OF PLAN	INCLUDES ACTS IDENTIFIED IN § 1307(c)	COURT MAY NOT CONVERT TO A CASE UNDER CHAPTER 7, 11 OR 12 IF DEBTOR IS A FARMER UNLESS DEBTOR REQUESTS CONVERSION CASE MAY NOT BE CONVERTED UNLESS DEBTOR MAY BE DEBTOR UNDER NEW CHAPTER

If the debtor has filed a chapter 11 case, the debtor may convert the case to a case under chapter 7 unless the debtor is not acting as debtor in possession (*i.e.*, a trustee has been appointed under § 1104(a)), the case was originally commenced involuntarily under § 303, or the case was previously converted to chapter 11 from another chapter other than on the debtor's request. § 1112(a). The court may also convert a chapter 11 case to a case under chapter 12 or 13 if the debtor requests the conversion, the court has not granted debtor a discharge under § 1141(d), and (in the case of a conversion to chapter 12) such conversion is "equitable." § 1112(d). The debtor must be eligible to be a debtor under the chapter to which the case is converted. § 1112(f).

A party in interest may seek conversion of a chapter 11 case to a case under chapter 7 under § 1112(b). If such a motion is made, the court must either dismiss the case or convert the case to chapter 7, "whichever is in the best interests of creditors and the estate," if the movant establishes "cause." § 1112(b)(1). Cause includes various acts enumerated in § 1112(b)(4). But this list is not exhaustive, and "cause" would also include the debtor's bad faith in filing. The court may also convert the case to a case under chapter 7, or dismiss the case, whichever is in the best interest of creditors and the estate, on request of the U.S. trustee if, in a voluntary case, the debtor fails to file its required information under § 521(a)(1) within 15 days after the filing of the petition or such additional time as the court may allow. § 1112(e).

There are three circumstances under which such a conversion will not be ordered. First, the court may not convert the case if "the court finds and specifically identifies unusual circumstances establishing that [such relief] is not in the best interests of creditors and the estate" and the debtor or another party establishes that there is a reasonable likelihood that a plan will be timely confirmed, and the grounds for conversion include an act or omission of the debtor (other than loss to the estate and the absence of a reasonable likelihood of rehabilitation) for which there is a reasonable justification and that will be cured within a reasonable period fixed by the court. § 1112(b)(2). Second, the court may not convert the case if the debtor is a farmer or corporation that is not a moneyed, business, or commercial corporation except on the request of the debtor. § 1112(c). Third, the court may not convert the case if the court determines that the appointment of a trustee or examiner under § 1104(a) is in the best interests of creditors and the estate. § 1112(b)(1). In all cases, the debtor must be eligible to be a debtor under the chapter to which the case is converted. § 1112(f).

The court must commence a hearing on a motion to convert a chapter 11 case not later than 30 days after the motion is filed, and must decide the motion not later than 15 days after the commencement of the hearing, unless the movant consents to a specified continuance or "compelling circumstances prevent the court from meeting the time limits." § 1112(b)(3).

The provisions on conversion of a chapter 11 case are visualized below.

CONVERSION OF CHAPTER 11 CASE
§ 1112

BY DEBTOR § 1112(a)		BY COURT § 1112(b)			
TO CHAPTER 7 § 1112(a) & (f)	TO CHAPTER 12 OR 13 § 1112(d) & (f)	STANDARD FOR CONVERSION § 1112(b)(1) & (2) & (e)	EXCEPTIONS § 1112(c) & (f)	CAUSE § 1112(b)(4)	TIMING § 1112(b)(3)
MAY CONVERT TO CHAPTER 7 UNLESS: 1) NOT ACTING AS DEBTOR IN POSSESSION, OR 2) CASE WAS INVOLUNTARY, OR 3) CASE WAS INVOLUNTARILY CONVERTED TO CHAPTER 11 CASE MAY NOT BE CONVERTED UNLESS DEBTOR MAY BE DEBTOR UNDER NEW CHAPTER	MAY CONVERT TO CHAPTER 12 OR 13 IF: 1) DEBTOR SO REQUESTS, 2) DEBTOR HAS NOT BEEN DISCHARGED, AND 3) IF REQUEST TO CONVERT TO CHAPTER 12, CONVERSION IS EQUITABLE CASE MAY NOT BE CONVERTED UNLESS DEBTOR MAY BE DEBTOR UNDER NEW CHAPTER	ON REQUEST OF PARTY IN INTEREST OR U.S. TRUSTEE, 1) AFTER NOTICE AND HEARING, COURT MAY CONVERT TO CHAPTER 7 FOR CAUSE, BUT NOT IF COURT FINDS AND SPECIFICALLY IDENTIFIES UNUSUAL CIRCUMSTANCES ESTABLISHING THAT RELIEF IS NOT IN BEST INTERESTS OF CREDITORS AND ESTATE, AND PARTY OPPOSING RELIEF SHOWS: A) REASONABLE LIKELIHOOD TIMELY PLAN WILL BE CONFIRMED, AND B) REASONABLE JUSTIFICATION FOR DEBTOR'S ACTS AND WILL CURE PROBLEM WITHIN REASONABLE PERIOD FIXED BY COURT; OR 2) COURT MAY CONVERT TO CHAPTER 7 OR DISMISS FOR FAILURE IN VOLUNTARY CASE TO FILE § 521(a)(1) INFORMATION WITHIN 15 DAYS AFTER FILING	COURT MAY NOT CONVERT CASE TO CHAPTER 7 IF DEBTOR IS A FARMER OR A CORPORATION THAT IS NOT A MONEYED, BUSINESS OR COMMERCIAL CORPORATION WITHOUT DEBTOR REQUEST OR CONSENT CASE MAY NOT BE CONVERTED UNLESS DEBTOR MAY BE DEBTOR UNDER NEW CHAPTER	INCLUDES ACTS IDENTIFIED IN § 1112(b)(4)	COURT MUST COMMENCE HEARING ON MOTION NOT LATER THAN 30 DAYS AFTER FILING, AND MUST DECIDE MOTION NOT LATER THAN 15 DAYS AFTER HEARING COMMENCED UNLESS: 1) MOVANT CONSENTS, OR 2) COMPELLING CIRCUMSTANCES PREVENT COURT FROM MEETING TIME LIMITS

Upon conversion of a case from one chapter to another, the conversion is deemed to be an order for relief, but the dates of the filing of the petition, the order for relief and the commencement of the case remain the same with two exceptions. § 348(a). First, when various sections of the Code in the chapter to which the case has been converted use the phrase "the order for relief under this chapter," the phrase is deemed to refer to the conversion of the case to that chapter. § 348(b). Second, the requirement for notice of the order for relief in § 342 is deemed to require notice of the conversion, and the time for assuming or rejecting executory contracts and unexpired leases under § 365(d) is deemed to run from the time of conversion rather than the time of the original order for relief. § 348(c).

Any trustee or examiner serving in the case under the chapter from which the case is converted is discharged. § 348(e). Claims against the estate or the debtor arising in the case prior to conversion (other than administrative expenses) are treated as if they had arisen prepetition in the converted case. § 348(d).

When a case is converted from chapter 13 to another chapter, property of the estate in the converted case consists of property of the estate as of the date of filing to the extent that it remains in the debtor's possession or under the debtor's control, § 348(f)(1)(A), unless the debtor converts the case in bad faith, in which event the property of the estate in the converted case consists of the property of the estate at the date of conversion. § 348(f)(2). Valuations of property and of allowed secured claims in the chapter 13 case apply if the case is converted to chapter 11 or 12, but not if it is converted to chapter 7. § 348(f)(1)(B). Allowed secured claims in a chapter 13 case converted to chapter 11 or 12 are reduced to the extent they were paid under the chapter 13 plan before conversion. *Id.* The claim of a creditor holding security as of the date of the petition remains secured as of the conversion date unless the full amount of the claim determined under applicable nonbankruptcy law (not merely the allowed secured claim determined under § 506(a)) was paid prior to conversion. § 348(f)(1)(C)(i). Unless any prefiling default is fully cured under the chapter 13 plan at the time of conversion, the default continues to have the same effect as under applicable nonbankruptcy law. § 348(f)(1)(C)(ii).

A visualization of the effect of conversion follows.

EFFECT OF CONVERSION § 348

ORDER FOR RELIEF	CLAIMS	TRUSTEE OR EXAMINER	CONVERSION FROM CHAPTER 13 CASE			
			PROPERTY § 348(f)(1)(A) & (2)	VALUATIONS § 348(f)(1)(B)	SECURITY § 348(f)(1)(C)(i)	DEFAULTS § 348(f)(1)(C)(ii)
CONVERSION CONSTITUTES ORDER FOR RELIEF BUT DATES OF FILING, ORDER FOR RELIEF AND COMMENCEMENT OF CASE DO NOT CHANGE EXCEPT: 1) "THE ORDER FOR RELIEF UNDER THIS CHAPTER" IN PROVISIONS IN NEW CHAPTER REFER TO DATE OF CONVERSION, AND 2) NOTICE UNDER § 342 MUST BE GIVEN OF CONVERSION, AND DATE FOR ASSUMPTION OR REJECTION UNDER § 365(d) RUNS FROM CONVERSION DATE	CLAIM ARISING AFTER ORDER FOR RELIEF BUT BEFORE CONVERSION IS TREATED AS PREPETITION CLAIM IN CONVERTED CASE (OTHER THAN ADMINISTRATIVE EXPENSES)	CONVERSION TERMINATES SERVICE OF TRUSTEE OR EXAMINER IN CASE PRIOR TO CONVERSION	PROPERTY OF ESTATE IN CONVERTED CASE IS PROPERTY OF ESTATE AT TIME OF CHAPTER 13 FILING THAT STILL REMAINS WITH DEBTOR, UNLESS CONVERSION IS IN BAD FAITH	VALUATIONS OF PROPERTY AND ALLOWED CLAIMS APPLY IN CASE CONVERTED TO CHAPTER 11 OR 12, BUT NOT CHAPTER 7, WITH CLAIMS REDUCED TO EXTENT PAID	CLAIM REMAINS SECURED UNLESS FULL AMOUNT OF CLAIM (DETERMINED UNDER NON-BANKRUPTCY LAW RATHER THAN § 506(a)) HAS BEEN PAID	ANY DEFAULT HAS EFFECT GIVEN UNDER NON-BANKRUPTCY LAW UNLESS FULLY CURED UNDER CHAPTER 13 PLAN

B. DISMISSAL

A bankruptcy case can be dismissed after filing, either by the debtor or by the court upon request by a party in interest. Under § 707(b)(1), the court may dismiss a chapter 7 case filed by an individual debtor whose debts are primarily consumer debts if it finds that the granting of relief would be an abuse of the provisions of chapter 7. A motion to dismiss under this section may be made by the court *sua sponte*, the U.S. trustee, the trustee in bankruptcy, and any party in interest unless the "current monthly income" (§ 101(10A)) of the debtor times 12 is equal or less than the median family income in the applicable state for the same size household. For below-median debtors, only the court, the U.S. trustee or the bankruptcy trustee may bring a motion to dismiss under § 707(b). § 707(b)(6). A presumption of abuse is created by § 707(b)(2), the so-called "means-testing" provision discussed in Chapter 1[D], *supra*. But the presumption of abuse created by § 707(b)(2) is not the only basis for dismissal of a chapter 7 case under § 707(b)(1). Even if the debtor passes the "means test" or is not subject to it, the chapter 7 case may be dismissed if the court concludes that chapter 7 relief would be an abuse. In considering whether relief would be an abuse, the court is directed to consider "whether the debtor filed the petition in bad faith" and "[whether] the totality of the circumstances . . . of the debtor's financial situation demonstrates abuse." § 707(b)(3).

If the court grants a motion under § 707(b), and the court finds that the action of the attorney for the debtor in filing a chapter 7 case violated Fed. R. Bankr. P. 9011, the court may order the attorney for the debtor to reimburse the trustee for all reasonable costs incurred in prosecuting the motion, including reasonable attorneys' fees, and may assess a civil penalty. § 707(b)(4)(A) & (B). By signing a bankruptcy petition, the attorney for the debtor is deemed to certify that the attorney has performed a reasonable investigation into the circumstances that gave rise to the petition and determined that the petition is well grounded in fact and warranted by existing law or a good faith argument for the extension, modification, or reversal of existing law and does not constitute an abuse of chapter 7. § 707(b)(4)(C). The attorney's signature on a chapter 7 petition is also a certification that the attorney has no knowledge after an inquiry that the information in the schedules filed with the petition is incorrect. § 707(b)(4)(D).

If any party in interest (other than the trustee or U.S. trustee) makes a motion to dismiss the chapter 7 case under § 707(b) and the court denies the motion, the court may award the debtor all reasonable costs, including reasonable attorneys' fees, incurred in contesting the motion if the position of the movant violated Fed. R. Bankr. P. 9011 or the attorney who filed the motion did not perform a reasonable investigation into the circumstances that gave rise to the motion and did not determine that the motion was well grounded in fact and warranted by existing law or a good faith argument for the extension, modification, or reversal of existing law and did not constitute an abuse of chapter 7, and the motion was made solely for the purpose of coercing a debtor into waiving a right guaranteed to the debtor under chapter 7. § 707(b)(5)(A).

Under § 707(a), the court may dismiss a chapter 7 bankruptcy case after notice and a hearing "for cause." "Cause" includes an unreasonable delay by the debtor that is prejudicial to creditors, nonpayment of filing fees and charges, and failure of the debtor in a voluntary case to file the information required by § 521(a)(1) within fifteen days after filing (or such additional time as the court may allow). § 707(a)(1)-(3). Most courts also consider "bad faith" cause for dismissal under § 707(a).

In addition, under § 707(c), on motion by a victim of a crime of violence or a drug trafficking crime (as such terms are defined in title 18 of the U.S. Code), the court may dismiss a voluntary case filed by an individual debtor who was convicted of such crime if dismissal is in the best interest of the victim unless the debtor establishes by a preponderance of the evidence that the filing of the chapter 7 case is necessary to satisfy a claim for a domestic support obligation.

A motion under § 707(b) or (c) may be filed only within 60 days after the first date set for the § 341 meeting of creditors unless the court extends the period during that time. Fed. R. Bankr. P. 1017(e)(1).

A visualization of the provisions dealing with dismissal of a chapter 7 case follows.

DISMISSAL OF CHAPTER 7 CASE § 707				
DISMISSAL FOR CAUSE § 707(a)	DISMISSAL FOR ABUSE § 707(b)			DISMISSAL FOR VICTIM OF CRIME OF VIOLENCE OR DRUG TRAFFICKING CRIME § 707(c)
COURT MAY DISMISS CASE AFTER NOTICE AND A HEARING FOR CAUSE, INCLUDING:	GROUNDS FOR DISMISSAL § 707(b)(1)	PRESUMPTION § 707(b)(2)	WHO MAY BRING MOTION § 707(b)(6)	COURT MAY, AFTER NOTICE AND HEARING, ON MOTION BY VICTIM OF CRIME OF VIOLENCE OR DRUG TRAFFICKING CRIME, DISMISS VOLUNTARY CASE OF INDIVIDUAL DEBTOR CONVICTED OF CRIME IF DISMISSAL IS IN BEST INTEREST OF VICTIM, UNLESS CHAPTER 7 CASE NECESSARY TO SATISFY DOMESTIC SUPPORT OBLIGATION
1) UNREASONABLE DELAY, 2) NONPAYMENT OF FILING FEES, AND 3) FAILURE TO FILE REQUIRED INFORMATION UNDER § 521(a)(1) ON TIMELY BASIS	COURT MAY DISMISS CASE OF INDIVIDUAL DEBTOR WITH PRIMARILY CONSUMER DEBTS IF GRANTING OF RELIEF WOULD BE ABUSE OF CHAPTER 7	PRESUMPTION OF ABUSE CREATED BY § 707(b)(2) IF DEBTOR FAILS TO PASS MEANS TEST	IF CURRENT MONTHLY INCOME (§ 101(10A)) OF THE DEBTOR TIMES 12 IS EQUAL OR LESS THAN THE MEDIAN FAMILY INCOME IN THE APPLICABLE STATE FOR THE SAME SIZE HOUSEHOLD, ONLY THE COURT, THE U.S. TRUSTEE OR THE BANKRUPTCY TRUSTEE MAY FILE MOTION OTHERWISE, ANY PARTY IN INTEREST MAY ALSO FILE MOTION	

At any time during a chapter 13 case, unless the case has previously been converted to chapter 13 from another chapter, the court must dismiss the case upon request of the debtor. § 1307(b). Although this provision is written in absolute and mandatory language, after the Supreme Court's decision in *Marrama v. Citizens Bank of Massachusetts*, 549 U.S. 365 (2007) (discussed in Section 11[A], *supra*), holding that the debtor's right to convert a chapter 7 case to a case under chapter 11, 12 or 13 under § 706(a) is qualified by a requirement of good faith, courts are divided over whether a debtor's right to dismiss a chapter 13 case is equally qualified by good faith. *Compare In re Williams*, 435 B.R. 552 (Bankr. N.D. Ill. 2010); *In re Hamlin*, 2010 Bankr. LEXIS 636 (Bankr. E.D.N.C. Mar. 1, 2010); *In re Polly*, 392 B.R. 236 (Bankr. N.D. Tex. 2008); *In re Davis*, 2007 Bankr. LEXIS 1751 (Bankr. M.D. Fla. May 16, 2007); *In re Campbell*, 2007 Bankr. LEXIS 4159 (Bankr. N.D. W. Va. Dec. 18, 2007) (debtor's right to dismiss under § 1307(b) is absolute), *with Jacobsen v. Moser* (*In re Jacobsen*), 609 F.3d 647 (5th Cir. 2010); *Rosson v. Fitzgerald* (*In re Rosson*), 545 F.3d 764 (9th Cir. 2008); *In re Caola*, 422 B.R. 13 (Bankr. D.N.J. 2010); *In re Armstrong*, 408 B.R. 559 (Bankr. E.D.N.Y. 2009) (debtor's right to dismiss is subject to good faith requirement of *Marrama*).

A party in interest or the U.S. trustee may also seek dismissal of a chapter 13 case. After notice and a hearing, the court may order such dismissal, or may convert the case to chapter 7, "whichever is in the best interests of creditors and the estate, for cause." § 1307(c). Examples of events constituting cause include unreasonable delay by the debtor that is prejudicial to creditors, nonpayment of required filing fees and charges, failure to file a plan timely, failure to commence making timely payments, denial of confirmation of a plan and denial of additional time to file a new plan or to modify the plan, material default under the plan requirements, revocation of a confirmation order and denial of confirmation of a modified plan, termination of a confirmed plan, failure to file required information under § 521(a)(1), or failure to pay postpetition domestic support obligations. *Id.* The court must either dismiss the case or convert it to a chapter 7 case, "whichever is in the best interest of the creditors and the estate," if the debtor fails to file a required tax return under § 1308. § 1307(e).

A visualization of the provisions relating to dismissal of a chapter 13 case follows.

DISMISSAL OF CHAPTER 13 CASE § 1307		
ON REQUEST OF DEBTOR § 1307(b)	ON REQUEST OF PARTY IN INTEREST OR U.S. TRUSTEE § 1307(c) & (e)	
ON REQUEST OF DEBTOR AT ANY TIME, IF CASE WAS NOT PREVIOUSLY CONVERTED TO CHAPTER 13, COURT MUST DISMISS CASE	GROUNDS FOR DISMISSAL § 1307(c) & (e)	CAUSE § 1307(c)
	ON REQUEST OF PARTY IN INTEREST OR U.S. TRUSTEE, AFTER NOTICE AND HEARING, COURT: 1) MAY DISMISS CASE FOR CAUSE, AND 2) MUST CONVERT TO CHAPTER 7 OR DISMISS FOR FAILURE TO FILE REQUIRED TAX RETURN	INCLUDES ACTS IDENTIFIED IN § 1307(c)

A party in interest may seek dismissal of a chapter 11 case to a case under chapter 7 under § 1112(b). If such a motion is made and the movant establishes "cause,", the court must either dismiss the case or convert the case to chapter 7 "absent unusual circumstances specifically identified by the court that establish that [such relief] is not in the best interests of creditors and the estate." § 1112(b)(1). Cause includes various acts enumerated in § 1112(b)(4). But this list is not exhaustive, and "cause" would also include the debtor's bad faith in filing. The court may also convert the case to a case under chapter 7, or dismiss the case, whichever is in the best interest of creditors and the estate, on request of the U.S. trustee if, in a voluntary case, the debtor fails to file its required information under § 521(a)(1) within 15 days after the filing of the petition or such additional time as the court may allow. § 1112(e).

There are two circumstances under which such a dismissal will not be ordered. First, the court may not dismiss the case if the debtor or another party establishes that there is a reasonable likelihood that a plan will be timely confirmed, and the grounds for dismissal include an act or omission of the debtor (other than loss to the estate and the absence of a reasonable likelihood of rehabilitation) for which there is a reasonable justification and that will be cured within a reasonable period fixed by the court. § 1112(b)(2). Second, if grounds to dismiss the case exist, but the court determines that the appointment of a trustee or examiner is in the best interests of creditors and the estate, the court may make such appointment instead. § 1104(a)(3).

The court must commence a hearing on a motion to dismiss a chapter 11 case not later than 30 days after the motion is filed, and must decide the motion not later than 15 days after the commencement of the hearing, unless the movant consents to a specified continuance or "compelling circumstances prevent the court from meeting the time limits." § 1112(b)(3).

The provisions on dismissal of a chapter 11 case are visualized below.

DISMISSAL OF CHAPTER 11 CASE § 1112(b)		
STANDARD FOR DISMISSAL § 1112(b)(1) & (2) & § 1112(e)	CAUSE § 1112(b)(4)	TIMING § 1112(b)(3)
ON REQUEST OF PARTY IN INTEREST OR U.S. TRUSTEE, 1) AFTER NOTICE AND HEARING, COURT MAY DISMISS FOR CAUSE ABSENT UNUSUAL CIRCUMSTANCES SPECIFICALLY IDENTIFIED BY COURT THAT RELIEF IS NOT IN BEST INTERESTS OF CREDITORS AND ESTATE, BUT NOT IF: A) REASONABLE LIKELIHOOD TIMELY PLAN WILL BE CONFIRMED, AND B) REASONABLE JUSTIFICATION FOR DEBTOR'S ACTS AND WILL CURE PROBLEM WITHIN REASONABLE PERIOD FIXED BY COURT; OR 2) COURT MAY CONVERT TO CHAPTER 7 OR DISMISS FOR FAILURE IN VOLUNTARY CASE TO FILE § 521(a)(1) INFORMATION WITHIN 15 DAYS AFTER FILING	INCLUDES ACTS IDENTIFIED IN § 1112(b)(4)	COURT MUST COMMENCE HEARING ON MOTION NOT LATER THAN 30 DAYS AFTER FILING, AND MUST DECIDE MOTION NOT LATER THAN 15 DAYS AFTER HEARING COMMENCED UNLESS: 1) MOVANT CONSENTS, OR 2) COMPELLING CIRCUM-STANCES PREVENT COURT FROM MEETING TIME LIMITS

Unless the court, for cause, orders otherwise, dismissal of a case does not prevent the debtor from filing another bankruptcy case (except as provided in § 109(g), *see* Chapter 1[C], *supra*) or from receiving a discharge in a later bankruptcy case of debts that could have been discharged in the prior case had it not been dismissed. § 349(a). A dismissal reinstates any avoided transfers or liens or setoffs and revests property of the estate in the entity that held such property prior to the bankruptcy filing. § 349(b). The following visualizes the effect of dismissal:

EFFECTS OF DISMISSAL § 349			
DISMISSAL DOES			DISMISSAL DOES NOT
REINSTATE 1) PROCEEDING OR CUSTODIANSHIP SUPERSEDED UNDER § 543, 2) ANY TRANSFER AVIODED UNDER § 522, 544, 545, 547, 548, 549 OR 724(a) OR PRESERVED UNDER § 510(c)(2), 522(i)(2) OR 551, AND 3) ANY LIEN VOIDED UNDER § 506(d)	VACATE ANY ORDER, JUDGMENT OR TRANSFER UNDER §§ 522(i)(1), 542, 550 or 553	REVEST PROPERTY OF ESTATE IN ENTITY IN WHICH VESTED PRIOR TO CASE	1) BAR DISCHARGE OF DISCHARGEABLE DEBTS, OR 2) PREJUDICE DEBTOR WITH RESPECT TO NEW FILING, EXCEPT PER § 109(g)

Chapter 12

SPECIAL SITUATIONS

A. CHAPTER 12

1. History

Under the Bankruptcy Act of 1898, farmers were originally treated just like any other debtor with one exception — they could not be forced into bankruptcy involuntarily. When the Bankruptcy Code was enacted in 1978, the only protections for farmers were the continued protection against involuntary bankruptcies (still in § 303(a)), and protection against involuntary conversion of a chapter 11 case or chapter 13 case to chapter 7 (still in § 1112(c) and § 1307(f)). "Farmer" is defined in § 101(20) for these purposes to mean a person who received more than 80% of such person's gross income for the taxable year preceding the taxable year of filing from a farming operation owned or operated by such person. "Farming operation" is defined in § 101(21) to include "farming, tillage of the soil, dairy farming, ranching, production or raising of crops, poultry, or livestock, and production of poultry or livestock products in an unmanufactured state."

The 1970s were a period of great prosperity for farmers, and farmers responded by expansion of production and incurring significantly more debt; the economic climate changed in the early 1980s. Interest rates rose, making it difficult for farmers to pay the debt they had previously incurred, and more difficult for them to borrow more. At the same time, production costs rose and commodity costs fell. The value of farm land declined. The confluence of these factors threatened the farmers' economic survival.

The provisions of the Code as they existed at that time were of little help to the financially-stressed farmer. They tended to have too much debt to satisfy the eligibility requirements for chapter 13, but chapter 11 was seen as too expensive, complicated and time-consuming for most farmers, and they were unlikely to be able to meet the requirements for plan confirmation without relinquishing ownership of the farm. The Supreme Court held in *Norwest Bank Worthington v. Ahlers*, 485 U.S. 197 (1988), that the absolute priority rule precluded a farmer/debtor from retaining an equity interest in the farm if the unsecured creditors were not being paid in full, and the new value exception to the absolute priority rule did not permit the equity holder (farmer) to contribute sweat equity (a promise of future labor) as new value.

In response to the economic troubles of farmers, Congress enacted a new chapter 12 as an emergency measure in 1986, and after various extensions it was made a permanent part of the Code in the 2005 amendments. Chapter 12 filings are infrequent, with 605 filings for the 12 months ending March 31, 2010 (compared to more than 1.1 million chapter 7 filings for the same 12-month period, and more than 400,000 chapter 13 filings). But chapter 12 cases are successful; empirical data suggests that most family farmers who file for chapter 12 are able to keep the farm and believe that chapter 12 worked for them.

2. Operation of Chapter 12

As discussed in Chapter 1[C], *supra*, only a family farmer (§ 101(18)) with regular income (§ 101(19)) or family fisherman (§ 101(19A)) with regular income (§ 101(19B)) is eligible to file for protection under chapter 12. § 109(f). The definitions of "family farmer" and "family fishermen" include certain debt limitations and requirements that at least 50% of gross income be received from the farming operation or commercial fishing operation, respectively.

In most respects other than the eligibility requirements, chapter 12 is much like a combination of chapter 13 and chapter 11. It is commenced under § 301 by filing a petition; there is no involuntary chapter 12 because § 303(a) allows for involuntary cases only under chapter 7 or 11, and even then not against a farmer (§ 101(20)) or family farmer (§ 101(18)). The filing of the petition creates an estate under § 541, but property of the estate in a chapter 12 case includes not only the property described in § 541, but also all property of the same kind that the debtor acquires during the case, and earnings from services performed by the debtor during the case. § 1207(a). The debtor remains in possession of all property of the estate unless the debtor is removed as debtor in possession. § 1207(b). A visualization of the property of the estate in a chapter 12 case follows.

PROPERTY INCLUDED IN THE CHAPTER 12 ESTATE § 1207
ALL PROPERTY SPECIFIED IN § 541
ALL PROPERTY OF THE KIND SPECIFIED IN § 541 THAT DEBTOR ACQUIRES AFTER COMMENCEMENT OF CASE AND BEFORE CASE IS CLOSED, DISMISSED OR CONVERTED
ALL EARNINGS FROM SERVICES PERFORMED BY DEBTOR AFTER COMMENCEMENT OF CASE AND BEFORE CASE IS CLOSED, DISMISSED OR CONVERTED

The filing of a petition commencing a chapter 12 case triggers the automatic stay under § 362 (which, like under § 1301 in a chapter 13 case, protects not only the debtor but also any person who is liable on a consumer debt with the debtor, § 1201). Although the same grounds for obtaining relief from the stay under § 362(d) apply, the normal definition of adequate protection under § 361 does not apply in a chapter 12. Instead, when adequate protection is required, the trustee must either make a cash payment or periodic cash payments to the entity entitled to adequate protection, or provide such entity an additional or replacement lien, or pay such entity for the use of farmland the reasonable rent customary in the relevant community (based on rental value, net income, and earning capacity of the property), or grant such other relief (other than providing an administrative expense claim) as will "adequately protect the value of property securing a claim or of such entity's ownership interest in property." § 1205(a). A visualization of the definition of "adequate protection" for purposes of chapter 12 follows.

ADEQUATE PROTECTION IN CHAPTER 12 CASE § 1205

1)	CASH PAYMENT OR PERIODIC CASH PAYMENTS TO EXTENT OF DECREASE IN VALUE OF INTEREST IN PROPERTY, OR
2)	ADDITIONAL OR REPLACEMENT LIEN TO EXTENT OF DECREASE IN VALUE OF INTEREST IN PROPERTY, OR
3)	PAYING REASONABLE RENT FOR USE OF FARMLAND IN AMOUNT CUSTOMARY IN COMMUNITY WHERE FARMLAND IS LOCATED, BASED ON RENTAL VALUE, NET INCOME AND EARNING CAPACITY OF PROPERTY, OR
4)	GRANTING OTHER RELIEF (OTHER THAN ADMINISTRATIVE EXPENSE PRIORITY) AS WILL ADEQUATELY PROTECT VALUE OF PROPERTY SECURING A CLAIM OR OF SUCH ENTITY'S OWNERSHIP INTEREST IN PROPERTY

As is true under chapter 11, the debtor acting as debtor in possession has all the powers and responsibilities of a trustee serving in a chapter 11 case, including the duty to operate the debtor's business, subject to any limitations the court imposes. § 1203. But there is also a trustee in a chapter 12 case, either a standing trustee for chapter 12 cases in the district, or another disinterested person appointed by the U.S. trustee. § 1202(a). This chapter 12 trustee performs the same functions as a chapter 13 trustee, but picks up the functions of a chapter 11 trustee that the debtor in possession does not perform (investigation of the debtor and the debtor's business and filing a report with the court). § 1202(b). The duties of a chapter 12 trustee are visualized below.

DUTIES OF CHAPTER 12 TRUSTEE
§ 1202(b) & (c)

BE ACCOUNTABLE FOR ALL PROPERTY RECEIVED

ENSURE DEBTOR PERFORMS INTENTION SPECIFIED IN STATEMENT OF INTENTION UNDER § 521(a)(2)(B)

EXAMINE PROOFS OF CLAIM AND MAKE APPROPRIATE OBJECTIONS

IF ADVISABLE, OBJECT TO DEBTOR'S DISCHARGE

FURNISH INFORMATION REQUESTED BY PARTY IN INTEREST

MAKE FINAL REPORT AND FILE FINAL ACCOUNT

IF THE COURT FOR CAUSE SO ORDERS, INVESTIGATE ACTS, CONDUCT, ASSETS, LIABILITIES, AND FINANCIAL CONDITION OF DEBTOR, OPERATION OF DEBTOR'S BUSINESS AND DESIRABILITY OF CONTINUING IT, AND OTHER MATTERS RELEVANT TO THE CASE OR TO FORMULATION OF A PLAN

FILE STATEMENT OF ANY INVESTIGATION AND TRANSMIT COPY OR SUMMARY TO ANY ENTITY COURT DESIGNATES

APPEAR AND BE HEARD AT HEARINGS ON:

  1) VALUE OF PROPERTY SUBJECT TO LIEN,

  2) CONFIRMATION OF PLAN,

  3) POST-CONFIRMATION MODIFICATION OF PLAN, OR

  4) SALE OF PROPERTY OF ESTATE

ENSURE DEBTOR BEGINS MAKING TIMELY PAYMENTS

IF DEBTOR CEASES TO BE DEBTOR IN POSSESSION, PERFORM ALL ADDITIONAL DUTIES OF CHAPTER 11 TRUSTEE (OTHER THAN FILING PLAN), OPERATE THE DEBTOR'S BUSINESS AND FILE PERIODIC REPORTS AND SUMMARIES OF OPERATIONS

IF THERE IS CLAIM FOR DOMESTIC SUPPORT OBLIGATION, PROVIDE NOTICE DESCRIBED IN § 1202(c) TO HOLDER OF CLAIM AND STATE CHILD SUPPORT ENFORCEMENT AGENCY

The debtor may be removed as debtor in possession on request of a party in interest "for cause, including fraud, dishonesty, incompetence, or gross mismanagement of the affairs of the debtor, either before or after the commencement of the case." § 1204.

If the chapter 12 trustee seeks to sell property of the estate under § 363, in addition to its rights under § 363(f) to sell property free and clear of an interest in that property, the trustee in chapter 12 is permitted to sell property under § 363 free and clear of any interest of another party if the property is farmland, farm equipment, or property used to carry out a commercial fishing operation (including a commercial fishing vessel), with the interest of the creditor attaching to the proceeds of the sale instead. § 1206. A visualization of the powers of the chapter 12 trustee to sell property free of interests follows.

SALE OF PROPERTY IN CHAPTER 12 CASE FREE AND CLEAR OF INTERESTS § 1206	
SALE FREE AND CLEAR UNDER § 363(f)	SALE OF FARMLAND, FARM EQUIPMENT OR COMMERCIAL FISHING OPERATION PROPERTY § 1206
PROPERTY MAY NOT BE SOLD FREE AND CLEAR OF INTEREST UNLESS: 1) APPLICABLE NONBANKRUPTCY LAW WOULD PERMIT SUCH SALE, 2) SUCH ENTITY CONSENTS, 3) THE INTEREST IS A LIEN AND THE PURCHASE PRICE IS HIGHER THAN ALL LIENS, 4) INTEREST IS IN BONA FIDE DISPUTE, OR 5) ENTITY COULD BE COMPELLED TO ACCEPT MONEY	AFTER NOTICE AND HEARING, TRUSTEE MAY SELL FARMLAND, FARM EQUIPMENT, OR PROPERTY USED IN COMMERCIAL FISHING OPERATION FREE AND CLEAR OF ANY INTEREST IN PROPERTY OTHER THAN THE ESTATE, AND INTEREST ATTACHES TO PROCEEDS OF SALE

3. Chapter 12 Plan

A chapter 12 case, like one filed under chapter 11 and chapter 13, proceeds towards confirmation of a plan. In a chapter 12 case (as in chapter 13), only the debtor may file a plan, and the plan may be filed with the petition, but must be filed within 90 days after the order for relief unless the court extends the time due to "circumstances for which the debtor should not justly be held accountable." § 1221 and Fed. R. Bankr. P. 3015(a).

The plan must comply with the requirements of § 1222, which mostly follow the requirements for a chapter 13 plan in § 1322. A chapter 12 plan must satisfy three requirements under § 1222(a). First, it must provide for the submission to the supervision of the trustee of whatever portion of the debtor's future earnings or other future income is necessary to carry out the plan. § 1222(a)(1). Second, the plan must provide for full payment, in deferred cash payments, of all priority claims under § 507. § 1222(a)(2). There are three exceptions to this requirement. One, if the claim is owed to a governmental unit and arises as a result of the sale, transfer, exchange or other disposition of any farm asset used in the debtor's farming operation, the claim is treated as an unsecured claim (rather than a priority claim) if the debtor receives a discharge. § 1222(a)(2)(A). This exception, added by the 2005 BAPCPA amendments, allows a chapter 12 plan to pay on account of these tax claims the same amount they would get as unsecured claims in a chapter 7 (usually nothing). For an examination of some of the ambiguities created by the new language, *see Knudsen v. Internal Revenue Service (In re Knudsen)*, 581 F.3d 696 (8th Cir. 2009). Two, the holder of a priority claim may agree to other treatment. § 1222(a)(2)(B). Three, a plan may provide for less than full payment of priority claims consisting of domestic support obligations that have been assigned to or are owed to a governmental unit, but only if the plan dedicates all the debtor's projected disposable income for a five-year period to make payments under the plan. § 1222(a)(4). The concept of "projected disposable income" will be discussed below in connection with confirmation of the plan. The third requirement for the chapter 12 plan is that, if the plan classifies claims, the plan must treat each claim within a particular class the same, unless the holder of a particular claim or interest agrees to less favorable treatment § 1222(a)(3). Classification of claims is discussed in Chapter 9[B], *supra*.

The mandatory provisions of a chapter 12 plan are visualized below.

REQUIRED PROVISIONS FOR CHAPTER 12 PLAN § 1222(a)	
MANDATORY PROVISIONS	EXCEPTIONS
PLAN MUST PROVIDE FOR SUBMISSION TO SUPERVISION AND CONTROL OF TRUSTEE OF DEBTOR'S FUTURE EARNINGS OR INCOME NECESSARY FOR EXECUTION OF PLAN	NONE
PLAN MUST PROVIDE FOR FULL PAYMENT IN DEFERRED CASH PAYMENTS OF ALL § 507 PRIORITY CLAIMS	1) CLAIM OWED TO GOVERNMENTAL UNIT ARISING AS RESULT OF SALE, TRANSFER, EXCHANGE OR OTHER DISPOSITION OF FARM ASSET USED IN DEBTOR'S FARMING OPERATION IS TREATED AS UNSECURED CLAIM IF DEBTOR RECEIVES DISCHARGE, 2) HOLDER OF CLAIM MAY AGREE TO DIFFERENT TREATMENT, AND 3) PLAN MAY PROVIDE FOR LESS THAN FULL PAYMENT OF DOMESTIC SUPPORT OBLIGATION OWING TO GOVERNMENTAL UNIT IF PLAN DEDICATES ALL DEBTOR'S PROJECTED DISPOSABLE INCOME FOR 5 YEARS TO MAKE PAYMENTS UNDER PLAN
IF PLAN CLASSIFIES CLAIMS, PLAN MUST PROVIDE SAME TREATMENT TO ALL CLAIMS IN CLASS	HOLDER OF PARTICULAR CLAIM OR INTEREST MAY AGREE TO LESS FAVORABLE TREATMENT

With the exception of these mandatory provisions, the chapter 12 plan may incorporate various permissive provisions described in § 1222(b), some of which have limitations or exceptions.

First, the plan may create a class or classes of unsecured claims. § 1222(b)(1). As discussed above, classification of claims in a chapter 12 plan is not mandatory, but if claims are classified, all claims within a class must be treated the same unless the holder of a specific claim agrees to less favorable treatment. § 1222(a)(3). In addition, if the debtor chooses to designate classes of claims, the debtor may not "discriminate unfairly against any class so designated," but may treat claims for a consumer debt on which an individual is a codebtor differently from other unsecured claims. § 1222(b)(1). The only reason for the debtor to designate classes of claims is to enable the debtor to afford different treatment to different classes. However, different treatment is not necessarily unfair discrimination. In determining whether unfair discrimination exists, courts look at such factors whether the disparate treatment has a reasonable basis, whether it is necessary to enable the debtor to complete the plan, whether it is proposed in good faith, and whether the extent of the different treatment is directly related to the rationale for it.

Second, the plan may modify the rights of secured or unsecured creditors, or leave their rights unaffected. § 1222(b)(2). Modifications could include changes to the principal amount, interest rate, term, or (for secured claims) collateral for the debt. The extent to which a chapter 12 plan may modify claims is limited by the confirmation requirements for chapter 12 plans, which are discussed below. There is no restriction on modification of home mortgage debt, as there is in chapter 13, nor is there a limit on materially altering the terms of a loan from certain pension and thrift savings plans described in § 362(b)(19) as under § 1322(f).

Third, the plan may provide for the curing or waiving of any default. § 1222(b)(3). If the debtor has failed to make a payment, this provision allows the plan to provide for that default to be cured by a payment under the plan. The cure amount is determined in accordance with the underlying agreement and nonbankruptcy law pursuant to § 1222(d), and may include postpetition interest if the agreement so provides. If the creditor has accelerated the debt on the basis of the default, the debtor may "de-accelerate" the debt, returning the parties to their respective positions prior to the default.

Fourth, the plan may provide for payments on any unsecured claim to be made at the same time as payments on any secured claim or any other unsecured claim. § 1222(b)(4). There is no requirement in a chapter 12 proceeding that secured creditors be paid before unsecured creditors, or that priority claims be paid before general unsecured claims.

Fifth, the plan may provide for any default to be cured "within a reasonable time" and for "maintenance of payments while the case is pending" on any secured or unsecured claim if the last payment on such claim is due after the due date for the final plan payment. § 1222(b)(5). As is true under § 1222(b)(3), the cure of a default may include "de-accelerating" debt as to which the creditor took action on the basis of the default. "Maintenance of payments" means meeting the current obligations on the debt as they come due, essentially reinstating the pre-default payment schedule. The right to "cure and maintain" is applicable only to long-term secured or unsecured debt, that is debt with respect to which the final payment is due after the plan is scheduled to be completed.

Sixth, the plan may provide for the assumption, rejection, or assignment of any executory contract or unexpired lease not previously rejected consistent with the requirements of § 365. § 1222(b)(6). *See* Chapter 6[D]. *supra.*

Seventh, the plan may provide for payment of a claim from property of the estate or property of the debtor. § 1222(b)(7). Property of the debtor includes property that would be exempt under § 522.

Eighth, the plan may provide for the sale, or distribution to those with interests in it, of all or any part of the property of the estate. § 1222(b)(8). Thus, a chapter 12 plan may be a liquidating plan, as under chapter 11.

Ninth, the plan may provide for the payment of allowed secured claims over a period exceeding the duration of the plan. § 1222(b)(9). The duration of the plan is limited, as discussed below.

Tenth, the plan may vest property of the estate in the debtor or in any other entity upon confirmation or the plan or at any later time. § 1222(b)(10). Unless the plan provides otherwise, confirmation of a chapter 12 plan vests all property of the estate in the debtor, free and clear of any claim or interest of any creditor provided for by the plan. § 1227(b) & (c).

Eleventh, the plan may provide for payment of postpetition interest on unsecured claims that are nondischargeable under § 1228(a) to the extent the debtor has disposable income available to pay such interest after all allowed claims are paid in full. § 1222(b)(11).

Finally, a chapter 12 plan may also include any other provision that is not inconsistent with the requirements of the Code. § 1222(b)(12).

A visualization of the permitted provisions of a chapter 12 plan follows:

PERMITTED PROVISIONS IN CHAPTER 12 PLAN § 1222(b)		
§ 1222(b)(1)	DESIGNATE CLASSES OF UNSECURED CLAIMS	MAY NOT DISCRIMINATE AGAINST ANY DESIGNATED CLASS, BUT MAY TREAT CLAIMS FOR CONSUMER DEBT ON WHICH INDIVIDUAL IS CODEBTOR DIFFERENTLY FROM OTHER UNSECURED CLAIMS
§ 1222(b)(2)	MODIFY RIGHTS OF HOLDERS OF SECURED OR UNSECURED CLAIMS	
§ 1222(b)(3)	CURE OR WAIVE DEFAULTS	
§ 1222(b)(4)	PAYMENTS ON ANY UNSECURED CLAIM MADE CONCURRENTLY WITH PAYMENTS ON ANY OTHER UNSECURED OR SECURED CLAIM	
§ 1222(b)(5)	CURE OF DEFAULTS AND MAINTENANCE OF PAYMENTS ON DEBT FOR WHICH LAST PAYMENT IS DUE AFTER LAST PAYMENT UNDER PLAN	
§ 1222(b)(6)	ASSUME, REJECT OR ASSIGN EXECUTORY CONTRACTS OR UNEXPIRED LEASES UNDER § 365	
§ 1222(b)(7)	PAYMENT OF CLAIMS FROM PROPERTY OF ESTATE OR PROPERTY OF DEBTOR	
§ 1222(b)(8)	SALE OF ALL OR ANY PART OF PROPERTY OF ESTATE OR DISTRIBUTION OF ALL OR ANY PART OF PROPERTY OF ESTATE TO THOSE HAVING INTEREST	
§ 1222(b)(9)	PAYMENT OF ALLOWED SECURED CLAIMS OVER PERIOD EXCEEDING PERIOD PERMITTED FOR PLAN	
§ 1222(b)(10)	VESTING OF PROPERTY IN DEBTOR OR ANY OTHER ENTITY UPON CONFIRMATION OF PLAN	
§ 1222(b)(11)	PAYMENT OF POSTPETITION INTEREST ON NONDISCHARGEABLE CLAIMS TO EXTENT OF DISPOSABLE INCOME REMAINING AFTER PAYMENT OF ALLOWED CLAIMS IN FULL	
§ 1222(b)(12)	ANY OTHER APPROPRIATE PROVISION NOT INCONSISTENT WITH CODE	

Section 1222(c) limits the duration of a chapter 12 plan. The chapter 12 plan may not provide for payments (other than under § 1222(b)(2) and § 1222(b)(9) described above) over a period longer than three years, "unless the court, for cause, approves a longer period" not to exceed five years. § 1222(c). A longer period might be necessary, for example, to enable the debtor to meet the requirements for confirmation of the plan, as by paying priority claims in full and curing arrearages on debt. There is no difference in plan length for above-median debtors as under chapter 13. The permissible length of a chapter 12 plan is visualized below:

DURATION OF CHAPTER 12 PLAN § 1222(c)
NOT LONGER THAN 3 YEARS UNLESS COURT, FOR CAUSE, APPROVES LONGER PERIOD NOT IN EXCESS OF 5 YEARS

The debtor may need to modify the plan originally filed because it becomes apparent that the original plan cannot be confirmed, or because the debtor's circumstances have changed since the plan was filed. Before confirmation, the debtor has an absolute right to modify the plan (so long as the modified plan still complies with § 1222). § 1223(a). After the debtor files the modification, the plan as modified becomes the "plan" for all purposes of future proceedings in the case without the need for any approval by the court or creditors. However, any secured creditor that previously accepted or rejected the plan may change its prior acceptance or rejection if its rights under the modified plan have changed from under the original plan. § 1223(b) & (c).

A visualization of the provisions relating to preconfirmation modification of a chapter 12 plan follows.

PRECONFIRMATION MODIFICATION OF CHAPTER 12 PLAN § 1223			
WHO	WHEN	LIMITS	RESULTS
DEBTOR	AT ANY TIME BEFORE CONFIRMED	MODIFIED PLAN MUST MEET REQUIREMENTS OF § 1222	MODIFIED PLAN BECOMES THE CHAPTER 12 PLAN HOLDERS OF SECURED CLAIMS WHO ACCEPTED OR REJECTED UNMODIFIED PLAN ARE DEEMED TO HAVE ACCEPTED OR REJECTED MODIFIED PLAN UNLESS THEIR RIGHTS WERE CHANGED AND THEY CHANGE THEIR ACCEPTANCE OR REJECTION

4. Confirmation

The court must hold a hearing on confirmation of the chapter 12 plan after expedited notice. In the absence of cause, the court must conclude the confirmation hearing not later than 45 days after the filing of the plan. § 1224. An objection to confirmation must be filed and served before the confirmation hearing under Fed. R. Bankr. P. 3015(f). Local bankruptcy rules may require that an objection be filed and served several days before the hearing. Any party in interest, the trustee or the U.S. trustee may object to confirmation of a plan. § 1224.

When neither the trustee nor the holder of an allowed unsecured claim objects to the chapter 12 plan, there are seven conditions to confirmation. § 1225(a). The first is that the plan complies with all provisions of chapter 12 and other applicable provisions of the Code. § 1225(a)(1). This provision allows enforcement of the requirements of § 1222 with respect to the content of the chapter 12 plan.

Second, all filing fees in connection with the case under 28 U.S.C. § 1930, and all fees required by the plan to be paid prior to confirmation, must be paid. § 1225(a)(2).

Third, the plan must be proposed in good faith and not by any means forbidden by law. § 1225(a)(3). In determining whether the plan was proposed in good faith, a court would likely apply the "totality of the circumstances" test used for the comparable confirmation requirement for chapter 13 cases.

Under § 1225(a)(4), a chapter 12 plan must provide property to each holder of an unsecured claim having a "value, as of the effective date of the plan," of not less than the amount that would be paid on such claim if the debtor's estate were liquidated under chapter 7 on that date. This requirement, familiarly known as the "best interest of the creditors" or "best interests" test, provides a statutory floor on distributions to unsecured creditors after giving effect to any modifications made to their rights under § 1222(b)(2). The floor is pretty low; most chapter 7 bankruptcies are "no asset" cases; unsecured creditors receive nothing after payment of priority claims, satisfaction of secured claims, and removal of exempt property by the debtor. Therefore, the best interests test in chapter 12 may be met easily in most cases. The phrase "as of the effective date of the plan" means that any value to be received by unsecured creditors after the effective date of the plan must be discounted to present value when it is compared with the single lump-sum amount that would be paid in a chapter 7 liquidation. In other words, interest must be paid on the deferred payments to compensate the creditors for the lost value of money received in the future rather than on the effective date of the plan.

In order to get a chapter 12 plan confirmed under § 1225, the plan must deal with secured debt in one of three specified ways under § 1225(a)(5). First, the holder of the secured claim must have accepted the plan (*i.e.*, agreed with the debtor's proposed means of satisfying the claim). § 1225(a)(5)(A). Second, the debtor can surrender the collateral to the holder of the secured claim. § 1225(a)(5)(C).

The third method, and the one most frequently employed, allows the secured creditor to retain its lien until the underlying debt is paid in full or discharged, and receive property under the plan with value, as of the effective date of the plan, of not less than the allowed amount of the secured claim. § 1225(a)(5)(B). Unlike the requirements for confirmation of a chapter 13 plan in § 1325(a)(5)(B)(iii) added by the 2005 BAPCPA amendments, periodic payments under chapter 12 to secured creditors need not be in equal monthly amounts nor need payments on account of personal property be in an amount necessary to provide the creditor adequate protection for the duration of the plan. Chapter 12 does not include a "hanging paragraph" like that in § 1325(a) which renders certain secured claims immune from strip-down.

There are two concepts in this requirement that require further examination. First, the value of property to which the secured creditor is entitled under the plan is measured by the allowed amount of its "secured claim." The allowed amount of a secured claim is determined under § 506(a)(1) and is limited to the value of the collateral securing such claim. If the total claim exceeds the value of the collateral, the secured claim is "stripped down" to the value of the collateral, and the excess of the total claim over that amount is treated as unsecured. *See* Chapter 4[A][1], *supra*.

Section 506(a) states that the value of collateral should be determined "in light of the purpose of the valuation and of the proposed disposition or use of such property." In the context of a chapter 13 plan under which the debtor proposes to retain the collateral, the Supreme Court decided in *Associates Commercial Corp. v. Rash*, 520 U.S. 953 (1997), that the property retained in a chapter 13 plan should be valued at its replacement cost (the price a willing buyer in debtor's place would pay to obtain like property from a willing seller, but without warranties, inventory storage or reconditioning charges) rather than its liquidation value. Congress codified *Rash* (with certain modifications) in § 506(a)(2) for chapter 7 and 13 cases, but did not refer to chapter 12 cases. The Supreme Court's analysis in *Rash* is equally applicable to a chapter 12 case. *See, e.g., In re Bishop*, 339 B.R. 595 (Bankr. D.S.C. 2005); *In re Bell*, 304 B.R. 878 (Bankr. N.D. Ind. 2003).

The second key concept in § 1225(a)(5)(B)(ii) is the requirement that property to be distributed under the plan to the secured creditor in respect of the creditor's secured claim must be valued as of the effective date (meaning on a present value basis). As is true in applying the "best interests" test of § 1225(a)(4), this means that if payments are to be received over time, interest must be paid on those payments to compensate the creditor for the time-value of money.

A plurality of the Supreme Court decided in *Till v. SCS Credit Corp.*, 541 U.S. 465 (2004), that the appropriate interest rate under § 1325(a)(5) is a "prime-plus" or "formula" rate under which you begin with the prime rate and then adjust it upward (perhaps by 1-3%) to reflect the risk of non-payment by this bankrupt debtor. Four dissenting Justices would have used the rate specified in the agreement between the secured creditor and the debtor as a presumptive rate; Justice Thomas would have used the prime rate alone (with no risk adjustment). The Supreme Court's analysis in *Till* is equally applicable to a chapter 12 case. *See, e.g., In re Tamcke*, 2010 Bankr. LEXIS 168 (Bankr. D. Mont. Jan. 14, 2010); *In re Schreiner*, 2009 Bankr. LEXIS 821 (Bankr. D. Neb. Mar. 30, 2009); *In re Torelli*, 338 B.R. 390 (Bankr. E.D. Ark. 2006).

A visualization of the confirmation requirements with respect to treatment of secured debt in a chapter 12 case follows:

REQUIRED TREATMENT OF SECURED DEBT IN CHAPTER 12 § 1225(a)(5)		
SECURED CREDITOR ACCEPTS PLAN	SECURED CREDITOR KEEPS LIEN UNTIL DEBT PAID OR DISCHARGED, AND RECEIVES PROPERTY WITH VALUE, AS OF EFFECTIVE DATE OF PLAN, OF NOT LESS THAN AMOUNT OF ALLOWED SECURED CLAIM	DEBTOR SURRENDERS COLLATERAL TO SECURED CREDITOR

The sixth confirmation requirement is that the debtor will be able to perform the requirements of the plan, often referred to as the "feasibility" requirement. § 1225(a)(6). In deciding whether the feasibility requirement is met, the court will consider the information included on Official Form 6, Schedule I (current income) and Schedule J (current expenditures), Official Form 7 (Statement of Financial Affairs), and the testimony of the debtor at the § 341 meeting, as well as the advice of the chapter 12 trustee. If the debtor is projecting farm income in excess of historic figures or has no room for contingencies, the plan will not be deemed feasible. A plan that provides for payment of debt by elderly debtors over a long period of time will also be suspect. But the income to pay under the plan does not have to come from farming operations, or even from the debtor, if someone else (such as a non-debtor spouse) agrees to supply funds.

Seventh, the debtor must be current in paying any required domestic support obligations for the period after the filing date. § 1225(a)(7).

The additional requirement for confirmation added by the 2005 BAPCPA amendments as § 1325(a)(7) (requiring that the action of the debtor in filing the petition was in good faith) was not included in chapter 12.

If the trustee or the holder of an allowed unsecured claim objects to the chapter 12 plan, the court may not confirm the plan unless it satisfies one of three additional requirements. § 1225(b)(1). First, the plan can be confirmed if the value of property to be distributed under the plan on account of such claim is not less than the amount of such claim (meaning the unsecured claim will be paid in full under the plan). This is not a likely scenario. Second, the plan may be confirmed if it provides that all of the debtor's "projected disposable income" to be received during the life of the plan (three years or any longer period up to five years approved by the court under § 1222(c)) be applied to make payments to unsecured creditors. Third, the value of the property to be distributed under the plan during the life of the plan must be not less than the debtor's "projected disposable income" for such period.

"Disposable income" is defined in § 1225(b)(2). It means "income which is received by the debtor and which is not reasonably necessary to be expended" for maintenance or support of the debtor or debtor's dependents or for a postpetition domestic support obligation, or for necessary expenditures for the continuation, preservation and operation of the debtor's business. There is no requirement that the computation use applicable monthly expense amounts specified under the National Standards and Local Standards within the meaning of § 707(b)(2) used in computing "disposable income" under § 1325(b)(2).

The debtor's projected disposable income to be received during the period of the plan is the minimum that must be distributed to creditors either in the form of payments or property under § 1225(b)(1) in order to confirm the plan over an objection, and is also the maximum that can be devoted to paying creditors under § 1225(a)(6) (to devote more would render the plan not feasible).

The requirements for confirmation of a chapter 12 plan are visualized below:

REQUIREMENTS FOR CONFIRMATION OF CHAPTER 12 PLAN § 1225	
IF NO OBJECTION BY TRUSTEE OR UNSECURED CREDITOR § 1225(a)	IF OBJECTION BY TRUSTEE OR UNSECURED CREDITOR § 1225(b)
1) COMPLIANCE WITH PROVISIONS OF CHAPTER 12 AND CODE,	AS OF EFFECTIVE DATE OF THE PLAN:
2) FILING FEES PAID,	1) VALUE OF PROPERTY TO BE DISTRIBUTED ON ACCOUNT OF OBJECTOR'S UNSECURED CLAIM IS NOT LESS THAN AMOUNT OF CLAIM,
3) PROPOSED IN GOOD FAITH,	
4) MEETS BEST INTEREST OF THE CREDITORS TEST,	2) PLAN COMMITS ALL DEBTOR'S PROJECTED DISPOSABLE INCOME (§ 1225(b)(2)) TO BE RECEIVED DURING PLAN TO PAY UNSECURED CREDITORS UNDER PLAN, OR
5) TREATS SECURED CREDITORS AS REQUIRED BY § 1225(a)(5),	
6) PLAN IS FEASIBLE, AND	3) VALUE OF PROPERTY TO BE DISTRIBUTED UNDER PLAN IS NOT LESS THAN DEBTOR'S PROJECTED DISPOSABLE INCOME (§ 1225(b)(2)) FOR SUCH PERIOD
7) DEBTOR HAS PAID ALL DOMESTIC SUPPORT OBLIGATIONS PAYABLE AFTER FILING	

5. Postconfirmation Issues

Once the court confirms the chapter 12 plan, it becomes binding on the debtor, each creditor, each equity security holder and each general partner in the debtor, whether or not the plan provides for such person's claim or interest, and whether or not such person has objected to the plan. § 1227(a). Confirmation of the plan vests all property of the estate in the debtor, free and clear of any claim or interest of any creditor provided for by the plan, except as otherwise provided in the plan or the confirmation order. § 1227(b) & (c).

The trustee retains payments and funds received by the trustee until confirmation or denial of confirmation of the chapter 12 plan; if the court confirms the plan, the trustee distributes the payments in accordance with the plan. § 1226(a). If the plan is not confirmed, the trustee returns any payments to the debtor after deducting any unpaid administrative expenses (*see* Chapter 4[A][3], *supra*), and the percentage fee fixed for any standing chapter 12 trustee under 28 U.S.C. § 586(e)(1)(B). § 1226(a). Before or at the time of making any plan payments, the trustee must pay any unpaid administrative expenses and the percentage fee fixed for any standing chapter 12 trustee under 28 U.S.C. § 586(e)(1)(B). § 1226(b).

If the court confirms a chapter 12 plan, the court may revoke the confirmation order, but only on very limited grounds. § 1230. A party in interest must request revocation of confirmation within 180 days after the date of entry of the confirmation order. The only ground for revoking confirmation is if the confirmation order was procured by fraud. If the court revokes the confirmation order, the court may either convert or dismiss the case under § 1207 unless the debtor proposes a modified plan that the court confirms. A visualization of the provisions for revocation of confirmation of a chapter 12 plan follows.

REVOCATION OF CONFIRMATION § 1230		
WHEN	WHY	RESULT
REQUEST OF PARTY IN INTEREST WITHIN 180 DAYS AFTER DATE OF ENTRY OF CONFIRMATION ORDER	ORDER WAS PROCURED BY FRAUD	COURT MUST CONVERT OR DISMISS CASE UNLESS, WITHIN TIME SPECIFIED, DEBTOR PROPOSES AND COURT CONFIRMS MODIFIED PLAN

After confirmation, the debtor may become unable to meet his or her payment obligations because of a change in circumstances since filing or because the original plan was unduly optimistic. On the other hand, the debtor's circumstances may have improved dramatically, as a result of which the amounts dedicated to creditors under the confirmed plan no longer represent all the debtor's projected disposable income. When the confirmed plan requires changes, under § 1229(a), modification may be sought by the debtor, the trustee or a holder of an allowed unsecured claim. Only three possible modifications to the plan after confirmation are permitted: (1) to increase or reduce the amount of payments on claims of a particular class, (2) to extend or reduce the time for payments on claims of a particular class, or (3) to alter the amount of distribution to a creditor to take account of payments outside of the plan. Other changes to a confirmed plan, such as modifying the amount of secured claims or recharacterizing claims from secured to unsecured, are not permitted. In particular, the plan may not be modified to increase the amount of any payment due before modification, nor may it be modified by someone other than the debtor to increase the amount of payments to unsecured creditors required for a particular month so that the aggregate of such payments exceeds the debtor's disposable income for such month. § 1229(d)(1) & (2). No one other than the debtor may modify the plan in its last year to require payments that would leave the debtor with insufficient funds to carry on the farming operation after the plan is completed. § 1229(d)(3).

Any modified plan must still comply with § 1222 and must meet the requirements for confirmation in § 1225. § 1229(b)(1). The modified plan may not exceed three years, counting from the time payment was first due under the unmodified original plan, unless the court for cause approves a longer period up to five years. § 1229(c). The modified plan becomes the "plan" for all purposes of chapter 12 unless, after notice and a hearing, the court orders otherwise. § 1229(b)(2).

A visualization of the provisions on postconfirmation modifications to a chapter 12 plan follows.

POSTCONFIRMATION MODIFICATION OF CHAPTER 12 PLAN
§ 1229

WHO	WHEN	LIMITS	PERMITTED MODIFICATIONS	PROHIBITED MODIFICATIONS	RESULTS
DEBTOR, TRUSTEE, HOLDER OF ALLOWED UNSECURED CLAIM	AT ANY TIME AFTER PLAN CONFIRMED AND BEFORE PAYMENTS COMPLETED	MODIFIED PLAN MUST MEET REQUIREMENTS OF § 1222, 1225 — MODIFIED PLAN MAY NOT PROVIDE FOR PAYMENTS OVER LONGER THAN THREE YEARS FROM TIME OF FIRST PAYMENT UNDER ORIGINAL PLAN UNLESS COURT FOR CAUSE APPROVES LONGER PERIOD NOT TO EXCEED 5 YEARS	INCREASE OR REDUCE PAYMENTS — EXTEND OR REDUCE TIME FOR PAYMENT — ALTER AMOUNT OF DISTRIBUTION TO CREDITOR PAID OUTSIDE PLAN	INCREASE AMOUNT OF ANY PAYMENT DUE BEFORE PLAN IS MODIFIED — OTHER THAN BY DEBTOR, INCREASE AMOUNT OF PAYMENTS TO UNSECURED CREDITORS REQUIRED FOR PARTICULAR MONTH BASED ON INCREASED DISPOSABLE INCOME TO CAUSE AGGREGATE OF PAYMENTS FOR SUCH MONTH TO EXCEED DEBTOR'S DISPOSABLE INCOME FOR SUCH MONTH — OTHER THAN BY DEBTOR, IN LAST YEAR OF PLAN, REQUIRE PAYMENTS THAT WOULD LEAVE DEBTOR WITH INSUFFICIENT FUNDS TO CARRY ON FARMING OPERATION AFTER PLAN IS COMPLETED	MODIFIED PLAN BECOMES THE CHAPTER 12 PLAN UNLESS DISAPPROVED BY COURT — HOLDERS OF SECURED CLAIMS WHO ACCEPTED OR REJECTED UNMODIFIED PLAN ARE DEEMED TO HAVE ACCEPTED OR REJECTED MODIFIED PLAN UNLESS THEIR RIGHTS WERE CHANGED AND THEY CHANGE THEIR ACCEPTANCE OR REJECTION

6. Discharge

A discharge under chapter 12 is intended to be granted upon completion of all payments required by the chapter 12 plan. There are three conditions that must be met before a court may grant a chapter 12 discharge if plan payments are completed. First, if the debtor is required to pay a domestic support obligation under any judicial or administrative order or statute, the debtor must have certified that all such obligations due on or before the date of certification (including prepetition amounts to the extent provided by the plan) have been paid. § 1228(a). Second, the debtor must not have executed a written waiver of discharge after the order for relief which has been approved by the court. § 1228(a). Third, after notice and a hearing held not more than 10 days before the date the court enters a discharge order, the court must find there is "no reasonable cause to believe" that the § 522(q)(1) limit on the debtor's homestead exemption may be applicable, see Chapter 3[B][1], supra, and there is pending any proceeding in which the debtor may be convicted of a felony under circumstances demonstrating that the filing of the bankruptcy petition was abusive, or the debtor may owe a debt arising from securities laws violations, fraud or deceit or manipulation in a fiduciary capacity or in connection with the purchase or sale of a registered security, a civil remedy under the Racketeer Influenced and Corrupt Organizations Act, or any criminal act or intentional tort or willful or reckless misconduct that caused serious physical injury or death to another individual in the preceding five years (§ 522(q)(1)). § 1328(h). This new provision is comparable to § 727(a)(12) applicable to chapter 7 cases and § 1328(h) applicable to chapter 13 cases. There is no limitation on the availability of a chapter 12 discharge based on a discharge received in a prior chapter 7 or chapter 13 case. Nor is there a requirement that the chapter 12 debtor complete a postpetition instructional course in personal financial management, as for chapter 7 and chapter 13.

If the debtor has not completed the plan payments, the court may grant the debtor a discharge but only if three additional conditions are met. First, debtor's failure to complete the plan must be "due to circumstances for which the debtor should not justly be held accountable," such as an unexpected change in financial position, illness, divorce or the like. § 1228(b)(1). Second, the "best interests" test must have been satisfied with respect to plan distributions actually made, that is, the value, as of the effective date of the plan, of the property actually distributed to creditors under the plan must not be less than the amount that would have been paid on their claims in a hypothetical chapter 7 liquidation on that date. § 1228(b)(2). Third, modification of the plan under § 1229 must be impracticable. § 1228(b)(3).

The conditions for a discharge in chapter 12 are visualized below.

CONDITIONS TO CHAPTER 12 DISCHARGE § 1228	
ALL DISCHARGES § 1228(a)	ADDITIONAL CONDITIONS TO DISCHARGE IF DEBTOR HAS NOT COMPLETED PLAN PAYMENTS § 1228(b)
DEBTOR WHO IS REQUIRED TO PAY DOMESTIC SUPPORT OBLIGATION BY JUDICIAL OR ADMINISTRATIVE ORDER OR BY STATUTE HAS CERTIFIED THAT ALL AMOUNTS PAYABLE ON OR BEFORE DATE OF CERTIFICATION HAVE BEEN PAID	DEBTOR'S FAILURE TO COMPLETE PLAN WAS DUE TO CIRCUMSTANCES FOR WHICH DEBTOR SHOULD NOT JUSTLY BE HELD ACCOUNTABLE
COURT HAS NOT APPROVED WRITTEN WAIVER OF DISCHARGE EXECUTED BY DEBTOR AFTER ORDER FOR RELIEF	VALUE, AS OF EFFECTIVE DATE, OF PROPERTY CREDITORS ACTUALLY RECEIVED UNDER PLAN WAS NOT LESS THAN AMOUNT THAT THEY WOULD HAVE RECEIVED IN HYPOTHETICAL CHAPTER 7 ON THAT DATE
COURT FINDS NO REASONABLE CAUSE TO BELIEVE THAT DEBTOR MAY BE SUBJECT TO § 522(q) AND PENDING FELONY PROCEEDING DESCRIBED IN § 522(q)(1)(A) OR POTENTIAL LIABILITY FOR DEBT DESCRIBED IN § 522(q)(1)(B)	MODIFICATION OF PLAN UNDER § 1229 IS NOT PRACTICABLE

A chapter 12 discharge (whether upon completion of plan payments or earlier) discharges the debtor from all debts provided for by the plan with the exception of debts that are not dischargeable under § 523 (*see* Chapter 10[B][1], *supra*) as well as debts that are cured and maintained under § 1222(b)(5) or that are secured claims specified to be payable over a period longer than the plan under § 1222(b)(9). § 1228(a) and (c). Upon the debtor's discharge, the court is directed to terminate the services of any trustee serving in the case. § 1228(e).

The chapter 12 discharge may be revoked only within one year after it was granted and only if it was obtained by fraud and the party seeking revocation did not know of the fraud until after discharge was granted. § 1228(d).

7. Conversion or Dismissal

A chapter 12 debtor may convert a chapter 12 case to a case under chapter 7 "at any time." § 1208(a). The right to convert is not subject to waiver. *Id.* Although this provision is written in absolute and mandatory language, after the Supreme Court's decision in *Marrama v. Citizens Bank of Massachusetts*, 549 U.S. 365 (2007) (discussed in Chapter 11[A], *supra*), holding that the debtor's right to convert a chapter 7 case to a case under chapter 11, 12 or 13 under § 706(a) is qualified by a requirement of good faith, it is unclear whether a debtor's right to dismiss a chapter 12 case is equally qualified by good faith.

In addition, on request of a party in interest (including the debtor) or the U.S. trustee, the court may convert a chapter 12 case to a case under 7, but only upon a showing that the debtor "has committed fraud in connection with the case." § 1208(d). The operative language of § 1208(a) is almost identical to that in § 706(a), and the rationale of *Marrama* may be equally applicable to these conversions. However, unlike conversion of a chapter 7 case under § 706(a) — which requires a motion by the debtor pursuant to Fed. R. Bankr. P. 1017(f)(2) — a chapter 12 case is converted without court order upon the debtor's filing of a notice of conversion under § 1208(a). Fed. R. Bankr. P. 1017(f)(3). This suggests that the court may lack authority to refuse to permit the conversion, although the court could subsequently dismiss the converted case if appropriate.

A visualization of the provisions relating to conversion of a chapter 12 case follows.

CONVERSION FROM CHAPTER 12 §1208			
BY DEBTOR §1208(a)		BY COURT §1208(d)	
WHEN AVAILABLE §1208(a)	EXCEPTION §1208(e)	TO CHAPTER 7 §1208(d)	EXCEPTION §1208(e)
AT ANY TIME DEBTOR MAY CONVERT CASE TO CASE UNDER CHAPTER 7	CASE MAY NOT BE CONVERTED UNLESS DEBTOR MAY BE DEBTOR UNDER NEW CHAPTER	ON REQUEST OF PARTY IN INTEREST OR U.S. TRUSTEE, AFTER NOTICE AND HEARING, COURT MAY DISMISS OR CONVERT TO CHAPTER 7 UPON SHOWING THAT DEBTOR HAS COMMITTED FRAUD IN CONNECTION WITH CASE	CASE MAY NOT BE CONVERTED UNLESS DEBTOR MAY BE DEBTOR UNDER NEW CHAPTER

At any time during a chapter 12 case, unless the case has previously been converted to chapter 12 from another chapter, the court must dismiss the case upon request of the debtor. § 1208(b). Again, the debtor's apparently unqualified right to dismiss the case may be qualified by good faith after the Supeme Court's decision in *Marrama*.

A party in interest may also seek dismissal of a chapter 12 case. After notice and a hearing, the court may order such dismissal "for cause." § 1208(c). Examples of events constituting cause include unreasonable delay by the debtor that is prejudicial to creditors, nonpayment of required filing fees and charges, failure to timely file a plan, failure to commence making timely payments, denial of confirmation of a plan and denial of additional time to file a new plan or to modify the plan, material default under the plan requirements, revocation of a confirmation order and denial of confirmation of a modified plan, termination of a confirmed plan, continuing loss to or diminution of the estate and absence of a reasonable likelihood of rehabilitation, and failure of the debtor to pay any postpetition domestic support obligation. *Id.*

In addition, upon request of a party in interest and after notice and a hearing, the court may dismiss the case or convert it to chapter 7 upon a showing that the debtor has committed fraud in connection with the case. § 1208(d).

A visualization of the provisions relating to dismissal of a chapter 12 case follows.

DISMISSAL OF CHAPTER 12 CASE § 1208		
ON REQUEST OF DEBTOR § 1208(b)	ON REQUEST OF PARTY IN INTEREST § 1208(c) & (d)	
ON REQUEST OF DEBTOR AT ANY TIME, IF CASE WAS NOT PREVIOUSLY CONVERTED TO CHAPTER 12, COURT MUST DISMISS CASE	GROUNDS FOR DISMISSAL § 1208(c) & (d)	CAUSE § 1208(c)
	ON REQUEST OF PARTY IN INTEREST, AFTER NOTICE AND HEARING, COURT MAY DISMISS CASE : 1) FOR CAUSE, OR 2) UPON SHOWING THAT THE DEBTOR HAS COMMITTED FRAUD IN CONNECTION WITH THE CASE	INCLUDES ACTS IDENTIFIED IN § 1208(c)

Chapter 12, unlike chapter 13, does not require the debtor to file tax returns for the four year period preceding the bankruptcy filing (*see* § 1308). Therefore, unlike under chapter 13, failure to file such tax returns does not constitute grounds for conversion or dismissal as under § 1307(e).

B. CHAPTER 9

1. History

The first municipal bankruptcy law was enacted as a temporary measure in 1934 in the wake of the Great Depression of the 1930s when hundreds of municipalities defaulted in the payment of their bonds because taxpayers defaulted on their property taxes. The new law was declared unconstitutional by the Supreme Court in 1936 as improperly interfering with state sovereignty. *Ashton v. Cameron County Water District No. 1*, 298 U.S. 513 (1936). Congress then passed a revised version of the law in 1937, and the new version withstood constitutional challenge, *see United States v. Bekins*, 304 U.S. 27 (1938), although there was more change in the composition of the Court than in the content of the law. In 1940, 104 municipalities filed for bankruptcy, the most in any year in history.

After the Great Depression, there were very few municipal bankruptcies until the 1970s, in part because of the impediments posed by the 1937 law. In order to file for bankruptcy, a municipality had to get creditors holding 51% of the municipality's debt to agree to a composition plan ahead of time. In addition, municipalities could not reject executory contracts, including labor contracts, so bankruptcy could not solve many of the problems facing modern municipalities.

In 1976 and 1988, the municipal bankruptcy provisions were amended to make bankruptcy more attractive, while attempting to ensure that municipalities retained their sovereign power to deal with their operations free from bankruptcy court control. Nevertheless, municipal bankruptcies are still very rare. From 1938 to 2007 there were fewer than 600 municipal bankruptcies in total. The most in any year since 1980 was 18 in 1987, after the stock market collapsed. In the 12-month period ending September 30, 2009, there were seven chapter 9 cases filed.

The largest municipal bankruptcy in U.S. history was the filing by Orange County, California in 1994. Orange County was at the time the fifth most populous county in the United States, with 2.5 million residents. The County budget exceeded $3.7 billion, and it had approximately 18,000 employees. More recently, the City of Vallejo, California filed for bankruptcy in May 2008, the largest city in California to declare bankruptcy.

2.   General Provisions Applicable to a Chapter 9 Case

A chapter 9 case is not governed by all of the provisions of the Code applicable to filings under other chapters. Except as set forth in § 901, the only provisions applicable to a chapter 9 case are those included in chapter 1 or in chapter 9 of the Code. § 103(f). Section 901 makes 76 sections or subsections of the Code applicable in a chapter 9 case. A visualization of these sections follows:

PROVISIONS APPLICABLE TO CHAPTER 9 CASE § 901(a)	
§ 301	COMMENCEMENT OF VOLUNTARY CASE
§ 333	APPOINTMENT OF PATIENT CARE OMBUDSMAN
§ 344	IMMUNITY FROM SELF-INCRIMINATION
§ 351	DISPOSAL OF PATIENT RECORDS
§ 347(b)	DISPOSITION OF UNCLAIMED PROPERTY
§ 349	EFFECT OF DISMISSAL OF CASE
§ 350(b)	REOPENING OF CASE AFTER CASE IS CLOSED
§ 361	ADEQUATE PROTECTION
§ 362	AUTOMATIC STAY
§ 364(c), (d), (e) & (f)	OBTAINING CREDIT
§ 365	EXECUTORY CONTRACTS AND UNEXPIRED LEASES
§ 366	UTILITY SERVICE
§ 501	FILING OF PROOFS OF CLAIM
§ 502	ALLOWANCE OF CLAIMS
§ 503	ADMINISTRATIVE EXPENSES
§ 504	SHARING OF COMPENSATION
§ 506	DETERMINATION OF SECURED CLAIM
§ 507(a)(2)	PRIORITY FOR ADMINISTRATIVE EXPENSES
§ 509	CLAIMS OF CODEBTORS
§ 510	SUBORDINATION
§ 524(a)(1) & (a)(2)	EFFECT OF DISCHARGE
§ 544	STRONG-ARM POWER AND RIGHT OF SUBROGATION
§ 545	STATUTORY LIENS
§ 546	LIMITATION ON AVOIDING POWERS
§ 547	PREFERENCES
§ 548	FRAUDULENT TRANSFERS
§ 549(a), (c) & (d)	POSTPETITION TRANSFERS
§ 550	LIABILITY OF TRANSFEREE OF AVOIDED TRANSFER
§ 551	PRESERVATION OF AVOIDED TRANSFER
§ 552	POSTPETITION EFFECT OF SECURITY INTEREST
§ 553	SETOFFS
§ 555	RIGHTS WITH RESPECT TO SECURITIES CONTRACT
§ 556	RIGHTS WITH RESPECT TO COMMODITIES OF FORWARD CONTRACT
§ 557	INTERESTS IN AND ABANDONMENT OF GRAIN ASSETS
§ 559	RIGHTS WITH RESPECT TO REPURCHASE AGREEMENT
§ 560	RIGHTS WITH RESPECT TO SWAP AGREEMENT
§ 561	RIGHTS WITH RESPECT TO MASTER NETTING AGREEMENT
§ 562	DAMAGE MEASURE UNDER VARIOUS FINANCIAL AGREEMENTS
§ 1102	CREDITORS' AND EQUITY COMMITTEES
§ 1103	POWERS AND DUTIES OF COMMITTEES
§ 1109	RIGHT OF SEC AND PARTIES IN INTEREST TO BE HEARD
§ 1111(b)	TREATMENT OF NONRECOURSE AND UNDERSECURED DEBT
§ 1122	CLASSIFICATION OF CLAIMS OR INTERESTS
§ 1123(a)(1)-(a)(5), (b) & (d)	CONTENTS OF PLAN
§ 1124	IMPAIRMENT OF CLAIM OR INTEREST
§ 1125	DISCLOSURE AND SOLICITATION
§ 1126(a)-(c), (e)-(g)	ACCEPTANCE OF PLAN
§ 1127(d)	MODIFICATION OF PLAN
§ 1128	CONFIRMATION HEARING
§ 1129(a)(2), (3), (6), (8) & (10)	CONFIRMATION OF PLAN
§ 1129(b)(1) & (b)(2)(A) & (B)	CRAMDOWN CONFIRMATION
§ 1142(b)	EXECUTION OF PLAN
§ 1143	DISTRIBUTION
§ 1144	REVOCATION OF CONFIRMATION ORDER
§ 1145	EXEMPTION FROM SECURITIES LAWS

Notable by their absence are provisions that impinge on state autonomy, and would therefore threaten the constitutionality of chapter 9 under the Tenth Amendment by allowing the bankruptcy court too much control over the municipal debtor. Some of the provisions that are not applicable in chapter 9 include:

- §§ 327, 328, 330 & 331 with respect to retention and payment of professional persons. This means that a chapter 9 debtor does not need court approval to retain counsel or other professionals and there is no provision for the court to order their payment.

- § 507(a) dealing with priority claims, other than § 507(a)(2) (administrative expenses). No other unsecured claims are entitled to any priority treatment in chapter 9.

- § 523 itemizing exceptions from discharge. There are no exceptions to discharge in a chapter 9 case except those described in § 944, discussed below.

- § 541 which creates the bankruptcy estate, §§ 542 and 543 requiring turnover of property to the trustee and § 554 providing for abandonment of property by the trustee. Property of the chapter 9 debtor is the property of the estate for purposes of a chapter 9 case and remains under the control of the debtor.

- § 363 which deals with use, sale or lease of property. The court has no control over the municipal debtor's use, sale, or lease of property, whether in the ordinary course or not.

- § 1101(1) which defines the "debtor in possession," and § 1107 which sets forth the rights, powers and duties of a debtor in possession. The prepetition debtor remains in possession of property of the estate and continues to run the debtor's operations, without judicial oversight.

- §§ 1104, 1105 and 1106 dealing with trustees and examiners. No matter what cause may be present, the court has no power to appoint a trustee to run a municipal debtor or an examiner to conduct an investigation into its affairs. As discussed below, the court may appoint a trustee to exercise one of the avoiding powers if the debtor refuses to do so.

- § 1108 allowing the court to take away the debtor's ability to operate its business.

- § 1112 dealing with conversion or dismissal of cases (although the court has a limited ability to dismiss the case under § 930 discussed below). A municipality cannot liquidate, and therefore cannot convert to a chapter 7.

- § 1113 dealing with collective bargaining agreements. This means that a chapter 9 debtor does not have to comply with the specific provisions of that section in connection with modifications to collective bargaining agreements, but must, consistent with *NLRB v. Bildisco & Bildisco*, 465 U.S. 513 (1984), negotiate in good faith for modifications before imposing them (*see* Chapter 6[E][1], *supra*).

- § 1114 limiting the ability of the debtor to modify retiree benefits; a municipal debtor need not comply with these special provisions with respect to its retirees. *See* Chapter 6[E][2], *supra*.

- § 1121 dealing with the debtor's period of exclusivity and the right of others to file a plan of reorganization. Only the debtor may file a plan in a chapter 9 case, and need do so only within the time fixed by the court under § 941.

In addition to those definitions included in chapter 1, chapter 9 includes five special definitions for use only in chapter 9 cases. The first, "property of the estate," when that term is used in any section made applicable to the chapter 9 case, means property of the debtor. § 902(1). There is a definition of the term "special revenues" in § 902(2), meaning various amounts received by the debtor targeted to service a particular project, and which may provide the sole source of recovery for certain holders of claims. § 927. The next two definitions of "special tax payer" and "special tax payer affected by the plan" are also defining potential limited recourse situations, in these cases to real property against which a special assessment or special tax has been levied. § 902(3) & (4). When used in any section made applicable to a chapter 9 case by § 901, the term "trustee" means the debtor, except with respect to § 926 discussed below. § 902(5). A visualization of these definitions follows.

CHAPTER 9 DEFINITIONS § 902				
PROPERTY OF THE ESTATE	SPECIAL REVENUES	SPECIAL TAX PAYER	SPECIAL TAX PAYER AFFECTED BY THE PLAN	TRUSTEE
MEANS PROPERTY OF THE DEBTOR	MEANS 1) RECEIPTS FROM TRANSPORTATION, UTILITY OR OTHER SERVICE PROJECTS OF DEBTOR, INCLUDING PROCEEDS OF BORROWING, 2) SPECIAL EXCISE TAXES IMPOSED ON PARTICULAR ACTIVITIES OR TRANSACTIONS, 3) INCREMENTAL TAX RECEIPTS FROM BENEFITED AREA IN TAX-INCREMENT FINANCING, 4) OTHER RECEIPTS FROM PARTICULAR FUNCTIONS OF DEBTOR, OR 5) TAXES SPECIFICALLY LEVIED TO FINANCE ONE OR MORE PROJECTS	MEANS HOLDER OF TITLE TO REAL PROPERTY AGAINST WHICH SPECIAL ASSESSMENT OR TAXES ARE LEVIED, THE PROCEEDS OF WHICH ARE SOLE SOURCE OF PAYMENT OF OBLIGATION ISSUED BY DEBTOR TO PAY COST OF IMPROVEMENT TO PROPERTY	MEANS SPECIAL TAX PAYER FOR WHOSE REAL PROPERTY THE PLAN PROPOSES TO INCREASE PROPORTION OF SPECIAL ASSESSMENTS OR TAXES	EXCEPT UNDER § 926, MEANS THE DEBTOR

The provisions of § 903 and § 904 are intended to ensure that nothing in chapter 9 infringes on state sovereignty in a way that would render the chapter unconstitutional. In § 903, Congress provided that nothing in chapter 9 limits or impairs the power of a state, legislatively or otherwise, to control a municipality of or in the state in the exercise of the municipality's political or governmental powers. There are only two exceptions to the unlimited state powers, and they are intended to prevent the states from enacting their own municipal bankruptcy laws in lieu of chapter 9. The two exceptions are that a state law providing for "a method of composition" of municipal indebtedness may not bind a nonconsenting creditor, and that a judgment entered under such a law may not bind a creditor who does not consent to the composition. § 903. The ability to bind nonconsenting creditors is unique to chapter 9.

Section 904 limits the ability of the bankruptcy court to interfere with any political or governmental powers of the debtor, any of the property or revenues of the debtor, or the debtor's use or enjoyment of any income-producing property through any stay, order or decree, except with the consent of the debtor or pursuant to the plan. A visualization of these protections of state sovereignty follows.

PROTECTION OF STATE SOVEREIGNTY § 903 & § 904			
RESERVATION OF POWER OF STATE § 903		LIMITATIONS ON POWER OF COURT § 904	
RETAINED STATE POWERS	EXCEPTIONS	LIMITATIONS	EXCEPTIONS
CHAPTER 9 DOES NOT LIMIT OR IMPAIR POWER OF STATE (BY LEGISLATION OR OTHERWISE) TO CONTROL MUNICIPALITY OF OR IN STATE IN EXERCISE OF MUNICIPALITY'S POLITICAL OR GOVERNMENTAL POWERS	STATE LAW PRESCRIBING METHOD OF COMPOSITION OF MUNICIPALITY'S INDEBTEDNESS MAY NOT BIND NONCONSENTING CREDITOR JUDGMENT ENTERED UNDER STATE COMPOSITION LAW MAY NOT BIND CREDITOR WHO DOES NOT CONSENT TO COMPOSITION	COURT MAY NOT, BY STAY, ORDER, DECREE OR OTHERWISE, INTERFERE WITH: 1) ANY OF POLITICAL OR GOVERNMENTAL POWERS OF DEBTOR, 2) ANY OF PROPERTY OR REVENUES OF DEBTOR, OR 3) DEBTOR'S USE OR ENJOYMENT OF INCOME-PRODUCING PROPERTY	DEBTOR CONSENTS, OR PLAN SO PROVIDES

3.   Administration of Chapter 9 Case

As discussed in Chapter 1[C], *supra*, only a "municipality" (§ 101(40)) may file for chapter 9 bankruptcy, and the municipality must satisfy the other requirements of § 109(c), including specific authorization by state law to be a debtor under chapter 9. A chapter 9 bankruptcy, like a chapter 12 or 13 case, must be voluntary, and is commenced by the filing of a petition under chapter 9 with the bankruptcy court under § 301. Section 303 makes an involuntary bankruptcy filing available only in chapter 7 and chapter 11 cases, and under § 901, § 303 is not applicable to a chapter 9 case. If the municipality is an unincorporated tax or special assessment district without its own officials, the district's governing authority or the board or body having authority to levy taxes or assessments to meet the municipality's obligations may file a petition under § 301 for such district. § 921(a).

A chapter 9 debtor does not have to file schedules of assets and liabilities, current income and expenditures, executory contracts and unexpired leases, or a statement of financial affairs required of other debtors under Fed. R. Bank. P. 1007(b), but must file a list of creditors. § 924. The creditors holding the 20 largest unsecured claims must be listed by name, address, and claim on Official Form 4. Fed. R. Bankr. P. 1007(d). The debtor must also file a list containing the name and address of each entity included on Schedules D (creditors holding secured claims), E (creditors holding unsecured priority claims), F (creditors holding unsecured nonpriority claims), G (executory contracts and unexpired leases) and H (codebtors) of Official Form 6. Fed. R. Bankr. P. 1007(a). This list must be filed "within such time as the court shall fix." Fed. R. Bankr. P. 1007(e). The court may modify the filing requirements on motion for cause shown. *Id.* A proof of claim is deemed filed for any claim appearing on the lists filed by the debtor, unless the claim is listed as disputed, contingent or unliquidated. § 925. The court will fix the time within which other proofs of claim must be filed. Fed. R. Bankr. P. 3003(c)(3).

The chief judge of the court of appeals for the applicable circuit selects the bankruptcy judge to whom the chapter 9 case will be assigned, unlike the usual random draw for other bankruptcy cases. § 921(b). If there is an objection to the petition, the court, after notice and a hearing, may dismiss the petition "if the debtor did not file the petition in good faith or if the petition does not meet the requirements of" the Code. § 921(c). In interpreting this requirement, courts look both at subjective good faith (as opposed to improper motive for the filing), as well as more objective good faith (whether the filing was an appropriate response to circumstances at the time after meaningful discussions of alternatives).

Unlike under the other chapters of the Code, the voluntary filing of the petition does not constitute an order for relief. If the court does not dismiss the petition, the court must order relief under chapter 9. § 921(d). If any party in interest appeals from the order for relief, the court may not delay any proceeding in the chapter 9 case and may not stay any such proceeding. § 921(e). If the bankruptcy court has authorized the municipal debtor to incur debt under § 364(c) or (d) prior to the appeal, and the appellate court reverses a finding of jurisdiction, such debt remains valid. *Id.*

The clerk, or such other person as the court may direct, must give notice of the commencement of the case and the order for relief. Fed. R. Bankr. P. 2002(f). Notice of the filing and notice of the order for relief must also be given by publication at least once a week for three successive weeks in a newspaper of general circulation published within the district in which the case is commenced, and such other newspapers as the court designates. § 923. Any creditor or indenture trustee may file a proof of claim (and must do so if its claim is not scheduled by the debtor or is scheduled as disputed, contingent or unliquidated) within the time fixed by the court (which time may be extended by the court for cause). Fed. R. Bankr. P. 3003(c).

A visualization of the provisions relating to the commencement of a chapter 9 case follows.

COMMENCEMENT OF CHAPTER 9 CASE				
PETITION § 921(a)	SCHEDULES § 924 & RULE 1007	ASSIGNMENT § 921(b)	NOTICE § 923	ORDER FOR RELIEF § 921(d)
DEBTOR MAY FILE VOLUNTARY PETITION UNDER § 301

IF DEBTOR IS UNINCORPORATED TAX OR SPECIAL ASSESSMENT DISTRICT WITHOUT OFFICIALS, IT CAN FILE BY ITS GOVERNING AUTHORITY OR BOARD OR BODY AUTHORIZED TO LEVY TAXES OR ASSESSMENTS FOR ITS OBLIGATIONS | DEBTOR MUST FILE LIST OF CREDITORS

DEBTOR MUST FILE LIST OF CREDITORS HOLDING 20 LARGEST UNSECURED CLAIMS

DEBTOR MUST FILE SCHEDULES D, E, F, G & H WITHIN TIME FIXED BY COURT

COURT MAY MODIFY FILING REQUIREMENTS ON MOTION FOR CAUSE | CHIEF JUDGE OF COURT OF APPEALS FOR CIRCUIT DESIGNATES BANKRUPTCY JUDGE TO CONDUCT CASE | NOTICE MUST BE GIVEN OF COMMENCEMENT OF CASE AND OF ORDER FOR RELIEF

NOTICE MUST BE PUBLISHED AT LEAST ONCE A WEEK FOR THREE SUCCESSIVE WEEKS IN AT LEAST ONE NEWSPAPER OF GENERAL CIRCULATION WITHIN DISTRICT WHERE CASE IS COMMENCED, AND IN SUCH OTHER NEWSPAPER AS COURT DESIGNATES | IF PETITION IS NOT DISMISSED UPON OBJECTION, COURT ENTERS ORDER FOR RELIEF |

As is true for all bankruptcy filings, the filing of a chapter 9 petition operates as a stay against various actions by all entities under § 362. *See* Chapter 2[B], *supra.* The chapter 9 stay also bars two types of actions not otherwise covered by § 362. The first is the commencement or continuation of any action or proceeding against an officer or inhabitant of the debtor that seeks to enforce a claim against the debtor. The second is the enforcement of a lien on or arising out of taxes or assessments owed to the debtor. § 922(a). Explicitly excluded from the scope of the stay (in addition to the general exclusions in § 362(b)) is application of pledged special revenues (§ 902(2)) used to pay secured indebtedness. § 922(d). The chapter 9 stay terminates, and is subject to motions for relief of the stay, in accordance with all the provisions of § 362(c)–(g). § 922(b). If the debtor provides adequate protection to avoid having the stay lifted under § 362(d)(1), and the adequate protection turns out to be inadequate, as is true under § 507(b), the claimant is given special priority, an administrative expense claim in chapter 9. § 922(c). The following visualizes the chapter 9 stay provisions.

AUTOMATIC STAY IN CHAPTER 9 § 922			
ACTIONS STAYED § 922(a)	**EXCEPTIONS** § 922(d)	**TERMINATION OF STAY** § 922(b)	**INADEQUATE ADEQUATE PROTECTION** § 922(c)
ALL ACTS DESCRIBED IN § 362(a), COMMENCEMENT OR CONTINUATION OF JUDICIAL ADMINISTRATIVE OR OTHER ACTION OR PROCEEDING AGAINST AN OFFICER OR INHABITANT OF DEBTOR SEEKING TO ENFORCE A CLAIM AGAINST DEBTOR, AND ENFORCEMENT OF LIEN ON OR ARISING OUT OF TAXES OR ASSESSMENTS OWED TO DEBTOR	ALL EXCEPTIONS DESCRIBED IN § 362(b), AND APPLICATION OF PLEDGED SPECIAL REVENUES TO PAYMENT OF INDEBTEDNESS SECURED BY SUCH REVENUES	ALL PROVISIONS OF § 362(c)-(g) ARE APPLICABLE	IF DEBTOR PROVIDES ADEQUATE PROTECTION UNDER § 362, 364 OR 922 AND, NOTWITHSTANDING THAT ADEQUATE PROTECTION, THE CREDITOR HAS A CLAIM ARISING FROM THE STAY UNDER § 362 OR § 922 OR FROM GRANTING OF A LIEN UNDER § 364(d), THEN SUCH CLAIM SHALL BE ALLOWABLE ADMINISTRATIVE EXPENSE UNDER § 503(b)

In addition to § 921(c), which permits the court to dismiss a chapter 9 petition if it was not filed in good faith, § 930(a) sets out other grounds constituting "cause" as a result of which the court may dismiss a chapter 9 case. These grounds include failure to prosecute the case or unreasonable delay by the debtor that is prejudicial to creditors, failure to propose a plan on a timely basis, failure to get it accepted within a time fixed by the court, denial of confirmation and denial of additional time to file another plan or a modified plan, material default under a plan, or termination of the plan pursuant to its terms, almost all of which have counterparts in § 1112. The court must dismiss a case if confirmation is refused. § 930(b). Grounds for dismissal of a chapter 9 case are visualized below.

GROUNDS FOR DISMISSAL OF CHAPTER 9 CASE § 921(c) & § 930	
PERMISSIVE	MANDATORY
AFTER OBJECTION TO PETITION, COURT MAY, AFTER NOTICE AND HEARING, DISMISS PETITION IF DEBTOR DID NOT FILE PETITION IN GOOD FAITH OR IF PETITION DOES NOT MEET REQUIREMENTS OF CODE COURT MAY DISMISS CASE AFTER NOTICE AND HEARING FOR CAUSE, INCLUDING: 1) WANT OF PROSECUTION, 2) UNREASONABLE DELAY BY DEBTOR PREJUDICIAL TO CREDITORS, 3) FAILURE TO PROPOSE PLAN ON TIMELY BASIS, 4) DENIAL OF CONFIRMATION AND DENIAL OF ADDITIONAL TIME FOR FILING ANOTHER OR A MODIFIED PLAN, OR 5) IF COURT HAS RETAINED JURISDICTION AFTER CONFIRMATION, MATERIAL DEFAULT BY DEBTOR UNDER PLAN OR TERMINATION OF PLAN PURSUANT TO PLAN PROVISION	COURT MUST DISMISS CASE IF CONFIRMATION OF PLAN IS REFUSED

In 1988, Congress added special provisions to chapter 9 to protect special revenue bonds (often issued for project financing, under which a designated source of revenue is pledged to pay the bonds). We already examined the new definitions for "special revenues," "special tax payer" and "special tax payer affected by the plan" in § 902. As discussed above, the automatic stay does not apply to application of pledged special revenues to payment of the indebtedness secured by such revenues. § 922(d). Although generally under § 552(a), applicable to chapter 9, prepetition liens do not attach to property acquired by the estate after the bankruptcy, § 928 states that "special revenues" remain subject to a prepetition lien. All payments on municipal bonds or notes are excepted from preference attack under § 547 pursuant to § 926(b). Creditors with claims payable only out of special revenues are not eligible to become recourse creditors under § 1111(b), and therefore may not get paid out of general funds of the municipality. § 927. Finally, leases to municipalities that are terminable in the event the debtor fails to pay rent (often part of such project financings) are not treated as executory contracts or unexpired leases for purposes of § 365, and therefore cannot be rejected. § 929.

As previously discussed, there generally is no trustee in bankruptcy in a chapter 9 case. If the debtor refuses to pursue an avoidance action, then, on request of a creditor, the court may appoint a trustee for the limited purpose of pursuing that action.

§ 926(a). Even the United States trustee, who generally supervises the administration of bankruptcy cases and trustees, has a more limited role in a chapter 9 case. Chapter 9 cases are excluded from the trustee's supervisory responsibilities under 28 U.S.C. § 586(a)(3) in order to avoid any improper interference with state sovereignty. Section 307, which allows the U.S. trustee to appear and be heard on any issue in any case or proceeding, is not applicable in a chapter 9 case. The only role the U.S. trustee has in chapter 9 cases is to appoint a committee of creditors holding unsecured claims and any additional committees of creditors under § 1102 (applicable in chapter 9 cases under § 901(a)).

Other parties may be interested in the case. Under Fed. R. Bankr. P. 2018(c), the Secretary of the Treasury of the United States may intervene in the chapter 9 case, and must do so if requested by the court. Representatives of the state in which the debtor is located are also entitled to intervene in the case with respect to matters specified by the court. *Id.* A labor union or employees' association, representative of employees of the debtor, is also entitled to be heard on the economic soundness of a plan affecting the interests of the employees. Fed. R. Bankr. P. 2018(d). The Securities and Exchange Commission and parties in interest have the rights to appear and be heard provided by § 1109, applicable to chapter 9 cases under § 901(a).

4. Plan of Adjustment

As is true for a chapter 11 debtor, a chapter 9 debtor aims at resolving its financial difficulties through confirmation of a plan for the adjustment of the debtor's debts. The chapter 9 plan of adjustment differs from the chapter 11 plan of reorganization in several respects. First, only the municipal debtor may file a plan. § 941. The plan must be filed with the petition or at such later time as the court fixes. *Id.* The debtor may modify the plan at any time prior to confirmation consistent with the requirements of chapter 9. § 942 and Fed. R. Bankr. P. 3019(a). There is no provision for modification of a plan after confirmation as in § 1127(b).

The contents of the chapter 9 plan are the same as those in a chapter 11 plan. *See* Chapter 9[B], *supra.* All mandatory and permissive provisions of § 1123 applicable to a municipality are applicable in chapter 9 under § 901(a). The requirements for classification of claims under § 1122 and the definition of impairment § 1124 also apply. The debtor prepares a disclosure statement that complies with § 1125 and may not solicit acceptance of the plan until the court, after notice and a hearing, approves the disclosure statement as "containing adequate information." § 1125(b). The voting requirements for holders of claims, and the provisions relating to potential designation of claims, in § 1126 are applicable in chapter 9. *See* Chapter 9[C], *supra.* If any holder of a claim covered by the plan accepts a new security from the debtor for that claim under the plan either prior to or after the filing of the case, that holder is deemed to have supported the plan. § 946. As under § 1128 in a chapter 11 case (made applicable to chapter 9 under § 901(a)), the court must hold a confirmation hearing.

The confirmation requirements for a chapter 9 plan are somewhat different from those applicable in a chapter 11 case. Only five of sixteen requirements for confirmation of a chapter 11 plan under § 1129(a) are applicable to a chapter 9 plan. *See* Chapter 9[E][1], *supra.* These are the requirements that the debtor comply with the applicable provisions of the Code; that the plan have been proposed in good faith and not by any means forbidden by law; that any governmental regulatory commission with jurisdiction over the rates of the debtor have approved any rate change proposed by the plan (or the rate change is expressly conditioned on such approval); that each impaired class of claims has accepted the plan; and that at least one class of impaired claims has accepted the plan (without regard to any acceptance by insiders). § 1129(a)(2), (3), (6), (8) & (10), made applicable in chapter 9 by § 901(a).

Chapter 9 includes seven additional confirmation requirements in § 943(b). First, the plan must comply with the provisions of the Code made applicable to chapter 9 cases under § 103(e) and § 901. Second, the plan must comply with the provisions of chapter 9. Third, although there is no requirement that the court approve the amounts payable for services and expenses as reasonable as under § 1129(a)(4), these amounts must be fully disclosed and must be reasonable. Fourth, the plan may not be confirmed if the debtor is prohibited by law from taking any action necessary to carry out the plan. Fifth, because only administrative expense claims get priority, the plan must provide that administrative expense claims only are entitled to be paid in full in cash on the effective date of the plan, unlike the mandatory treatment for other priority claims in § 1129(a)(9). Sixth, confirmation is conditioned upon obtaining any regulatory or electoral approval necessary to carry out any provision of the plan, such as the acquisition or disposition of property or the incurring of indebtedness or imposition of tax increases. (This requirement is broader than the also-applicable requirement of § 1129(a)(6) that government regulatory commissions with authority over rates approve any rate change in a plan.) Finally, because there is no such thing as a municipal liquidation, the best interests test (the requirement in chapter 11 under § 1129(a)(7) that each creditor receive at least as much under the plan as it would have received in a chapter 7 liquidation) does not apply to a chapter 9 plan. Instead, there is an express requirement that the plan be "feasible" and "in the best interests of creditors." "Feasible" means that the court believes that the debtor will be able to fulfill the requirements of the plan. "Best interests of creditors" is undefined, but may require a comparison between what creditors are receiving under the plan, and what they would have received outside bankruptcy.

A chapter 9 plan may also be confirmed on a cramdown basis (when not all classes of impaired claims have voted to approve the plan), and the requirements for such a confirmation are the same as for a chapter 11 plan with respect to secured and unsecured claims under § 1129(b)(1) and § 1129(b)(2)(A) & (B), made applicable to chapter 9 under § 901(a). The plan may be confirmed over the objection of one or more classes of impaired claims if the plan "does not discriminate unfairly, and is fair and equitable, with respect to each class of claims" that is impaired and objects to the plan. § 1129(b)(1). The term "fair and equitable" with respect to secured claims requires the same treatment as under chapter 11. § 1129(b)(2)(A). *See* Chapter 9[E][2], *supra*. For unsecured claims, the term "fair and equitable" in a chapter 11 case implements the absolute priority rule; if the objecting class of impaired unsecured claims is not paid in full, no holder of a claim or interest with a lower priority can receive any distribution. § 1129(b)(2)(B). However, because there are no equity holders in a chapter 9 bankruptcy with interests junior to unsecured creditors, unsecured creditors have no protection in a chapter 9 cramdown plan other than the requirement that one impaired class support the plan.

A visualization of the confirmation requirements for a chapter 9 plan follows.

CONFIRMATION REQUIREMENTS FOR CHAPTER 9 PLAN			
NON-CRAMDOWN PLAN		CRAMDOWN PLAN	
§ 1129(a)(2)	PLAN PROPONENT COMPLIES WITH APPLICABLE PROVISIONS OF CODE	§ 1129(b)(1)	ALL REQUIREMENTS EXCEPT § 1129(b)(8) ARE MET AND PLAN DOES NOT DISCRIMINATE UNFAIRLY AND IS FAIR AND EQUITABLE WITH RESPECT TO EACH OBJECTING IMPAIRED CLASS
§ 1129(a)(3)	PLAN HAS BEEN PROPOSED IN GOOD FAITH AND NOT BY ANY MEANS FORBIDDEN BY LAW		
§ 1129(a)(6)	ANY GOVERNMENTAL REGULATORY COMMISSION WITH JURISDICTION OVER RATES OF DEBTOR HAS APPROVED ANY RATE CHANGE PROVIDED FOR IN PLAN	§1129(b)(2)(A)	FAIR AND EQUITABLE TREATMENT FOR SECURED CLAIMS
§ 1129(a)(8)	EACH CLASS OF IMPAIRED CLAIMS HAS ACCEPTED PLAN	§ 1129(b)(2)(B)	FAIR AND EQUITABLE TREATMENT FOR UNSECURED CLAIMS (ABSOLUTE PRIORITY RULE)
§ 1129(a)(10)	IF ANY CLASS OF CLAIMS IS IMPAIRED, ONE CLASS OF IMPAIRED CLAIMS HAS ACCEPTED PLAN		
§ 943(b)(1)	PLAN COMPLIES WITH PROVISIONS OF CODE MADE APPLICABLE TO CHAPTER 9		
§ 943(b)(2)	PLAN COMPLIES WITH PROVISIONS OF CHAPTER 9		
§ 943(b)(3)	ALL AMOUNTS TO BE PAID FOR SERVICES OR EXPENSES IN CASE HAVE BEEN FULLY DISCLOSED AND ARE REASONABLE		
§ 943(b)(4)	DEBTOR IS NOT PROHIBITED BY LAW FROM TAKING ANY ACTION NECESSARY TO CARRY OUT PLAN		
§ 943(b)(5)	PLAN PROVIDES FOR ADMINISTRATIVE EXPENSES TO BE PAID IN FULL IN CASH ON THE EFFECTIVE DATE OF THE PLAN		
§ 943(b)(6)	ANY REGULATORY OR ELECTORAL APPROVAL NECESSARY TO CARRY OUT PLAN HAS BEEN OBTAINED		
§ 943(b)(7)	PLAN IS IN BEST INTERESTS OF CREDITORS AND IS FEASIBLE		

If the plan is confirmed, the plan binds all creditors, whether or not they filed proofs of claim or voted against the plan. § 944(a). The court may revoke an order of confirmation before 180 days after its entry only if the order was procured by fraud under § 1144 (made applicable to chapter 9 under § 901(a)).

The debtor is discharged from all debts when three conditions are met. First, the plan must be confirmed. Second, the debtor must deposit any consideration to be distributed under the plan with a disbursing agent appointed by the court. Third, the court must determine that any security so deposited will be a valid legal obligation of the debtor after distribution, and that any provision made to pay or secure payment of such obligation is valid. There are two types of debts excluded from the chapter 9 discharge. § 944(b). One is those debts excepted from discharge under the plan or confirmation order. The other is a debt held by an entity that had no notice or actual knowledge of the case before confirmation. The permanent injunction of § 524(a) comes into effect upon a discharge. A visualization of the provisions relating to the chapter 9 discharge follows.

CHAPTER 9 DISCHARGE § 944(b)			
CONDITIONS TO DISCHARGE	DEBTS DISCHARGED	EXCEPTIONS TO DISCHARGE	PERMANENT INJUNCTION
1) PLAN IS CONFIRMED, 2) DEBTOR DEPOSITS ANY CONSIDERATION TO BE DISTRIBUTED UNDER PLAN WITH DESIGNATED DISBURSING AGENT, AND 3) COURT DETERMINES THAT ANY SECURITY SO DEPOSITED WILL BE VALID AFTER DISTRIBUTION AND ANY SECURITY FOR ANY OBLIGATION IS VALID	ALL DEBTS	DEBTS EXCEPTED FROM DISCHARGE UNDER PLAN OR CONFIRMATION ORDER, AND DEBT HELD BY ENTITY THAT HAD NO NOTICE OR ACTUAL KNOWLEDGE OF CASE PRIOR TO CONFIRMATION	PERMANENT INJUNCTION OF § 524(a)(1) AND (2) COMES INTO EFFECT UPON DISCHARGE

The court may retain jurisdiction over the case after confirmation and during implementation of the plan. § 945(a). When administration of the case is completed, the court is directed to close the case. § 945(b).

C. CHAPTER 15

1. History

In a global economy, it is becoming more and more likely that a business's financial troubles will not be local in nature; not only will a corporation have operations that extend beyond the borders of a single state, they may also have operations that extend beyond the borders of a single country. When an international entity files for bankruptcy, significant issues of choice of law and jurisdiction of U.S. and foreign courts ensue.

The general rule internationally on insolvent businesses has traditionally been one of territoriality — each country in which the business operated would grab local assets and administer them according to the local law of that jurisdiction. Territoriality has serious disadvantages. A reorganization may becomes difficult or impossible when local assets necessary for ongoing operations are seized by local creditors. Even if the business is sold, the value that can be realized for those assets may be adversely affected if they must be sold by nationality rather than by division or subsidiary or another logical organization. Distributions between creditors in different countries may end up being significantly different based on the assets in each country and the priority rules that country utilizes, which seems arbitrary and unpredictable and therefore bad for international business. Debtors can game the system, moving assets from jurisdiction to jurisdiction to ensure that insiders or favored creditors will benefit. Foreign creditors tend to be discriminated against in local insolvency proceedings, if not overtly at least practically because of language differences and lack of notice and lack of accessibility. For all of these reasons, the United States has joined some other countries in moving away from the territorial approach towards "universalism" in transnational bankruptcy issues.

In the 1978 Bankruptcy Code, Congress took the first steps towards universalism by enacting § 304. Section 304 could be invoked if there was a "foreign proceeding" for the liquidation or reorganization of a debtor. "Foreign proceeding" was defined as a proceeding in a foreign country "in which the debtor's domicile, residence, principal place of business, or principal assets were located" for the purpose of liquidating an estate, adjusting debts or effecting a reorganization. This meant that the foreign proceeding had to be the main bankruptcy proceeding, and the U.S. courts were simply being asked to help in connection with that foreign proceeding.

A foreign representative (meaning a trustee or other representative of the estate in the foreign proceeding) could commence something called an "ancillary" case in U.S. bankruptcy court by filing a petition. If no party in interest objected to the filing of the petition, the U.S. bankruptcy court could enjoin various actions against the debtor and the property involved in the foreign proceeding, order turnover of property to the foreign representative, or order other appropriate relief. In deciding whether to grant such relief, the U.S. court was directed to be guided by the goal of "an economical and expeditious administration of the estate" consistent with certain goals:

(a) just treatment of all holders of claims against or interests in the estate,

(b) protection of claim holders in the U.S. against prejudice and inconvenience in the processing of claims in the foreign proceeding,

(c) prevention of preferential or fraudulent dispositions of property of the estate,

(d) distribution of proceeds of the estate substantially in accordance with the U.S. priorities,

(e) comity, and

(f) if appropriate, the opportunity for a fresh start for an individual debtor.

There was no requirement in § 304 that the foreign jurisdiction in which the foreign proceeding had been commenced have similar procedures to assist in U.S. bankruptcy cases, but it was hoped at the time that reciprocity would develop; that didn't happen for many years. The first major step towards international cooperation in transnational bankruptcy cases came in 1997 when the United Nations Commission on International Trade Law (UNCITRAL) promulgated a Model Law on Cross-Border Insolvency, which was approved by the General Assembly of the United Nations. Legislation based on the Model Law has been adopted by at least 14 countries or territories, including Great Britain, Japan and Mexico, although some countries have made significant changes to its provisions.

In 2005, Congress repealed § 304, and replaced it with a new chapter 15 to the Code, which is intended "to incorporate the Model Law on Cross-Border Insolvency" with the objectives of cooperation between courts of the U.S. and those of other countries, legal certainty for trade and investment, fair and efficient administration of cross-border cases, maximization of value of the debtor's assets, and protecting investment and preserving employment. § 1501(a). Meanwhile, the European Union adopted the EU Regulation on Insolvency Proceedings 2000, which entered into force in 2002 and is binding on the 14 member states of the EU. The EU Regulation provides for automatic recognition of cross-border insolvency proceedings within the European Union, and establishes rules for determining which courts have jurisdiction over them, as well as choice of law rules. The EU Regulation was drafted before the Model Law, and the Model Law adopted some of its provisions; as a result, case law interpreting the EU Regulation is helpful in interpreting similar provisions in the Model Law, and therefore in interpreting chapter 15. Indeed, under § 1508, in interpreting chapter 15, the court is directed to "consider its international origin, and the need to promote an application of this chapter that is consistent with the application of similar statutes adopted by foreign jurisdictions."

2. Scope of Chapter 15

The first major difference between chapter 15 and the old § 304 is in its scope, *i.e.*, the situations in which it operates. Whereas § 304 operated only when there was a foreign main proceeding, chapter 15 operates whenever there is any "foreign proceeding," now defined in § 101(23) to mean any collective judicial or administrative proceeding in a foreign country under a law relating to insolvency or debt adjustment in which the assets and affairs of the debtor are subject to control or supervision by a foreign court for the purpose of liquidation or reorganization. As discussed below, chapter 15 still distinguishes between "foreign main proceedings" and "foreign nonmain proceedings" and defines those terms in § 1502(4) & (5).

Chapter 15 applies in four situations under § 1501(b). First, it applies when assistance is sought in the U.S. by a foreign court or a "foreign representative" in connection with a foreign proceeding. A foreign representative is defined in § 101(24) as a person or body authorized (either permanently or on an interim basis) in a foreign proceeding "to administer the reorganization or liquidation of the debtor's assets or affairs or to act as the representative of the foreign proceeding." Second, it applies when assistance is sought in a foreign country in connection with a U.S. bankruptcy case. Third, it is applicable when there are concurrent bankruptcy proceedings in the U.S. and in a foreign country with respect to the same debtor. Finally, chapter 15 applies when creditors or other interested persons in a foreign country have an interest in requesting commencement of, or participation in, a U.S. bankruptcy case.

Section 1501(c) specifically excludes from the scope of chapter 15 three proceedings and entities. First, chapter 15 does not apply to a proceeding concerning an entity not eligible to be a debtor under chapter 7 pursuant to § 109(b), except foreign insurance companies. *See* Chapter 1[C], *supra*. Second, chapter 15 does not apply to individuals lawfully resident in the U.S. who have debts within the limits for chapter 13 under § 109(e). Third, chapter 15 does not apply to an entity subject to a proceeding under the Securities Investor Protection Act of 1970, a stockbroker subject to subchapter III of chapter 7, or a commodity broker subject to subchapter IV of chapter 7.

A visualization of the scope of chapter 15 follows.

SCOPE OF CHAPTER 15 § 1501	
WHEN CHAPTER 15 APPLIES § 1501(b)	**WHEN CHAPTER 15 DOES NOT APPLY § 1501(c)**
1) FOREIGN COURT OR FOREIGN REPRESENTATIVE SEEKS ASSISTANCE IN U.S. IN CONNECTION WITH FOREIGN PROCEEDING, 2) ASSISTANCE IS SOUGHT IN FOREIGN COUNTRY IN CONNECTION WITH U.S. BANKRUPTCY CASE, 3) FOREIGN PROCEEDING AND U.S. BANKRUPTCY CASE WITH RESPECT TO SAME DEBTOR ARE PENDING CONCURRENTLY, OR 4) CREDITORS OR OTHER INTERESTED PERSONS IN FOREIGN COUNTRY HAVE INTEREST IN REQUESTING COMMENCEMENT OF, OR PARTICIPATING IN, U.S. BANKRUPTCY CASE OR PROCEEDING	1) PROCEEDING CONCERNING ENTITY WHO MAY NOT BE A DEBTOR UNDER CHAPTER 7 PURSUANT TO § 109(b), OTHER THAN FOREIGN INSURANCE COMPANY, 2) INDIVIDUAL OR INDIVIDUAL AND SPOUSE WHO ARE CITIZENS OF U.S. OR LAWFUL PERMANENT RESIDENTS OF U.S. WHOSE DEBTS FALL WITHIN LIMITS OF § 109(e) FOR CHAPTER 13 ELIGIBILITY, OR 3) ENTITY SUBJECT TO PROCEEDING UNDER SECURITIES INVESTOR PROTECTION ACT OF 1970 OR STOCKBROKER OR COMMODITY BROKER SUBJECT TO SUBCHAPTER III OR IV OF CHAPTER 7

If chapter 15 conflicts in any respect with an obligation of the U.S. arising out of a treaty or other international agreement, the requirements of the treaty or agreement prevail. § 1503. A court may refuse to take an action governed by chapter 15 "if the action would be manifestly contrary to the public policy of the United States." § 1506.

3. Access and Recognition

A foreign representative (§ 101(24)) has limited rights in a U.S. court unless it gets recognition of its foreign proceeding. It may take any action that is extra-judicial in nature, one that does not require comity or cooperation of the U.S. court, without obtaining recognition *See, e.g., In re Loy*, 380 B.R. 154 (Bankr. E.D. Va. 2007) (allowing foreign representative to file lis pendens against debtor's U.S. property). But to obtain access to U.S. courts, the foreign representative must obtain recognition of the foreign proceeding.

It does so by commencing a case under chapter 15 pursuant to § 1504 by filing "a petition for recognition of a foreign proceeding under § 1515." The foreign representative is authorized to file such a petition under § 1509(a). "Recognition" is the entry of an order granting recognition of a foreign main proceeding or foreign nonmain proceeding. § 1502(7). The distinction between a foreign main proceeding and foreign nonmain proceeding is discussed below.

A petition for recognition must be accompanied by certain documents. First, the foreign representative must present either the decision commencing the foreign proceeding and appointing the foreign representative (translated into English), or a certificate from the foreign court affirming the existence of the foreign proceeding and the appointment of the foreign representative (translated into English), or in the absence of either of those documents, any other evidence acceptable to the court as to the same subject matter. § 1515(b) & (d). Second, the foreign representative must provide a statement identifying all foreign proceedings with respect to the debtor known to the foreign representative. § 1515(c). A visualization of the requirements for the application for recognition follows.

REQUIREMENTS FOR APPLICATION FOR RECOGNITION § 1515		
PETITION FOR RECOGNITION UNDER § 1504	EITHER: 1) CERTIFIED COPY (TRANSLATED INTO ENGLISH) OF DECISION COMMENCING FOREIGN PROCEEDING AND APPOINTING FOREIGN REPRESENTATIVE, OR 2) CERTIFICATE (TRANSLATED INTO ENGLISH) FROM FOREIGN COURT AFFIRMING EXISTENCE OF FOREIGN PROCEEDING AND APPOINTMENT OF FOREIGN REPRESENTATIVE, OR 3) ANY OTHER EVIDENCE ACCEPTABLE TO COURT OF EXISTENCE OF FOREIGN PROCEEDING AND APPOINTMENT OF FOREIGN REPRESENTATIVE	STATEMENT IDENTIFYING ALL FOREIGN PROCEEDINGS WITH RESPECT TO DEBTOR THAT ARE KNOWN TO FOREIGN REPRESENTATIVE

The court is entitled to presume that these supporting documents submitted with the petition for recognition are authentic and to presume the truth of their contents. § 1516(a) & (b). Pursuant to § 1518, the foreign representative must promptly provide a notice of change of status concerning any substantial change in the status of the foreign proceeding or the appointment of the foreign representative, and any other foreign proceedings that become known to the foreign representative.

The clerk, or some other person designated by the court, must give notice of a petition for recognition to the debtor, all persons or bodies authorized to administer foreign proceedings of the debtor, all entities against whom provisional relief is being sought under § 1519 (discussed below), all parties to litigation pending in the U.S. in which the debtor is a party at the time of the filing of the petition, and such other entities as the court may direct, at least 21 days prior to the hearing on the petition. Fed. R. Bankr. P. 2002(q)(1). The notice must specify whether the petition seeks recognition of the foreign proceeding as a foreign main proceeding or a foreign nonmain proceeding. *Id.* If the petition seeks recognition of a foreign nonmain proceeding, the clerk must forthwith issue a summons for service on the debtor, any entity against whom provisional relief is sought under § 1519, and on any other party as the court may direct. Fed. R. Bankr. P. 1010(a). Any party in interest may contest the petition. Fed. R. Bankr. P. 1011(a).

While the petition for recognition is pending, "provisional" relief may be granted by the bankruptcy court "where relief is urgently needed to protect the assets of the debtor or the interests of the creditors." § 1519(a). Relief may be denied if it would interfere with the administration of a foreign main proceeding. § 1519(c). All relief is also subject to the public policy exception in § 1506.

The types of provisional relief that are available include staying execution against the debtor's assets; entrusting administration or realization upon U.S. assets to the foreign representative to the extent that they are perishable, susceptible to devaluation or otherwise in jeopardy; barring any transfer, encumbrance or disposition of assets; providing for examination of witnesses or acquiring evidence or information; and granting any additional relief, except for relief under one of the avoiding powers. The court may not provisionally enjoin a police or regulatory act of a governmental unit (including a criminal action or proceeding), or certain acts excluded from the automatic stay. § 1519(d) & (f).

Any provisional relief granted is subject to modification or termination upon request of the foreign representative or an entity affected by the relief, or at its own motion. § 1522(c). The court may grant provisional relief, or may modify or terminate any relief granted, only "if the interests of the creditors and other interested entities, including the debtor, are sufficiently protected." § 1522(a). Provisional relief is subject to the standards, procedures and limitations applicable to an injunction. § 1519(e). Provisional relief terminates when the petition for recognition is granted, unless the court extends it. § 1519(b).

A visualization of provisional relief in chapter 15 follows.

PROVISIONAL RELIEF PENDING RECOGNITION			
WHEN PROVISIONAL RELIEF IS AVAILABLE § 1519(a) & (c) & § 1522(a)	TERMINATION OF PROVISIONAL RELIEF § 1519(b)	TYPES OF PROVISIONAL RELIEF § 1519(a) & (d)	PROVISIONAL RELIEF THAT MAY NOT BE GRANTED § 1519(d) & (f)
AFTER FILING OF PETITION FOR RECOGNITION WHERE RELIEF IS URGENTLY NEEDED TO PROTECT ASSETS OF THE DEBTOR OR INTERESTS OF CREDITORS INTERESTS OF THE CREDITORS AND OTHER INTERESTED ENTITIES, INCLUDING THE DEBTOR, MUST BE SUFFICIENTLY PROTECTED RELIEF MUST NOT INTERFERE WITH ADMINISTRATION OF FOREIGN MAIN PROCEEDING	UPON GRANT OF PETITION FOR RECOGNITION, UNLESS EXTENDED BY COURT UNDER § 1521(a)(6)	1) STAYING EXECUTION AGAINST DEBTOR'S ASSETS, 2) ENTRUSTING ADMINISTRATION OR REALIZATION OF ALL OR PART OF DEBTOR'S U.S. ASSETS TO FOREIGN REPRESENTATIVE OR ANOTHER PERSON AUTHORIZED BY COURT IN ORDER TO PROTECT AND PRESERVE VALUE OF ASSETS THAT ARE PERISHABLE, SUSCEPTIBLE TO DEVALUATION OR OTHERWISE IN JEOPARDY, 3) SUSPENDING RIGHT TO TRANSFER, ENCUMBER OR OTHERWISE DISPOSE OF ANY ASSETS OF DEBTOR, 4) PROVIDING FOR EXAMINATION OF WITNESSES, THE TAKING OF EVIDENCE OR DELIVERY OF INFORMATION CONCERNING DEBTOR'S ASSETS, AFFAIRS, RIGHTS, OBLIGATIONS OR LIABILITIES, OR 5) GRANTING ANY ADDITIONAL RELIEF AVAILABLE TO A TRUSTEE, OTHER THAN RELIEF AVAILABLE UNDER §§ 522, 544, 545, 547, 548, 550 AND 724(a)	COURT MAY NOT ENJOIN POLICE OR REGULATORY ACT OF GOVERNMENTAL UNIT COURT MAY NOT STAY ACTS EXCEPTED FROM AUTOMATIC STAY UNDER § 362(b)(6), (7) OR (27) OR § 362(o)

The court must decide upon a petition for recognition "at the earliest possible time," § 1517(c), and must recognize the foreign proceeding (unless it would be "manifestly contrary to the public policy of the United States" § 1506) if it meets three requirements. First, the foreign proceeding must be a "foreign main proceeding" or "foreign nonmain proceeding" (and will be recognized as one or the other if the petition is granted, § 1517(b)). § 1517(a)(1). A "foreign main proceeding" is defined as a foreign proceeding pending in the country where the debtor has the "center of its main interests" (known as the "COMI"). § 1502(4). This phrase comes from the EU Regulation, where the regulation adopting the Regulation described it as "the place where the debtor conducts the administration of his interests on a regular basis and is therefore ascertainable by third parties."

It is presumed (in the absence of contrary evidence) that the COMI is where the debtor's registered office, or habitual residence (for an individual), is located. § 1516(c). If there is evidence that the COMI is in a different jurisdiction than the country of the registered office or habitual residence, the foreign representative has the burden of showing that the COMI is in the same place as the registered office or habitual residence. The foreign representative also has the burden of rebutting the presumption if the foreign representative wishes to establish that the COMI is in a different jurisdiction from the registered office or habitual residence.

Some of the factors considered by the court in deciding where the COMI of a non-individual debtor is located include the location of the debtor's headquarters, the location of the debtor's managers, the location of debtor's primary assets, the location of a majority of debtor's creditors, and the jurisdiction of the applicable law that would apply to most disputes. *See In re SPhinX*, Ltd. 351 B.R. 103, 117 (Bankr. S.D.N.Y. 2006), *aff'd*, 371 B.R. 10 (S.D.N.Y. 2007). Using these factors, courts frequently find the COMI is not where the registered office is, applying something comparable to a "principal place of business" analysis. *See, e.g., In re Tradex Swiss AG*, 384 B.R. 34 (Bankr. D. Mass. 2008) (Swiss corporation held to have Boston COMI when trading platform was based at Boston office, more operations were conducted there, signing authority was manager of Boston office); *In re Bear Stearns High-Grade Structured Credit Strategies Master Fund, Ltd.*, 374 B.R. 122 (Bankr. S.D.N.Y. 2007), *aff'd*, 389 B.R. 325 (S.D.N.Y. 2008) (Cayman Islands was jurisdiction of registration, but court held U.S. was COMI).

Factors considered by a court in deciding where the COMI of an individual debtor is located include where the debtor has a residence and employment, whether debtor has intent to return to former place of residence, length of residence in current location, where a majority of creditors are located, where principal assets are located, where the debtor has citizenship or permanent legal residence status, governing law applicable to most disputes and location of debtor's finances. *See Lavie v. Ran (In re Ran)*, 607 F.3d 1017 (5th Cir. 2010).

A visualization of the determination of the debtor's COMI follows.

DETERMINATION OF COMI FOR FOREIGN MAIN PROCEEDING § 1502(4)				
DEFINITION	**PRESUMPTION**	**BURDEN**	**FACTORS CONSIDERED**	
CENTER OF THE DEBTOR'S MAIN INTERESTS (PER EU REGULATION) IS "THE PLACE WHERE THE DEBTOR CONDUCTS THE ADMINISTRATION OF HIS INTERESTS ON A REGULAR BASIS AND IS THEREFORE ASCERTAINABLE BY THIRD PARTIES"	IN ABSENCE OF CONTRARY EVIDENCE, DEBTOR'S REGISTERED OFFICE, OR HABITUAL RESIDENCE OF INDIVIDUAL, IS PRESUMED TO BE COMI	FOREIGN REPRESENTATIVE HAS BURDEN OF OVERCOMING PRESUMPTION, OR OF ESTABLISHING THAT PRESUMPTION IS CORRECT IF CONTRARY EVIDENCE IS PRESENTED	INDIVIDUAL DEBTOR 1) LOCATION OF PRINCIPAL ASSETS, 2) LOCATION OF MAJORITY OF CREDITORS, 3) JURISDICTION WHOSE LAW WOULD APPLY TO MOST DISPUTES, 4) HOW LONG DEBTOR AND FAMILY HAVE LIVED IN CURRENT LOCALE, 5) WHETHER DEBTOR HAS INTENT TO RETURN TO PRIOR RESIDENCE, 6) WHERE DEBTOR HAS RESIDENCE AND EMPLOYMENT, 7) CITIZENSHIP AND/OR PERMANENT LEGAL RESIDENCE, AND 8) LOCATION OF FINANCES	NON-INDIVIDUAL DEBTOR 1) LOCATION OF HEADQUARTERS, 2) LOCATION OF MANAGERS, 3) LOCATION OF PRIMARY ASSETS, 4) LOCATION OF MAJORITY OF CREDITORS, AND 5) JURISDICTION WHOSE LAW WOULD APPLY TO MOST DISPUTES

A "foreign nonmain proceeding" is defined as one not a foreign main proceeding pending in a country where the debtor has an "establishment." § 1502(5). An "establishment" is any place of operations where the debtor carries out a nontransitory economic activity. § 1502(2). Note that all foreign proceedings do not fall in one of the two categories, *i.e.*, there are foreign proceedings that are neither foreign main proceedings nor foreign nonmain proceedings, in which case recognition will be denied. For example, if a foreign proceeding is commenced other than in the debtor's

COMI where the debtor has assets but no establishment, the foreign proceeding does not qualify for recognition under § 1517(a)(1). *See Lavie v. Ran (In re Ran)*, 607 F.3d 1017 (5th Cir. 2010) (denying recognition to Israeli bankruptcy receiver for case that was neither foreign main proceeding nor foreign nonmain proceeding).

The second requirement for recognition is that the foreign representative is a person or body. § 1517(a)(2). This would include foreign representatives who are the debtor in possession under the relevant foreign law rather than a trustee.

The third requirement for recognition is that the petition meets the requirements of § 1515 discussed above, meaning it has all the required documentation and is submitted by the foreign representative. § 1517(a)(3).

The requirements for recognition are visualized below.

REQUIREMENTS FOR RECOGNITION OF FOREIGN PROCEEDING § 1517(a)		
FOREIGN PROCEEDING IS "FOREIGN MAIN PROCEEDING" (§ 1502(4)) OR "FOREIGN NONMAIN PROCEEDING" (§ 1502(5))	FOREIGN REPRESENTATIVE IS A PERSON OR BODY	PETITION MEETS REQUIREMENTS OF § 1515

Upon recognition of a foreign proceeding as a foreign main proceeding, certain provisions of the Code automatically apply with respect to property of the debtor within the U.S. § 1520(a). The automatic stay of § 362 and adequate protection requirements of § 361 apply with respect to the debtor and U.S. property of the debtor. Sections 363 (limiting the use, sale or lease of property), 549 (limiting postpetition transfers) and 552 (limiting the effect of prepetition security interests) apply with respect to transfers of an interest of the debtor in U.S. property to the same extent as they would apply to the property of the estate. The foreign representative is given the powers of the trustee to operate the debtor's business and exercise the trustee's rights under § 363 and § 552, unless the court orders otherwise. And § 552 applies to U.S. property of the debtor.

The foreign representative has certain additional rights to participate in a U.S. bankruptcy court upon recognition. The foreign representative may participate as a party in interest in a U.S. bankruptcy case involving the debtor upon recognition of the foreign proceeding under § 1512. The foreign representative may commence a bankruptcy case, either voluntary (under § 301 or § 302) or involuntary (under § 303(b)(4)). § 1511(a). The foreign representative must inform the court where the petition for recognition was filed of the foreign representative's intent to commence a case prior to such commencement. § 1511(b). The foreign representative may also seek dismissal or suspension of a pending bankruptcy case under § 305(a)(2), which the court may grant if a petition for recognition of a foreign proceeding has been granted and the court determines that the purposes of chapter 15 would best be served by such a dismissal or suspension. § 305(a)(2).

Filing a petition to commence an involuntary case under § 303, seeking dismissal or suspension of a pending case under § 305, or filing a petition for recognition under § 1515, does not subject the foreign representative to the jurisdiction of U.S. courts for any other purpose. § 306, § 1510. However, if the court grants recognition to the foreign proceeding, subject to any limitations the court may impose, the foreign representative has the capacity to sue and be sued in a U.S. court. § 1509(b)(1). Foreign representatives may also apply directly to a U.S. court for appropriate relief in that court, and a U.S. court must grant comity or cooperation to the foreign representative. § 1509(b)(2) & (3).

Upon recognition, the foreign representative has standing to commence an avoidance action in a U.S. bankruptcy case of the debtor. § 1523(a). If the recognized foreign proceeding is nonmain, the court must determine that the assets subject to the avoidance action are assets that should be administered in the foreign nonmain proceeding before granting the relief sought. § 1523(b).

The foreign representative may, upon recognition, intervene in any proceedings in state or federal U.S. court in which the debtor is a party. § 1524.

The rights conveyed automatically by recognition are visualized below.

RIGHTS OF FOREIGN REPRESENTATIVE UPON RECOGNITION	
§ 1511	COMMENCE AN INVOLUNTARY CASE UNDER § 303(b)(4), OR COMMENCE A VOLUNTARY CASE UNDER § 301 OR § 302
§ 305(b)	SEEK DISMISSAL OF CASE OR SUSPENSION OF PROCEEDINGS UNDER § 305(b) IF PURPOSES OF CHAPTER 15 WOULD BEST BE SERVED BY SUCH DISMISSAL OR SUSPENSION
§ 1509(b)	1) CAPACITY TO SUE OR BE SUED IN U.S. COURT, 2) MAY APPLY DIRECTLY TO U.S. COURT FOR APPROPRIATE RELIEF IN THAT COURT, AND 3) COURT IN U.S. SHALL GRANT COMITY OR COOPERATION TO FOREIGN REPRESENTATIVE
§ 1512	PARTICIPATE AS A PARTY IN INTEREST IN A BANKRUPTCY CASE REGARDING DEBTOR
§ 1520	1) §§ 361 AND 362 APPLY WITH RESPECT TO DEBTOR AND PROPERTY OF THE DEBTOR WITHIN U.S., 2) §§ 363, 549 AND 552 APPLY TO TRANSFER OF DEBTOR'S INTEREST IN PROPERTY WITHIN U.S. TO SAME EXTENT AS IF PROPERTY WERE PROPERTY OF ESTATE, 3) FOREIGN REPRESENTATIVE MAY OPERATE DEBTOR'S BUSINESS AND EXERCISE RIGHTS OF TRUSTEE UNDER § 363 AND § 552, AND 4) § 552 APPLIES TO PROPERTY OF THE DEBTOR WITHIN U.S.
§ 1523	STANDING TO INITIATE ACTION UNDER § 522, 544, 545, 547, 548, 550 OR 724(a) IN DEBTOR'S U.S. BANKRUPTCY CASE, BUT IF FOREIGN PROCEEDING IS NONMAIN, COURT MUST BE SATISFIED THAT ASSETS SHOULD BE ADMINISTERED IN FOREIGN NONMAIN PROCEEDING
§ 1524	INTERVENE IN ANY PROCEEDINGS IN A U.S. STATE OR FEDERAL COURT IN WHICH DEBTOR IS A PARTY

Other relief that is not granted automatically by statute may be granted upon application to the court in any recognized foreign proceeding, whether main or nonmain, "where necessary to effectuate the purpose of [chapter 15] and to protect the assets of the debtor or the interests of the creditors." § 1521(a). All relief is subject to the public policy exception of § 1506. The types of discretionary relief that may be granted by the court to the foreign representative include broadening the scope of the stay; imposing additional limitations on the ability of the debtor to transfer, encumber or dispose of property; providing for the examination of witnesses or the taking of evidence or delivery of information; entrusting the administration or realization of debtor's U.S. assets to the foreign representative or someone else; extending any provisional relief that was previously granted; and granting any additional relief that is available to a trustee, other than the right to bring an avoidance action. The court may also entrust the distribution of all or part of the debtor's U.S. assets to the foreign representative if "the interests of creditors in the United States are sufficiently protected." § 1521(b).

No discretionary relief may be granted in a foreign nonmain proceeding unless the court is satisfied that "the relief relates to assets that, under the law of the United States, should be administered in the foreign nonmain proceeding or concerns information required in that proceeding." § 1521(c). Typical example of assets that should be administered in the foreign nonmain proceeding would be assets that had been fraudulently transferred from the foreign jurisdiction where the foreign nonmain proceeding is pending.

The court may not enjoin a police or regulatory act of a governmental unit (including a criminal action or proceeding), or certain acts excluded from the automatic stay. § 1521(d) & (f). Any relief granted is subject to modification or termination upon request of the foreign representative or an entity affected by the relief, or at its own motion. § 1522(c). The court may grant relief, or may modify or terminate any relief granted, only "if the interests of the creditors and other interested entities, including the debtor, are sufficiently protected." § 1522(a). Any discretionary relief with respect to the stay or limiting the right to transfer, encumber or dispose of property must meet the requirements for injunctive relief. § 1521(e).

A visualization of the provisions relating to the grant of discretionary relief upon recognition of a foreign proceeding follows.

DISCRETIONARY RELIEF AVAILABLE UPON RECOGNITION			
WHEN RELIEF IS AVAILABLE § 1521(a) & § 1522(a)	TYPES OF RELIEF § 1521(a)	DISTRIBUTION OF U.S. ASSETS § 1521(b)	RELIEF THAT MAY NOT BE GRANTED § 1521(d) & (f)
UPON RECOGNITION OF FOREIGN PROCEEDING, WHERE NECESSARY TO EFFECTUATE THE PURPOSE OF CHAPTER 15 AND TO PROTECT ASSTS OF DEBTOR OR INTERESTS OF CREDITORS INTERESTS OF CREDITORS AND OTHER INTERESTED ENTITIES, INCLUDING DEBTOR, MUST BE SUFFICIENTLY PROTECTED	1) STAYING COMMENCEMENT OR CONTINUATION OF ACTION OR PROCEEDING CONCERNING DEBTOR'S ASSETS, RIGHTS, OBLIGATIONS OR LIABILITIES, 2) STAYING EXECUTION AGAINST DEBTOR'S ASSETS, 3) SUSPENDING RIGHT TO TRANSFER, ENCUMBER OR OTHERWISE DISPOSE OF ASSETS, 4) PROVIDING FOR EXAMINATION OF WITNESSES, TAKING OF EVIDENCE OR DELIVERY OF INFORMATION, 5) ENTRUSTING ADMINISTRATION OR REALIZATION OF ALL OR PART OF DEBTOR'S U.S. ASSETS TO FOREIGN REPRESENTATIVE OR OTHER AUTHORIZED PERSON, 6) EXTENDING PROVISIONAL RELIEF, AND 7) GRANTING ADDITIONAL RELIEF OTHER THAN UNDER § 522, 544, 545, 547, 548, 550 OR 724(a)	COURT MAY ENTRUST DISTRIBUTION OF ALL OR PART OF DEBTOR'S U.S. ASSETS TO FOREIGN REPRESENTATIVE OR ANOTHER AUTHORIZED REPRESENTATIVE IF INTERESTS OF U.S. CREDITORS ARE SUFFICIENTLY PROTECTED	COURT MAY NOT ENJOIN POLICE OR REGULATORY ACT OF GOVERNMENTAL UNIT, INCLUDING CRIMINAL ACTION OR PROCEEDING COURT MAY NOT STAY ACTS THAT ARE NOT SUBJECT TO AUTOMATIC STAY UNDER § 362(b)(6), (7), (27) OR § 362(o)

The court may also provide additional assistance to a foreign representative upon recognition under § 1507(a). The nature of this assistance is not described in the statute. However, in deciding whether to grant additional assistance, the court is directed in § 1507(b) to consider whether the assistance, "consistent with the principles of comity," will reasonably assure the following factors, identical to those included in the former § 304. The additional assistance provision can be visualized as follows.

ADDITIONAL ASSISTANCE UPON RECOGNITION § 1507	
AVAILABILITY OF ADDITIONAL ASSISTANCE § 1507(a)	CONSIDERATIONS IN GRANTING ADDITIONAL ASSISTANCE § 1507(b)
IF RECOGNITION IS GRANTED, COURT MAY PROVIDE ADDITIONAL ASSISTANCE TO FOREIGN REPRESENTATIVE UNDER CODE OR OTHER LAWS OF U.S.	COURT SHALL CONSIDER WHETHER ADDITIONAL ASSISTANCE, CONSISTENT WITH PRINCIPLES OF COMITY, WILL REASONABLY ASSURE: 1) JUST TREATMENT OF ALL HOLDERS OF CLAIMS AGAINST OR INTERESTS IN THE ESTATE, 2) PROTECTION OF CLAIM HOLDERS IN THE U.S. AGAINST PREJUDICE AND INCONVENIENCE IN THE PROCESSING OF CLAIMS IN THE FOREIGN PROCEEDING, 3) PREVENTION OF PREFERENTIAL OR FRAUDULENT DISPOSITIONS OF PROPERTY OF THE ESTATE, 4) DISTRIBUTION OF PROCEEDS OF THE ESTATE SUBSTANTIALLY IN ACCORDANCE WITH THE U.S. PRIORITIES, AND 5) IF APPROPRIATE, THE OPPORTUNITY FOR A FRESH START FOR AN INDIVIDUAL DEBTOR

If recognition of a foreign proceeding is denied, the court may enter appropriate orders to prevent the foreign representative from obtaining comity or cooperation from U.S. courts. § 1509(d).

4. Treatment of Foreign Creditors

Chapter 15 gives foreign creditors the same rights to be involved in a U.S. bankruptcy case as domestic creditors. § 1513(a). They can commence an involuntary case and can participate in a case to the same extent as domestic creditors. The claims of foreign creditors under § 507 or § 726 cannot be given a lower priority than that of general unsecured creditors solely because they are held by foreign creditors. § 1513(b)(1).

Known creditors who do not have an address in the United States are also entitled to receive notices given to creditors generally, or to creditors of a specific class or category to which they belong. § 1514(a). If a foreign creditor's address is not known to the debtor, the court may order that appropriate steps be taken to notify any such creditor. *Id.* Notification to a foreign creditor must be given individually (as opposed to by publication or other means) unless the court approves another method. § 1514(b). Notice of the commencement of a bankruptcy case must indicate when and where proofs of claim are to be filed, and must indicate whether secured creditors need to file proofs of claim. § 1514(c). It must also include any additional information required to be included in such notice under the Code and orders of the court. *Id.* If the court finds that a notice mailed within the time prescribed by the Federal Rules of Bankruptcy Procedure would not be sufficient to give a creditor with a foreign address to whom notices are mailed reasonable notice under the circumstances, the court may order that notice be supplemented with notice by other means or that the time prescribed for notice by mail be enlarged. Fed. R. Bankr. P. 2002(p)(1).

Foreign creditors must be given a reasonable amount of additional time beyond that given domestic creditors to file proofs of claim. § 1514(d). Under Fed. R. Bankr. P. 2002(p)(2), unless the court for cause orders otherwise, a creditor with a foreign address to which notice has been mailed must be given at least 30 days' notice of the time fixed for filing a proof of claim.

A visualization of the provisions relating to treatment of foreign creditors follows.

TREATMENT OF FOREIGN CREDITORS		
RIGHTS OF FOREIGN CREDITORS § 1513	NOTIFICATION OF FOREIGN CREDITORS § 1514(a)-(c)	FOREIGN PROOFS OF CLAIM § 1514(d) & RULE 2002(p)(2)
FOREIGN CREDITORS HAVE SAME RIGHTS TO COMMENCE AND PARTICIPATE IN BANKRUPTCY CASE AS DOMESTIC CREDITORS CLAIM OF FOREIGN CREDITOR UNDER § 507 OR § 726 SHALL NOT BE GIVEN LOWER PRIORITY THAN THAT OF GENERAL UNSECURED CLAIM WITHOUT PRIORITY SOLELY BECAUSE IT IS HELD BY FOREIGN CREDITOR	NOTICE GIVEN TO CREDITORS GENERALLY OR TO CREDITORS OF ANY CLASS OR CATEGORY OF CREDITORS MUST BE GIVEN TO KNOWN CREDITORS GENERALLY OR OF THAT CLASS OR CATEGORY THAT DO NOT HAVE U.S. ADDRESS INDIVIDUAL NOTICE MUST BE GIVEN TO CREDITORS WITH FOREIGN ADDRESS UNLESS COURT CONSIDERS SOME OTHER FORM OF NOTICE MORE APPROPRIATE NOTIFICATION OF COMMENCEMENT OF CASE MUST: 1) INDICATE THE TIME PERIOD FOR FILING PROOFS OF CLAIM AND SPECIFY PLACE FOR FILING, 2) INDICATE WHETHER SECURED CREDITORS MUST FILE PROOFS OF CLAIM, AND 3) CONTAIN ANY OTHER INFORMATION REQUIRED BY LAW OR BY COURT TO BE INCLUDED	UNLESS THE COURT FOR CAUSE ORDERS OTHERWISE, A CREDITOR WITH A FOREIGN ADDRESS TO WHICH NOTICE HAS BEEN MAILED MUST BE GIVEN AT LEAST 30 DAYS' NOTICE OF THE TIME FIXED FOR FILING A PROOF OF CLAIM

5.   Cooperation and Coordination

Both the bankruptcy court and the trustee or any examiner is directed to "cooperate to the maximum extent possible with a foreign court or a foreign representative." § 1525(a), § 1526(a). The court is authorized to communicate directly with, or to request information or assistance directly from, a foreign court or a foreign representative. § 1525(b). The clerk, or some other person authorized by the court, must give the debtor, all persons or bodies authorized to administer foreign proceedings of the debtor, all entities against whom provisional relief is being sought under § 1519, all parties to litigation pending in the U.S. in which the debtor is a party at the time of the filing of the petition for recognition, and such other entities as the court may direct, notice by mail of the court's intention to communicate with a foreign court or foreign representative. Fed. R. Bankr. P. 2002(q)(2). The trustee or other person (including an examiner) authorized by the court may also communicate directly with a foreign court or a foreign representative, subject to the supervision of the court. § 1526(b).

Other forms of cooperation that may be pursued by the court or by a trustee or other authorized person include appointment of a person or body to act at the direction of the court; communication of information by any appropriate means; coordination of administration and supervision of the debtor's assets; approval or implementation of agreements concerning coordination of proceedings; and coordination of concurrent proceedings regarding the same debtor. § 1527.

The court may also authorize a trustee or another entity to act in a foreign country on behalf of a bankruptcy estate. § 1505. Anyone so acting must do so in compliance with foreign laws.

The provisions dealing with cooperation and communication are visualized below.

COOPERATION AND COMMUNICATION WITH FOREIGN COURT AND FOREIGN REPRESENTATIVE		
DIRECT COMMUNICATION § 1525(b) & § 1526(b)	OTHER FORMS OF COOPERATION § 1527	AUTHORIZATION TO ACT IN FOREIGN COUNTRY § 1505
COURT MAY COMMUNICATE DIRECTLY OR REQUEST INFORMATION OR ASSISTANCE DIRECTLY FROM FOREIGN COURT OR FOREIGN REPRESENTATIVE AFTER GIVING NOTICE OF INTENT TO DO SO UNDER RULE 2002(q)(2) TRUSTEE OR OTHER PERSON AUTHORIZED BY COURT MAY, SUBJECT TO COURT SUPERVISION, COMMUNICATE DIRECTLY WITH FOREIGN COURT OR FOREIGN REPRESENTATIVE	1) APPOINTMENT OF PERSON OR BODY, INCLUDING AN EXAMINER, TO ACT AT DIRECTION OF COURT, 2) COMMUNICATION OF INFORMATION BY ANY APPROPRIATE MEANS, 3) COORDINATION OF ADMINISTRATION AND SUPERVISION OF DEBTOR'S ASSETS AND AFFAIRS, 4) APPROVAL OR IMPLEMENTATION OF AGREEMENTS CONCERNING COORDINATION OF PROCEEDINGS, AND 5) COORDINATION OF CONCURRENT PROCEEDINGS REGARDING DEBTOR	TRUSTEE OR ANOTHER ENTITY, INCLUDING AN EXAMINER, MAY BE AUTHORIZED BY COURT TO ACT IN FOREIGN COUNTRY ON BEHALF OF A BANKRUPTCY ESTATE

If there is a foreign proceeding regarding the debtor pending at the same time as a U.S. bankruptcy case for that debtor, so-called "concurrent proceedings," the role of the U.S. court depends on whether the foreign proceeding is a foreign main proceeding or foreign nonmain proceeding, and which case preceded the other. In all cases, the court is directed to seek cooperation and coordination under §§ 1525, 1526 and 1527. § 1529.

If a foreign main proceeding is recognized at a time when there is no U.S. bankruptcy case pending, a U.S. bankruptcy case may not be commenced unless the debtor has assets in the U.S., and then the effects of such case are restricted to those assets and, to the extent necessary to implement cooperation and coordination under § 1525, § 1526 and § 1527, other assets of the debtor within the court's jurisdiction and not subject to the jurisdiction of the foreign proceeding. § 1528.

If a U.S. case is commenced after recognition of a foreign proceeding or after the filing of a petition for recognition of a foreign proceeding, any provisional relief in effect under § 1519 and any discretionary relief in effect under § 1521 must be reviewed by the court and will be modified or terminated if inconsistent with the case in the U.S. and, if the foreign proceeding is a foreign main proceeding, the automatic application of § 362 and § 361 with respect to the debtor and the property of the debtor within the U.S. must be modified or terminated if inconsistent with the relief granted in the case in the U.S. § 1529(2). Recognition of a foreign main proceeding is, absent evidence to the contrary, proof that the debtor is generally not paying its debts as such debts become due for purposes of an involuntary bankruptcy petition under § 303. § 1531.

If the U.S. case is pending at the time the petition for recognition of a foreign proceeding is filed, § 1520 does not apply even if the foreign proceeding is recognized, and any provisional or discretionary relief granted under § 1519 or § 1521 must be consistent with any relief granted in the U.S. case. § 1529(1).

If there is more than one foreign proceeding pending with respect to the debtor, any provisional or discretionary relief granted under § 1519 or § 1521 to a representative of a foreign nonmain proceeding after recognition of a foreign main proceeding must be consistent with the foreign main proceeding. § 1530(1). If a foreign main proceeding is recognized after recognition of a foreign nonmain proceeding (or after the filing of a petition for recognition of such a proceeding), any provisional relief in effect under § 1519 and any discretionary relief in effect under § 1521 must be reviewed by the court and will be modified or terminated if inconsistent with the foreign main proceeding. § 1530(2). If a subsequent foreign nonmain proceeding is recognized after recognition of a foreign nonmain proceeding, the court must "grant, modify, or terminate relief for the purpose of facilitating coordination of the proceedings." § 1530(3).

A visualization of the provisions relating to coordination of concurrent proceedings follows.

COORDINATION OF CONCURRENT PROCEEDINGS			
U.S. CASE COMMENCED AFTER RECOGNITION OF FOREIGN MAIN PROCEEDING § 1528	PETITION FOR RECOGNITION FILED WHEN U.S. CASE PENDING § 1529(1)	U.S. CASE FILED AFTER PETITION FOR RECOGNITION FILED OR AFTER RECOGNITION § 1529(2)	MORE THAN ONE FOREIGN PROCEEDING § 1530
U.S. CASE MAY BE COMMENCED ONLY IF DEBTOR HAS U.S. ASSETS EFFECT OF U.S. CASE IS LIMITED TO U.S. ASSETS AND OTHER ASSETS WITHIN JURISDICTION OF U.S. COURT AND NOT SUBJECT TO JURISDICTION OF FOREIGN PROCEEDING	ANY RELIEF GRANTED UNDER § 1519 OR § 1521 MUST BE CONSISTENT WITH RELIEF GRANTED IN U.S. CASE, AND § 1520 DOES NOT APPLY	ANY RELIEF IN EFFECT UNDER § 1519 OR § 1521 MUST BE REVIEWED BY COURT AND MODIFIED OR TERMINATED IF INCONSISTENT WITH CASE IN U.S., AND IF FOREIGN MAIN PROCEEDING, STAY AND SUSPENSION IN § 1520(a) MUST BE MODIFIED OR TERMINATED IF INCONSISTENT WITH RELIEF GRANTED IN U.S. CASE	ANY RELIEF GRANTED UNDER § 1519 OR § 1521 TO REPRESENTATIVE OF FOREIGN NONMAIN PROCEEDING AFTER RECOGNITION OF FOREIGN MAIN PROCEEDING MUST BE CONSISTENT WITH FOREIGN MAIN PROCEEDING, IF FOREIGN MAIN PROCEEDING IS RECOGNIZED AFTER RECOGNITION OR FILING FOR RECOGNITION OF FOREIGN NONMAIN PROCEEDING, ANY RELIEF IN EFFECT UNDER § 1519 OR § 1521 MUST BE REVIEWED BY COURT AND MODIFIED OR TERMINATED IF INCONSISTENT WITH FOREIGN MAIN PROCEEDING, AND IF FOREIGN NONMAIN PROCEEDING IS RECOGNIZED AFTER RECOGNITION OF ANOTHER FOREIGN NONMAIN PROCEEDING, COURT MUST GRANT, MODIFY OR TERMINATE RELIEF FOR PURPOSES OF FACILITATING COORDINATION OF PROCEEDINGS

The final provision of chapter 15, § 1532, is sometimes called the "hotchpot" rule. It states that, without prejudice to any rights that a creditor may have as a holder of a secured claim or in rem, if a creditor gets payment on its claim in a foreign proceeding, that creditor may not get payment on that claim in a U.S. bankruptcy case regarding the debtor until other creditors of the same class receive proportionately at least as much. After other creditors have received the same proportion of their claims, everyone continues to share proportionately in U.S. distributions. This provision on coordination of distributions is visualized below.

COORDINATION OF DISTRIBUTIONS § 1532
WITHOUT PREJUDICE TO SECURED CLAIMS OR IN REM RIGHTS, CREDITOR WHO RECEIVES PAYMENT ON CLAIM IN FOREIGN PROCEEDING MAY NOT RECEIVE PAYMENT ON SAME CLAIM IN U.S. BANKRUPTCY CASE UNTIL ALL OTHER CREDITORS OF SAME CLASS RECEIVE SAME PROPORTIONATE AMOUNT ON THEIR CLAIMS

6. Jurisdiction

Because a case under chapter 15 is a case under title 11, it is within the original and exclusive jurisdiction of the district court under 28 U.S.C § 1334(a). However, unlike other title 11 proceedings, proceedings in a chapter 15 case are not subject to permissive abstention under 28 U.S.C. § 1334(c)(1).

Under 28 U.S.C. § 157(a), each district court may provide that any or all bankruptcy cases and any or all proceedings arising under title 11 or arising in or related to a case under title 11 be referred to the bankruptcy judges for that district. All districts have adopted standing rules providing for such referrals. In order to avoid rendering the bankruptcy system unconstitutional by conferring authority on non-Article III judges that they cannot exercise, *see Northern Pipeline Constr. Co. v. Marathon Pipe Line Co.*, 458 U.S. 50 (1982), 28 U.S.C. § 157 sets out the division of authority between bankruptcy judges and district court judges by allowing bankruptcy judges to hear and determine the case and all "core" proceedings, but only hear noncore proceedings and make recommendations to the district court. Upon the adoption of chapter 15, § 157(b)(2) was amended to provide that recognition of foreign proceedings and other matters under chapter 15 are "core" proceedings.

There is a special venue provision for cases under chapter 15 in 28 U.S.C. § 1410 which is discussed in Chapter 1[E], *supra*.

TABLE OF CASES

[References are to pages]

[References are to pages]

TABLE OF STATUTES

[References are to pages.]

[References are to pages.]

[References are to pages.]

[References are to pages.]

INDEX

[References are to chapters and sections.]

B

C

[References are to chapters and sections.]

[References are to chapters and sections.]

[References are to chapters and sections.]

[References are to chapters and sections.]

[References are to chapters and sections.]

[References are to chapters and sections.]